THE DANUBE

THE DANUBE

A JOURNEY UPRIVER FROM THE
BLACK SEA TO THE BLACK FOREST

Nick Thorpe

YALE UNIVERSITY PRESS
NEW HAVEN AND LONDON

For information about this and other Yale University Press publications, please contact:
U.S. Office: sales.press@yale.edu   www.yalebooks.com
Europe Office: sales@yaleup.co.uk   www.yalebooks.co.uk

Set in Adobe Garamond Pro by IDSUK (DataConnection) Ltd
Printed in Great Britain by CPI Group (UK) Ltd, Croydon, CR0 4YY

Library of Congress Cataloging-in-Publication Data

Thorpe, Nick.
   The Danube : a journey upriver from the Black Sea to the Black Forest / Nick Thorpe.
      pages cm
   ISBN 978–0–300–18165–4 (cl : alk. paper)
   1. Danube River Valley—Description and travel. 2. Danube River Valley—History, Local.
3. Danube River Valley—Social life and customs. 4. Thorpe, Nick—Travel—Danube River
Valley. I. Title.
   DJK76.4.T47 2013
   914.96045—dc23

A catalogue record for this book is available from the British Library.

10 9 8 7 6 5 4 3 2 1

This book is for Andrea

Contents

Illustrations and Maps

Plates

Maps

Acknowledgements

THE DANUBE has wound its way through the many years I have lived in Hungary and eastern Europe – sometimes straight as an arrow, sometimes wild and meandering. As I began to write this book, my relationship with the river became more intimate. It was as if the river looked back and watched me for the first time. When I arrived at the end of the journey in Donaueschingen, I realised that I now carry the whole river within me.

Many people, friends and strangers, helped make this journey and this book possible. The list below is seriously incomplete.

My wife Andrea first took me down to the river and gave me a home beside it. In the winter of 1991, before the Danube was diverted, we walked late at night beneath willows pure white in the snow and the hoarfrost at Ásványráro.

In Romania Mihai Radu was an indefatigable researcher, translator and driver. In the Danube delta, Radu Suciu introduced me to the sturgeon, and Daniel and Eugen Petrescu, Grigore Baboianu and Adrian Oprisan guided my travels. Todor Avramov saved me when I was stranded at the mouth of the river, and his wife Maria told me stories from her childhood.

The staff of the National History and Archaeology Museum in Constanța, and Marian Neagu of the Museum of the Lower Danube in Călărași were generous with their time. In Sulina Aurel Bajanaru and in Dervent Father Atal deserve special mention. Doru Oniga was an excellent host on several visits to the Iron Gates.

In Bulgaria I would like to thank especially Nikolai Nenov, Eskren Velikov, Milan Nikolov, Momcilo Kolev and Theodora Kopcheva in Ruse, Todor Tsanev in Červena Voda, Nikolai Kirilov and his team and Father Iliya in Lom, and Mitko Natovi and his whole family in Vidin.

In Serbia, Lacka Lakatos and Milorad Batinić drove me through the long reaches of the summer night. After so many wars it was a relief to cover the story of a river in peacetime with them. Andrej Starovic explained the intricacies and controversies of the Vinča culture.

In Hungary, Adam LeBor first suggested the Danube as a theme, the crew of the Tatabánya took me all the way to Esztergom, and Szilárd Sasváry and Gábor Karátson generously shared their knowledge of the river. Viktor Filipenko translated texts from Russian, and Andrea Iván translated the story of Teddy Weyr and my interview with Todor Tsanev from Bulgarian. Onur Yumurtaci of the University of Eskişehir translated the Turkish songs from the Danube delta.

In Austria, I would like to thank in particular Bethany Bell, Lana Šehić, Omar Al-Rawi, Seda Atsaeva and her whole family, Hermann Spannraft and Refik.

Many environmentalists, the whole length of the river, shared their time and knowledge with me. Apart from those mentioned already, I must thank Orieta Hulea, Stela Bozhinova, Tibor Mikuska, Claudia and Arno Mohl, Jaromír Šibl, Philip Weller, Georg Frank, Hannes Seehofer and Siegfried Geissler.

The main maps I used throughout the journey were the excellent four-volume *Bikeline* editions of the Esterbauer publishing house, designed especially for long-distance cyclists. By pretending to be on a bicycle even when I was in a car, I was able to stay within sight and smell of the river for almost the whole journey.

No English writer or traveller in eastern Europe can escape the magnificent legacy of Patrick Leigh Fermor, who passed away in June 2011, as I was in mid-stride on my own journey. Neal Ascherson's *Black Sea* was a great inspiration, and without him the precious Danube snail might never have found refuge between these pages. *The Ottoman Empire* by Patrick Kinross was invaluable as a source on the Turkish period, and I have quoted liberally from his work. I first read *Danube* by Claudio Magris when it was first published in English in 1989. While my own book is very different, I enjoyed his literary company throughout my journey. For my understanding of the archaeology of the Danube, *The Lost World of Old Europe – The Danube Valley 5000–3500 BC*, edited by David W. Anthony, was a constant reference work, as was the book so many of its authors challenge, *The Goddesses and Gods of Old Europe* by Marija Gimbutas. The archaeologist John Chapman kindly corresponded with me to clarify the origins of the spiny oyster shell, *Spondylus gaederopus*. Donald Wesling of San Diego introduced me to 'The Willows', the astonishing short story by Algernon Blackwood about the Danube between Hungary and Slovakia. Gary Snyder's writings, from the faraway Sierra Nevada in northern California, have been a precious reminder since my youth of the power and importance of wilderness.

In Britain, I would like to thank especially Robert Baldock of Yale University Press for his unstinting support, and also at Yale, Steve Kent, Tami Halliday, Samantha Cross and Candida Brazil. My agent Sara Menguc enthusiastically backed the project from the start. Loulou Brown painstakingly copy-edited the book.

Many friends walked under the willows over the years, encouraging me to write: Gerard Casey and Louise de Bruin, Roger Norman, Simon Pilpel, Jim Oppé, Bill Brockway, Nicola Balfour, Steve Johnstone, Frances Land, Stephen Batty, Frances Hatch, Art Hewitt, Charlie Foster-Hall, Nikola Leudolph and Mark Frankland. At the BBC, among many friends and colleagues, Tony Grant, the editor of *From Our Own Correspondent* was a tower of strength and enthusiasm.

Finally, I would like to thank my mother Janet, my sister Mish, my brother Dom, and last but not least my friend and faithful champion Xandra Bingley.

The Lips of the Danube

I do not know much about gods; but I think that the river
Is a strong brown god
T. S. ELIOT, 'THE DRY SALVAGES'[1]

Yet the river almost seems
To flow backwards, and I
Think it must come
From the East.
FRIEDRICH HÖLDERLIN, 'DER ISTER'[2]

History flows backwards now
Gathering in its wide pages
This terrible river:
Water spills, from three mouths of the Danube,
But from the fourth, blood.
ANDREI CIURUNGA, 'CANALUL'[3]

HISTRIA. A thin column of smoke leans inland from its roots among the reeds. The sharp north-easterly breeze brings tears to my eyes. There's a flicker of flame; I can just see the heads of two men above the reeds, beside their fire. Two small fishing boats pass northwards up the coast, like racehorses, side by side. Their bows cut the rough grey surf. There are twin figures in the stern, one in the bow. Are the men by the fire fishermen, come ashore to cook, or reed cutters, who have reached the end of the world? Has the mariner built his last or his first desolate fire on this coast?

Here on the fraying fringes of Europe, between the Greek and Roman ruins of Histria and the rising waters of the Black Sea, I begin my journey up the River Danube. Suddenly an explosion splits the fabric of the morning. We crouch for shelter, but find none among the ruins. The roar rolls slowly round the rim of the horizon. The Persians, under Darius the Great? The Iranians under Mahmoud Ahmadinejad? The Romanian coast is only two hours' flying time from Baghdad or Tehran. But it is only the Romanian navy, or their close allies the Americans, testing the firepower of their frigates far out at sea. The ruins take no notice. These walls were overrun for fourteen hundred years. Histria was established by Greek colonists from Miletus in time for the Olympic Games in the mid-seventh century BC, and abandoned in AD 700, when silt from the southernmost lip of the Danube turned its sheltered bay into an inland lake.

To travel the Danube upriver, from the Black Sea to the Black Forest, I must first explore the hinterland of Dobrogea – the 'good land', according to one etymology[4] – between the Danube and the Black Sea coast. In the National History and Archaeology Museum at Constanța, forty-five kilometres down the coast from Histria, stands a coiled snake made from purple marble, its head erect. Known as Glykon, the sweet one, a Roman god of healing, the snake has the face of a lamb, the ears of a man, and the tail of a lion, signifying gentleness, attentiveness and courage. It was found during excavations beneath the old railway station in the city in 1962, with thirteen other gods, most probably deliberately hidden to save them from the Christians, with their passion for destroying pagan images. Did the owners expect the Christians to pass like a sudden squall, after which the snake could re-emerge, unscathed? At the start of this journey up the Danube, the serpent is for me the river herself, a single body, green, brown, white, yellow, grey, blue, silver and black, her moods and her surface colours constantly changing.

Up the Danube? Many people I met on this long journey thought I must be mad to attempt the river the wrong way. I clung on for dear life in the stern of Adrian Oprisan's small fibreglass dinghy, riding the waves at Sulina in the Danube delta; I battled on my bicycle along the dyke into a fresh north-westerly wind near Mohács in southern Hungary, as immaculately dressed Swiss and English cyclists glided effortlessly past me in the other direction, their mouths wide open in amazement, catching the fruit-flies of late summer; and finally I chased the tail of the Danube in my car, snaking away among suburban German hills.

Rivers follow a certain inevitable course from the mountains to the sea. Intrepid travel-book writers emerge from coffee shops in Furtwangen and Donaueschingen, gorged on Black Forest gateaux, to follow the same route downstream, with growing apprehension as they reach less and less familiar lands. But what do east Europeans think, in their palaces and hovels by the river, in towns whose names few geography teachers in Bonn or Brighton, Basel or Barcelona, ever utter? In Brăila or in Călăraşi, in Smederevo or Baja? And what of the steady procession of migrants and traders, soldiers and adventurers who travelled in my direction, *up* the Danube, in search of a better life. What was on their minds and in their satchels? And what did they leave behind?

Only for a brief period, from 1740 to 1790, did the Swabians of Ulm board their *Kuppe* – simple wooden boats with long rudders, powered by oars – and head downriver to resettle lands in Hungary laid waste by war and disease. And even they would probably have stayed at home had it not been for the persuasive charm of the Habsburg empress Maria Theresa.

With all due respect to the noble efforts of past writers, I feel I can offer something different. After half a lifetime living in eastern Europe, it seems high time for a journey westwards, upriver, to cast new light on the continent as people coming from the east see it, rising early in the morning, following their own shadows. One man, at least, understood my journey. Ilie Sidurenko, a retired fisherman in the village of Sfântu Gheorghe, on the southernmost tip of the Danube, roared with approval when I told him my plan. 'You will be like the sturgeon!' he laughed. Heading upriver to spawn.

As I travelled, I became aware of the Danube's contribution to Europe, in the sense that it carved a path, or laid a trail, for people to follow westwards. Europe was populated and 'civilised' from the east. Around 6200 BC, farmers from Anatolia settled in south-eastern Europe, bringing with them cows and sheep, goats and seeds. Analysis of the genetic structure of milk traces found on shards of Neolithic pottery shows that their cows mated with aurochs, the wild bulls of the European continent.[5] The settlers brought with them a knowledge of metallurgy. They built kilns that reached a temperature of 1,100 degrees Celsius to smelt copper from the greenish-brown rocks of the northern Balkans at Rudna Glava in Serbia and Ai Bunar in Bulgaria. From this new material of such dazzling beauty they fashioned exquisite jewellery, tools and weapons.[6] These were traded far and wide, and the longer the river, the greater the reach. Not much later, gold was extracted from rich seams, or washed from the tributaries of the Danube.

Between 5000 and 3500 BC, large villages or towns grew up across south-eastern Europe, especially between the Danube and Dnieper rivers. The largest, at Majdanetskoe and Tal'janki, boasted 2,700 households and around 10,000 inhabitants, five hundred years before the foundation of the Sumerian city states between the Tigris and the Euphrates.[7] This was at a time when most other inhabitants of mainland Europe were clustered in small clans, chewing on bones in dank caves. Such towns or large villages grew physically higher from the surrounding countryside into tells or raised cities, as successive generations built on the ruins beneath them. This cluster of independent cultures, known to archaeologists as Tripol'ye-Cucuteni, Hamangia, Gumelniţa, Karanovo and Vinča, established the European continent's first long-distance trade in beautiful pinkish-white spiny oyster shells, *Spondylus gaederopus*.[8] The translucent shells did not just reflect the light; they seemed to carry it within themselves, catching and storing the moonlight across the Aegean Sea where they were gathered. This was in vivid contrast to the dark, graceful pots with intricate lines, the animal-headed lids and handles of the same cultures. The *Spondylus* shells were buried with their owners, both male and female, as sacred objects to smooth the difficult journey to the next world. Salt was as important to the peoples of the region as the ornaments and tools they used. The white gold quarried from the mines near Tuzla in Bosnia, Varna in Bulgaria, Turda in Transylvania and Hallstatt in Austria enabled them to preserve and trade over vast distances the meat and fish they hunted.[9]

These civilisations were named 'Old Europe' by the American-Lithuanian archaeologist Marija Gimbutas, and the name still seems more appropriate than the 'New Europe' label attached to eastern Europe by American statesmen and British comedians. Many thousands of miniature clay figurines, mostly female, with lines and spirals drawn on their bodies, have been found throughout the Lower and Middle Danube region. Marija Gimbutas has argued that these represent proof of the spiritual and social power of women, and named the groups 'councils of the goddess', evidence of a matriarchal society.[10] More recently, archaeologists have argued that they were mere playthings, household objects which tell us more about their owners' fashion-sense than their beliefs.[11]

There is more controversy over the markings on the beautiful pottery of the same civilisations. Some researchers claim that these represent a 'Danube script', even earlier than the Sumerian and still undeciphered.[12] The marks found on pottery in graves are rather different from those found in households, suggesting a distinction between the information which might be useful in this life and the next. The civilisation of this Copper Age beside the Danube was shattered by the invasion of Bronze Age peoples, carrying more robust weapons, riding newly domesticated horses, but with less knowledge of working the land. Although the quality of the pottery declined, that of sharp metal and its uses improved. One school of thought suggests a sharp break at this point, between a matriarchal, peace-loving world, and a patriarchal, war-loving one.

Greek colonies were founded, crumbled, then re-fortified by Roman ones – a rare example in the region of civilisation arriving from the West. Christianity put a spear in the hand of the Thracian horseman, a dragon beneath his hooves, and renamed him Saint George. The Romans built roads, and imposed some order on the landscape, then fell to the 'barbarians' in their own ranks. The Scythians and Sarmatians, Alans, Huns and Slavs rode their horses down the same route as Bronze Age invaders, from the steppes north of the Black Sea, down the narrow strip of land between the elbow of the Carpathians and the sea, then turned west when they hit the Danube.

The Ottoman Turks brought another wave of civilisation from the East and rebuilt thermal baths neglected since Roman times. Their tolerance of Christianity and Judaism encouraged orthodox Russians to take refuge from the persecution of the Tsars, and gave shelter to Jews fleeing from the cruelties of the Spanish kings. Little clay oil-lamps found at the large military camp of Viminacium near Belgrade reveal the Roman passion for candle-lit bathing before they set out eastwards along the Danube to fight the Dacians.[13]

The surviving thermal baths of Buda, with their magnificent chambers and copper roofs, are proof of a similar passion for cleanliness among the

Turks. In the Middle Ages, the Roma arrived from the East in Europe and dazzled audiences with their skills in metal-working, music, and in taming animals. Their westward journey continues, despite the efforts of successive French governments to send them 'home'.

This book has several wellsprings. In February 1995 I found myself high over Africa, flying home to Budapest from Nairobi in Kenya on a crystal-clear winter's morning. The plane followed the White Nile, nine thousand metres below, like a migrating bird. For hour after hour I watched the blue line in the sand, sometimes thicker, sometimes thinner, bulging to accommodate islands and marshes, turning from silver to blue then back to silver. I saw the Blue Nile attach its waters to the White, watched it split Cairo like an axe, then fan out into the great lake of the Mediterranean. We crossed Cyprus, semi-detached, floating cloud-like above the sea, Anatolia, then the corner of the Black Sea pond. Soon the Nile seemed to begin again, this time a blue line winding across green plains, knifing between mountains still white with snow. The thought struck me that the Nile and the Danube are just one river. The Danube as the Upper Nile, and the Nile as the Lower Danube. And just as the Victorian explorers Richard Burton and John Hanning Speke set out to find the sources of the Nile, why not try to rediscover the sources of the Danube? Egypt was the 'gift of the Nile' wrote Herodotus.[14] Might not Europe be the 'gift of the Danube'?

Another reason for travelling up the river is political. During the many years I have lived in Budapest, within a stone's throw of the Danube, I have witnessed the dismantling of the ugliest eyesore that marred the mental and physical horizon of the European continent: the mass of concrete and steel, of look-out towers and fortifications, known as the Iron Curtain. When I first came to live in eastern Europe, I encountered people who had never seen a Dutch tulip, or the perfect blue waters of the Adriatic, only a few hours drive away. I have met people to the west of the Curtain, who could not tell, and still cannot tell, the difference between Budapest and Bucharest, Slovenia and Slovakia.[15]

As an observer of the reunification of a Europe through which the Danube flows, I have witnessed the arrogance of the West towards the East. For me, the revolutions of 1989 were a triumph of the human spirit, a celebration of the need for freedom in all its forms, including, but not limited to, the economic. I saw no 'triumph of capitalism' or 'Cold War victory'. The tearing down of the Iron Curtain was inspired by the desire to think, write, travel, work and play without the cold breath of an authoritarian state on your neck, listening to your phone, opening your letters or blackmailing your friends.

By travelling the Danube from East to West, my intention is to represent the lives and views of the people who live from, and beside, the river. I do not intend to romanticise the East. There are deep economic and structural problems, largely solved in the more fortunate west of the continent. Above all, there is a problem of story-telling. Large chunks of the recent past remain undigested. The terrible story of the Holocaust of eastern European Jews has been told, and told well.[16] But other tragedies have been less well documented, and, where told, rarely translated. There are the Roma, robbed of their music and their mobility by the communists, in exchange for a mattress in a workers' hostel and a factory job, then robbed of their livelihoods by the onset of capitalism. There are also the dwindling peasantry of eastern Europe, who won back their lands in the 1990s, only to lose them to land speculators in the 2000s or simply to weeds when their own children and grandchildren refused to get their hands dirty. And there are the children of Romania and Bulgaria who were left behind when their parents disappeared to Spain and Italy in search of work. The Danube flows through a region of multiple identities, but the river alone, constantly changing, is one.

I set out from the Danube delta in Romania in March 2011 and reached the sources of the Danube in Germany in March 2012, travelling in several stages. Between trips, I returned to Budapest, to make a living as a reporter and to spend time with my family. I travelled mostly by car, but also on foot, by bicycle, boat, train, plane and, just once, along the footpath at Kladovo in Serbia, on my son Matthew's skateboard.[17] I swam in the river at every opportunity, usually in the early mornings of summer, in lazy lakes upstream of dams, or barely making progress against a current flowing at a muscular six kilometres per hour.

The backbone of this book is a new journey up the Danube, but I have also occasionally woven other journeys into the narrative. In the mid-1980s, I risked expulsion from Hungary to report on the protests against the Gabčíkovo-Nagymaros hydroelectric project on the Danube, between Hungary and Czechoslovakia. My secret police file in Hungary has detailed reports of conversations on those marches. 'The so-called journalist makes little secret of his sympathy for the protesters,' reads one of my favourite entries, compiled by an informer standing beside me at the ferry crossing in Esztergom. On April Fool's Day 1986 I was walking with friends through the Danube wetlands in Szigetköz in western Hungary when it started to rain. We did not realise that the gentle rains contained the first radiation from the Chernobyl nuclear disaster one thousand kilometres further east. In 1991 Hungary withdrew unilaterally from the hydroelectric scheme, but the Slovaks pressed ahead with a project which they saw as a matter of national pride, regardless of the environmental damage it would cause. In October 1992 four-fifths of the river along a thirty-kilometre section were diverted into a canal. The old bed of the Danube dried out in a matter of hours, and fishermen waded ankle deep in the marshlands that remained, trying to rescue the same fish they used to try to catch. People on both sides of the river are still counting the cost.

In March 1999 I watched from the Hyatt Hotel in New Belgrade as NATO missiles rained down on Batajnica, the Yugoslav military airfield to the north, and Pančevo, an oil refinery right on the Danube.

In 2000 I filmed pelicans in the Danube delta, in their largest remaining natural habitat in Europe. In 2005 I returned to the delta with a less pleasant task – to document the impact of bird-flu on rural communities which depend as much on their hens and geese as on fish for their livelihoods.

In late March 2010, the first traces of radioactive iodine from the nuclear disaster at Fukushima in Japan, ten thousand kilometres away, were found in the milk of sheep grazing near the Danube in Romania.[18]

In conversation with people on and by the river, I have also sought to write about their dreams and songs, their visions and nightmares. In his prison camp at Belene, an island on the river in Bulgaria, Todor Tsanev watched the mosquitoes eat his body and the bed bugs suck his blood for ten long years. In Orşova, near the Iron Gates dam, Ahmed Engur, a former inhabitant of the island of Ada Kaleh, still dreams that he is walking through the streets of the old Turkish town, before the buildings were dynamited and the floodwaters drowned it. For one man to dream of his old home would not be so surprising, but others tell the same story. From his dream, a new history of the past fifty years is spun. Perhaps, in a world not so dissimilar to our own, the Iron Gates hydroelectric project never happened. Perhaps the dam and turbines were never built at Gabčíkovo. Perhaps Ferenc Zsemlovics still pans for gold in the Danube at Zlatná na Ostrove, and did not have to become an ostrich farmer after all.

Colin Thubron wrote that the traveller's voice is 'the sound of one civilisation reporting on another'. I hope my own voice will have a stereo effect. I stake my claim both as a traveller from the West rediscovering the East, and as a traveller from the East, rediscovering the West. I thought I knew the river, more or less, before I set out, but was often astonished, delighted, and only occasionally disappointed. There is more archaeology in this book than I expected, more traces of the Romans and their predecessors, more food and wine, and even more remarkable characters than I dared hope for.

These are the stories of the people of the Danube, and their dark, dreamy river.

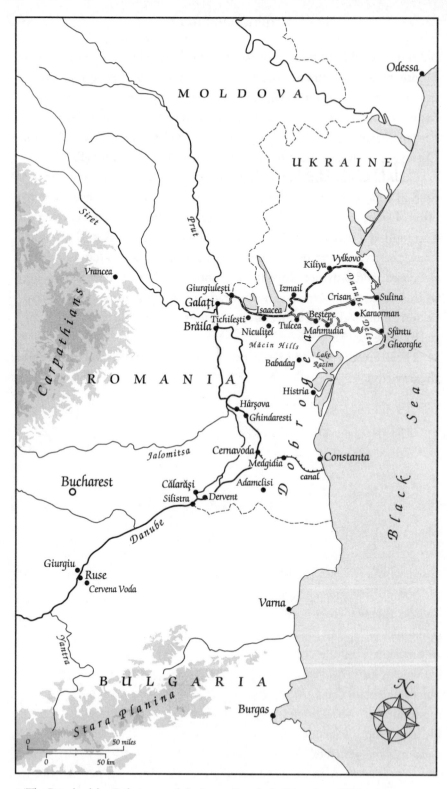

1. The Danube delta, Dobrogea, and the Lower Danube in Romania and Bulgaria.

CHAPTER 1

The Beginning of the World

According to the Thracian account the country beyond the Danube is
infested by bees, which makes further progress impossible; to my mind,
however, this is an improbable story, as bees are not creatures which can
stand the cold . . .

HERODOTUS[1]

'The Danube snail (*theodoxus danubialis*) is recognized by its shell with
transversal dark zig-zag stripes on lighter, usually yellowish ground. In
the east it may also be plain black . . . [it] prefers clean streaming water
rich in oxygen and with stony ground. Where such waters are dammed,
the populations usually disappear.'[2]

THE STURGEON, Radu Suciu tells me, is an armoured fish. Images of long-
nosed whiskery crusaders, underwater knights in full armour battling up
the bed of the muddy Danube, wild-eyed through their visors, propelled
by iron flippers, crowd my mind. What he means is that it doesn't have
skin and a long, thin backbone, like most other fish; this is a fish which is
all cartilage, a bundle of muscles, a masterpiece of design.

We are sitting in Radu's office at the Danube Delta Research Centre in
Tulcea, the main delta town in Romania, surrounded by jars of pickled fish,
mountains of papers, computer screens and shelves bursting with books.
He hands me a Romanian translation of the Hungarian author Mór Jókai's
Golden Man,[3] which tells of the lost island of Ada Kaleh, far up the Danube

near the Iron Gates. Those who fall in love with the Danube do so with the whole river, with her entire body, even those parts they have never seen.

On the walls outside his office, curved, wicked-looking hooks are fixed to the wall like clothes hooks, those once used by fishermen to catch sturgeon. This is not a fish to nibble nervously at bait on the end of anglers' lines. This is a fish that can live for a hundred years, can grow to several hundred kilos, and can store a man's weight of caviar in its belly.

There are five kinds of sturgeon in the Danube: the beluga, the ship's sturgeon, the Russian sturgeon, the stellate and the sterlet. The ship's sturgeon, with its curved snout and rounded whiskers is the closest to extinction, but none are exactly flourishing in the wild. This is the oldest fish on earth, once the pride of the river, and the most abundant. Ancient Dacian tribesmen caught them in a fence made up of stakes driven into the bed of the river, with hooks protruding between the wooden bars. The Dacian word for this device, *garda*, can still be found in modern Serbian. When the Romans conquered the Dacians, in two bloody campaigns from AD 100 to 113, they forced their captives to teach them how to catch sturgeon before they killed them or marched them off to the slave markets. The base of Trajan's Column in Rome shows bearded, trousered men cowering beneath the swords of triumphant legionaries, distinguished by their clean-shaven faces and short tunics. As a piece of war propaganda rather than faithful reportage, there are no images of bearded men teaching the Romans to fish.

Roman engineers adapted the Dacian model into a lobster pot, fixed to the riverbed. The technology has changed little. In the museum at Baja in Hungary, I saw wooden bars arranged like the side of a child's cot, with hooks protruding between them. The hooks get stuck in the fishes' armour, and the more they struggle, the deeper the barbs embed themselves in their sides. These 'fish fences' are then hauled up beside the boats, and the fish extracted.

Radu rattles his visitor's box, a simple shoebox full of fish bones and fish skeletons. The sturgeon, he explains, 'is a great climber and a poor swimmer'. He demonstrates with his arms the way the fish fixes its dorsal fins firmly at its side, and digs them into the riverbed as anchors on its long migrations up the River Danube. He produces two fins from his box, long and yellow and sharp, more like knitting needles than pins. When the fish reached the cataracts which once lined certain sections of the riverbed, they would anchor their bodies with these fins, swim a bit, then anchor again to rest behind a suitable rock. In that way they could climb the steep, swift-flowing uphill gradient.

The oldest fossils of sturgeon are two hundred million years old. These fish have swum beneath the waters of the earth ten times longer than man has run along the surface. In that time they have hardly changed. The fossils show the long-noses of the beluga just as they are today, hunting the ledges of the Black Sea and the Caspian, where once they hunted in the Pannonian Sea. The beluga is the largest, and can reach a length of six metres and a weight of up to a tonne. Filmed underwater, they look like giant space ships, twisting and turning between the galaxies.

'There are people who have lived their whole lives beside the river, and never seen a sturgeon,' says Radu. It insists on staying close to the bottom of the river. In the Black Sea, where three of the five Danube species spend most of their adult life, the fish also rarely surface. Little was known about their movements at sea until a joint Romanian–Norwegian research project was launched in 2009.[4] Small satellite transmitters, each costing as much as a laptop computer, were fixed to five teenage fish, which were returned to the Danube at Hârsova, far upriver.

In the Neptune restaurant that evening in Tulcea, beneath murals of trident-wielding gods, over plates of fried pikeperch washed down with white wine from the Niculiţel region, Radu tells me more about the project. Harald was the most successful so far, a twelve-year-old male named after the King of Norway. A healthy sixty kilos, he headed out to sea as soon as he was released into the Danube. He spent that winter on an underwater ledge, only sixty metres deep, in the north-west corner of the Black Sea, off Odessa. This was the first scientific proof that this was where sturgeon gather in winter, where they are most vulnerable to trawlers – crucial information for conservation-ists. The small gadget attached to his back was programmed not to broadcast all the time, but simply to store the data, then send it up to the satellite when the fish finally reached the surface. Exactly 164 days after he was released, Harald resurfaced 11 kilometres off the Crimea. During that first night, according to the information beamed to the Argos satellite, he travelled at a steady fifteen kilometres an hour – presumably on the deck of a fishing boat. Harald had been caught. He was still alive, probably, but only just.

Another remarkable feature of the sturgeon is its ability to live for days out of water. A huge beluga caught by Serbian fishermen at Apatin in 2003 was wrapped in a fisherman's blanket on the shore for several hours, then succeeded in unwrapping itself and rolling back down the bank into the water to escape. Before it eluded them, its captors noted the remains of several rusting hooks in its side. That was more than twenty years after the Iron Gates dam on the Romanian–Serbian border cut off the sturgeon from its traditional breeding grounds in the Danube shallows between Hungary and Slovakia. The fish must either have been stranded upriver when the dam was built, or slipped into the locks beside a laden barge, to continue a migration route denied to the rest of its species.

After Harald was caught and brought ashore, the satellite tracked him for two more days. The last signal came from the nearby railroad station, in Saki. Harald was about to start travelling inland by train. One wonders what those who caught him, or bought him, made of his transmitter. The project has revealed much about the migration routes |of sturgeon, but few of the fish have sent back as much information as Harald. Some have still not resurfaced. Others have done so, but the data they sent to the satellite was garbled. The skies above the Black Sea hum with satellite signals between Russian naval ships and the military base at Sevastopol. The Black Sea is Russia's window on the wars and revolutions of the Middle East.[5]

The pride of Radu's shoebox is a small, perfect sturgeon, barely longer than his hand, the gift of his professor, Nicolae Bacalbaşa. In the early 1970s, Professor Bacalbaşa realised that sturgeon were dying out in the Danube. Over-fishing, pollution, and the construction of the Iron Gates hydroelectric dam devastated sturgeon stocks, just as the building of the Volgograd dam in Russia had in the Volga, a decade earlier. Only a tenth the number of beluga sturgeon were caught in 1980 compared to that in 1930. Bacalbaşa dedicated the remaining decades of his long life to try and save them.[6]

His first problem was with the fishermen – they refused to tell him where sturgeon could be caught. This was a closely guarded family secret, taciturn Romanian fishermen explained, handed down from father to son. Undeterred, Nicolae Bacalbaşa parked his Trabant near the bridge at Hârsova, where men still stand at the roadside, their arms spread akimbo, to mime the huge catfish of their buckets or their imaginations, and wandered upstream. He was in no hurry. Each evening he pitched his tent, and all day he chatted to anyone he met along the banks of the river. After three days he struck gold. A casual glance into the wooden barrel beside a lone angler revealed his first sturgeon. The angler came from faraway Moldova each year, fished until his barrel was full, salted them, then drove his catch home, to feed his family for the winter and sell off the surplus. Embarrassed to be told by the learned professor that he had caught a rare species, he implored his visitor to take it away. And that was the perfect specimen which Radu now handed me. From the size of the fish and the season, Bacalbaşa deduced that sturgeon overwinter in the Danube, rather than returning to the warmer, saltier waters of the Black Sea.

Bacalbaşa and his team taught themselves to catch sturgeon from such titbits of information, culled from fishermen and their own observations. Young adult fish enter the Danube every three to five years to spawn, while older fish make the journey only every ten to fifteen years. Hybrid fish – a cross between different varieties of sturgeon – become more attached to the river than others, as though reluctant to return to the sea. The scientists noticed a remarkable fact: sturgeon were most plentiful in exactly those places where the Romans had built their forts. The commanders of Roman border garrisons, with units of a hundred soldiers or more to feed, were no fools. Sturgeon lived and bred in the Danube at that time in such numbers that their succulent pink flesh and black caviar became a staple food for soldiers garrisoned far from home. Civilisations rise and fall, but old sturgeon habits die hard.

As I drive towards the delta from the West I see my first wind turbines, spaced out across the hills like dandelions, or the advance guard of a Roman army. The wind always blows in Dobrogea, keeping the hillsides bare and the grasses short and steppe-like. This is the southernmost, westernmost outcrop of the great grassland steppe regions of southern Russia, across which nomads in prehistory swept on horseback. They had the prevailing, northerly wind, known as *crivăţ* in Romanian, at their backs. They must have felt quite at home on these low, worn granite hills. Their *kurgans* (burial mounds) still dot the landscape.

Dobrogea, the land between the Danube and the Black Sea, is a wild, empty, moody landscape, little known even to most Romanians. The only book I can find on the region in the best bookshops of Bucharest is a massive tome of photographs by Razvan Voiculescu, a man on a motorbike that can take him to places best reached by sea, or on horseback.[7] There are granite cliffs like giant's teeth, with a single mulberry at the foot like the gift of a goddess. 'In the depths of the night . . . I still hear the creaking of the boats moored at the foot of Citadel hill. There are roads there that lead nowhere, but which the locals stubbornly insist on roaming . . . The bridge with rusted rails between two dry hills, the infinity of sunflowers, the churches clumsily cast among fields of wild wormwood and rocks,' Voiculescu writes in the preface. The beginning of the world, he emphasises, not the end of it. The place to begin my own journey, up the Danube.

The villages I drive through have Turkish-sounding names like Saraiu and Topalu, small mosques, barely bigger than a prayer room, and thin, spiky minarets. Most of Romania's eighty thousand remaining Turks and Tatars live in Dobrogea. Like most invaders over the centuries, they fell in love with the place and stayed. Their great-granddaughters, shy girls with deep brown eyes and smiles to tame wild animals, sell little bunches of purple flowers, flashes of purple in brown hands as we pass.

Sheep wander in flocks at the roadside, through a smudged cloud of smoke, downwind of a man bent over to burn off last year's grass. Threadbare carpets hang to dry on a line, hens peck in a yard beside a wooden shed packed high with corn cobs, and a policeman with a white-topped cap saunters wearily up the side of Razvan Voiculescu's road to nowhere.

The image of dandelions for the wind turbines proves more appropriate than that of soldiers. Four hundred and fifty have sprung up in barely two years. Four thousand are planned for the whole of Dobrogea, many in the path of the millions of birds who migrate to and from the delta.

On a blustery March morning, Daniel Petrescu drives me to Beştepe, which means 'five hills' in Turkish, overlooking Mahmoudia and the Sfântu Gheorghe arm of the river. Daniel is tall, with an easy grin and a massive pair of binoculars slung around his neck. Lake Razim, below Beştepe, is the largest in Romania, and stretches almost to the southern horizon. On the other side of the hills, the southernmost band of the Danube winds the last hundred kilometres to the sea. There's a strong breeze from the north and the skies are grey. A lone hooded crow swoops into the wind, then small clusters of chaffinches and brambling cross the hill northwards, chattering as they fly. 'Not spectacular birds, but they can travel, even in this weather. These hills are like Mecca, a magnet for migrating birds. They approach from these flat and watery areas, and use the ascending, thermal currents of the hill to gain height. And from high above here they glide down the other side of the hills, in autumn towards the south, in spring towards the north.'

The hills are a nature reserve because of the fragile species of moss and plants growing there, rather than the birds. There are wild thyme, tufted grasses called *festuca*, rosehip bushes and even a small, stunted mulberry tree, sheltering in a gully. In communist times there was a quota in schools to bring silk caterpillars from the mulberries, to revive the Romanian silk industry. 'It's a good tree for birds, because of its long fruiting period,' Daniel says. 'The rose-coloured starlings like them a lot.' The caterpillars feed on the leaves of the white mulberry. Silk was brought from China to Europe from the first century AD. In AD 552, during the reign of the Byzantine emperor Justinian the Great, two monks succeeded in smuggling a bamboo stick full of silkworms back to Constantinople.[8] From then on, the mulberry spread rapidly through Greece and the Balkans as many regions developed their own silk production.

The Danube divides into three branches at Tulcea. The northernmost, Chilia arm arches along the shore of Ukraine to the Black Sea. The city of Izmail guards the entrance and its coat of arms depicts a Christian cross on a red background divided by a sword from the crescent moon of Islam.

Danube's swiftly flowing waters
Are at last in our firm hands;
Caucasus respects our prowess,
Russia rules Crimean lands.

Turkish-Tatar hordes no longer
May disturb our calm domain.
Proud Selim won't be the stronger
evermore, as Crescent wanes.[9]

The poem is by Gavrila Derzhavin and comprised the first Russian national anthem. Selim was the Turkish sultan. It was written to commemorate the capture of the supposedly unassailable Turkish fortress of Izmail by the

Russian commander Alexander Suvorov in 1791. The aftermath was not so heroic. Forty thousand Turkish men, women and children were massacred by Russian troops after the siege, as soldiers went from house to house – hence the red background, perhaps, on the crest. When it was all over, Suvorov went to his tent and wept.[10] Today it is a town of nearly ninety thousand people, with a large Chinese community.

The middle, Sulina, branch of the Danube is the busiest route, straightened by an Englishman, Charles Hartley, on his way home from fighting in the Crimean War. He went on to widen the Suez Canal, and participated in the straightening of a route through the meandering Mississippi delta.[11] But he cut his teeth on the Danube, and started a battle between transport engineers keen to get their goods to market as quickly as possible, and environmentalists who love the twisting, turning, changing river, which continues to this day.

The southernmost arm, Sfântu Gheorghe or 'Saint George' branch, which stretches to the horizon beneath us on Beştepe hill, is the oldest. From where we stand, we look across at hills, polished smooth by the sleeves of the wind. There are few trees, and even those that have gained a root-hold in this windswept place are small and bent like flags. And there is little rainfall, barely forty centimetres a year.

Where the birds feed depends on the water levels in the delta. In the late spring, when rain and melting snow upstream swell the river to a swirling brown flood, pelicans and waders have to go further afield to fish. Neither of the two pelican species in the Danube can dive, so they need shallow water to feed in. Human interference in the landscape – such as the building of wind farms – forces the pelicans to make wider and wider detours. And the longer they spend away from their nests, the less chance their chicks will survive. Daniel's story reminds me of a fisherman I met many years ago in the Lofoten Islands off Norway. As a young, newly married man, he was rarely away on his boat for more than a week at a time. As the years passed, however, he might be away for six months, trawling the pale waters of the Barents Sea in search of a diminishing supply of fish.

In communist times, the authorities tried to turn Razim from a salt water lake fed by the sea into a freshwater lake fed by the Danube. Dykes were built to seal it off, and artificial channels dug from the river. The experiment proved a disaster.[12] There have been tentative attempts ever since to restore these areas to their natural state. Similar efforts were made with the land. A vast network of dykes was built to win land for maize and rice. Some were successful at first, but rising salt in the soil destroyed the crops. The dream of the Romanian dictator Nicolae Ceaușescu, the son of a village cobbler, to overcome 'rural backwardness' has been replaced by the dream of environmentalists to restore rural wilderness.[13]

We strike out across the hilltops. Visibility gets worse, despite the wind, and out of the swirling fog we catch glimpses of tall wind turbines in the distance, as though striding towards us. Attempts by the construction companies to erect them inside the delta have foundered on account of the opposition of the Greens, but almost everywhere else in Dobrogea construction continues at breakneck speed. The hunger of local councils for investment, subsidies from Brussels, and above all the powerful Dobrogean winds, keep the builders coming. Daniel fears for the migrating birds, for those that nest here all year round, and he worries about the impact of roads and power cables, the concrete and steel on the fragile ecosystem. 'This is one of the wonders of Europe, and it shouldn't be destroyed by this kind of investment. But in Romania, the big money wins all the time. The developers snap up the land, build first and ask questions afterwards.' On the road from Mahmoudia to Tulcea we follow striped concrete mixers, like wasps in a cloud of dust. Spanish, German, Romanian, French and American companies all compete for the same land and the same wind. 'We're not against development, and we're not against wind energy, but whenever anything turns into this industrial scale, it's bound to cause harm. You just cannot have thousands of rotors, each the diameter of a football field, spinning round without a major impact. Most species of birds migrate at night. The birds are not stupid; they can dodge a few turbines, but what happens if they fly into hundreds of them? It's even worse for bats. They don't even need to be hit by the blades; the difference in pressure caused by the rotors makes their lungs implode as they pass.'

Environmental impact studies are funded by the investors themselves, and suggest no grounds for concern. But when ornithologists try to study the ground under the turbines for the corpses of birds, they are chased away by private security guards.

We drive in a wide loop to Murighiol – 'purple lake' in Turkish – named after the particular hue of the water – to see herring and black-headed gulls, and a gaggle of greylag geese. The poplar trees wear the dark nests of rooks on their branches like rings on their fingers. Many have been taken over by red-footed falcons. No hunting is allowed on land owned by the Biosphere Reserve, so birds take refuge here.

We continue on through the village of Plopu, once famous for its thatchers. Most have migrated up the Danube to Britain or the Netherlands in search of better paid work. A line of white-fronted geese flies high over roofs on which red tiles have replaced the traditional covering. Thousands of black-tailed godwits rise in a cloud from a former fish pond. 'They're just resting, fattening themselves up for the journey to Russia,' says Daniel. Like curlews, godwits have beaks with a flexible tip, to grab the worms and crustaceans they find in the holes they dig in the mud. Fine dwarf reed lines the shore of the lake, the best quality for thatching, pure gold against a grey sky.

Coming into Tulcea, the rain beats against the windscreen and the road is crowded with concrete mixers. Is no compromise possible with the turbine builders? I ask. Couldn't a map be drawn up to avoid the areas most sensitive for migrating birds? 'There was such an attempt, but the investors arriving now say it discriminates in favour of those who have already started work. They build wherever they find land that is suitable. I'm afraid this will continue until the profits drop, or the subsidies disappear.'

Grigore Baboianu is Director of the Danube Delta Biosphere Reserve. On the wall of his modern glass office, overlooking the harbour in Tulcea, is a photograph of him with Jacques Cousteau. The famous French environmentalist travelled the length of the Danube from 1990 to 1992, gathering information on the health and diseases of the river from the pollutants he found stored in shells.[14] 'You are lucky,' Cousteau told Baboianu in Tulcea, 'the Danube is still a living river, compared to the Rhine, but it will need a lot of help.'

In the 1950s, communism brought rapid, crude industrialisation to half of Europe still dozing in a semi-feudal slumber. The village of Pentele in Hungary became first Sztálinváros (Stalintown), then Dunaújváros (Danube New Town). Cities swelled on the banks of the rivers as babies boomed and people moved from the countryside to housing estates, which resembled the battlements of medieval castles. All human, chemical and animal waste flowed back into the river, which processed and cleaned what it could in the reed beds and root systems of its remaining wetland flood plains, and spat out what it could not digest into the Black Sea. In the early 1990s, hundreds of giant communist era industrial plants along the Danube banks went bankrupt and closed down. When state subsidies and the vast bureaucratic energy of the totalitarian state were withdrawn, they stood little chance of survival.

The story with the farms was a little different. Huge state farms and cooperatives, from the Austrian border with Hungary all the way to the delta, turned the fields of the Middle and Lower Danube basin into food machines. Grain harvests grew year by year, with the soil pumped full of chemical fertilisers. Chemical factories lined the river, producing fertilisers and explosives. The factories flushed their waste into the river, while barges carried their products to market. Grain was transported down to Constanța for shipment across the oceans of the world, or upriver to Austria and Germany to feed the capitalist masses. When communism collapsed, the Danube breathed a massive sigh of relief.[15] The pollutant stream in the drainage ditches from pig farms slowed from a flood to a trickle. Gypsies stripped the metal from the closed industries on the shores, to be sold as scrap, carried across the seas, and melted into iron girders to reinforce the concrete of the building boom in China and India. State farms were broken up into small units and peasants got back land, or compensation for it, which had been stolen from them in the great wave of nationalisations in the late 1940s. For a decade there was a dearth of tractors small enough to plough the small plots, with the Soviet and East German monsters rusting in the weeds. In the twenty-first century there is still a dearth of capital in the countryside. Some agribusinesses have been resurrected, often with foreign capital. There is a steady concentration of land in ever fewer hands, as the sons and daughters of the peasants who got back their patrimony decide they do not want to work it and sell it off. The food industry and breweries of Romania and Bulgaria, Hungary and Slovakia were snapped up by foreign companies in the first wave of privatisations in the 1990s. Big supermarkets and hypermarkets have partly replaced the traditional open-air markets where people used to buy their fruit and vegetables and freshly slaughtered hens direct from the producers, but many markets still survive, because the food tastes better, you can see who grew it, and the tomato on your plate can only gain from not having travelled two thousand kilometres from the plant which produced it.

Some factories have resumed work, with tighter laws on discharges into the river. Big European Union-backed projects to build state-of-the-art sewage works for cities such as Vienna and Budapest have helped clean up the waters. Now one of the biggest pollutants is plastic bottles, which float down on the current, bereft of messages, save that someone upstream was careless enough to leave them on the shore. Washed out into the Black Sea, they eventually disintegrate into a poisonous sludge on the sea bed that will be there for all time.

The task of the Biosphere Authority is to protect the delta after the depredations of the Ceaușescu years, and to help local communities make a living. Unfortunately, however, the two tasks do not always sit comfortably side by side. Local farmers and fishermen resent what they see as the interference of 'the ecologists', as they call employees of the Biosphere Authority. High unemployment in the 1990s left men in the delta with nothing to do except fish. Some use nets with illegally small mesh. Others attach electrodes to a car battery and plunge them into the water, which kills everything within a wide radius. Upstream in Serbia, hand grenades made plentiful by the wars of the 1990s are used to blow fish out of the water. In 2006 Romania banned sturgeon fishing. This was a good move to save the fish from extinction, but a heavy blow to the dedicated band of fishermen, especially in the delta, for whom sturgeon was by far the most valuable prize. Creative ways have been sought to help fishermen make a living. One idea Grigore Baboianu supports is for fishermen to be allowed one week in the year when they can fish for sturgeon. But that would be difficult to introduce just when Bulgaria, Serbia and Ukraine, after years of Romanian pressure, have brought in a general ban on sturgeon fishing in their own sections of the river. Another idea is aquaculture, that is breeding sturgeon artificially and reintroducing them to the river. There are already two sturgeon farms in Romania, one at Isaccea on the Danube, another near Bucharest. The Norwegian–Romanian project plans to introduce 'sturgeon tours' of the Danube.[16]

I first met Grigore in 2000 when I came to film pelicans in the delta. He gave us the use of a boat and a guide, while we paid the diesel for the outboard motor. The Authority was so short of funds its rangers could hardly patrol the vast, semi-wilderness of the delta to prevent poaching. The trick with pelicans, our guide explained, is to behave like them. As such enormous birds themselves, they are not easily alarmed by other large creatures, such as humans, drifting down towards them on the current. We were almost among them before the more nervous birds identified us as short-beaked aliens, while the wiser, older birds, or perhaps just those who had been filmed so many times, remained tranquil on the calm waters among the reeds. The financial situation has not improved much since then, Grigore confesses, though the border police are better equipped, better funded, and in a much better position to protect the delta. Nets are confiscated, and those who fish during spawning periods when a ban is in force are punished. Only the humble pike can be caught in April and May.

On a Sunday morning in Tulcea, I go in search of the imam at the mosque a little way up the hill towards the museum. He's rushing to a funeral, but will be back later, and we can talk then, God-willing. But God has other plans for him, and at the appointed time there's no one in sight. After a brief wait in the cold of a March evening, I ring the doorbell at the Turkish–Romanian Friendship Association opposite, a low town house of just a single storey. The Turks governed Dobrogea for nearly five hundred years, and only lost their territories here in the 1870s. The remaining Turks have been transformed from rulers to an ethnographic oddity, but they have kept some of their treasures intact. A woman comes to the door and welcomes me inside like a prodigal son. A Turkish women's group has gathered for their weekly singing session: Vezza Sadula, Sabis Mahmet and Sabiha Ali lead the troupe. Some of the songs they have learnt on their annual trips to the Turkish heartlands, which they perform at folk festivals. But the best are old Turkish ballads from Dobrogea, about the Danube.

I saw a Romanian girl down by the Danube shore . . .
With no father or mother, her hands bound by strangers,
'– Romanian girl, tell me the truth –
Where is your mother?'
'I have neither mother nor father,
I'm alone in the world, orphaned and alone'
– 'You an orphan, me a poor fellow
Let us be married!'

'Marry you?' she replied,
'And wrap us both in this land of homesickness?'[17]

Why a Romanian lass would feel homesick beside the Danube, and where
the Turkish lad arrived from, remain hidden in the mists of time. Tulcea
was always a town for people in transit. It looks out towards the sea, and
back up the Danube.

   After four or five songs, the ladies are tiring, and one has lost her mobile
phone. Soon the whole group is hunting high and low for it, and even the
final chorus falls victim to the disappearance of new technology. Back in
the small hotel in the harbour, I eat another perch then have an early night,
lulled to sleep by the sound of waves lapping against the harbour and the
cries of gulls.

CHAPTER 2

The Kneeling Oak

The crew our companions, were good lads
unchanging in the changing days
they did not grumble at the labour
the thirsts, the night frosts
like trees, like waves
they accepted the wind, the rain
the night cold, the heat of the sun . . .
GEORGE SEFERIS, 'Argonauts'[1]

THE BOAT from Tulcea down the Sulina arm of the Danube delta is packed with people and goods. Sacks of oats for the horses of Sulina, nappies for its babies, Greek oranges, Spanish tomatoes, Bolivian bananas, but above all people. Ladies with flowered headscarves, anchored to the deck with shopping bags, two narrow-hipped teenage girls on their way to visit their grandmother, middle-aged lovers making a new start, gazing into the wake of the boat, but most of all an army of chiselled-faced men, brooding over the stern in their Baltic-blue workers' jackets, smoking in silent clusters on the deck.

Willows line the riverbanks, the old men of the river, their gnarled and twisted roots reaching down to the water for one last drink. Fast-growing Canadian poplars crowd behind them, like teenagers trying to get into a party. In one place a whole forest of them has been massacred, levelled to the ground. The Danube smells like the sea I grew up beside, in southern England, but greener, more pungent, unsalted. There are seagulls, though, and cormorants. Black, hook-necked, then straight-backed as soldiers with yellow noses, slow and dignified in their movements as surgeons, perched on driftwood on the banks of the river, diving gracefully as arrows into the water. Lone herons, cranes, storks and egrets. Only ducks and geese fly together in groups. All the others fish by themselves, with a wary eye on their fellow birds, or human interference with the life of the riverbank.

The ferry takes four and a half hours from Tulcea to Sulina, sixty kilometres east, on the Black Sea coast. There are no roads, just a labyrinth of creeks and marshes. The delta has the biggest concentration of reed banks on earth. The Black Sea into which the yellow-brown Danube pours is an inland lake, isolated from the Atlantic Ocean by the long, lazy body of the Mediterranean. Bold sailors passing through the straits of Gibraltar, the Dardanelles and the Bosphorus must have wondered if they would ever see the Bay of Biscay again. In places, sand-dunes and soil have settled long enough to allow a village to spring up. Milea 23 is named after 'Mile 23' from the Danube mouth. C. A. Rosetti, on the Chilia arm, is a cluster of villages named after a nineteenth-century Romanian novelist, though the settlement was actually created by shepherds whose sheep found just enough dry land to lead them on towards the beckoning surf. Constantin Rosetti was also a politician, whose support for the 1848 revolution nearly led him to the gallows. Rescued by the pleas of his English wife, Mary, the sister of the British consul in Bucharest, he later served as Minister of Police.[2]

I go out on deck into the grey afternoon. The Danube is grey, the sky is grey, even the forests on each side of the river are shades of grey. The scene is brightened only by the occasional splash of colour of the peasant houses and the sea-stained hulls of passing ships. Upriver they carry bauxite ore from Russia or Brazil to the aluminium works in Tulcea. Other ships are empty, high in the water, on their way to fetch laminated sheets from the steel mills of Galați; the *Belfin*, and the *Burhan Dizman*, registered in Istanbul, the *Ayane* from Valletta.[3] Like rare birds, lone sailors stand gazing down from the gangways at our crowded river ferry into a world in which families and friends still travel together. If my children were with me, we would wave. Instead, I sweep their decks with my binoculars, trying to catch a glimpse of the man at the wheel, his face set against the dying day.

There are a few villages beside the river, spreadeagled along the shore on either side as though the river were the main street. Tidy stacks of cut reed are piled high beside houses with thatched or tin roofs. Rowing boats with black-tarred hulls are moored by wooden jetties, or turned upside down like seashells by the path. The houses are wooden, their window frames painted blue, or white or green. Cockerels call from the shore. White-coated geese waddle self-importantly, like doctors on a tour of a hospital ward. Fishermen, always in pairs, cast off in their black boats. One man rows while the other patiently feeds the floats of a net out between his fingers.

There is not a bare head to be seen in the river world. The men wear Cossack-style hats, flat caps or baseball caps; the older women scarves or knitted woollen hats. Even the birds seem to be wearing hats, the tufted plumes of their feathers. The river is wide, ten to fourteen metres deep, and there is plenty of space for all manner of craft to pass. The blue, yellow and red Romanian ensign, the blue and yellow of Ukraine, and the Dutch tricolour are stiff in the afternoon breeze.

Our boat arrives in Sulina right on time at five-thirty. A crowd of people and a horse and cart are waiting on the quay. The gangplank clatters down and thick wire ropes are looped around the stanchions. A bubble of laughter bursts as relatives fall into each other's arms, elderly couples peck each other on the cheeks, then reach for their bags. Much of the rest of the town, with no one in particular to meet, has wandered down to the shore to watch the new arrivals. Cut off from the rest of the world by water and reed banks, the visit of the daily boat from Tulcea is a landmark in their lives.

I book into the Hotel Jean Bart, just along the shore from the ferry landing. It has a Wild West feel, with heavy, wooden panelling in the dining room and hibernating geraniums on the window ledge of my high-ceilinged bedroom, smelling of black pepper. From the outside, the hotel is striped dark red and white like a raspberry ripple. I'm in a rush to reach the Black Sea before darkness falls.

On the unmade road east to the sea beyond Sulina is the town graveyard. A young couple are just leaving as I reach the gate. Their eyes are not grave-yard red, but their lips are fresh from kissing. There's a little chapel with a wooden tower and a weather vane, and just behind it is the British section of the cemetery. The English names seem particularly desolate beside the Danube, so far from the Tyne and the Thames, the Mersey and the Medway.

'Sacred to the memory of Thomas Rutherford of Houdon Pans, England, Chief Engineer of the Steam Ship *Kepler* of North Shields, who

departed this life on the 26th day of July 1875 at Sulina, aged 36 years.'
This is followed by a quote from Psalm 39: 'Thou makest my days as a
handbreath, and my years are as nothing before thee.' James Mason, of the
Phoenician of Sunderland, died at Sulina on 3 October 1852, aged twenty
years. William Simpson died at Sulina on 28 July 1870 aged forty-six
years. His stone was erected by the European Commission of the Danube,
'by whom Mr Simpson was employed for 13 years as foreman of the
works'. I wonder if old Charles Hartley attended the funeral, exposed his
bowed head to the burning August sun as they lowered Bill Simpson into
the ground. There are four names on the next stone, seamen from HBMS
Recruit, all drowned in the Danube between 1859 and 1861. How could a
ship be careless enough to lose four sailors in just two years? 'And also for
Peter Gregor, stoker, who died from the effects of climate.'

The wrecks marked on shipping charts, on either side of the Danube
mouth, are proof that this is not always such a placid river.

Finally, with a beautifully carved olive branch at the top of the stone:
'In loving memory of Isabella Jane Robinson, eldest and dearly beloved
daughter of E. A. and E. D. S. Robinson of South Shields, aged 28, who
drowned off Sulina on 27 September 1896, by the foundering through
collision of the S/S *Kylemoor*.'

Near the entrance of the graveyard, I see the freshest grave of all. A low
shoulder of hard sand and a bunch of flowers. Ion Valentin, it says on his
simple wooden cross, born 2011, died 2011.

Sulina is a town founded by pirates, made famous by consuls, which
survives on an uneasy diet of fish and foreigners. It was first mentioned by
the Byzantine emperor Constantine VII in a long letter to his fourteen-
year-old son in AD 950, about the tribes he might expect to have to deal
with when he inherited the throne. 'The Russians come down the Dnieper
river to the Black Sea each year in dug-out boats,' Constantine wrote, 'past
the Danube mouth to the Selinas (Sulina) river, and are constantly harried
by the tribe of Pechenegs, who pick off any boats that stray from the rest,
all the way down the coast to Constantinople.'[4]

The far gate of the graveyard is already locked for the night, so I clamber
over the fence and press on towards a sea I can no longer see but can hear
more clearly, resounding off new houses, poised in the sand like crabs
beyond the cemetery. Seabirds call from close at hand among the

whispering reeds, their preparations for sleep disturbed by my intrusion. Then the sand is suddenly soft beneath my bare feet, followed by the painful crackle of shells, and I see the white lines of the waves on a dark canvas. For once, the Black Sea is really black. A lighthouse pulses white at the end of a long jetty. I walk for a long time, alone along the shore.

The sun rises next morning over the sea. I lean out from my wrought iron balcony at the Jean Bart, straining to catch the first rays on my face. A single seagull perches on the top of each lamp post with a similar plan to my own, and the tops of the willow trees on the shore turn to gold. There is a bustle of people rushing for the six-thirty boat back to Tulcea, boys pushing bicycles, and women with three or four shopping bags in each hand.

Over morning coffee in the wood-panelled bar, the owner of the hotel, Aurel Bajenaru, tells me his story. He came here aged twenty, and is now fifty-two. When he arrived there were fifteen thousand inhabitants employed in the fisheries, at the fish-canning factory, the big ship repair yard or the naval barracks. Now there are only four thousand and the factories have gone. 'I used to like it here, but democracy has changed it, harmed it,' he says. His three daughters have grown up and left, and he would leave too, if he were twenty years younger. He thinks the only chance for the town is tourism, but everything he tries to do is weighed down by bureaucracy, and by the incapacity of the townsfolk to work together. On the television behind his head, set high in the wooden panelling, I see a black-and-white film of a man and woman in passionate embrace. The news has just broken that the actress Elizabeth Taylor has died.[5] Until the previous December, immune to the rise and fall of the stars of the silver screen, each family was allowed to catch three kilos of silvery fish a week for their own consumption. That was abolished because the authorities believed people were exceeding their quota, and it was impossible to police. In order to buy fish to serve in the hotel restaurant, Aurel now has to take his boat once a week to Tulcea to buy from the main fish company, to whom local fishermen are obliged to sell their catch. People have to pay three separate taxes: to the town hall, the biosphere authority, and the state. Outside his hotel it is hard to tell which parts of the town are being built up and which are falling down. Bulldozers dig through the back-streets, turning the soil beneath the torn-up tarmac to mud. There is no central heating in the newer, four-storey blocks of flats which sprang up along the shore in communist times. Such is the anarchy of capitalist Romania, one flat is heated by wood, another by gas, another by electricity. The town hospital is so short of funds it may close down.

Aurel is happier talking about the former glory of Sulina. At the end of the Crimean War in 1856, the idea of a united Europe was born here. A European Commission was set up by the great powers: Great Britain, Russia, Austro-Hungary, Turkey, Prussia, France and Italy. The town became a thriving, cosmopolitan centre, where the common language was Greek. In 1900 there were twenty-three nationalities, easily led by the Greeks with 2,500, then 803 Romanians, 444 Armenians, 268 Turks and 173 Jews.[6] The sprinkling of nationalities at the bottom of the list is as interesting as that at the top – what did the five Ethiopians, ten Senegalese and twenty-four English people make of Sulina then? How did they spend the long summer days or the long winter nights? Aurel tells a Romeo and Juliet story of an Englishman and a beautiful cabaret dancer of mixed Greek and African parentage. The boy's parents bitterly opposed their marriage, and when she fell overboard from a boat in the midst of the drama he dived into the Danube to save her; they were both drowned. Their bodies were found entwined, the story goes, though I somehow missed their graves in the cemetery the previous evening.

The buildings of Sulina are an odd mix, each in a different architectural style. The Jean Bart Hotel had Maltese owners before the war, who got it back after the 1989 revolution and eventually sold it to him. Jean Bart was the pen-name of the writer Eugeniu Botez, whose novel *Europolis* (1958) is set in Sulina.[7] July and August are the only busy months in Sulina now. The hotel is frequented mostly by French and Germans, with a sprinkling of Italians who come for the hunting. For a long time water was a serious problem in the town, but that was finally solved by a generous visitor. When her Royal Highness Queen Emma of Holland stepped down from her ship in 1897, wiped her brow and asked for a glass of water, there was consternation on the quay. It took some minutes before one could be rustled up for her. Upset by the embarrassment her humble request caused, she paid for the construction of a water tower.[8] It stands there to this day, a sledge-hammer of a building on the western approaches to the town. But

Sulina's most important landmark is the lighthouse. This is where any journey up the Danube begins: mile, or kilometre zero. The Danube is measured upriver from the lighthouse, not downriver from the source like other rivers. My own progress upriver should be easy to measure. The three miles between the lighthouse and the sea are not counted in its official length – a kind of no-man's-land, the soft gums of the river mouth. They help contribute to the general confusion about just how long the river is. Some authors even refer to two different lengths in the same article. But because I start with the lighthouse and end with the pool in the gardens of the Furstenberg Palace in Donaueschingen, I am in no such danger.

I climb the spiral staircase to the top of the chunky white tower, pausing for breath and to gaze out of the three round portholes that run up the front of the tower like black buttons on a white dinner jacket. Then I step out through a low iron door on to a rickety balcony. If I shut my eyes, I can see all the way upriver to Germany, 2,860 kilometres upstream. Sulina lounges in the spring sunshine beneath me – old ships rusting apart into the marshes, streets of single-storey homes laid out, higgledy-piggledy towards the reed banks, the onion-domed towers of churches in the town centre. Through my binoculars the Ukrainian church looks the most frail and the most beautiful, its pale blue wooden panels framing an icon that might be Saint Demetrius. The lighthouse has a rather quaint glasshouse in the middle, with a tiled roof and a weather vane on the top. There are no light bulbs, but the original French crystal, which once refracted the beam far out to sea, is still in place, in rings around the sockets like dragonfly wings. Downstairs, a brass plaque in French at the entrance states that its construction was agreed at the Treaty of Paris at the same time that the European Commission was established there, on 30 March 1856, to improve the navigability of the mouths of the Danube. It was completed in November 1870 and would not look out of place on the shores of the English Channel.

Maria Sinescu is the custodian. She was born and bred in Sulina, left for a few years, then came back to look after her elderly parents. The level of the Black Sea is rising as a result of global warming. The great sandy beaches of Romania and Bulgaria are rapidly disappearing. In fifty years time, they will be gone completely if no way is found to save them. 'Might that not restore the importance of her lighthouse, now stranded so far inland?' I ask. 'Certainly not,' she insists, 'the sand will continue to pile up at the river mouth, and more houses are under construction between the graveyard and the sea.' In fact, the opposite is happening: the lighthouse is still moving towards the town centre.

And might Sulina blossom again?

'I cannot guarantee that it will; I can only hope. History always works in cycles.'

That evening in a restaurant on the river shore, I order grilled sturgeon from a blonde waitress, who flits between the tables like a goldfish. Innocently I ask her where my fish comes from, neglecting to mention that sturgeon fishing has been banned in Romanian waters since 2006. She shrugs her pretty shoulders, but tells me where to find her husband's grand-mother, Aunty Nicolina, who knows everything there is to know about fish. My dinner arrives, rather small, but with an exquisite taste, like wild salmon. I drink a glass of the white wine of the Măcin hills, dry as granite.

Nicolina is not at home the next morning, but her husband Simion is. I find his house easily, the only one with a horse and cart tethered outside. Simion is seventy-two, his eyes barely opening on a face beaten by Danube winters and scorched by Sulina summers. He wears two grey jumpers over his shirt and a black Cossack hat which looks as though he never takes it off. We talk outside in the street as he gets his horse ready for a trip to his vegetable patch. The horse is expensive to keep, but worth having because he can plough his land with it and carry his crops home. The winter has been long, and the hay he cut the previous summer has run out. He has just bought oats – the sacks I saw unloaded from the boat I arrived on – to keep his horse going until the grass grows again. He needs five kilos a day. His winter wood supply is also exhausted, and the nights are still cold. He came here from Tulcea originally, to work on the dykes under construction in communist times, and met his future wife at a wedding. He asked her to dance, and that was it. He likes the peace and quiet of Sulina, and the fact that there are no thieves – no one bothers to lock their homes. As we speak a trader, a Roma from the mainland, comes down the road, selling clothes. Simion farms a swathe of land on the edge of the town, and grows potatoes, tomatoes and cabbages. The soil is poor, because of the salt so close to the sea, but it can be improved with plenty of manure, which he gets from his cows. But he can't tell me anything about fishing: 'I can't stand the taste of fish, never could,' he explains. He's a cheese and milk man, and keeps five cows to make sure of his supplies. For his wife, on the other hand, 'a day without fish to eat is a sad day indeed!'

Inside the house, a thirteen-year-old boy, Simion's grandson, does not look up from the computer screen. His mother has been working in Spain for three years, and left her three children at home with the grandparents. At least the youngest likes books. But none of them helps him with the animals. Soon there will be no cattle in the delta, he says, because the young have no interest in working with them and his generation will die out.

Adrian Oprisan has short, reddish fair hair, a firm handshake and a small, green fibreglass boat. He lives with his wife and small child right on the Danube at Crisan, half way between Sulina and Tulcea, and rents an island of reeds in the delta from the Danube Biosphere Authority. The reeds, cut in January and February, are nearly ready, and on my first journey upriver he takes me to see his harvest.

The Danube is milky-green beneath the soaring hull of his boat. Leaving Sulina, we load up with fuel from a floating filling station, then head upstream. Like cars, ships that are no longer in use rapidly lose their shine. A hydrofoil, the S.F. *Maria*, registered in Constanţa, dozes fitfully on the right bank. A couple of mammoth grey-hulled hulks, straight out of a horror film, stretch against a crumbling concrete dock on the left. I imagine bats flitting in and out of the dark windows of the bridge. We leave Sulina far behind. Brown horses graze peaceably on the shore, flocks of ducks flee our approach, and our wash lifts and drops the car-tyres tied to makeshift jetties for boats to moor alongside. Only one cargo ship seems to be in use: the *Anglia*, flying the Maltese cross, registered at Batumi at the far end of the Black Sea in Georgia, moves ponderously upstream. Adrian swerves his boat into a side channel, south of the main stream and we enter another world, the real delta. Reeds encroach on all sides; willows overhang the water so low we have to duck not to lose our heads, and birds of all kinds, silent raptors, watch from the bigger trees. The reeds are thick with ducks, geese, egrets, and smaller birds, so light they can balance on a single stem. The channel gets narrower. Adrian turns off the engine and poles with a single oar. Solid ground turns out to be afloat, and he pushes the clumps of earth aside. Invading armies were once lured into this labyrinth and picked off one by one by the arrows of local tribesmen who alone knew exactly where to tread. Many of the reeds grow on floating islands. The islands rise and fall with the tide, or the flood waters. When you cut reeds all day, the tree which seemed so tall in the early morning has shrunk to a bush by lunch time. What has happened is that the floating island on which you work has risen like a lift on the tide. Columns of grey-black smoke drift on the far horizon. When the reeds have been cut, farmers burn off the chaff to act as fire breaks. If fire breaks out accidentally elsewhere, there is less chance of it raging right through the delta. The delta stretches across nearly six thousand square kilometres, a large part of which is covered by reeds. Over the golden stems, rustling gently in the wind, the columns of smoke give an impression of homes burning in wartime.

A dark brown dog called Caesar bounds through the reeds and jumps with joy at Adrian's approach. Three men feed bundles of cut reeds through what looks like a giant red sewing machine. This produces reeds of uniform lengths for thatching or fence-making, and tidies them into neat bundles which are then stacked into wigwams. A clump of plastic soft-drink bottles is positioned to warn the workers of a hole in their island – a step there would plunge you into water four metres deep.

This will be a good year for the reeds, Adrian says. A winter cold enough but not too cold, long but not too damp. He needs thirty to forty good cutting days in the four months of winter. When it is too cold, or the snow is too damp and heavy on the reeds, they cannot be cut. Damp reeds turn dark brown. Reed is like gold, he says, but there is no great profit from it, because of the high cost of the cutting. He will make fifteen thousand bundles this year, graded according to quality and length. The breeze stirs the flowers at the top of the reeds, creating a whispering sound but quite unlike the wind in the leaves of trees.

On the way to Crisan, a cold wind sends cat's-paws, shadows like sudden shivers, over the water. A grey heron, then a purple one, lift effort-lessly from the shore, then peel away to one side. Behind his house in Crisan Adrian shows me his combine harvester, specially built for the reeds, with four massive rubber tyres that float on the water, and a plat-form on the back where the newly cut reeds are stacked – up to a tonne per load. It looks like a moon-buggy or a *Starwars* Lego toy.

'It's beautiful, in its way,' I tell Adrian, but he will have none of it.

'It's a working machine. It has nothing to do with beauty!' A single tyre, made in Denmark, costs eighteen hundred dollars, and lasts five years. He could buy them more cheaply in Budapest, but they might burst in their second season.

That evening, after a fine catfish dinner, I meet his wife's grandparents. Mihai Tecliceanu is a former history teacher from Bucharest. His wife, Elena, is a Ukrainian from Karaorman, half an hour's journey through the reeds to the south. Mihai first visited the delta as a schools' inspector in communist times. Motorboats were rare in those days, and most fishermen rowed or sailed. As Mihai arrived in the region to inspect the schools, a fisherman asked for a tow alongside his motorboat for the last few kilometres of the journey. 'It was snowing, though it was only early November, and that man with his beard full of snow and his long boots made a very powerful impression on me,' Mihai remembers. 'I thought I had arrived in the land of the Eskimos!' He found them so congenial that he decided to spend the rest of his life here.

Elena was born in 1947, at the time of the post-war famine. Karaorman is a largely Ukrainian village, though in the toughest communist years the inhabitants were not allowed to speak their own language. This came as something of a surprise to people who had welcomed the Russians after the war as fellow Slavs. But communism also had its good sides, Elena says. 'People were more honest then . . . not so busy chasing after money.' She is only three-quarters Ukrainian, she tells me proudly, because her great grandfather on her mother's side was a Romanian shepherd, and came from the Carpathian Mountains near Sibiu with his sheep. Transhumance, the custom of bringing the sheep down from the mountains for the winter to travel great distances with the flocks in search of pasture, is still practised in Romania.[9] Brindza, a delicious salty white sheep's cheese akin to Greek feta, is still made in Poiana Sibiului, the mountain region where Elena's ancestors came from, some 650 kilometres from Karaorman. On a visit there many years before, I met a shepherd who walked his flock each autumn as far as Satu Mare in north-eastern Romania, then back in time for Easter, when families celebrate the return of the men, and their wives and children go with them and the flocks up on to the high mountain pastures. The cheese is still made in large wooden barrels, notwithstanding the efforts of the hygiene inspectors to move the sheep folds closer to the road and mix the milk in stainless steel vats. 'The cheese would not taste the same,' they say in the mountains.

During Ottoman times, Romanian shepherds walked their flocks as far as the Crimea, and might be away for several years at a time. They carried wooden passports, recognised by the Habsburg, Ottoman and Russian empires, with the details of their flocks carved in the wood. It must have been on one of these trips that Elena's great grandfather fell in love with his future wife, and never returned to the mountains.

Mihai interrupts our conversation to go and round up his cows to milk them in the last light. They are wandering wild along the grassy dyke, but run away when they see me, a stranger. I have to hide behind the milking shed for Mihai to coax them inside. Back in her kitchen, Elena unscrews a tall plastic bottle of sour-tasting wine, which improves with each glass, and sings old Ukrainian songs.

Very early the next morning we eat a breakfast of fried eggs and brindza, with coffee. Elena watches us eat approvingly, her back to the woodburning stove, with all the pleasure of a woman who has spent her whole life making men food, and still delights in watching them eat it. Then we walk down the towpath, ankle-deep in bird feathers and the plastic flotsam and jetsam thrown up by the river, to Adrian's boat.

It's a religious holiday in Karaorman when we arrive, windblown from the journey across the lakes. The wide, unmade-up streets are almost empty. Every chimney wears a plume of smoke; the families are inside in the warm by their woodburning stoves, celebrating. Adrian asks around for someone who could take me to the forest – the strange expanse of oak and ash trees, growing on sand dunes, which gives Karaorman its name. The Danube does not just flow from the Black Forest to the Black Sea. *Karaorman* means 'black forest' in Turkish. The river flows from one black forest to another.

I'm up in the wooden belfry of the village church tower, inspecting a fine brass bell, when a man pulls up below with his horse and cart. The date '84' is clearly visible on the bell, but I can't decide if it's 1884 or 1784. Through the fly-strewn window, I study the green-painted cart with red wheels, a worthy successor to Adrian's boat for the next leg of my journey. Bogdan is a broad-shouldered, red-faced fellow with a chequered jacket and a black woolly hat. He drives a hard bargain for a couple of hours ride to the forest and back, but I don't grudge it to him as I've torn him away from his family. His horse, called Marcel, also has the air of an animal that until a few minutes ago had been looking forward to a well-deserved rest. I climb up beside Bogdan onto a wooden seat, and we set out at a steady pace on the waterlogged and rutted tracks out of the village. There are storks' nests overhead, and the forest looms on the horizon, more dark brown than black, above an expanse of close-cropped yellow grass. White-tailed eagles and hooded crows nest in the tall trees, and rare flowers and mosses grow beneath them. There is a strong smell of horse and cow dung, and the cry of cockerels and the barking of dogs follow us from the village.

As we enter the forest, the sounds change suddenly. The horse's hooves and the wheels of the cart rustle over dry leaves, then strain silently through thick sand and splash loudly through deep water as the horse stumbles to find the track in the mud. One particular bird calls repeatedly. Bogdan cannot name it, in Romanian or Ukrainian, but produces an excellent imitation of its cry. The Kneeling Oak, the goal of our journey, rises majestically at the edge of a clearing. Two great branches rest their knees, or elbows, in the grass, then rise again from the ground, straight in front of it. This is the first big tree of my journey, and its girth reminds me of the lighthouse in Sulina. 'The Kneeling Oak' would make an excellent name for a pub in England. The previous evening in Crisan, Mihai Tericleanu had told me how it got its name. During Turkish times, according to legend, a young shepherd's wedding was rudely interrupted by Turkish soldiers who rode into the middle of the festivities, seized the bride and rode off. Outraged, the lads of the village, led by the furious bridegroom, rode after them, and thanks to their better knowledge of the area, headed them off. They rescued the girl and killed the Turks. The oak tree grew on that very place, and obligingly knelt down on the ground where the Turks are buried – to keep them down there, explained the teacher, 'and make sure they don't come up again to give us any more trouble!' The oak tree has been a local landmark ever since. Bogdan came to celebrate his eighteenth birthday here, and spent the night under its branches, 'with plenty of beer and girls'. There's also a well, dug in 1989 beside the tree. 'Good people,' reads the plaque, 'we found out that at the kneeling oak tree in this faraway forest there was no water. So the decision was taken to dig this well.' The plaque bears four names, Paul Stama, Ion Fotescu, Ilie Fotescu and Marin Sultan, 'lovers of animals, people and nature'.

On our way back, Marcel, the horse, stops frequently to drink. 'He's not really thirsty, he's just tired, so he pretends to drink to give himself an excuse to stop,' Bogdan laughs. He bursts into a melancholy song which rises and dips like our progress out of the woods, about an impoverished girl who resists the attentions of a rich man. 'Don't you want to be rich like me?' runs the refrain. In the end she gives up her resistance and marries him. 'And was she very unhappy?' I ask. Certainly not; they both lived happily ever after, sings Bogdan.

In the village, an elderly couple invite us into their yard to talk about the old days. As we sit in their porch, under an arbour of vines, they scale and gut a whole bucketful of freshly caught carp, to keep their grandson Alexander going during the week in Tulcea where he goes to university. The grandfather came here from Odessa, further around the Black Sea coast. When he arrived there were barely a dozen houses. Apart from two years in the army in Transylvania, where he learnt to read, write and speak Romanian, he has lived his whole life here. They always spoke Ukrainian at home. There was never enough time for school; he spent his childhood looking after several hundred sheep his father owned. In those days there were three mills in the village, for corn, wheat and oats, and all you could buy in the shops were sugar, vinegar and rice. He remembers the Russian soldiers coming at the end of the war. 'At first we welcomed them, we embraced them like long lost brothers – we spoke almost the same language. They came to our house because someone told them we were rich – because my father owned sheep. But when they saw that he slept on a pallet on the hard ground, they laughed and left us in peace, "we have thousands like him in Russia!" they said.' He also remembers, with bitterness, the nationalisation of property in the late 1940s, and how the peasants pleaded in vain to keep their land. As a child he used to take the sheep to the Kneeling Oak. 'They liked to rub their backs under one of its knees, but the other knee was too high in those days – only my donkey was tall enough for that one!'

The homemade wine is red and potent, and Alexander refills my glass too often. 'The grapes didn't ripen quite enough, so we added a little saccharine . . .' I sip it a little more cautiously after that. 'Life was better under communism,' he says. 'Everyone had animals, and work. There were three thousand head of sheep in the village then – now there are less than fifty. People had more children then too – between five and ten in a family.'

He and his wife make a quick calculation to count how many children there are today in the ten houses between their own and the church. Only three.

'Is nothing better now?' I ask. He shakes his head for a while, then cheers up. 'Just one thing,' he says. 'Under communism, the police would sometimes come to the village and beat us. They don't do that any more. They've been *democratised*!' He uses the word with deep irony.

The delta region is as rich in Russians and Ukrainians as it once was in Turks and Greeks. Like the Serbs, they celebrate Christmas two weeks later than the Romanians, according to the old rite. But Easter is marked at the same time as by Romanian Orthodox and Catholic believers. The one year they held Easter later, a terrible hailstorm decimated their crops, and the villagers took it as a sign that they should leave Easter where it was. For all their physical and cultural similarities, there's an uneasy rivalry between Ukrainians and Russians. 'They keep their traditions too, but they don't raise cattle like us.'

'Fishermen came here from Volkovo in Ukraine to fish for sturgeon, and we learnt some songs from them,' says his wife. She remembers one from school, and sings it to us, pausing first to wipe the fish scales off her hands. Even the cockerels fall quiet to listen. Old fishing nets hang on the wire fence, dreaming fitfully of fish. 'The song is about a girl, harvesting in the fields,' she says. 'A young man rides by, and offers to help. "No," she says, "because if you help me, all the boys in the village will want to too."'

To reach Mahmoudia by motorboat from Karaorman is several hours ride, and we've dawdled too long to easily intercept the ferry from Tulcea to Sfântu Gheorghe. Adrian guns the engine through narrow channels over wide expanses of lake. We pass the first tourists of the year, barbecuing fish on the shore, and silent anglers like cormorants, wrapped up in their thoughts. A young couple paddle by in a canoe with a tent and rucksacks, hardy explorers in the late March cold. The water is shallow here, only a metre and a half in places. The wind whips up the waves and the boat skims over them like a stone. We make it to Mahmoudia with only five minutes to spare before the afternoon catamaran appears around a headland in the river. The *Delta Express* is twin-hulled, with a single, Cyclopean eye in the middle from which the crew steer the boat. Adrian sets out back north, all the way home to Crisan, standing in his seashell of a craft, bouncing across the waves. I set out for Sfântu Gheorghe to start my journey up the Danube again, this time from the southernmost tip of the delta.

Sfântu Gheorghe, unlike Sulina, has no pretensions to be a town. This is a remote fishing village, with its back to the land, its face to the sea, and its shoulder to the river. It seems to belong here among the sand dunes and the birds and the sea-horses, much more than to the interior of the conti-nent. In summer it boasts a film festival, and its internet pages brim with images of tented youths silhouetted against the sunset.[10] For the rest of the year the wind, the water and the fruits of the deep provide the main entertainment.

High on an outside wall of the church, facing west, away from the preda-tions of the winds, are paintings of Christ as a fisher of men in the Sea of Galilee. In an alcove by the gate is an icon of a youthful Saint George, hardly old enough to be a patron saint, spearing a monster of the deeps. An oil lamp flickers in front of him. The alcove is designed to protect the flame, whatever the strength of the winds off the sea or the river. Inside the church, people kneel in a semi-circle round the priest, their eyes tight shut, singing with him in a service in memory of the dead – all the dead, not just the recently departed. People mostly stand in Orthodox churches; few sit or kneel. In another Orthodox country, Greece, I have seen old ladies struggling up steep hills or wandering far from their villages in the last light of day, to light a candle or an oil lamp in front of a shrine. There is still an instinctive, blind faith in God in eastern Europe, from Finland to Greece, which neither the material faiths of capitalism or communism have quite managed to erase. There is a stubborn insistence on contemplating the mystery of one's own existence and its conclusion. In the words of the Bosnian poet Mak Dizdar: 'And in the deepest depths of death the colours will be clearer then.'[11]

The beach in March is a great bow of sand, embedded with millions of shells, on to which huge trunks of trees have washed up like heads, some still wearing strange horned helmets. This southern mouth of the Danube is more tangible, simpler than the one in Sulina and uncluttered by piers or lighthouses. Offshore, the sweet waters of the Danube merge boister-ously with the salt waters of the Black Sea, like a rugby scrum first making progress against a bigger adversary by the sheer energy of their charge, then finally slowing to a halt as the home team digs in its heels, flexes its muscles, and drives them back. The most spectacular floods over the centuries have been caused by wind and tide combining to block the river, and then the Danube shrugs its vast shoulders on to the lands instead and drowns the villages.

This is the time of year, just before Easter, of the 'howling'. It starts up like an orchestra rehearsing, a straining of strings and a gurgling and a crying and a longing, mingled together. Local people say it is the herring, tempting fishermen to follow them, further and further out to sea, never to return. Out over the sea a line of cormorants and a single pelican fish together. The pelican's long, humorous beak gives it a leisurely air, which makes even the movement of the cormorants seem hurried. Over the southern lip of the delta a single column of black smoke rises from burning reeds. I walk barefoot in the seawater for a while, then turn inland, upriver again.

According to Greek legend, Jason and the Argonauts, in their ship the *Argo*, sailed up the Danube to flee the wrath of King Aeëtes of Colchis at the far, eastern end of the Black Sea, in what is now Georgia. The Argonauts stole the Golden Fleece with the help of the King's daughter Medea.[12] 'There are two ways back to Greece,' Phrixus' son Cytisorus told them. 'One is the route by which you came. The other is via the Danube, a great, broad river we can sail up till we come to another sea, which will take us round to the Aegean in the West.' Notwithstanding the dubious geography of the proposal, the journey was made, and the *Argo* must have sailed past this very headland.

There is also a Romanian folk story according to which Helios, the Sun, wanted to get married, but could find no bride more beautiful or desirable than his own sister Ileana Cosinzeana.[13] For nine years he travelled around the world in search of a bride, pulled in his chariot by nine horses, then came back and told his sister to prepare for her wedding. His mission had failed, and now he was determined to marry her. He found her in a shady glade, weaving at her loom in an *argea*, a hut used by the women to work in and give birth, half buried in the soil. The bashful girl protested that the union of brother and sister was unheard of, but in vain, and eventually she gave in. But she made the Sun promise that they would be married in a wax church, attended by a wax priest, at the far end of a wax bridge. Nothing was too difficult for the Sun, and soon all was prepared. But as they walked towards the white church, the bridge beneath them melted, and they fell into the water. God took pity and rescued them, placing the sun on one side of the sky and the moon on the other, so they can always see one another but never meet. One of Ileana's names was Diana, another was Luna, and a third was Selina, or Sulina. The green, shady glade was somewhere in the Danube delta, and the island to which they were walking to be wed might have been Sacalin Island just off the Black Sea coast. The story was told by the late nineteenth-century ethnologist Nicolae Densusianu in his epic work *Prehistoric Dacia*.[14] One of his most extraordinary claims is that the Dacians founded ancient Rome, and that Latin is actually a dialect of Dacian.

The map near the quay in Sfântu Gheorghe, which I consulted before setting out for the sea shore, also has a rather legendary quality. As I walk wearily beside the river, there is no sign of the footpath which was clearly marked on it. So I follow the river itself, skirting round low, overhanging branches by venturing deeper into the water, up to my knees. The river is cold and there is not a boat in sight, just the roar of the surf behind me, the call of sea and river birds in my ears. The smoke from the burning reeds on the far side is diluted and almost disappears into the grey sky. Suddenly to my side, I hear a whistle, then another. My heart misses a beat, expecting bandits to leap out of the marshes and overpower me. Then I discover the culprit: a single reed, taught to whistle by short blasts of the wind through its dry stem. A wall of reeds blocks my path, too thick and marshy to go through, and the water is too deep in the main channel to walk around. I have to cut inland, into a thorny thicket. I find a path which leads to an abandoned house. There once must have been an easy route for those who lived here into the village, but if there was, it's gone now, and there is nothing but bogland and the low, square concrete hulk of a bunker, overgrown with moss, built by the Germans during the Second World War. Surely the efficient Germans must also have had a road? But even to reach their fortifications, I would have to swim across a deep, narrow channel. I don't want to retrace my steps all the way back to the mouth of the river, so I ring the fisherman I'm due to meet: Tudor Avramov. Twenty minutes later his small boat purrs round the headland and I wade out to it. This is a part of the world where water transport still trumps the land routes.

Back in the village we sit in a café, though he refuses a drink. He's in a hurry; it's the height of the Danube herring season, and he wants to get back to his nets by his hut on the far side of the river. Radu Suciu in Tulcea gave me Tudor's name, as a former sturgeon fisherman involved in the Norwegian–Romanian sturgeon sustainability project. Once they travelled to Norway together. What impressed Tudor most was how organised the Norwegian fishermen were. 'We have an association of fishermen here too, but we need a proper trade union,' he says. The lone fishing company in the delta uses its monopoly position to keep the prices paid to fishermen low. Yet they are obliged by law to sell all their fish to it. Why doesn't he organise a trade union himself? 'I tried once, in 2005, to get fishing rights for us in several lakes in the delta. And they threw me out. I wouldn't want to be seen as a trouble-maker.'

Tudor has spent his whole life here. His first memories of the Danube are of stealing his father's boat as a child, and trying to row out to sea. His father had to rescue him. He has no romantic nostalgia for the Romania of his childhood. 'Everything is easier now than it used to be. In those days, everyone rowed. There were no engines before the 1989 revolution. That was very hard.' He regrets the ban on sturgeon fishing, but says it must be respected. His main contempt is reserved for those of his colleagues who use illegal methods to fish, such as electrodes attached to car batteries. 'They ought to be electrocuted themselves!' he says, and I don't think he's joking. Sturgeon was always the hardest fish to catch. 'First we had to sharpen the hooks. Then we had to know exactly where to lay them.' The best beluga sturgeon Tudor ever caught was a 280 kilo female, with forty kilos of caviar. 'Where did you sell it?' 'To the fish collecting point. We had no choice . . .' He's impatient to go back to his fish, but I persuade him to tell one last story. 'We fear the fog here in the mouth of the Danube more than any other weather. It comes down suddenly, out of nowhere. There were a lot of us out on the river, fishing one day, when that happened. It was so thick, you could hardly see your own hands, let alone the end of the boat. The women and children came out on the shore when they realised we were lost, and beat pots and pans together to guide us back to the village. But it was no good. The sounds seemed to come from all sides. It took me hours to find my way to the shore.'

Tudor's wife Maria is planting onions in the small garden in front of her house. We talk in her kitchen. 'Life is better here than in other parts of

Romania, because we have fish. Even if my husband doesn't catch enough to sell, he always brings some home to eat.' She likes all kinds. 'We cook them in the same ways we cook meat – fried, baked, boiled, in bread-crumbs or as fishballs.' She gives me her fishball recipe. 'First remove the backbone, then put the whole fish through a grinder. Add the onion, garlic, two eggs, breadcrumbs, a grated raw potato, cover them in a light dusting of flour and fry them till they're ready. Then eat them with tomato sauce, or put them in a sandwich – they're healthier than salami!' Living here at the fraying edge of the Danube, she watches the climate change and worries how it might affect their precarious existence between a sinking river and a rising sea. Her birthday is in a few days time, on 29 March. 'Each year, my mother used to go and look under the snow, to find the first few snowdrops to pick for my birthday. Now look at the thermometer! Its twenty degrees at the end of March!' There were years when the Danube was still frozen solid here on 15 March. She misses the spring and autumn most. 'Nowadays we pass straight from cold to hot.'

Sorin is a different kettle of fish to Tudor Avramov. I meet him near the harbour, near his Chinese-made boat, the 'King of Rubbish'. 'Rubbish' appears to be a mistranslation of 'junk' – in homage to his craft's Far Eastern origins. Sorin is as talkative as Tudor was quiet. He swiftly fleeces me of a handful of small denomination *lei* notes, and talks me into a fish dinner at his house and an all-night fishing trip afterwards. He is a foun-tain of stories or legends about his years as a soldier and a fisherman. He served in Somalia, Iraq and Afghanistan, he says, and came home in the end because he could not bear to live without the Danube. He has a high forehead, round jaw, blue eyes, alternately fierce with anger or wet with tears, big biceps and an anchor tattooed on his forearm. The day he was released from the army he rang his father to get his rowing boat ready. When he stepped off the ferry from Tulcea, he climbed straight down into his own boat, without a word to his relatives, and set off alone into the familiar labyrinths of the delta. For three days and nights he fished and slept and fished, cleansing himself of a life of war and obedience to authority. In his outhouse, his young girlfriend remains almost mute as Sorin cleans and fries small crucian carp. His best tales are about his grand-father. Born around 1907, he fought on both sides in the Second World War, eventually opting for the Germans because they treated their soldiers better. 'I got both brandy and chocolate,' he told his grandson. The Russians treated him even worse as a prisoner of war than as their own soldier. Captured on the Eastern Front in 1943, he spent nine years in a prison camp in Siberia. Potato peelings were a rare luxury. Released in 1952, he made his way back as far as Izmail. Just across the river from the city, he could see the sparse lights of Romania, glittering like beads along the shore. He asked about a boat to get him across, but was told that none existed. When he announced his intention to swim instead, he was told he would be shot. One night he went downriver to Vlkovo, where the Danube is wider still, but there were fewer border guards and swam several miles across to the Romanian side. Nowadays Vlkovo is treasured by Ukrainians for its early strawberries, which you can buy in the marketplace in Odessa.

Sorin is very proud of his grandfather. 'He was one of twelve brothers, and he went out to fish at the age of nine, to help feed the family – they lived only from fishing.' Even now, he says, there are people who come up to Sorin in the street, and tell him how his grandfather saved them when their boats capsized. His family were Don Cossacks, offered land by Catherine the Great in the Crimea. But the Crimean Tatars pushed them southwards, all the way to the Danube. Sorin used to go to Izmail by boat in the 1990s, to bring food and alcohol back to sell in Romania. 'Everything was so cheap there – you could buy a whole head of cheese, big as a wheel, for almost nothing!' He now makes a living from the tourist trade in summer, and from fishing. The winds in the delta each have a name. The south wind is called the *moriana*, and fishermen say that when it blows you just have to put your nets in the water and they fill with fish. The north wind, the *crivăţs*, comes from Russia, and brings us nothing, he says. It is so strong it makes currents in the water, and breaks nets thicker than his thumb. He holds it up, for dramatic effect, still covered in the entrails of the fish he is gutting for our supper. 'But the wind is fickle, it can turn around from one moment to the next, and blow a squall from the other direction.' I remember the British graves in Sulina and all the deaths from collisions and drownings. His fried carp are tasty and plentiful, but full of bones. They might have been better suited to Maria Avramov's fish balls. The level in the two-litre plastic bottle of wine he picked up from a ramshackle bar with the money I gave him plunges downwards dangerously. We part company after supper, and he says he will pick me up in an hour from my hotel for our fishing trip. The hours pass, and by the time he arrives roaring drunk after midnight I have gone off the plan altogether.

The next morning, to make sure that no feelings are hurt on either side, and to lessen the danger that I will ask for the money back, he takes me by boat to the fish-collecting centre. There is a floating platform with a metal shed at the back, where fish are stacked to the ceiling in plastic crates. The man in charge is busy on his mobile phone. At first he is suspicious of me. This is nowhere near the tourist season and my story about writing a book about the Danube sounds far-fetched. Reluctantly, he answers my questions. The herring come in from the sea when the Danube reaches 6 or 7 degrees centigrade. The migration takes place every five years. They take forty-five days to swim upriver, as far as the Iron Gates dam that blocks their way. There they spawn, before swimming back to the sea, which takes only fifteen days downstream. He pays five to six *lei* per kilo for the fish (under two dollars) and sells them wholesale to the shops. The fish will go for four times that price in the markets of Constanța and Bucharest.

I decline a lift back to town with Sorin, and set out on foot down a street of neat peasant houses, wood panelled, painted pastel shades of blue and green. Black rowing boats that will never again go to sea are beached in back gardens and yards, keel up, elegant as musical instruments in their final resting places. Hens roost in some, children play in others.

Ilie Sidurenko and his wife are in their front garden, pruning the vines. 'So you're going upriver, like the sturgeon!' he remarks with delight, when I tell him about my journey. 'The sturgeon is a smart fish, if he smells nets, you can't catch him . . . The best time is when the bed of the river or the sea is muddy, and he gets confused. We used to lay hooks, three, five, seven kilometres out to sea. Only the older fishermen knew the secret, and now it is not passed on, it will be lost.' He hardly interrupts his work, methodically tying his vines as we speak. The biggest sturgeon he ever caught was a male, 400 kilos, 'not a long fish, but a fat one!' Then in December 2004, just before Christmas, he was alone on the Danube – a rare event, as the fishermen always fish in pairs. He landed a female, 209 kilos, with 35 kilos of caviar. 'I sold it to the fish-collecting centre in the village,' says Ilie, showing no emotion. 'I don't care what they did with it.'

CHAPTER 3

Mountains of the Fathers

We came to the town known by the name of Baba Saltuq. They
relate that this Saltuq was an ecstatic devotee (dervish), although things
are told of him which are reproved by the Divine Law. This is the last
of the towns possessed by the Turks, and between it and the territory
of the Greeks is a journey of eighteen days through an uninhabited
waste, for eight days of which there is no water.
IBN BATTUTA, FOURTEENTH-CENTURY TRAVELLER[1]

SOUTH OF Tulcea on the road to Constanţa is the town of Babadag. There
are woods, unusual for the bare, rolling landscape of Dobrogea, fresh water
springs, a hotel and restaurant with a rather Turkish feel, and the oldest
mosque in Romania. The Polish writer Andrzej Stasiuk got here before
I did, and wrote a book called *The Road to Babadag*,[2] but his book is about
his journey there, not his arrival.

In my suitcase I carry an old, red hardback copy of *The Travels of Ibn
Battuta*, an Islamic traveller of the fourteenth century. He reached Babadag in
1332 and used his time to re-provision his caravan for the long journey south
to Constantinople, still in the 'territory of the Greeks', before the Ottoman
conquest of 1453. 'A provision of water is laid in for this stage, and carried in
large and small skins on the wagons. Since our entry into it was in the cold
weather, we have no need of much water, and the Turks carry milk in large
skins, mix it with cooked *dugi* and drink that so that they feel no thirst. At
this city we made our preparations for the crossing of the wasteland.'

Babadag means 'the mountain of the father' in Turkish. Just a few kilometres inland from the Black Sea, its relationship to the Danube is hard to
define. As a centre of miracles and a place of pilgrimage for devout
Muslims, the small wooded hill towers over the surrounding landscape,
guarding the southern approaches to the river. Nearby, the US military
share a training ground with the Romanian army, to practise manoeuvres
for the next wars in the Islamic heartlands as though hoping to tap some
of its magic. Videos posted on the internet show spidermen in combat
fatigues, weighed down with a paraphernalia of gadgets and weaponry,
leaping from helicopters and taking cover behind tanks. The 'father' in the
name is Sari Saltuq, who arrived here with forty warriors by flying carpet
from Central Anatolia, according to one source, to convert Dobrogea to
Islam. Many wonders are told about him, not least that he saved the
daughter of the King of Dobrogea from a dragon and cut off its seven
heads with his wooden Bektashi sword.[3] A peculiar variant of the story
suggests that a Christian monk claimed credit for this feat, in order to win
the hand in marriage of the King's daughter – the prize announced by her
father for anyone who could rid him of the dragon. Sari Saltuq proposed
to the monk an ordeal by fire, to find out which of them was telling the
truth about the defeat of the dragon. They were both boiled alive in the
same cauldron, suspended over the flames. The monk perished in agony,
while Sari Saltuq emerged unscathed. In other legends he is paired with
Saint Nicholas, the patron saint of children.

At Blagaj in Bosnia, where the River Buna – 'the good' – flows fully
formed out of a cliff face, a handsome dervish lodge clings to the cliff ledge
beside it. Ancient stone steps lead down straight into the crystal clear water,
where the dervishes used to come to wash before prayers. Up in the lodge
the rooms hum with silence and devotion. Off one room is a domed stone
roof, with star-shaped holes cut into it through which the rain can fall: an
Islamic shower room. In a small shrine at the side of the building is one of
the tombs of Sari Saltuq, royally clad in green and gold, with his rounded
dervish hat at the raised end. During the 1992–95 war, Muslim refugees
took shelter here, and the Croats who shelled Blagaj tried and failed to drop
mortars on the roof. Each night Zijo, the self-appointed caretaker of the
place, would put cups of water out beside the raised coffins. Each morning
he would find the cups empty.[4] There is another, sadder story told about

Blagaj. Close to where the Buna emerges from the cliff are two restaurants, famous for their excellent trout, freshly caught from the river. The cliff above was once home to eagles. Just before the war, in the winter of 1991, the restaurant owner believed the eagles were stealing his hens, and put out the poisoned carcass of a sheep for them to eat. The eagles died. According to local legend, war would engulf Bosnia if the eagles ever disappear from Blagaj. The conflict began the following April. Another tomb of Sari Saltuq, at Krujë in Albania, resides high in the mountains looking down on to the Adriatic. Another small domed *turbe*, arched with thin, wafer-like bricks. Another fine, slanted coffin, dressed in green and gold cloth, mounted with a dervish mitre. Outside you can rest in the shade of tall mulberry trees and enjoy the sweet scent of fig trees baking in hot sunshine. Vines, honeysuckle and pomegranates grow from the cracks in the walls.[5]

Thin, tentative threads tie distant Albania and Bosnia to the Danube. The Drina river turns its back on the White and Black Drin rivers and the Neretva, which all flow westwards to the Adriatic. The Drina flows north and east into the Morava, which meets the Danube before Belgrade. Sari Saltuq has seven tombs in all and is said to have been buried in each of them, so no one knows where his body really lies. 'Through tolerance and piety . . . Sari Saltuq influenced the non-Muslims and contributed a great deal to the spreading of the Islamic religion in the Balkans. He won the non-Muslims' affection, maintaining open lines of communication with them, and thus for centuries Muslims and non-Muslims have been living in peace and harmony in Dobrogea,' reads the information booklet, available at the mosque. The mosque itself has another tomb, just behind the main building, of Gazi Ali Pasha, who was the governor of Buda in the early seventeenth century.

The snowdrops of Babadag, Memnune tells me sternly, have the most beautiful scent. 'But what do they *actually* smell of?' I ask her, casting aside a lifetime of certainty that while snowdrops may have many other qualities, they are certainly odourless. 'Freshly laundered linen on a winter's day,' she says, confidently.

Memnune serves cups of strong black Turkish coffee as we sit in her neat, middle-class living room discussing Sari Saltuq. I asked in the street of the town who could tell me about the saint and was directed straight here. She is a matronly woman, with intelligent brown eyes and a passion for flowers and history. Sari Saltuq's grave disappeared for a while, she tells me, only to be rediscovered by a man called Koyun Baba, while walking with his sheep. Koyun means 'sheep' in Turkish. Babadag was once threatened by a huge flood, pouring from a hole in the ground, but Koyun Baba saved the community by pushing barrow-loads of cotton into the hole. The British orientalist F. W. Hasluck mentions another Bektashi saint, Pambuk Baba, 'who seems to have succeeded, or to be identical with the Bektashi saint Koyun Baba'.[6] Pambuk means 'cotton' in Turkish. Both men were disciples, like Sari Saltuq, of Hajji Bektash, the founder of the Bektashi order of dervishes, the mystical order most closely associated with the janissaries, the elite of the Ottoman armies. There are still Bektashi strongholds in Albania and Macedonia. Miskin Baba, from the island of Ada Kaleh in the Danube, and Gül Baba, still honoured upstream in Budapest, were also Bektashis. The Danube carried the Islamic faith upriver into Europe. The track up the mountain is steep and well worn, through young woods of oak and acacia, sprouting out of a carpet of bluebells. As the path levels at the top of the hill, the bushes are tied with strips of coloured rags, like man-made blossom impatient for spring. Koyun Baba's grave is rather humble, with a crescent moon at its head, set in crude granite. He didn't actually want a grave at all – unlike Sari Saltuq – and each time the villagers made one for him, the story goes, he scattered the rocks, which came to resemble sheep on the meadows around the mountain. On his latest grave, not yet self-vandalised, stands a single candle. The rags on the bushes were tied by Muslim Gypsies, Memnune told me, who make pilgrimages and picnics here every year on 6 May, Saint George's Day according to the Gregorian calendar. A single robin hops curiously from branch to branch, watching me closely. A battered tin sign admonishes visitors, in Romanian and Turkish, that it is a sin to ask for anything from the dead, a warning defied by every strip of rag tied to the branches. From far below this pudding-shaped hill come the barking of dogs and the shouts of men engaged in some sporting activity. Rain starts to fall lightly on Koyun Baba's grave. Before leaving, I pick a small handful of snowdrops. Delicate, but fully scented, just like fresh linen sheets, plucked, stiff to the touch, from a washing line on a cold winter's day.

When we meet again Memnune is so pleased to hear that I have taken the trouble to visit Koyun Baba, she tells me her dream. Some years earlier, on the night before the Muslim feast of Bayram, she dreamt that she should sacrifice a white ram on the right side of the courtyard of the mosque in Babadag. Muslims do sacrifice rams during Bayram, but this would normally be done in one's own yard. The strangest feature of her dream was that the gardens and yard of the mosque were laid out in a different pattern to how they really were at the time. She obeyed the dream and, with her brother-in-law's help, found an animal and sacrificed it in the place she had been told. Some time later, with funds from Turkey, the land around the mosque was re-landscaped and now corresponds exactly to the way she saw it in her dream. Across eastern Europe, the former empires quietly nurse what is left of their heritage, the Turks their mosques, the Russians their war memorials.

Memnune calls a friend to take me to Sari Saltuq's tomb. It is a simple, handsome affair, with the traditional green-draped coffin in the centre of the room and an arched, beehive-shaped roof made of thin, white-washed bricks. The brickwork is like the roof of the Bajrakli mosque in Belgrade. The floor is paved with stone. Memnune used to come here as a child with her grandmother every Friday to light candles, 'to honour the heroes', she explains. And to make wishes, one with each candle. They always lit white candles, she stresses, not the thin, yellow beeswax ones favoured by the Orthodox Christians. Opposite Sari Saltuq's tomb is a spring famous for the healing qualities of its waters. A young Gypsy girl, perhaps fourteen years old with a cigarette dangling from her lips, arrives with her younger brother on a horse and cart. They smile sweetly at us, then wrestle a big blue plastic container down off the cart and start filling it. There is no running water in most houses in the Roma district.

In his front room on a low hill on the far side of the town, Recep Lupu, the unofficial head of Babadag's Roma community, talks about the pride and the shame of his people. 'We don't have a language of our own, it's more like a dialect,' he says, sitting with his wife and mother-in-law in their living room, just off the steep, unmade road that is the Gypsy high street. On the wall hangs a huge carpet depicting the 'Abduction of the Seraj'. His wife sits cross-legged on the bed, mythically beautiful in the traditional, bright long skirts and headscarf of her people. Her mother sits beside her, a picture of stern, silent dignity. 'We speak a mixture of words . . .' Recep continues, 'Bulgarian, Russian, Romanian, Gypsy and Turkish – it changes all the time – we shift between them. We are too ashamed to speak our own language.'

Unlike most of the Roma in Babadag, Recep and his family are Pentecostalists. He has a very earthly explanation for giving up Islam. 'If you are a Muslim, you have to marry a fellow Muslim. In the Pentecostalist church, you can marry who you wish!' I look over at his wife, who smiles, shyly. 'All her family are Christians too . . .' The evangelical Protestants arrived in the Dobrogea region at the end of the twentieth century, and have launched an aggressive recruitment drive among the Muslim Gypsies to 'save their souls'. The community has a parallel justice system, accepted by the Romanian state in disputes where only Roma are involved. Instead of punishment or retribution for crimes, the emphasis is on respect, honour and repairing the torn fabric of the community. The council of elders sits to hear all sides in the dispute, then issues a verdict designed to satisfy the injured party. The offender must pay compensation, or find other ways to make up for the harm generated by his act.

Recep and his wife have only two children. That is unusual. 'Most have five or six, occasionally ten or eleven. For myself, two is enough . . . but if God wants us to have one more . . .' He exchanges another gentle smile with his wife. His youngest son accepts the gift of my pencil and sits down to draw.

'The biggest problem here is poverty and the lack of education,' his wife explains. 'The boys just go to school to get a driving licence.' You have to have finished eight grades of school in Romania to apply for a licence. 'The girls finish four grades or even less. They have to stay at home to take care of the little ones because their parents go to work in other villages. The children get married very young. It used to be at eleven or twelve, now more often at fourteen or fifteen.' Their main work is trade. 'We buy clothes, cutlery, dishes, or animals in the wholesale market, then take them from village to village, to sell.' Few Roma, if any, own land.

'Do the young people today respect the traditions?' I ask Recep's mother-in-law.

'The young do not respect us. Many used to wear baggy trousers – a traditional item of dress among Muslim women – now they only wear them occasionally.'

The number of Roma is hard to calculate. Recep estimates 3,500 in Babadag, but 'many are on the road, travelling from place to place'. A sizeable number – several hundred, he believes – are in Portugal, but he cannot remember where. Like Roma throughout eastern Europe, they establish an unofficial twinning system with one particular place, often the suburb of a small or larger town. Those with a foothold abroad help more to come, and the income they make becomes a significant lifeline for the families back home. The bright yellow Western Union sign has become as important a landmark in Romania as the local post office. Outside in the street, we stop to talk to some girls of about twelve or thirteen years. Why aren't you at school? 'Our parents need us at home, to take care of our brothers and sisters.' What do you sing to them? A burst of laughter, then a somewhat raucous rendition of a lullaby, sure to wake up any baby for miles around. More children come running from neighbouring streets, to hear Regina and Sibella sing to the strangers. 'And anyway,' Regina adds, 'if we stayed at school, the boys would steal us.'

The road out of Tulcea to the east leads past vineyards, brown and bedraggled in the spring rain, along the southern shore of the Danube. Ukraine, on the far bank, looks uninhabited. There are no watchtowers, and the barges at anchor near Isaccea are nationless and motionless; no flags stain the morning. Izmail, the port city where Sorin's grandfather could not find a boat and where Sorin bought whole heads of cheese to sell in Romania, is somewhere on the far side. The two half-brothers, Ishmael and Isaac, face each other across the Danube. Isaccea is a small, dozy village, with a war memorial, a mosque with a slim, green capped minaret, and a stone quarry set on a hill, its gaze always downwards towards the river.

Under the heading 'dead', thirty-four names are listed on the war memorial, from 1916 to 1919, and four are still classified as 'missing'. It was a hard war to cost a place as small as this thirty-eight of its young men. Some of the first and last names are the same: Ion Ion; Emin Emin . . . The mayor of Văcăreni, Stelică Gherghișan, is not at home as we pass through, but I will nevertheless tell his story. In 1999 when work ran out at the fish farm where he was employed, he turned his hand to fishing for wild sturgeon. The regular sturgeon fishermen jealously guarded the stretch of river they had occupied, so he was forced further downstream. He landed a 450-kilo female, with 82 kilos of caviar. That fish changed his life. The caviar can fetch up to ten thousand dollars a kilo in New York. Sterian bought a house, then another house. A car, then another car. In no time he was elected mayor. And since then he has been re-elected several times. Romanians, like everybody else, are impressed by success. The loss of those eggs was another disaster for the diminishing sturgeon stocks in the Danube, however.

In Tulcea I tried in vain to find a boat that would take me across to Izmail. One former fisherman might take me, illegally, I was told, 'but he costs a lot'. A name and phone number were scribbled down on a scrap of paper, but I never rang the number. While half of Asia and Africa hammers on the doors of western Europe, was I really going to pay to smuggle myself into Ukraine? A small, unsignposted road leads off the Tulcea to Galaţi road. After several kilometres skidding in and out of potholes I come to a gate with a large sign: 'Tichileşti Hospital, Leprosarium.'

The rain stops and a damp-eyed sun tries to negotiate a passage between the clouds. Vasile Olescu is pruning his vines up on the slopes of this protected valley. His father taught him to prune when he was twelve, he says, though his father had no legs. He would be carried or wheeled, or sometimes drag himself out to the edge of the vineyard. But his hands were strong, and he could practise the right way to grip the cutters in his son's small hands and call to him which branches of the untidy tangle of vines to cut, or which rare stem should be allowed to stay and how many knots along it should be severed. Vasile was born at the lepers' colony in 1955. Now he is one of the youngest patients. Both his parents were lepers. His mother was sent here when she was fourteen, his father when he was eighteen. They fell in love. Leprosy is an illness which can be both inherited and caught from others, so to be born to leper parents surrounded by other leprosy cases is a poor start in life, though there is a hope for each child that she or he will not develop the disease. Vasile grew up in a bubble of hope, helping his parents and the other patients. In all, fifteen children were born here. As long as they remained healthy, they seemed miraculous, the perfect red grapes produced by diseased vines. When they grew up they were sent away 'to freedom' as Vasile puts it, making it sound like exile. When Vasile was given a clean bill of health he was sent out into the world to earn his fortune. In communist Romania, where work was compulsory, that was not too difficult. He got a bed in a worker's hostel in Constanţa and a job in the shipyards, unloading the ships of all the world. He worked for two years before he realised he was ill. The same fate befell most of the other children born at Tichileşti. One by one they developed the tell-tale signs of the illness – a wound that would not heal, the loss of feeling in first one toe, then another. Then the gradual flaking and rotting of the flesh. He is a man who likes to get things done, not to speak of them. As we talk, crouched side by side among his vines, he works fast, cutting and tying and tidying the piles, hardly pausing for a moment to think or to rest.

From a bacteriological point of view, leprosy is a curable disease, meaning that it is possible to prevent patients infecting others, says Alexe Vasiliu, the colony doctor. But little can be done to stop the evolution of the disease in a leper's own body. Each patient is afflicted in a slightly different way: some go blind; some lose fingers or toes. There has not been a new case of leprosy in Romania for more than thirty years. This is the only remaining colony of its kind in Europe, though there are several hospitals with leprosy patients in Spain, Italy and Turkey. It took a very long time to develop the complex of drugs to treat it, because laboratory animals cannot be infected. It is a disease carried exclusively by humans. Vasile is something of a hero to the other inmates at Tichileşti. He has lost all feeling in his hands, but he can still prune the vines because his father taught him the technique. He just has to watch his fingers closely, because he would not feel the pain if he cut into them with the sharp blades. But the wine he makes from the 'pearl' and 'a thousand and one' grape varieties keeps the whole colony, its medical staff and its visitors, going for the year. And it gives him a sense of purpose. Among the vines on the steep hillside, wires are hung with strips of rag and bells. In September, he explains, he sits all day at one side of his vineyard. He has built this elaborate system of wires and pullies to frighten the blackbirds away.

Ioana Miscov is one of the oldest inmates in the colony, where many live to a ripe old age. Born in 1929, she has been here since 1948. She lets me help her feed her chickens, spooning cooked pasta from a bowl into the dirt. There are thirteen, and she calls out to each of them by name: 'Pilpica,

Scumpa, Gulerada . . .' *Scumpa* means 'the lame one'. Ioana herself is so
tiny and fragile, perhaps the hens think she is one of their own. Clutching
a small walking stick, she shuffles precariously over the paving stones that
lead from her little two-roomed house. She has no toes on either foot, and
no fingers on either hand. Her wrists are veined and polished stumps. But
she still manages to crouch and chop grass for the chickens on a chopping
board, gripping an almost blunt axe between her strong wrists. She giggles
like a thirteen-year-old. One of the sadnesses of her life is that her husband
never saw their daughter, who was born here in the colony. He went blind
a month before she was born. Her daughter lives in Tulcea. She never
became ill, worked for thirty years as a seamstress, and visits her mother
often. Ioana bears her fate stoically. She delights in her daughter's visits,
and in the progress of the little tomato and paprika plants in yoghurt pots
dotted along her window sill, each with six or eight leaves already. 'Everyone
admires my tomato plants every year – tell them, nurse!' Then she takes
me to see the little Baptist church. We walk side by side up the steps. I offer
her my arm, but she's happier with her stick and the railing. There are two
churches in the colony, one for the Baptists, one for the Orthodox. Even
during the toughest years of communism, when the state denied that the
colony existed and the Baptists were persecuted elsewhere in Romania,
they were allowed to continue worshipping here. It is not hard to imagine
the conversation between two Party officials.

'What about the lepers' church?' asks one.

'Ah . . . Let them keep it. They take so many other drugs – why not a
little opium too?'[7]

Ioana bought her house from the preacher. Before that, she recalls lying
in a hospital ward, sharing a bed with her mother who was also sick. 'I kept
falling out of the bed!' She remembers her mother reading from a Bible the
preacher brought her. The preacher taught the children at the colony to
read and write. 'He was not afraid of us.' She shows me the pictures on the
wall of her room, especially those of her grandson's wedding. 'I was there!'
she says proudly, 'and I was not ashamed of myself. And my grandson was
very pleased that I came.'

Costica Serban is a year younger than Ioana and is completely blind.
He lies in his room on a couch beside a window he can no longer see
out of, with the radio on, day and night. 'It keeps me company,' he says,

'I couldn't sleep without it.' He lost the sight of one eye in 1986, then the other one 'during the revolution . . . it just exploded . . .' He pauses for effect, as though he were out on the barricades himself, or storming the Bastille in Paris in 1789. There's just a space where that eye used to be. His first eye is simply white. 'I remember the famine after the Second World War in Romania. I had no father or mother. I collected sunflower seeds in the fields, roasted them, then sold them at railway stations and pubs, mostly to the soldiers, coming back from the war . . .' In 1947 he noticed the first signs of leprosy on his body, and was sent here to Tichileşti – 'to get well', the doctor said. He's been here ever since. The patients were tightly confined during the communist era. But since the revolution they can leave if they wish. Most have stayed. Those with relatives go on visits, to Tulcea or beyond, for several days at a time, but always return. 'They like to be here, because of the sense of community,' the doctor explains. 'This is their home. And they get free medication . . .'

I walk up into the little graveyard, on a hill near the main gate. There are small wooden or granite crosses, wrought iron fencing, names, dates, loving memory . . . the same as any village graveyard. In the Tichileşti booklet, there is a quotation from Psalm 139: 'If I say, Surely the darkness shall cover me; even the night shall be light about me.'

At its peak, the colony had nearly two hundred inmates. Most of them are here now, no longer any different from their fellow human beings, finally healed of their affliction by death. In the valley below, there are only twenty-one left alive. When they have gone, Dr Vasiliu plans to turn the institution into an old people's home. 'It would be a shame if all this infra-structure, built up over nearly a hundred years, went to waste.'

At Niculiţel, a short distance up the road towards Galaţi, I turn off to the left, into a rather different vineyard. At first sight it feels like Goldilocks country, waiting for the arrival of the three bears. The wine showroom is open, the tables spread with bottles, ready to be opened. The cellar and the offices upstairs and downstairs are all open to unexpected visitors. I call out, but finding no one set out up the gently sloping hillside through young vines.

'We are ten miles north of the 45th Parallel, just like Tokaj, Rioja and Bordeaux,' Sorin Ignat, the technical manager of the vineyard explains when I finally track him down. He is a ruddy-faced man with an easy smile that hints at dark green bottles, readily uncorked, fine wine already drunk or still to be imbibed.

Burebista, a Dacian king, grew vines here before the Romans arrived. The Greeks transported wine home to the Greek mainland by sea in the tall amphora on display in the entrance hall of the museum in Tulcea. Similar pots contained olive oil sent from the Greek mainland – no olive trees grow east of Thrace. Where the Danube flows due East, the Romanian vineyards face northwards, but that is not a problem. 'The river creates its own microclimate,' Sorin explains. 'It diminishes the extremes of temperature and increases the humidity in the heat of summer.' He produces a bunch of several hundred keys and opens the main warehouse. Crates are stacked high in the cavernous room, red wines made from Merlot and Romanian Feteasca Neagra grapes, whites from Aligote grapes, brought here from the Burgundy region of France in the 1950s, but rarely grown there any more. Soon Aligote will be a Romanian wine, Sorin predicts happily. It is not hard to imagine the joy of Romanian agricultural engineers, in their stiff, identical suits, boarding the plane from communist Romania to capitalist France at the height of the Cold War, on their strange mission to bring back some of the delights of the valley of the River Saône to the valley of the Danube. But here the picture in my head grows fuzzy round the edges. Were secret police agents sent with them, to ensure they did not slander the Party or its leader Gheorghe Gheorghiu-Dej, even as the second bottle was being uncorked? Did one of the younger engineers slip away from the main party, hand in hand with a French girl he had met the evening before, not to be allowed to return to his homeland until his poor father was dead, his younger brothers and sisters grown up, his old school buried under the ruins of the 1977 earthquake? Or was the whole situation reversed? Did French agricultural engineers follow our Romanian friends back to Niculiţel to see how their cuttings were getting on in the thick limestone soil above the ancient granite seam of the Măcin mountains? Was one seduced by a raven-haired Securitate agent? And did he, perhaps, settle down in some Bucharest suburb, finding less and less consolation as the years passed in his dusty copies of Sartre, Camus and André Breton in the Editions du Seuil? I would need to spend many more weeks in Sorin Ignat's company, and drink much more of his excellent Aligote with its hint of stilled volcanoes to find out the truth.

By the late 1950s the Romanian Communist Party leadership was already rolling its eyes at the Soviet Union, and looking for ways to assert a little more independence. In 1958 Gheorghiu-Dej managed to persuade Nikita Krushchev to withdraw Soviet troops from Romania, which was a remarkable feat considering that the Red Army had only just re-invaded neighbouring Hungary to crush the revolution of October 1956, an action of which Gheorghiu-Dej warmly approved. The failure of the Hungarian revolution and Yugoslav defiance of Moscow both served the Romanian communist leadership very well. They won more elbow room within the Soviet bloc to counter Soviet plans to establish Comecon, a carbon copy of the European Union in western Europe. According to the Comecon blueprint, drawn up in Moscow, each Soviet ally was allotted a speciality: the Czechoslovaks would produce cars, the Hungarians buses, while the Romanians felt insulted to be told that they should supply the raw materials, the oil and food, for the Soviet empire. They wanted giant, prestige industries of their own. The iron and steel works up the river in Galați, my next overnight stop, became a symbol of their pride, and of their comradely tussle with the Kremlin.

Surrounded by his wine, Sorin Ignat spells out the hopes and dreams of the vineyard. With European Union subsidies more vines will be planted, to increase its size from four to five hundred hectares. Production should increase gradually from one million to two or three million litres a year, while the quality of the wine should also improve. There are plans to build a small port to ship the wine upriver on the Danube. Perhaps one or two bottles of Aligote from Niculițel will one day reach Burgundy. According to the legend of the Argonauts, when the *Argo* could travel no further on the Danube, its powerful crew carried their ship on their shoulders to the Rhône in France, and from there sailed back down to the open sea. The Greek chroniclers are silent on what beverages sustained them on the marbled river after they left the wine-dark sea, but it seems reasonable to assume that a barrel or two of the wines of Niculițel would have found a space in the hold, to brighten their impossible journey.

Before I leave, Sorin takes me out past a line of barking dogs to a circle of broken concrete, overgrown with weeds. This was the helicopter landing pad used by Gheorghiu-Dej's successor, Nicolae Ceaușescu, who came to power in 1965. He and his wife Elena liked the wines at Niculițel very much, perhaps as much as anything because of their name. He named his first son Nicu. When I applied for an interview with him in 1988 and began to imagine our encounter, I planned to begin the meeting with reference to the similarity of our names. But my application was politely refused. 'The President is not in the habit of granting interviews in a cell at Otopeni airport,' George Albuț, the press secretary at the Romanian embassy in Budapest, told me. 'Because that is as far as you will get, if you ever try to visit our country again.' I remember my sense of relief that I would not, after all, have to shake the dictator's cold, clammy hand. At the ruined helipad Sorin points out a mound just visible on the horizon: a lookout point built in the Copper Age from which to guard against the arrival of Bronze Age invaders from the north, with their heavier, more lethal, spears.

Weighed down with bottles, and promising to return, I set out to try to find the hump. A farm track leads into an orchard of apple trees, all recently pruned, with mountains of branches underneath. The sun has just set, so I have to hurry. The trees block my view in all directions, so I weave between the rows, searching for the last place I caught a glimpse of the hill. From the top the view is tremendous – the silver ribbon of the Danube, stretching back to the delta, and on, up into Europe. Smoke rises in columns from the slopes of the valley, with flashes of flame at the base, where peasants burn off the dry stems of winter. Down on the shore the silver spreads inland, remnants of early spring floods. Willows protrude from the waters near the river edge like shaving brushes. Further inland, sloping up to where I stand, the apple trees seem bare and amputated, so thorough was the pruner's saw. Other trees, not yet pruned, stand bushy beyond a certain line, like long-haired men queuing for the haircut that will qualify them to become soldiers. The hump itself is lined with paths – a large one made by visiting humans, and smaller, subtler lines, made by rabbits or foxes through the grass. There is no sign of the barbarians.

It is dark by the time I reach Brătianu, to take the car ferry across the Danube to Galați. A beautiful starlit night, the hunter Orion poised above the horizon as though advancing, silent as the river itself, to seek his prey among the myriad lights of the city. The tall river control tower, 120 metres high, barely brushes his ankle. There are only three other cars on the ferry, and a long truck. The water is calm, mirroring the lights of the city and the stars. Then the long metal lip of the boat touches the shore, a sailor hurls the long coiling snake of a cable to his mate, a barrier slides noisily aside, and the vehicles rumble ashore. All the streets in Galaţi slope down to the Danube. I find a cheap hotel near the port in a mess of streets dug up to lay new sewage pipes, then go in search of a restaurant. The Marco Polo has a name to attract long-distance travellers. There's a big pizza oven, rather frumpy waitresses in identical blue jeans and red T-shirts, and a few romantic diners. Back in the hotel the rooms are enormous, and echo with the desperate love-making of men on shore leave from the ships in the harbour. The television sets are small, dwarfed by the size of the rooms. I flick through the channels. Each programme is a caricature of itself: Brazilian soap-operas with olive-eyed, red-lipped girls; news channels with over-earnest reporters and over-elegant presenters; football matches with terrible misses and empty stadiums. In this port town I feel like Herman Melville in Nantucket on his way to find a whaler.

I have to be at the border-crossing at Giurgiuleşti by eight in the morning. A cluster of low, modern buildings, freshly tarmacked roads, and police officers with a spring in their step are waiting for me. Part-funded by the European Union, this is one of the EU's newest frontiers with Moldova. They show me the latest X-ray equipment for searching lorries and a gleaming scanner designed to detect radioactive goods – donated by the Americans. It looks as though it has never been used.

The real war at this border-crossing point is on tobacco. Cigarettes have long held a special magic in Romania. In communist times, imported packets of Kent almost became an alternative currency. An American colleague once took out a packet and lit one in a Bucharest restaurant. The place fell silent as people watched in horror. It was as if he had produced a handful of banknotes and set fire to them. Nistor Dorin takes me from warehouse to warehouse, stacked to the roof with cigarettes. All the famous brands are here, alongside some rather quaint imitations – Chinese-made Camels with a picture of a goat on the packet. About half the cigarettes are genuine, my guide explains, manufactured by the big tobacco companies in Ukraine, Russia and Moldova, with only the smallest tax slapped on them by the state. Since Romania and Bulgaria joined the EU in 2007, new compulsory taxes have doubled and quadrupled the price. Neither petty traders nor large-scale smugglers need a degree in mathematics to grasp the money to be made. Legally, you are allowed to bring two packets into Romania a day. The same packet of Marlboro or Kent costs eighty eurocents in Moldova, two and a half Euros in Romania. A single, unemployed man receives a pitiful twenty-five Euros a month from the state. If he crosses every day for a month, bringing over only his quota, then sells them for two Euros a packet on the black market, he can earn seventy-two Euros. He would almost be foolish not to. A successful smuggler, however, who gets a big quantity into the country – concealed in a shipment of barbecue charcoal, a false petrol tank or a shipment of detergent – can buy a nice flat in the city and still have money left over.

The trade is causing such a dent in the profit margins of the big manufacturers that Philip Morris considered closing down their state-of-the-art cigarette factory in Bucharest and moving out of the country. The authorities responded by stopping the Duty-Free shops – where about a third of all smuggled cigarettes originate – from selling tobacco products or alcohol and introducing more checks at borders. Suspicious-looking vehicles are driven through a giant scanner at Giurgiuleşti. Police intelligence operations have been stepped up. Dorel Fronea, the head of Romanian customs tells me that nationwide seven new sniffer dog teams have been trained, in addition to the three existing ones. A customer-awareness campaign has also been launched – it's dangerous to smoke what you buy in the street because you don't know what's in it. It is difficult not to smile at this point in the conversation; surely it's also dangerous to smoke because you *do* know what's in it? Surveys show, Mr Fronea assures me, that five out of every hundred Romanians will not smoke a cigarette if they know it is counterfeit, but taken another way, this proves a healthy, or perhaps an unhealthy, disrespect for the state in all its glory. The authorities are hurt by the claims of cigarette companies that one in three cigarettes smoked in Romania has been smuggled. They suggest the true figure is closer to one in five. A hundred and twenty million cigarettes were seized at the borders in 2009.

There are three border crossings at Giurgiuleşti: one on the road, one on the railway and the third on the river. The road and rail bridges cross the River Prut, which forms much of Romania's long border with Moldova. A police launch is waiting to take me down the Prut, to its confluence with the Danube, then back up the Danube to Galaţi. The Polish-built, harpoon fibreglass police launch is like a stone, skimming waves of liquid glass, her stern anchored in the water, the bow bouncing, breathless and brave. Marcel the helmsman bends down to shout something in my ear, above the roar of the outboard motor, and as he does so the collars of our orange lifejackets rub together. 'We have to be careful,' he bellows, gripping the steering wheel with one hand and looking over my shoulder as he shouts, 'because if we hit one of those, we'll sink in seconds!' He nods to a whole tree trunk, tumbling past in the grey waters, only a metre to starboard. The boat is small with a cabin for two, with room for two more in the cockpit. From the Prut we reach the Danube, a vast backhand of waters, divided by knuckles, thin stands of trees. The waves get bigger. It is hard to tell which are islands and which the tail-ends of forest in this borderland of rivers. The Danube is in flood, shouldering its way round the last lap of its long race. But there is no competition. The Danube is the queen of rivers, and any which join it now are more like fans or admirers, jogging the last stretch before the finishing line on the Black Sea shore.

To our left are the cranes of Giurgiuleşti, the round barrels of an oil terminal, and a big blue aunt of a ship moored alongside. Beyond that, further down, the Moldovan border gives way to the Ukrainian and Chilia arm. We pass lone, sullen anglers, wary of police who might deny them their catch, even their nets. In places here, the Danube is fifty or sixty metres deep, swirling whirlpools of brown and green water. Barges pass in both directions, carrying gravel or ore, as do sea-going ships bound for Galaţi or Brăila, the last ports with waters deep enough and harbours big enough to load and unload sea-going cargoes. The sun comes out just as we bounce into Galaţi. On the grass beneath the harbour-master's control tower, surrounded by housing estates on three sides and the river on the fourth, vehicles confiscated from tobacco smugglers are on display. Trucks, coaches, cars, camper vans and power boats stand side by side. A change in Romanian law allows the vehicles smugglers use to be confiscated, then auctioned. Confiscated cigarettes also used to be sold, but the temptation to pocket a packet or two was so great they are now burned. On my way into a warehouse in a disused, red-brick school, I see nets in the first room – seized from fishermen during the spawning season, or because the mesh is finer than that sanctioned by law. In an inside room, more cigarette packets are stacked high to the ceiling. Viceroy, L & M, Pall Mall, Winston, and Regal are joined by the more religious St George. The room is infused with the dark, delicious smell of illicit tobacco.

Captain Virgiliu Cioban looks out from his window at the port of Galați. As deputy director of the Harbour Authority, he is responsible for keeping the broad Danube here safe for navigation – for the buoys, lighthouses and signals connected with the river. That means keeping the main navigable channel along the 170-kilometre stretch from Brăila to the Black Sea seven metres deep, so that sea-going vessels can pass. But there's less and less traffic on the river, he laments. In the early 1990s, there would be forty ships passing at a time, and two hundred waiting. That was the time when the forests of Romania, especially from the slopes of the Carpathians in the north, on the border with Ukraine, were being chopped down for export. 'Millions of trees passed down the Danube, bound for Britain, France, the north of Europe, and even North Africa,' he recalls. Now traffic is down to 2,500 to 3,000 ships a year. Of those, about two hundred stop at the shipyard in Galați for repairs. Iron ore, bauxite, coke and coal are the main goods coming upriver, mostly from Russia and Ukraine. Petroleum products, steel and grain make up the rest.

There's an exhibition just opening at the Galați History Museum when I arrive, dedicated to the city's large Greek community. Rodika Zamfiropol takes me under her wing. The exhibition mostly consists of books and photographs. There have been Greeks in Dobrogea for 2,700 years – about 2,000 years longer than the Turks, the Greeks like to mention – but the communist years were hard on them. Seven hundred Greeks live in Galați today, and there's something of a revival. The treasures of the exhibition include all four volumes of Nicolas de Nicolae's *Orientation et Navigation Orientale*, printed in Lyon in 1568. My namesake fought the Austrians at the battle of Perpignan in 1542, then served three French kings as soldier, diplomat and geographer. His book is a description of his journey in 1551, together with Henry II's ambassador Gabriel d'Aramont, to hold talks with Suleiman the Magnificent in Constantinople, and includes 'descriptions of the clothing of the men, as well as of the women', in the countries he visited. In another hall of the museum a series of caricatures mocks the quarrels between the great powers for control of the Lower Danube in the nineteenth century. One shows a youthful-looking Charles Hartley, the British engineer who regulated the Sulina arm, standing astride the

St George branch of the river with a rather overweight Frenchman behind him, both wielding curved, Turkish-style swords. Out at sea is a windmill, with the flags of the UK, France, Russia and Austria fixed to its sails. 'Don Quixote, (Charles Hartley)', reads the caption, 'chief engineer, tilting at windmills on the Lower Danube.' The lighthouse at Sulina is next to the Englishman's right foot and large sailing boats enter the Danube between his legs.

Down in the harbour a paddle steamer, the *Tudor Vladimirescu*, is moored to the pier. Built in 1854, she's the oldest paddle steamer still on the river. The first, the aptly named *Argo*, arrived in the city just twenty years earlier, in 1834. In the nineteenth century the Austrians, and later the Hungarians, dominated shipping on the river. The *Tudor Vladimirescu* was originally named the *Croatia*, and built at the Ganz-Danubius shipyard in Budapest. Sixty metres long and fifteen wide, she was handed over to Romania by Hungary as part of the reparations for the First World War, and renamed after a Romanian revolutionary from the early 1820s. After the Second World War, many ships were seized by the Russians when they occupied Romania. The ship – by then known as the *Sarmizegetusa*, the capital of the Dacian king Burebista – escaped requisitioning because she was considered too old. She was kept in service as a passenger ship between the Iron Gates and Tulcea, and was finally restored to her ancient glory in 2003, with dark green funnels embossed with the letters NR for Navrom, the Romanian state shipping company which owns her, and a big brass bell on the bow. As we talk on deck, an elderly man comes down the gangplank, selling orange windsocks he has made himself – 'Captain's pricks', as they are known in Romanian. On the Danube beside us, a Ukrainian ship, the *Petrozavodsk*, passes slowly downstream. The *Tudor Vladimirescu* can take a hundred passengers in style on its irregular journeys on the river. Such trips are not cheap, as it costs five thousand Euros just to start the engines and keep them running for twenty-four hours to reach the right pressure. He takes me down into the engine room, where the oil was originally mixed with sheep's fat to keep it at the right consistency. The original wooden paddles have now been replaced with steel ones, since one used to break on every trip.

I leave Galaţi at lunchtime, closely following the Danube on the road to Brăila, my head humming with the red wine from the Greek reception.

On the right, the huge steelworks, which once employed fifty thousand men and women, stretches along the horizon. I lose count after twenty chimneys. Now owned by Mittal Steel, less than nine thousand work there today. The factory is on the shore of the Siret river, whose name means 'love' in Hungarian. Flowing parallel to the Prut, the Siret brings the snow-melt down from the eastern slopes of the Carpathians, its source 700 kilometres away in northern Bukovina.

There has been no road sign for a while, so I stop to ask a man with a handsaw, crossing the river. Straight on for the river ferry he reassures me. Does he need a lift himself? But he only has a few hundred metres left to walk, to the woods at the confluence of the Siret and the Danube, where he is going to cut himself a nice new handle for his rake.

The ferry across the Danube is called the *Racheta*, 'the rocket', but is as quiet as a mouse. Her counterpart, the *Condor*, passes us in midstream. White seagulls stand out against the rust-brown waters of the river. An elderly couple ask for a lift to the town of Măcin, just down the road. The man has just collected his wife from hospital, and buses are few and far between on this stretch. He used to quarry granite at Măcin. His job was to drill holes in the rock face for sticks of dynamite, but he fell ill with silicosis after twenty-four years and was forced to retire. It's a mark of local pride that granite from here was used at the Olympic Games in Munich in 1972, though no one seems to know exactly what for. His wife made corks for the Niculiţel wine bottles. Huge flocks of birds follow a red tractor, ploughing the fields at the foot of the Măcin hills. 'Somewhere up there,' says the woman, pointing from the back seat, 'there's a holy spring, and a monastery.' Her reverent tone suggests that it is thanks to those healing waters that she and her husband are still alive, rather than the hospital she has just visited.

No sooner have they said goodbye than a younger couple flag me down. 'The wind from the East ripens the harvest, but dries everything out,' the man tells me. He doesn't fish in the Danube, just in the fishing ponds, but even they have been privatised, he complains. He was an apprentice in November 1987 at the Red Flag Truck Factory in Braşov when the uprising against the Ceauşescu dictatorship began. After the revolution, he went to work in Italy. They have three sons, two working in Turin, one in Tulcea. There's no work in Romania. Soon he will return to Italy himself.

The hills of western Dobrogea roll like waves towards the sea. I turn off right from the main road to the large Russian village of Ghindăreşti, where Nicu Artion and David Kondrat are waiting for me in the village hall. Nicu has a striking silver beard, typical of the Russian men of Dobrogea. 'We don't actually have to have beards any more,' he confesses, 'I shaved it off once . . . but then it grew back . . . We've been here 360 years,' he says, as if he remembers every one of them personally, and relates the foundation story of his community, how the reforming Patriarch Nikon ordered the Orthodox faithful in Russia to cross themselves in a different way. Nikon's aim was to harmonise Russian Orthodox with what he believed was the more ancient Greek Orthodox practice in ritual and liturgy, to return to the 'roots' of the Orthodox Church. In fact, the Greek liturgy had been steadily revised, and Russian practice was closer to the old writings, though this was not apparent at the time. Nikon was strongly backed by Tsar Alexis I, who welcomed the idea of Russia liberating all Orthodox Christians from Muslim rule. The Old Believers, several hundred thousand people who clung to the old ways, fled into exile rather than accept the new practice. They were welcomed in the Ottoman empire, in the best tradition of Islamic tolerance of other faiths, and given land to farm. Forty thousand still live in Dobrogea. By the time Tsar Nicholas II introduced an Act of Religious Freedom in 1905 it was too late to tempt them back.[8]

Their only problem in this particular village was its name – Ghizdar – which in Romanian slang refers to a particularly intimate part of the female anatomy. When the remaining Turks in the village left, the village was renamed Ghindăreşti. Today, almost all the six thousand inhabitants are Russians. The walls of the village hall are lined with black-and-white photographs of them: Mitrica Procop, a sprint canoeist who won a gold medal in the 2000 Sydney Olympics, Miron Ignat who represents the Russian minority in the Bucharest parliament, and, in pride of place, nameless fishermen, heroically hauling in their nets. One shows three men grappling with a beluga sturgeon, the side of the boat tipping precariously down to the water, their square jaws contrasting with the long snout of the fish. Men from this village are in great demand in the building industry, they tell me, 'throughout the world'. They are known as 'bearded excavators' on account of their capacity for diligent, hard work. Those who go abroad are mostly in Spain, Portugal and Italy. Those who stay are dedicated to one purpose only: fishing. Twenty or thirty black boats line the shores of the Danube, just waiting to be launched. As we walk down to the river, past the newly restored, cream-painted, copper and gold onion-domed church, I see smoke rising from a fire, down on the distant beach, and the figures of men repainting the hull of their boat with tar.

Already afloat on the dark green waters, Nikita Ivan is seventy, his companion Mitya Alexi sixty-eight. Nikita is unravelling a net the colour of his flowing white beard, and speaks not a word. There's a thin blue rope along the outside edge. Mitya's face is burnt brown by the sun, and his eyes are so narrow when he smiles he might be from the Russian Far East. Both men wear black Cossack caps. No one in the village uses a motor on their boat. They row upriver, sometimes as far as Cernavodă, then let their nets out, weighed down with lead weights, and trawl for fish. What was the biggest sturgeon they ever caught? 'One hundred and fifty kilos! As we were getting it into the boat, it hit the side with its tail, and knocked my companion clean into the water! I couldn't decide which of them to save!' he guffaws. Even Nikita permits himself a rare smile at this. Eventually he got both the fish and his companion into the boat, 'and we rowed back to the village singing all the way!' Would they sing that song for me, now? Both men look at me as if I am mad. 'What, during Lent?' I'm invited back after Easter and promised as many songs as my ears and my heart can bear, and as much fish to eat and brandy to drink as my stomach and brain can cope with. 'Did that sturgeon make you rich?' I ask them. Mitya grins. 'We sold it to the cooperative . . . for peanuts. In my household, money is like the Danube. . .' and he holds his hands up in the air to demonstrate, 'it . . . flows through our fingers!'

On the outcrop of rock which forms a headland above the village, a tall, white Russian Orthodox triple cross stands dramatically on a black marble plinth. Gold letters are embossed against the black background: *Kresty tvoemy poklonyaemsya vladiko I svyatoye voskresenie tvoye slavim* ('We worship your Holy Cross, O Lord, and we glorify thy Holy Resurrection').[9] On another side of the plinth, there's the stylised crest of the village, the rising sun, a boat and a bird over the river, and the words 'In Honour and Respect for our ancestors, the Russian Old Believers who settled in these lands in the name of saving their Pravoslav faith.' On a third side, 'In eternal memory of those Russian-Lipovans who fell in the wars, defending the homeland of their ancestors'.

In the distance, white smoke billows out over the river from the tar-burners' fire. Black horses graze among the black boats on the shore. On a long island in mid-stream the poplars and willows are still in their bleak winter underwear. A man stumbles out of the village blind drunk to harangue us in Russian and Romanian. But there's no anger with him from my companions for showing this other side of village life, towards the end of a winter that is taking its time to finish. Just a light-hearted acceptance of the bumbling fool, and a concern that he doesn't knock the guest flying into the river far below.

As I leave, I take a photo of three girls, giggling on a bench outside a house. Apart from the teenage beauty of their faces, the other striking features of the picture are the wavy, delicately wrought iron frames of the fence, the windows and the doors, like a non-figurative painting of the river itself.

CHAPTER 4

The Colour of the River

But the Old European sacred images and symbols were never totally
uprooted; these most persistent features in human history were too
deeply implanted in the psyche.
MARIJA GIMBUTAS[1]

Alas, we who hoped to lay the foundations of kindness, could not
ourselves be kind.
BERTOLD BRECHT[2]

IN THE delta the Danube was green, unwinding like a whole family of snakes
from the grey-brown of the winter foliage on its banks. Then upriver it was
grey, absorbing and reflecting the March sky and the cities of Galaţi and
Brăila on its banks. In Cernavodă it is black – the name means 'black water'.

Two black figures sit on the grass in front of Reactor Hall Zero at the
Cernavodă nuclear power station. The woman's right knee is raised, while
her left foot is doubled back, under her bottom. Her hands rest delicately
on her raised knee, and her oval face looks straight ahead, her eyes slightly
raised as though fixed on a point just above the horizon. The pose is both
sensual and authoritative. She knows who she is and what she wants. Next
to her on the grass sits a male figure on a tiny stool. His elbows rest on his
knees, his head is framed in his hands, he gazes straight ahead; unlike his
partner, however, he sees nothing but the images inside his own head. He is
known as 'The Thinker', or 'The Sorrowful God', and the female as 'the

Great Goddess of Hamangia', or, less kindly, 'the thinker's girlfriend'. The originals are just eleven centimetres tall, made of brown-black burnt clay, and belong to the Romanian National History Museum in Bucharest.[3] They were discovered by archaeologists excavating late Neolithic graves in 1956, ahead of work on the canal. Made in about 5000 BC, they have become iconic figures of modern art. A copy has been sent into space, as one of the ten items chosen to represent terrestrial culture to life-forms on other planets. How could Stone Age 'barbarians' from early farming communities produce such objects? How did the artist make the move from 'polishing stone and bone implements', as that epoch of human history is often described, to finding the leisure to fashion objects like this in his own image? It is the fact that the couple were seated, lost in thought rather than hunting game or grinding meal, that is so powerful. What was the man so sorrowful about? If a vegetation god, was he sad about the state of his creation? And if a man, did he feel already then at the mercy of the whims of the gods? The couple seem so much like us, seven thousand years on.

'Cernavodă is famous for two things, these figurines and this nuclear power plant,' explains the director of the latter, Ionel Bucur, as we head past the couple towards the reactor control room. 'So we thought we ought to have them here with us.' Cernavodă is pronounced 'cherna-voda' and has the public relations problem of sounding rather like Chernobyl, the nuclear power station in Ukraine that exploded in 1986. So he is at pains to stress the safety of his own operation – the more so since my visit coincides with the first anniversary of another nuclear disaster, at Fukushima in Japan.

I have to leave my mobile phone, my camera and my tape-recorder in a locker before entering the reactor building. If I had any chewing gum in my pocket, I would have had to leave that behind too, though polite enquiries fail to reveal why. Two Canadian-designed CANDU reactors here produce 20 per cent of Romania's electricity. They are surprisingly low, squat buildings, more like gas tanks in the rolling hills rippling back from the Danube. Water to cool them is taken straight from the Danube canal, and the water returned to the river through a tunnel and an open channel, 6 degrees Celsius warmer.

Inside the dark blue painted control room, Ionel Bucur tells me about his professional career. He studied nuclear engineering in Russia in the

1970s, and returned to Romania to build a Soviet-designed VVER on the shores of the River Olt, a tributary of the Danube, but it was not to be. The 1977 earthquake struck almost exactly at the spot where the new power station was to be built. Even dictator Nicolae Ceauşescu's ambitions could not resurrect that project from the ruins. Instead, plans were drawn up for a power station at a different site: Cernavodă. Apart from the Canadian design – a rarity in a half-continent dominated by things Soviet – the project had the additional glory for a nationalist like Ceauşescu that the fuel was home-grown. Uranium would be taken from the mines of Transylvania and converted into heavy water near the Danube at Turnu Severin. It was to be both fuelled by the Danube and cooled by it.

Nuclear power stations around the world have been forced to reassess their safety procedures in the light of Fukushima. In European Union countries, each reactor has been subjected to stress-tests, to explore potential weaknesses to natural disasters. Cernavodă is just sixteen metres above sea-level. 'When we built this plant, one of the main safety concerns was flooding from the Danube. But our experience has been rather of years of drought. And that has caused problems for the cooling of the reactors,' says Bucur. In the summer of 2003, the water level in the Danube sank to almost zero. The reactors had to be shut down for twenty-two days, but they still had to be cooled. Emergency wells were drilled, six hundred metres deep. That was the summer when unknown wrecks emerged from the river, and archaeologists and bounty hunters scoured the unusually exposed riverbed. It was also when swords, hurled into the waters centuries before to placate the river god, were returned to human hands. What if such summers become the norm, rather than the exception, as the climate of the planet warms up? What if the Danube runs drier and drier?

'We need 105 cubic metres of water a second to cool two reactors. There are big reserves of water here. I'm not worried about that.'

Bucur has already installed a second set of diesel-powered generators as a back-up power supply in case the lights go out. His main fear is not of an accident, but that there might be less political will, after yet another nuclear disaster, to build two more reactors at Cernavodă on which he has set his heart. I am reminded of the words of a Czech nuclear engineer at Temelín in the soft hills of South Bohemia. 'Every nuclear power plant is an experiment. As an engineer, I love the challenge of making them work. But as a member of the public, taking into account the enormous risk, I would never allow them to be built.'

In the Romanian capital Bucharest, I meet Romania's foremost expert on earthquakes, Gheorghe Marmoreanu. His mobile phone buzzes constantly, each buzz a text message reporting another earth tremor somewhere on the planet. He receives more than six thousand such messages a day, which gives the impression that the solid ground under one's feet is in constant, restless motion. But he dismisses fears of a nuclear disaster at Cernavodă. The epicentre of all Romanian earthquakes is Vrancea, in the south-eastern corner of the Carpathian Mountains, he explains. Several kilometres underground, its effects are normally felt far away, not here in Romania. One of his favourite tales is of the baby Pushkin, pushed by his nanny through the grounds of a monastery in Moscow in 1800. Tiles suddenly began falling from the roof of the church, and the quick-witted nanny steered the pram and its precious cargo out on to the open ground. That was the effect of Vrancea, Marmoreanu tells me, with delight, 'but even that was not enough to rob Russia of a future writer of genius'. In Vienna, the International Atomic Energy Authority has declared that new nuclear plants must be designed to withstand a major earthquake every ten thousand years – double the previous requirement of five thousand. The oval faces of the couple on the grass in Cernavodă gaze into the future, as well as into the past. Seeing and unseeing.

The Thinker and the Goddess were not alone. The Hamangia culture to which they belong forms a semi-circle, inland from the Black Sea coast, from the Danube delta to Varna in Bulgaria. They belong to a civilisation or span of parallel civilisations that flourished in south-eastern Europe, along the Danube, Prut, Siret, Dnieper, Sava, Drava and Tisza rivers, as far inland as the borders of modern Hungary, from around 6000 to 3500 BC. Together, the civilisations that thrived here are known as 'Old Europe', a term coined by the American-Lithuanian archaeologist Marija Gimbutas. This controversial, fiercely feminist archaeologist has dared to suggest that the civilisation was matriarchal, devoted to worship of the mother goddess, and that this was overthrown by patriarchal, Bronze Age invaders from the Russian steppes, north of the Black Sea. 'They independently discovered the possibility of using copper and gold for ornaments and tools, and even appear to have evolved a rudimentary script. If one defines civilisation as the ability of a given people to adjust to its environment and develop adequate arts, technology, script, and social relationships it is evident that Old Europe achieved a marked degree of success,' she wrote.[4]

That success is not disputed. Huge villages or towns of several thousand inhabitants were built in the Danube valleys, at a time when most other people in Europe were eking out a nomadic existence in little scattered clusters. These settlements were maintained for hundreds of years in the same place. Copper was mined, smelted and used for tools, weapons and jewellery. Gold was produced in small quantities, although few would have been lucky enough to see it. Salt was quarried and transported hundreds of kilometres to allow a constant supply and meat – mostly red deer – and fish were exported up and down river. The people lived in similar sized homes, with no apparent hierarchy in life – only in death, when the grave goods they took with them on their journey to the next world varied considerably. The first physical objects to be traded long-distance were the beautiful pink-white *Spondylus* – spiny oyster – shells from the Aegean or the Adriatic. These are also found extensively in their graves. The archaeologists John Chapman and Bisserka Gaydarska poetically contrast the luminous effect of the shells with the dark, burnished pottery of the Tripol'ye-Cucuteni culture found on the shores of the Prut, Siret and Dnieper, reminiscent of the full moon shining off the waters of the Danube.[5]

The exact relationship of the different peoples to one another, their belief systems and their forms of organisation are the subject of fierce debate. The discussion focuses particularly on the discovery of several thousand tiny, wide-hipped, exquisitely decorated female figurines at sites across the region. Many were found in the sitting position, with tiny thrones or chairs – the Thinker at Cernavodă was also portrayed on a small stool. These were central to the matriarchal theory of Marija Gimbutas. She named one such collection of figurines 'the council of the goddesses'. A younger generation of archaeologists, led by the American Douglass Bailey, has challenged the matriarchal theory, suggesting that there is no proof of this whatsoever, and that such theories have more to do with the feminism of the 1970s or to Lithuanian folklore than to the mysterious pots, jewellery, tools, weapons and settlement plans of the late Stone Age.[6] He accuses Marija Gimbutas of leapfrogging millennia, to suggest an unbroken continuity of folk beliefs and religious practices from the late Stone Age to pre-modern times. These were settled peoples with a regular supply of food from agriculture, fishing and hunting, Bailey argues – they had no need to invoke goddesses or gods. Instead he suggests we should look rather at the size of the figures. 'Contemporary psychological studies have shown that something very odd happens to the human mind when one handles or plays with miniature objects . . . we enter another world, one in which our perception of time is altered and in which our abilities of concentration are affected.' The figurines should rather be seen as playthings, easily made and easily discarded, he suggests, telling us more about fashion – the lines on their bodies suggest close fitting tunics, or even body paint – than their beliefs.

For myself, a stranger following the snaking river inland from the sea, I find much to admire in both approaches, and no real contradiction. But only Gimbutas gives clues to the kind of world which people might have entered as they fingered the figurines.

The nuclear power station gives Cernavodă a modern, nervous, self-important air, with policemen checking cars at the roadside, more expensive hotels than elsewhere in Dobrogea, and electricity pylons marching off impatiently through the vine-clad hills like men with a mission. There are even ladies of easy virtue, dawdling in doorways in a small street near the canal.

Ionel Bucur might have mentioned a third wonder of the town – the Anghel Saligny Bridge. Saligny was just thirty-three years old when he designed Romania's longest and boldest bridge, to take the new Bucharest to Black Sea railway across the Borcea arm of the Danube. The tender was won against fierce foreign competition, not least from British firms that were already busy laying the country's new railways. On 15 September 1895, twenty thousand people flocked from all over the country to see the opening of this architectural miracle, at four thousand metres the longest steel structure at that time in Europe.[7] King Carol I was there in person, with five hundred guests of honour. Would the steel structure hold for its first test? Fifteen heavy locomotives tore over it at eighty kilometres per hour. To prove his unflagging faith in his own creation, Anghel Saligny sat under the bridge in a rowing-boat, calmly smoking his pipe. The bridge held, and the way was open for goods and passenger transport to the Black Sea at Constanța. The bridge is still there, though it has now been bypassed by a less elegant, more utilitarian, creation. The removal of the wooden sleepers and the track has stripped it of some of its original glory, but two stone soldiers still stand guard, and there is a statue of the young Saligny himself, triumphant. Underneath, horses graze on the spring grass, next to bush willows along the banks of the Danube, and a lone cow with a bell round its neck, clanking as she munches. A goods train passes slowly, endlessly over the new bridge, bound for the coast, hooting mournfully. Then the sound of the birds swells up again around it, interrupted only by the *zag, zag* of passing cars. The river is mud brown, ponderous, lost in its own memories. To one side is a long, low building and an enclosure of wooden fence-posts. A herd of sheep, somewhat the worse for wear, fan out across the rivery landscape. If the grass and the foliage were lusher it might have been painted by Turner.

The Danube canal stretches, straight as a bullet, eastwards towards Constanţa, sixty-five kilometres away. First conceived in 1837, it took the brutality of the communist system, its industrialising frenzy and a cheap supply of human lives to get it started in 1949. Up to a hundred thousand men and women worked here, and several tens of thousands died of poor food and medical care, the cruelty of the conditions, and the harshness of winter, before the project was suspended in 1953. The route taken to the coast proved too hard. Today's canal was resumed, along a simpler route, and completed in 1984. In the early 1950s, this was a dumping ground for all social and political opponents of the communist regime, better-off peasants, priests and anyone else the authorities took a dislike to.[8] There was little earth-moving equipment, so the inmates had to work with shovels and spades. Elena Sibiscanu was born in 1938, and still lives on the hill near the cemetery, looking down on the Columbia district below. Columbia was one of the most notorious prison colonies. As a child in 1949 she remembers going to play on the cliff overlooking it. 'After seven or eight in the evening, we would hear the women singing sad songs, on the steps of their barracks. My father used to take bricks and other materials in his cart inside, and he would sometimes smuggle out notes from the prisoners to their relatives. He also used to take cheap cigarettes in for them, though he was strictly forbidden to speak to the prisoners.'

The most dangerous work her parents did was to act as go-betweens for family members, some of whom would come to their house, late at night, when her parents thought the children were fast asleep. But the children knew something was afoot, and listened behind the door. 'I remember one family telling my parents they were from Timişoara – in the west of Romania – and that their relatives had been sent to the camp for not fulfilling the quota of food they had to give to the state as peasant farmers.' There were three layers of barbed wire fence, nine to twelve feet high around the colony. In the morning the inmates would be marched along the section of the canal they had already dug, to a point in front of where the nuclear power station is now, where they were digging through a hill. 'The winters were particularly cold, and the wind was bitter. In the winter of 1952 two or three inmates died a day. They would bring the bodies in wooden carts, after dark, up near our house to the cemetery. We used to run along behind. The cops (she uses the Romanian slang, *caraliu*) would point their guns and shout at us to go away, but we followed them into the cemetery, and watched them dump a pile of bodies into a mass grave, right behind the church.' She shows me the place, overgrown and strewn with rubbish, though the rest of the graveyard is nicely kept. We look in silence over the town. The red bridge over the canal, built at the request of the power station, contrasts with the bright green cap of the minaret. Communism could never brook dissent, least of all in the 1950s, the years of iron and steel. It was as blind a faith as that of the medieval churches, but without the figure of Christ or the hope of redemption. The camp was finally shut down in July 1953 when Stalin died, and work temporarily abandoned. Historians estimate that 100,000 people took part in the forced labour on the canal, and that at least 10,000 of them died.

From Cernavodă the road runs east beside the canal. Just after Poarta Albă a concrete column stands like a totem pole between the road and the waterway. Eleven massive concrete crosses, three on the ground, eight stacked in a child's tower above them, stand in an 'L' shape, with the words: 'In memory of the martyrs'. Each cross carries the name of a prison camp: Constanţa, Midia, Peninsula, Galesul, Noua Culme, Poarta Albă, Medgidia, Saligny, Columbia. Poarta Albă was the largest, with up to 12,000 inmates. In Romanian it means 'the white gate'. A poem, written by a survivor, is carved in the concrete at the foot of the column.

Water spills, from three mouths of the Danube,
But from the fourth, blood.

Further east along the canal lies the small town of Murfatlar. The crisp, fruity white wine produced here is not the most delicious of the Romanian vintages, but is the best marketed. A huge wooden barrel on a vine-clad hill marks the entrance to the vineyards. I drive on with an altogether different goal in mind – the tenth-century cave churches of Basarabi.

Huge trucks laden with limestone form a constant thundercloud in front of the wooden scaffolding that covers a cliff face. The guardian of the cave complex, a woman with a large Alsatian dog, emerges from behind her washing lines and points me over a rickety wooden bridge. Discovered in 1957 during efforts to expand the limestone quarry next door, the caves are still not open to the public. Romania's own little Cappadocia – chapel after chapel with curious, intricate, crude shapes carved in white rock – is almost unknown. There are madonnas and saints, water-birds observed in the wetlands of the Danube, monsters and dragons, and what looks like a Viking ship, evidence of a Viking trade route from Scandinavia to Constantinople.[9] To reach the chapels, you walk along wooden platforms and stairways built up against the cliff face. Even the sound of the trucks passing below fades to nothing in the inner recesses of places of worship abandoned a thousand years ago. The Romans quarried limestone blocks from here in long terraces, to build three 'Trajan's walls' across Dobrogea to keep out the tribes invading from the north. When the Romans left, the Christians of the Byzantine empire burrowed inwards from the terraces in the soft rock to escape their enemies, or for a little peace and quiet for their worship. They carved out naves and chapels, arches and apses, the same shapes, only smaller, as the basilicas of the early Christians.

There are also runic inscriptions, little hooked letters, carved over haloed saints. These figures are a bone of contention between Romanians and Bulgarians.[10] The Romanians trace their origins to a happy marriage between the Dacians, a tribe that inhabited the Lower Danube region, and the Romans who arrived to conquer them in AD 101. The Roman emperor Trajan defeated the Dacian chief Decebal and destroyed his capital Sarmizegetusa in AD 106. The provinces of Moesia and Wallachia were annexed to the Roman empire, bringing it right down to the shores of the Black Sea. Some Classical Greek authors called the Dacians the Getae, while others believed the Getae were the easterly branch of the Dacian tribe, with the same language but different gods. Whoever they were, they adopted the language of the conquerors. When the Romans left in around AD 300 the native Romanians remained and became an integral part of the Byzantine empire, runs this particular narrative. But there are missing pieces in the puzzle. There is no story of the conversion of the Romanians to Christianity, a crucial milestone in the history of any Christian nation. There is no further trace of the Latin-based language that Romanian was to become until the twelfth century. And to make matters worse, Bulgarian linguists claim evidence of their own conversion to Christianity in these very caves.

Central to the Bulgarian argument are the Alans, a people closely associated with the proto-Bulgarians, who lived in western Ukraine and the Dobrogea region in the first centuries after Christ. Seven of the runic characters found at Murfatlar are contained in an inscription from southern Ukraine, which has been interpreted as 'the Khan (or leader) of the Alans'. In the Basarabi caves, a man with a fine, drooping moustache, clearly dressed in a monk's habit, with a halo round his head and a large stylised cross in his left hand, is identified in the runes as Saint John the Baptist – converting the Bulgarians. Bulgarian researchers also claim to have deciphered a whole sentence at Basarabi, in the Alano-Kassogian alphabet: THE SOWING OF THE HOLY TEMPLE OF GOD WATERS AND FEEDS LIKE AN IRRIGATOR THE DRYNESS. Romanian scholars, however, say this is fanciful. 'Only some Bulgarian scientists try to assign Runic inscriptions, as well as the entire complex, to Bulgarians, an opinion not accepted by the scientific community,' wrote Constantin Chera. 'The monuments in Basarabi confirm Byzantine writers Cedren and Attaleiates' information about the existence of Romanians in the Lower Danube, as well as other, much less numerous populations, in Dobrogea.'[11]

In 2007, the name 'Basarabi' was changed back to its old Turkish name 'Murfatlar'. This comes from the Turkish *murvet*, which means 'a generous man' – as good an etymology of a town as I have ever heard, and one likely to bring blessings of one sort or another.

After so much time in Dobrogea, I begin to worry if I will ever make progress upstream. But I should visit one last person in Medgidia before I move on. The town is a bastion of the Turkish-Tatar people and the Islamic faith in Romania. Originally a humble village called Karasu, or Black Water, it was rebuilt by the Ottomans in the mid-nineteenth century on a carefully planned grid of streets, and renamed after Sultan Abdul Medjid. The population was swollen with Muslim refugees from the Crimean War. That was how Ayhan's family, Tatars from the Crimea, reached the Dobrogea.

Ayhan is just nineteen and already an imam. He has been appointed in the village of Negru Voda, a place which, like almost every other name here, means black water in Romanian. Black permeates the landscape of Dobrogea – Black Sea, Black Forest and Black Water. I was first introduced to Ayhan by his teacher at the Turkish-Romanian high school on an earlier trip, but this time we talk alone, in a Turkish restaurant, with a Turkish soccer game on a big television screen above our heads, over a hearty lunch of long, thin Turkish pizzas, like elegant slippers. His family settled in Techirghiol, about thirty miles to the east, at the beginning of the twentieth century. He tells a story about the lake. A man called Techir was trying to get rid of his lame donkey, and walked it into the waters of the lake (*ghiol* in Turkish). But then he saw that the mud of the lake healed the animal's legs. People have treasured it ever since. King Carol II of Romania even had a holiday home there, where his son Michael learnt to ride and hunt. Ayhan's father worked in the shipyards in Constanţa, making ropes known as *parima*, with which the ships were tied to the shore. When Ayhan decided to become an imam his mother was not pleased, but he took inspiration from his paternal grandfather, who was also a man of faith. As for himself, 'I would like to marry a Turkish or Tatar girl,' Ayhan says. According to the 2010 census there are fifty thousand Turks and Tatars left in Romania, most of them in Dobrogea. 'But God is great, he alone knows what will happen . . .' To be a Muslim, he says, means to respect one's parents and the elders of the community, to pray five times a day, and to keep the feasts. He has no qualms about studying in Romanian schools where modern history is taught as the story of battle after battle to shake off the Turkish yoke. 'One of my teachers nicknamed me "Ottoman", which hurt me at first, until I got used to it.' He feels no disadvantage from belonging to a religious and cultural minority. His dream is to study at university in Turkey. He has been there several times, and wept with joy at the beautiful way the morning prayer, the *ezan,* was sung in the city of Edirne. Not long before our meeting Osama Bin Laden was killed by US forces in Pakistan. Ayhan shrugs, as if I had asked him about a football team in a distant city. 'I didn't feel anything for Bin Laden,' he says. And he has never come across any signs of radical Islam in Romania. Nonetheless, he hopes for a revival of Islam in his own community and sees some indication of it. His maternal grandfather worked on the Danube canal in the 1970s. Once Ceauşescu visited the project, and announced that when he came again, in three months' time, the canal should have reached a certain tree. No matter how hard the men worked, they were still far from the tree as the deadline approached. With their foreman's connivance, the tree was carefully cut down and reassembled at the point they actually had reached. Even the leaves of the tree were painted green, to please the mad dictator.

We spend one night in Medgidia, in this canal port, before returning to the river. I eat catfish in a restaurant, then find a quiet hotel, with windows that look out on to the main square, and cakes in a display case in the main entrance that you can eat, day or night. A group of young, rather rowdy, Germans is watching Germany play the Netherlands in the European Championship on the television in the common room. They're winning, and the empty bottles of Ursus, a rather drinkable Romanian beer brewed in Cluj with a bear on the label, are piling up around their ankles. 'Germans,' whispers the waitress, with a hint of pride in her voice because they have chosen her establishment, 'they're with the windmills . . .'

At exactly the same time that Saligny and his men were building their bridge, a team of Romanian archaeologists was working just up the road from Cernavodă on another, very different, monument to Romanian pride: a Roman ruin. A monument, not to man's ingenuity, but to his raw power. There is no one in the little glass booth at Adamclisi to sell us tickets, but a lone guard dog, a brown-and-white-faced animal with wolf-like eyes, bounds up to greet us instead, and leads us down a cobbled avenue to what looks like a round stone fortress, a carbuncle growing on Romania's unblemished face.

The Dacians were 'the noblest as well as the most just of all the Thracian tribes', according to Herodotus.[12] Their totem was a wolf's head, carried on their banners into battle. The strange look of the mongrel at the gate was no accident. The Romanian historian of religions, Mircea Eliade, has proposed that the name 'Dacia' may come from the Phrygian *daos* meaning 'wolf'. Another etymology suggests the word means 'the enemy'.

The Roman emperor Trajan marched through the Iron Gates gorge on a treacherous path carved into the sheer cliffs above the River Danube, to crush the Dacians twice, first in AD 101, then again in 106. The monument is a fat cylinder, thirty metres tall and forty metres in diameter, built to celebrate Trajan's final victory. Friezes around it – copies of the much eroded originals – depict bloody scenes from the Roman triumph: full-bearded Dacian tribesmen in leggings, trampled under the hooves of the Roman cavalry, or squewered on their lances, their own curved swords rendered useless by the superior reach of the clean-shaven invaders. The Romans shun trousers in favour of short, chain-mail skirts in the battle fashion of the second century after Christ. Above the pictures of the fighting is another row of friezes showing Dacian prisoners being led away in chains. When Sarmizegetusa fell, and Decebal committed suicide rather than face capture, the entire population was taken away into slavery, according to Roman historians. Instead of mourning such a cataclysmic defeat, the Romanians celebrate it as the 'birth certificate' of their nation – the marriage in the heat of battle of the Dacians and Romans. Copies were made of the original friezes in the 1970s, and the monument has a rather suspicious, socialist-realist look, as though the Roman statues on top were the prototypes of the 'new man' of the socialist era. Only one or two rather beautiful carvings of sheep soften the austere and violent depiction of war. There is a mound that contains the remains of four thousand Roman soldiers who fell in battle, but no record of the Dacian losses. Few traces of the Dacian language remain, but place names ending in -*dava*, such as Moldava, the Drava river, and possibly Plovdiv in Bulgaria, are believed to be among the last such.[13]

In AD 117 Trajan died and was succeeded by Trajan. In Marguerite Yourcenar's *Memoirs of Hadrian*, published in 1951, the Roman emperor Hadrian reminisces on his deathbed.[14] He describes a secret ritual performed by Roman soldiers, an initiation into the rites of the cult of the god Mithras. The cult, Yourcenar has Hadrian say, 'won me over tempo-rarily by the rigours of its stark asceticism, which drew taut the bowstring of the will, and by its obsession with death, blood, and iron, which elevated the routine harshness of our military lives to the level of a symbol of universal struggle'.

'My initiation took place in a turret constructed of wood and reeds on the banks of the Danube . . . I remember that the weight of the bull in its death throes nearly brought down the latticed floor beneath which I lay to receive the bloody aspersion.'

'Each of us believed that he was escaping from the narrow limits of his human state, feeling himself to be at the same time himself and his own enemy, at one with the god who seems to be both the animal victim and the human slayer. Victory and defeat were mixed like rays of the same sun.'

'Those Dacian footsoldiers whom I crushed under my horse's hoofs, those Sarmatian cavalrymen overthrown in the close combat of later years when our rearing horses tore at each other's chests, were all struck down the more easily if I identified myself with them.'

The name of the bow, Heraclitus wrote, is life. It's work is death.[15]

I lie down in the long grass behind the monument, on the tomb of a Roman officer. The birds are deafening – swallows flitting above a sea of wheat and corn, pigeons perched high on Roman soldiers' heads, and cuckoos asking questions of each other in the scrub-like trees around the column. All around are the rolling plains where Hadrian defeated his enemy. A horse and cart passes along the edge of the field, ridden like a motorbike by two teenage lads with hoods on their heads, looking neither left nor right, as though on their way to a murder.

I drive through sparse, deserted villages which feel as though they have been unpopulated since the Romans withdrew, and reach the Danube in time to watch a blood-red sun sink through vineyards among the forested islands of the river. The monastery at Dervent rears up out of the gathering gloom like the warhorse of an ally, and offers a bed for the night. Outside, an agile fellow with a long stick is dislodging fragments of swallows' nests from the high rafters above the entrance to the church, as agitated swallows fly in all directions. I suppress a Franciscan cry of outrage. 'We try to keep just this one area free, so that people going into or coming out of church don't get shat on,' explains the monk with the stick. A rapid glance around the eaves of the rest of the quadrangle confirms his story. The monastery is a city of swallows, their undisturbed nests packed into every conceivable space. The birds swarm like biblical locusts. There are so many swallows, it seems the monks themselves might be just rare, seasonal visitors.

I go into the church. A group of monks, some of almost Old Testament age, are gathered at the front, near the iconostasis. Some sing the lead, others the refrain. The older monks sing with their eyes shut. The younger men sing from an enormous old Bible, leaning earnestly over each other's shoulders to read the words. There are also one or two men in civilian clothes and younger women as well in the church, keeping a respectful distance. It is lit only by candlelight. The icons are glorious, reds and golds, silver and deep blue.

After the service I find a monk who speaks English. Father Atal is young, perhaps in his early thirties, and a little reticent. He has duties to perform, but sits down with me in a small courtyard by the wall, looking down on the silvery Danube below. There are ancient anchors beside us, a little covered pagoda, and various rocks – perhaps from the river as well, and carefully tended flower-pots. He agrees to talk on condition that it doesn't take long. And of course I can stay the night. The monastery has guest rooms. Another monk will show me to my quarters when we are finished. There is no charge, but I am welcome to make a contribution to the monastery. First I ask about the Danube. It's the right question. He gives a long sigh, then speaks about the river with a religious passion. 'My first memory of the Danube is when my father threw me into it to learn to swim. I must have been four or five . . .' He learnt his lesson, though, and has been swimming in its waters ever since. When the visitors to the monastery, with all their troubles, get too much, he takes a small rowing boat across to the island in the middle of the river, Pacuiul de Soare. The boat belongs to the archaeologists. They're excavating the Roman and Byzantine ruins on the island, and have already found the remains of a flourishing ship-building yard and a ninth-century cathedral. 'I go to the island when I need a break. Sometimes I swim, and I enter into communion with the river. This is how I have felt since I was a child. I saw people swimming in the Danube, and realised they didn't know how to use the Danube, because the river has currents and helps you to get to the shore. Likewise in life, some people do not know how to use whatever God gives them, how to live life to the highest intensity.'

Father Atal first visited the monastery by chance, with no intention of becoming a monk. 'It was February 2002. I had already done my military service, and was studying engineering at university in Bucharest. I don't know what happened to me. I just knew I had to come here.' So he sold all his books, spent two weeks tying up all the loose strands of his life, and moved to Dervent. 'I like the autumn the most, the range of colours, from raw green to dark brown. I also like the sunlight in summer, in August, when it casts a special colour . . . which foresees the fall.' The hardest time, he says, is between January and mid-March when no visitors come at all. If he closes his eyes, I ask, what colour does he see the Danube? Blue he says, to my surprise. On my own travels, I haven't often seen the river blue. Mostly dark green . . . or silver. 'Once some monks found an old anchor in the mud, and dragged it up here.' It stands to one side of the courtyard, a double anchor with four hooks – the archaeologists would be interested. 'The anchor is like our belief, our faith . . . There was also a crucifix found on the island. The figure of Christ on it is dressed as a monk. On the back there are the waves of the Danube; it's a unique piece, there is nothing quite like it in the world.'

The monastery also owes its existence to another miracle – the discovery of an ancient stone cross, washed ashore in 1936. Father Atal takes me to see it in a little chapel next to the church. It is a large chunky piece, polished by the fingers of the faithful, softened by their beeswax.[16] Another time we could have drunk some of the monastery's excellent wine together, he says, but now it is Lent, and he has chores to attend to. We take our leave, and I drive into the next village to buy bread and wine for my supper. I eat a simple meal overlooking the darkening river, turning slowly silver beneath a full moon.

Early the next morning I walk down the track to the healing spring. I have a slight limp from a footballing injury. I check there's no one around to offend with my nakedness, then undress and bathe my bad knee in the chill waters. Then I walk back to the church for the start of the early morning service. There are snail tracks in the dust, transparent in the dawn.

CHAPTER 5

The Dogs of Giurgiu

Anything I subsequently experienced had already happened in
Ruse. There, the rest of the world was known as 'Europe', and if
someone sailed up the Danube to Vienna, people said he was going
to Europe. Europe began where the Turkish Empire had once ended.
ELIAS CANETTI, *MEMOIRS*[1]

ON A wide meadow, a headland overlooking a sweeping bend in the
Danube, just before the Romanian–Bulgarian border at Silistra, I catch
sight of a man striding purposefully beside a line of blue and yellow
beehives, evenly spaced like floats on a net across the river. From a distance
he looks like a giant. As I walk towards him, he seems to shrink to only a
little more than my own height. Standing in front of him, shaking his
hand, I notice that he has two or three bee-stings on his face.

'Our first child was born about the time of the revolution,' Vasile Brici
tells me. He has broad, muscular shoulders, and a stripy, Breton T-shirt.
'I was working in the dockyards in Constanța at that time, loading ships.
My wife ran out of breast milk to feed the baby, so we decided to move to
the countryside, to buy a cow to replace the missing milk. I had to find a
new job, and tried my hand at bee-keeping. I got hooked! . . . It's like a
game of chess. There are twenty frames in each hive. When I open a hive,
I have to decide if there is enough wood in each frame, if the queen is old
and should be replaced, when the hive needs cleaning, and when the
frames should be changed . . .'

He has 160 hives, twenty thousand bees in each, and follows the flowers each spring. As each new flower comes into bloom he arrives with his bees. He travels in a large white truck, carefully designed for his hives. 'They don't enjoy the travelling, but after two days in a new place they settle down and find the flowers they need.' Now they are busy with the oil-seed rape which paints the meadows above the Danube an intense, fluorescent yellow. Soon the acacia will start – I have been watching its overhanging branches breaking into blossom as I drive down long avenues of trees. 'Acacia is the best. I can get half as much again for acacia honey – up to six dollars a kilo.' He earns about ten thousand dollars a year from the honey, he says – by Romanian standards, a living wage. Over more than twenty years, spending seven months a year living with the bees, he has noticed the climate change. 'The acacia should be over by now, but it hasn't even started.' The winter was mild, but too long. Before he moves to a new area, he contacts the local farmers' association to check the crops haven't been sprayed recently; if they have, he avoids the place, to minimise the risk to his bees' health.

The daughter he moved to the country for has grown up and left home. Now she lives in Italy. His wife is content in their village. And he is happy out here by the Danube, playing chess with his bees.

It's still early morning at the ferry crossing from Silistra to Călăraşi on the left bank. I need a coffee and something to eat, but the girl behind the counter in a wooden shack is sullen; her coffee is lukewarm and tastes burnt. There are no fresh pastries, just soggy croissants in plastic wrapping. Behind her in the shop, packets of biscuits and snacks from all over the world line the walls. But if there ever was a baker in this part of town, he has gone. There are just a few shrivelled apples and peppers in a cardboard box in front of her shop.

A stubby little tug with a big voice drags the platform which serves as a ferry across the wide green Danube. The *Cardinal* pushes mine north, the *Perla* pushes the other, coming the other way, bound for the southern shore. We pass in midstream, and nobody waves. But the helmsmen, high in their turrets, share an almost imperceptible nod, a twitch of their bushy eyebrows. On my ferry there are four cars, a truck carrying timber and two or three men with very short hair and wrap-around sunglasses, their ears glued to mobile phones into which they mutter veiled threats. The river gurgles beneath the bows with supreme disinterest. It has mafiosi like these for breakfast.

On the far shore, I reach Călăraşi just in time for my appointment with Marian Neagu, director of the Museum of the Lower Danube. He has promised me thirty minutes, but when I start to ask questions close to his archaeological heart, he closes the door behind us, orders coffees from his secretary, and gives me his whole morning. 'We think the Danube was a cradle of civilisation, the oldest in Europe and one of the oldest in the world,' Marian explains. 'At that time, the river was not a barrier, as it has become in modern times, but a bridge, linking similar civilisations.' I like the way in which he lumps the Romans with their pouting Venuses, ardent Priaps and river forts, among the 'moderns'.[2]

In prehistory, the Danube delta began here, and spread all the way to the Black Sea. Large communities grew up among the maze of islands, thanks to an abundance of fish, new farming techniques such as ploughing and the absence of enemies. Most of his excavations are on islands in the middle, or on the banks, of the river. He has been working on some settlements for decades. Trade and migration routes, from Anatolia and Thrace to the south-east, and the steppes north of the Black Sea, criss-crossed here. The cows they brought with them provided milk, cheese and meat, and bones for tools and idols.

In the basement of his museum, Marian carefully unwraps a small object from tissue paper, and hands it to me. A figurine, beautifully shaped, surprisingly light, in the palm of my hand. No face – just a beaked, bird-like nose. Unquestionably a woman – small, firm breasts at the touch of my thumb, buttocks patterned with spirals, a meander on the navel. If she were perched on my desk, I would never be able to take my eyes off her. 'If you look carefully, you will see that she is in the early stages of pregnancy.' The woman on whom this figure was modelled gave birth two thousand generations ago. The figurines in his collection portray different stages of pregnancy – three, six and nine months – these last with spreading legs and emphasised genitals, as though at the very moment of giving birth. Not only the shape of the bellies, but the arching of the back is exactly observed in each case, a local obstetrician told him. Some of the figurines stretch their arms skywards in prayer. Most are missing their heads, in a process known as 'fragmentation' – the deliberate breaking off of the head at the neck, a ritual practice in many cultures. The heads of those lucky enough to still have them are thin, inexpressive, with tiny, beak-like noses, and there are lines incised on the thighs, the buttocks and the back – triangles and diagonals and curvilinear lines on the burnt clay. The lines give the figures a special lightness, like curls of smoke, as if they made it possible for the figures to rise slowly through the firelight.

Upstairs in his museum Marian shows me round. There are two graves with the skeletons buried on their left side, their heads to the east – down-river – in the foetal or 'hocker' position, knees raised towards the chest as if in the mother's womb. Red ochre is often found in tombs, symbolising blood, and all the other jewellery and tools the dead might need in the next life. One peculiar feature of Tripol'ye-Cucuteni culture further east is that very few graves have been found. Life in such communities, however prosperous, was short. Few skeletons are found older than thirty years of age. One woman lived to her mid-fifties, and met a violent death with a blow which cracked her skull. 'Someone thought she had lived too long,' Marian suggests.

There are also reproductions of kilns, with clay bases punctured with holes underneath, in which beds of straw and reed were kept burning that could reach 1,100 degrees Celsius, the temperature needed to smelt copper. There is, too, a ceramic jug carefully designed with a spout resembling a woman's nipple, and a tiny hole through which a Copper Age baby sucked. One of the great frustrations of Marian's work is that there is so little money available to pursue it properly. Archaeologists in eastern Europe are dependent on the projects of big foreign universities and archaeologists. The Americans arrive and want to explore the details of relationships between settlements ten miles apart. Local archaeologists have been doing that for years, and would prefer to explore the trade and contact between settlements several hundred miles apart, and to meet and discuss with archaeologists from the Near and Middle East to compare the strange markings on their pots.

I leave Marian Neagu with his dreams of future cooperation on the shores of the Danube and walk down to the water. This is the small Danube, the less navigated, while the mass of water flows on the far side, around the island of Pacuiul de Soare. Călăraşi was a steel town in commu-nist times, and by the mid-1970s boasted the most modern steel mill in

Romania. But capitalism has been cruel to steel production on the Danube. The Călăraşi steel mill has stopped completely. Gypsies, hunting for scrap metal, have stripped away anything of value from the factory. The whole complex resembles a ghost town, the windows broken, a sea of chimneys protruding through clean air. Down on the shore, a steel sculpture made of twisted metal petals with filigree trimmings is the flower which made this town famous. But the steel industry has lost its shine. On an earlier visit I saw a couple kissing passionately on the base of that sculpture at sunset, their feet dangling over the river, the soft curves of their human shapes merging, contrasting with the jagged edges of the steel, black against the huge red sun.

I cross back to Silistra, this time pushed by the *Perla*, to drive into Bulgaria. I have to buy Bulgarian road tax, but have no *leva*, the Bulgarian currency. There is no bank in sight, and they will not accept Euros or Romanian *lei*.

'Do you see that car parked over there? There's a man sitting in it who changes money! Get some from him!' suggests the helpful border policeman. I make a small transaction, fix the sticker to my windscreen, and set off slowly through the quiet town of Silistra lined with horse-chestnut trees, just coming into flower. Everything feels a little different on the Bulgarian side of the border. While Romania has tried hard to fix the surface of its main roads, to spruce up its main buildings and kit out its filling stations to resemble those of Austria or Germany, Bulgaria gives the impression of caring as little for the trappings of capitalism as its border police care for banks. There's a Balkan feeling in the air, where 'Balkan' is something positive, even heroic, suggesting a certain approach to life which values human relationships, including the right to sleep or make love in the afternoon, rather than earn a living. The mood is put succinctly in *The Shade of the Balkans,* a collection of Bulgarian folksongs and proverbs collected in the late nineteenth century:

> And softly then as the stars to the twilight sing
> So slept the voice that spoke to the mountain-king.
> And as he looked to the gloom of the woodland glades
> The chin of the Balkan drooped and his lips were dumb
> And he was sunk in a dream of days to come.[3]

That approach to life was also encouraged by one of Silistra's most unusual sons. Eliezer Papo was a Sephardic rabbi from Bosnia. Born in Sarajevo in 1785, he died in Silistra at the age of only forty-one in 1826, and had made such a strong impression that the town is still a place of pilgrimage for devout Jews. Papo taught that while work is important, keeping God's commandments and laws is the main purpose of life. His most famous work was the *Pele Yoetz*, a moral treatise arranged according to the letters of the Hebrew alphabet, which begins with the love of God and ends with the word *Teshuvah*, salvation. According to the entry in the *Jewish Encyclopaedia*, 'it implores us to seek salvation not just as a nation, but also as individuals, who place their trust in an omniscient Creator. In between are many of the most fundamental principles, essential philosophical tenets and ethical teachings of Judaism. Each entry in the book is written in a beautiful and articulate language that is accessible and inspiring to all people.'[4]

The road west from Silistra cuts inland, past the pelican reserve at Srebarna. The Danube river plain stretches between the Balkan mountains to the south, and the Carpathians to the north. The plain only narrows at the Iron Gates, far upriver. Like the travellers and itinerant preachers of old, I feel myself funnelled westwards, unimpeded. There are fewer horses and carts on the road than on the Romanian side, but fewer cars as well. The Danube meanders between many islands. As other sections of the river have been denied to them, the sturgeon take refuge here, in a river landscape constantly changing with the whims of the river. As the banks erode, trees fall into the water, and if the current does not take them away a new sandbank grows around them as sedimentation from upriver gets trapped against their trunks – good for fish, frustrating for ships' captains. A Romanian project to fix a bottom ledge or sill to one section of the river, to slow sedimentation and provide a standard 2.5 metre deep waterway year round, has drawn protests from the World Wide Fund for Nature (WWF), the guardians of the river.[5] 'The project . . . threatens the last naturally reproducing populations of wild sturgeons in European watersheds,' warns the WWF. Transport companies complain that their barge convoys have to be broken up, and that in low water conditions they have to make a hundred-kilometre detour around islands in the river. There are many weeks in the year when this stretch cannot be navigated at all.

The transport lobby has the upper hand, and the most the environmentalists have been able to achieve is that fish will be monitored for signs of harm as the project goes ahead.

In Turkish times, Romanian shepherds would travel with their flocks down the Danube, then across the Black Sea to Constantinople to sell the animals in the markets. As they couldn't afford to keep their dogs with them on the boat, they left them behind in the harbour at Giurgiu. There they would howl for their lost masters. Hence the threat still used in modern Romanian: 'I will hit you so hard, you will hear the dogs barking in Giurgiu!'

The reputation of Giurgiu in modern times is hardly more attractive. For years, the chemical works spewed out tonnes of toxic fumes across the Danube to the more beautiful city of Ruse on the Bulgarian shore. The bridge of Friendship and Unity, built in 1954 as a prestige project between two communist allies, became a bridge of hatred and suspicion. By 1988 the people of Ruse had had enough. They marched on the Communist Party headquarters, women pushing prams, students, old people, demanding the Romanian factories be closed. Unwilling to be left out, the communist youth movement joined them. The Romanian comrades tried to complain about factory chimneys on the Ruse side too, but they could hardly argue with the direction of the prevailing wind – north-westerly, taking their bad breath to Bulgaria. Out of all this a movement called Ecoglasnost was born, and grievances about environmental pollution soon spread to other frustrations with single party rule. Just as at Nagymaros, upstream in Hungary, the Bulgarian protest movement that brought down the communist regime in 1989 owed much to the people of the Danube.[6]

Years before, at the Romanian end of the bridge, I watched a Turkish truck, loaded to the roof with televisions, taken apart by zealous Romanian customs officers searching for drugs. Sniffer dogs leapt in vain between the cardboard boxes. Vast X-ray machines examined every nook and cranny. The Turkish driver looked on, stroking the two-day growth of beard on his chin with a mixture of frustration and resignation. Eventually he was sent on his way, minus one day of his life.

I arrive late in the evening in Ruse, and the first three hotels are full. Ruse has always attracted visitors, and when they arrive they tend to come in hordes. I end up in my last choice, the tall skyscraper Hotel Riga, the pride of communist Ruse. Scantily clad, peroxide blonde girls, affiliated to a travelling disco, negotiate the reception area on stiletto heels. In the first floor restaurant there are ironed linen tablecloths, and waiters who look as though they have never smiled in their lives. But the room is cheap and clean, the view of the river is wonderful, and I can sleep off the dust of the encroaching Bulgarian summer. It is already May. At a restaurant on the shore, I arrange to meet a friend of a friend, Theodora. She remembers my hotel as the place where, as a child, she was introduced to the communist leaders of Romania and Bulgaria, Nicolae Ceaușescu and Todor Zhivkov. 'We were triplets, at a nursery school named after Zhivkov's wife. Our parents were away, studying in Bucharest, living in a students' hostel. Our father was 23 then, our mother only 21. Romanian was always the secret language in our family – my mother's mother came from Silistra when it belonged to Romania. We were invited to the Riga hotel during a big state visit, to the "red hall" on the second floor. Everything was decorated with red velvet. My brothers handed the flowers to the visiting guests. "What is your name?" Nicolae Ceaușescu asked. "Nicolae . . ." replied my brother – well, as you can imagine, that went down very well! Then my chance came. I read a greeting in Romanian to them. I knew some Romanian, but the teacher had written it out for me, phonetically, in Cyrillic letters to make it easier. I was four years old. They gave us cherries. It was the first time in my life I'd tasted cherries in winter! . . . The pollution used to be really awful here. We used to walk to school holding handkerchiefs in front of our faces. It went on for seven or eight years. Twenty thousand people moved away from Ruse in the 1980s because of it.'

Early the next morning I go down to the Danube in fog so thick it obscures the top half of the hotel. A big cruise liner, the *Viktoria*, is just docking, and through the misty windows I can see passengers finishing their breakfasts in time to explore the town. In front of the *Viktoria*, the *Amadeus Diamond* is already moored, a seemingly identical ship, but flying the German ensign and registered in Passau. The flags of the tour operators dangle in the fog on the quay, and a line of coaches waits for the passengers. Back to the Riga for an early breakfast. A big television screen above the tables inhibits conversation. There's been an earthquake somewhere, but I can't quite work out where.

I was given Nikolai Nenov's name by Marian Neagu in Călăraşi. As
director of the Regional History Museum, with a new exhibition just
opening, he's eager to get back to work, but he's proud of his town and his
museum and we talk over cups of strong coffee. A tell or raised mound
excavated at Ruse gives the layout of the original settlement, on a hill overlooking the river. In Neolithic and Copper Age graves excavated on both
banks, the dead are buried on their sides. The Romans valued Ruse above
all for its winter harbour, so-called because it never froze over. They built
two fortresses, at Sexaginta Prista and Ialtus. Sexaginta is named after the
sixty galleys that fitted into the harbour, their entire Lower Danube fleet.[7]
The remains of a Thracian settlement have also been found where the Lom
flows into the Danube, with shards of pots that have been traced to the
island of Rhodes in Greece. The Slavs and Bulgars sent the Romans
packing, and the Bulgarians founded their first kingdom here in the
seventh century AD. Unlike the Romanians, they draw a clear line between
themselves and the Romans, just as they do with the Soviet empire. As in
the Danube delta, the townsfolk developed a special affinity with Saint
George. Giurgiu on the far bank was called 'Little Georgetown', and Ruse
'Big Georgetown'.

All conversations in Ruse inevitably lead to Elias Canetti, a son of Ruse
and winner of the Nobel Prize in Literature in 1981. He wrote of its people
and their adventures at the height of their cosmopolitan glory at the turn
of the nineteenth century. 'Ruschuk was an old port on the Danube, which
made it fairly significant. As a port, it had attracted people from all over,
and the Danube was a constant topic of discussion. There were stories
about the extraordinary years when the Danube froze over; about sleigh
rides all the way across the Danube to Romania; about starving wolves at
the heels of the sleigh horses . . . Wolves were the first wild animals I heard
about. In the fairy tales the Bulgarian peasant girls told me, there were
werewolves, and one night my father terrorized me with a wolf mask on
his face.'[8]

Ruse had the first bank, the first brewery and the first railway in
Bulgaria, and its citizens also enjoyed the first electricity supply. Canetti's
family, like that of Eliezer Papo in Silistra, were Sephardic Jews, expelled
from Spain in 1492, who took refuge in the Ottoman empire. Though he
left Ruse with his family in 1911 at the age of six, lived for most of his life

in Austria and Switzerland, wrote in German, and is buried in Zurich, his autobiographical writings about Ruse have done much to put the town on the literary map of the world, and his town is deeply grateful.

In the main exhibition hall of the museum, Nikolai Nenov's colleague Eskren Velikov shows me a boomerang, the only one of its kind in Europe. Fashioned from bone in around 4500 BC, it was probably used to hunt birds. There are gold bracelets from the same period as the treasure in Varna, and bone amulets, carved in the shape of a woman, with holes for her breasts and eyes. Set in the floor is 'Ernestina', the skeleton of a teenage girl, buried on her left side in the hocker position, her head to the north-east. The pit in which she was found was burned, to cleanse it before her body was placed inside. Archaeologists have found traces of red ochre and coal, to symbolise her blood and decorate her eyes in the next life. There is also a musical stone, with a hole carved in the centre, carefully designed to produce a monotonous sound if it is swung round and round in the air. The relief of a Thracian horseman, carved in a cliff, is portrayed in a faded photograph. There is also a single gold coin from the time of the Roman emperor Trajan. It was found in the stomach of a ram that swallowed it while grazing in the fields near the old Roman town. There are Thracian helmets, worn either by children or by people who had much narrower heads than we do today. And seven Hunnish swords.[9]

Eskren feigns a historian's interest in prehistory and medieval times, but gets into his stride when we reach his own period, the nineteenth and twentieth centuries. Midhat Pasha became governor of the Danubian Principalities of Bulgaria in 1864 and oversaw the arrival of the first railway in the town.[10] The track from Varna, two hundred kilometres away on the Black Sea coast, brought goods from the sea port, which were then shipped up the Danube on barges to Vienna and beyond. When the Turks left after the Treaty of St Stefano in 1878, their officials handed over the keys to the city, then took the train home – to Varna, then the boat to Constantinople.

Eskren was born in 1984 and finished school in 2003. 'Pop music didn't just reach Ruse over the radio waves, it also came down the Danube.' Bulgarian sailors smuggled vinyl records into the city, despite the best efforts of the communist authorities to protect Bulgarian youth from such 'corruption'. Eskren has interviewed disc-jockeys from the 1970s and 1980s for an oral-history project. 'The Twist' was the first dance which the regime tried to ban, as an 'unhealthy' activity, on the grounds that it was 'bad for the knees'. Then, in an attempt to keep up with the times, the 'Disco Decree' was passed in 1985, which stated that discos would be permitted provided they played 50 per cent Bulgarian music, 25 per cent from other socialist countries, and the remaining 25 per cent from the West. I imagine sour-faced secret agents, scowling beside the dance floor, jotting the statistics down in grubby notebooks. Western music was not completely banned, just frowned on. One DJ played a Nazareth song at full blast through the loudspeakers of his secondary school and was slapped hard in the face by the school principal. Other music fans, caught trying to bring records across the Bridge of Friendship from Romania, watched in horror as zealous border guards smashed their records and tossed the pieces into the Danube, sixty metres below.

Eskren tells another good tale about the bridge. According to the original plans created by a Ukrainian sculptor, the bridge should have been flanked by huge stone eagles. They were left out at the last moment because they resembled Roman eagles, which had been especially favoured by the Third Reich. One was actually made, but never put in place. He cannot say in which yard or cliff top it now rests.

I set out through the town in search of the remnants of Elias Canetti's cosmopolitan Ruse. I find it in the central park, built on the site of an old Muslim mosque and graveyard, with palm trees, banana trees and cactuses, and in the so-called 'Profit-Yielding Building', designed by Viennese architects, in the theatre, library and casino, and in the Teteven Grand Hotel. But I want to find it in the people, too.

I see the camels of the Koloseum Circus first, then the big tent as I speed past on the main road. Their great mocking faces are outlined against the housing blocks of communist Ruse, in supreme contempt. I slam on the brakes, park the car, and ask for the boss. The receptionist directs me to Momcilo – 'everyone calls me Momi' – Kolev, who is also the circus clown. He's only twenty-six, was born into the circus, and loves his trailer as his home, though he has a flat in Sofia as well, for the long winter months when it's too cold to tour. But nine months of the year he travels the roads of Bulgaria with his band of twenty-six performers, two camels and a clutter of ponies and goats. 'We have acrobats, good ones, we have a flying trapeze, excellent acts, but what do the children ask when they queue with their parents to buy tickets? What animals do you have? So we reply that we have two camels, the pony, the horse, the goats, the birds . . . And? they ask. It's a big problem.' Increasingly strict European Union rules against cruelty to animals have made it harder for circuses to keep live animals. 'In my childhood we had bears, lions, tigers, monkeys . . .' Momi laments, 'but the show must go on!' The show lasts two hours, is put on every evening, and costs five Euros for adults, three Euros for children. 'We cannot charge more. Bulgaria is a poor country.'

Momi Kolev admits he doesn't like Gypsies. He's had bad experiences with them, he says – though there are exceptions, such as the three he employs himself. He tried working in America for a while, where his mother and his cousins are in the circus, but didn't like it and came home. 'Life in America is no good. Work-home-work-home-work-home. If you try and persuade someone to come to the movies with you, they say they can't because they have to work tomorrow! . . . In Bulgaria I love my friends. We drink coffee, watch films, watch football – we enjoy life!'

We wander out to see his camels, passing his father-in-law who is putting a pony through its paces under the big dome. 'This is Sultan . . .' Sultan is four years old and gets up reluctantly to be admired. As camels can live to eighty years old, he is a baby, and there's actually not a great deal to admire about him at the moment. He's in the middle of his spring moulting, and his coat looks like the floor of a barber's shop. Next to him is Emir, half a year younger. Momi paid a thousand Euros apiece for them in Kirgizistan. It took four months to bring them back to Bulgaria, across four countries, and the journey cost more than the price of the camel, there were so many documents to be filled in, and everyone demanding back-handers along the way. He prefers the two-humped, Central Asian camels to African ones. It might be easier to bring them to Bulgaria by ship from Tunis, but African camels can't stand the Bulgarian winters, he says. His circus is among the five largest in Bulgaria. He likes touring the bigger cities best – Sofia, Ruse, Plovdiv – places where they can stay for two weeks at a time and are guaranteed a full house every night. Smaller, poorer towns such as Vidin on the River Danube are less attractive as venues. People cannot afford the tickets, and it is a lot of work to put up the show, perform for only two nights, then take it all down again and move on. Camels are stubborn, but more like cows than donkeys, Momi says. 'They kick and jump and spit . . . you have to break them in slowly, like horses. Only then can you let the children take rides on them.'

Before I leave, we meet his wife and their one-year-old son in their caravan. She's stunningly beautiful, a sixth-generation circus performer, and has more important things to talk to her husband about than small talk for the benefit of foreigners. I leave them preparing for the night's show.

The road south east out of Ruse leads towards Červená Voda: red water. It won't be hard to find Todor Tsanev, they told me in Ruse, everybody knows him. I have no phone number for him, so my visit is completely unannounced. The first elderly couple I ask point me straight to his house, just off the main square, with pride that such a man lives in their village. All I know about him is that he was a former political prisoner at the notorious Belene prison camp, just upriver from Ruse, and that he served briefly as mayor of Ruse, thanks to his anti-communist credentials, after the return of democracy. His wife answers the door and waves me into their garden. Todor arrives looking frail but in good humour, and we sit down in a corner overhung with flowers while his wife rustles up coffee and plates overflowing with biscuits. 'I got a paper saying I was in prison, but they never wrote down why! It might have been for stealing a chicken, or killing a man . . . but the fact was, I was a political prisoner. I was not happy with what the authorities did, how they handed the country over to the Russians. I had a democratic temperament, just like my father, and that's why they put us in prison together. I just couldn't stop myself speaking out about what they were doing to the country. But why resist them? Why bother? We could hardly have liberated the country from them. We simply had to stand up and show them that we opposed them, like the great Bulgarians of old stood up against the Turks.'

He was fourteen when the Second World War ended and Soviet troops occupied Bulgaria, to enforce the communist takeover of power.[11] He was nineteen when he was arrested: 'The National Agricultural Party of Nikolai Petkov showed the most steadfast resistance. There were always those who said communism could have a human face, but when they finally showed it, the Berlin Wall collapsed! If you rule with violence, you have to maintain the violence, and if you don't the whole structure collapses, which is what actually happened . . . When I was arrested in 1951, there were so many trials, and not a few ended in death sentences. I got a twenty-year sentence for organising protests. I was in several prisons, but ended up at Belene in 1954. I served eleven years altogether. It was a tough prison, and very hard to escape from. Romania on one side, Bulgaria on the other, and there we were in the middle of the wide, fast-flowing Danube, with armed guards everywhere. In the early days a lot of people were shot trying to get away. I lost several of my friends like that. Then the prisoners realised that it was practically impossible, so they stopped trying. From the other prisons I was in, there were always a few who managed to escape. But not from Belene.'

'The river to me was like a great force, which one could never overcome. There were two camps there, number one and number two. The prisoners in number one were those who hadn't been sentenced yet. They were proper concentration camps, like those Hitler built, or Stalin set up in Siberia. There were barbed wire fences, and a look-out tower every thirty or forty metres, manned by guards with machine guns. Beyond the barbed wire were ditches full of water. Even if they didn't shoot you there, you couldn't have got off the island. There were several islands. There were even women prisoners on one of them, but not where we were. There were lots of theatre people. Even a famous singer, Lea Ivanova. And because they wanted to maintain the lie that there were no political prisoners in Bulgaria, they invented all kinds of crimes that we were supposed to have committed. But it was all a lie. The Interior Ministry decided how long we would stay there.'

'I had to have a hernia operation, but they wouldn't call a doctor. Another convict had to perform the operation on me, in atrocious conditions. But I survived it, because I was young. My father only lived another three years after his release. The older ones couldn't bear what they put them through. The humiliations, the heavy work, the poor food, everything. But we younger ones survived. If we had thought we would really have to serve twenty years there, it would have killed us. But we always believed that the democratic world would somehow stifle the appetite of Stalin and the others. But that's not the way it happened. The system only got better long after we were released.'

'The mosquitoes were terrible. It is hard to imagine what we endured. At sunset millions of mosquitoes would descend on us, and start to attack. They bit into every bit of flesh that was not covered. Our faces, necks, arms, hands, feet, legs were all swollen with bites. But there was something which was even worse than the mosquitoes. The bedbugs. I was on the upper bunk, because I could climb easily. But we couldn't sleep in summer because of the bedbugs, sucking our blood. During the day the mosquitoes, during the night the bugs. Those were the weapons they used against us.'

'Let me tell you about the work. We called it "Chinese style". Because in China there are a lot of people. Our job was to build dykes. Some would build the walls, others would fill them in. And when there weren't dykes to build, we had to carry tree trunks four or five kilometres. Even a light tree gets heavy if you have to carry it a long way on your shoulders . . . We weren't allowed to fish, though there were a lot of fish there, and it was easy to catch them. There were many lakes and ponds on the islands. The trick was for one person to wade in, stir up the mud, so the fish had to come up for air, and then you grabbed them. But they searched us on our way back into the camp. If they found a fish on you, they put you in solitary. But sometimes people managed to smuggle them in . . . In winter there was no heating of any kind. We had our clothes and some blankets. You wrapped yourself up as best you could. And we survived it. We lived in barracks on Belene, fifty metres long. I don't know how we survived the cold. We survived the summer heat much better than the winter cold.'

Those serving the longest sentences were entitled to the least food and the fewest letters from their families. A single letter, censored by the camp authorities, and three kilos of provisions every three months. It was hard to get real information about the outside world or send information of their own. The only safe way was when someone was released. He would be asked to memorise hundreds of messages to relatives of the convicts stuck inside.

Todor Tsanev survived the long years on Belene, he says, with a lot of faith and a lot of hope. 'If a person's spirit is broken, that's the end, he is annihilated. You have to believe in the good, and that the bad will finally be over one day. And we younger ones, we always asked for pig fat from home, and we toasted our bread in the morning, on an open fire, and spread pig fat on it, and that was when we talked, and encouraged each other, saying that this will not last forever. And physically, the human body knows what to do. It knows its limits. We had to work, or we would have been killed like dogs, but we worked slowly, we tried to pace ourselves, not to get over-exhausted. You don't need anyone to tell you what to do, you don't need anyone to organise you. Your body knows. And all the time, even if you're not working, you act as if you are. If I hadn't known what to do, I wouldn't be here with you now. And I'm eighty years old! . . . I don't dream often about Belene any more, though I did for a long time after I was released. Nightmares. Nowadays only rarely, and they're not so bad as they were. For a time I had nightmares every night. Not any more . . . I try to stay healthy. I walk a lot. I don't have a car. I stay out of politics. I was very active in politics for a while, after 1990, but now I see that everything is lost. There's no way of putting the state back together. Those who say they can are just play-acting.'

He resents the luxury, the palaces of former communists, and those he calls 'the mafia'. And he blames the communist leadership for what was done to him, and his country. 'I don't blame those I knew who gave in to them, who capitulated. I blame those at the top, who ran the whole system. And since that system collapsed, they stayed on, to torture us in the new one!' There's no true democracy in Bulgaria he concludes.

I drive slowly back up river, chastened by our meeting.

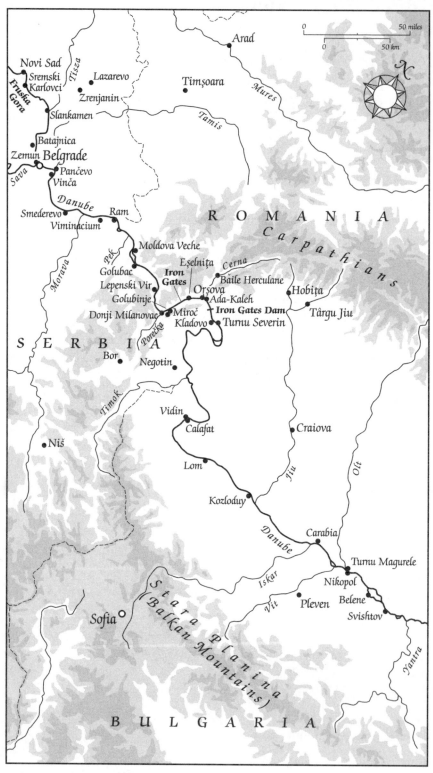

2. The Lower-Middle Danube, including the Iron Gates and the plains of Vojvodina.

CHAPTER 6

Gypsy River

Everyone likes to laugh at Roma monkeys . . . they add colour.
NIKOLAI KIRILOV[1]

The Western knights, with no enemy to fight, treated the whole operation in the spirit of a picnic, enjoying the women and the wines and the
luxuries they had brought with them from home, gambling and engaging
in debauchery, ceasing in contemptuous fashion to believe that the
Turk could ever be a dangerous foe to them.
PATRICK KINROSS[2]

THIRTY KILOMETRES west of Ruse, the first poppies of spring grow beside the
architect Kolyo Ficheto's bridge across the Yantra river, which flows down to
the Danube from the Stara Planina mountains. To the north, the Danube is
fed by the Olt and the Jiu rivers flowing down from the Carpathians. Barn
swallows dart beneath the ten handsome stone arches of Ficheto's bridge,
and the wavy, broken line built into the stone beneath the parapet gives a
sense of movement, a nod towards the majesty of the river flowing beneath
it. This was Kolyo Ficheto's trademark, imprinted on almost all the buildings
he designed.[3] On the Danube shore in Svishtov, the roof of the Church of
the Holy Trinity has the same wavy line, as though imitating the waves of the
Danube or the Black Sea. The carved ends of the pews in the church at
Balatonkenese in Hungary, the floor tiles of a friend's house in Mindszentkálla,
have the same, quiet human tribute to the rhythms of nature.

The heart of the nineteenth-century Bulgarian writer Aleko Konstantinov is preserved in a jar in a museum named after him in Svishtov.[4] Next to it is the blood-stained jacket he was wearing when an assassin's bullet ended his life in 1897 at the age of only thirty-six. Konstantinov created the fictional character Bay Ganyo Balkanski, whose adventures were published in his 1895 best-seller *Bay Ganyo Goes to Europe*. Konstantinov won many enemies with his sarcastic portrayal of a provincial Bulgarian setting out to the West in peasant costume and returning home in elegant West European garb, having learnt the basics of capitalism during his sojourn among the peoples up the Danube, but none of their manners or restraint. 'While Ganyo is simply a comic, primitive buffoon in the first part of the book that follows his exploits in Europe, he becomes the authentic and dangerous savage only on his return, among his own, where he is the *nouveau riche* and newly hatched corrupt politician,' writes Maria Todorova.[5] Konstantinov thought up *Bay Ganyo* on a trip to Chicago for the World Fair in 1893, but the character is based on his own experiences in Bulgaria as a judge, before he quit in disgust at the political corruption of his profession. Konstantinov sought refuge from his life and times in humour, and joined a circle of artists known as 'Merry Bulgaria'. He wrote under the ironic pseudonym 'Shtastlivetsa' – 'The Happy One'. His family disowned him and he clashed frequently with the authorities, but the character he created lives on to haunt the imagination of Bulgarians finding their way in the European Union, not the ugly caricature of an outsider, mocking their worst characteristics, but of an insider. 'Critics disagree on whether Bay Ganyo represents "Bulgarianness". In his character, "national" features are combined with those of any upstart; thus he can also be interpreted as representative of human shamefulness,' wrote Sonia Kanikova.[6] Konstantinov also wrote about the flaws of other societies. His description of his visit to America, *To Chicago and Back*, was published in 1894. According to Kanikova, 'he regards the American way of life as anti-human and foresees some of the disastrous effects of technological progress and civilisation'. A soul brother, then, for Momi Kolev at the Koloseum Circus in Ruse.

Belene, the oversized village where Todor Tsanev suffered so long, presents a double-face to the world. A huge, unfinished nuclear power station lies along the low cliffs like a mortally wounded lion. An endless building site shelters behind a tall fence, decorated with coils of barbed wire. A hundred security guards provide at least a little local labour. 'Belene NPP – Energy for the Future' proclaims an information board in the centre of the town. 'Construction period – 59 months. Design lifetime – 60 years.' The reality has proved a little harder. Begun in the 1970s, it was abandoned for lack of money in 1990, restarted and abandoned again several times. In January 2013, a referendum called by the opposition Socialist Party aimed at restarting Belene was approved by the public. But the governing party carefully changed the wording at the last minute into support for an unnamed nuclear reactor. Opponents argued that Belene would cost every Bulgarian dear, and that money in the European Union's poorest member state would be better spent on health care, pensions and safer energy.

Petar Dulev, the mayor of the municipality, is a firm believer in all things nuclear. 'We always supported construction here. Despite the recent problems in Japan, we believe that nuclear power is the safest and cheapest source of energy, and will provide seven thousand jobs during the construction phase.' 'And the prison camp?' I ask, cruelly. 'The concentration camp is a black spot on the history of Belene. We try to build our prestige in other ways now. But perhaps in future it will attract tourists here, as a place of commemoration – like Alcatraz.' As I leave, he presents me with a compact disc of Bulgarian folk songs by a group of local singers called 'Danubian dawn', backed by the musicians of Belenka and Dimum. The local paper, *Dunavski Novini* (Danube News), has a photo of the musicians on the back cover: two accordion players, a violinist and a drummer. The music alternates between the rousing and the melancholy, but is all rather fine. My favourite tracks are 'Saint George, break in horse', and 'Why didn't you come yesterday night, elder brother Maria'ne?'

A high security prison has replaced one corner of the old, sprawling barracks of the prison camp, and the still undiscovered graves of those who died here. The rest of the island, and some twenty islands which surround it, have been turned into a national park. Out of the darkness of the past, something green and hopeful seems to be emerging.

Down on the shore, opposite Belene Island, is an elegant, modern building set on green lawns gently sloping down to the river. Here as much effort is going into preserving and restoring nature as once went into destroying it. The park is part of a World Bank and European Union effort to reduce the load of nutrient pollution in the Black Sea, most of which arrives through the Danube, the Dniester and the Dnieper – the great flush toilets of Europe. Thanks to both the prison and the nature protection area, the twenty or so islands of the Belene archipelago are almost inaccessible to the public, a blessing for shy and rare birds like the white-tailed eagle and the pygmy cormorant that nest there. The park authority's job is to undo the damage caused by decades of forced labour by the inmates of the prison camp – the vast dykes that cut the Danube off from the wetland forests, built at such a cost in human misery, which deprived the fish of the spawning grounds they need and the birds of the fish they need to survive. If Todor Tsanev could see what is happening here, I think he would be glad. A system of sluices and waterways has been built on the island, to allow periodic, controlled flooding. After the first intervention, in 2008, monitors from the park recorded a surge in the number of birds. Whiskered terns, mistle thrushes, purple herons and mute swans appeared as if from nowhere. Floating watermoss, mouse garlic, yellow floating heart, fen ragwort and spring snowflake all flourished in the new conditions.

'A big part of our work is to explain to local people, especially children, why restoring the wetlands is a good idea,' said Stela Bozhinova, director of the Persina Nature Park.[7] 'Some people understand what we're doing, others resent the fact that we seem to be undoing their life's work, protecting the shoreline from flooding.' The largest island, Persina, is fifteen kilometres long and six kilometres wide at its fattest point. The water is unusually low for May, which is disappointing for Stela and her team as it makes it harder to flood the forests for any useful length of time. A constant problem for the park is the functioning of the massive Iron Gates dam on the Romanian–Serb border. When water is released at the dam it creates a wave that travels down the river, still sixty to eighty centimetres high when it reaches Belene. That erodes the islands and damages the confluence of tributaries of the Danube such as the Yantra. Even so, the work to nurse the rarest species back from the brink of extinction is bearing fruit. Four of Bulgaria's fourteen white-tailed eagles nest on Persina Island – two adult pairs. This year one nest has two eggs in it, while they have not been able to get close enough to the other to count. If just two chicks survive from each nest, that would mean a nearly 30 per cent increase in Bulgaria's white-tailed eagle population.

Stela notices climate change in several ways. During the eight years she has worked as director of the park, the Danube has not frozen over once, although this used to be commonplace. But extremes of weather seem to be increasing in other ways, with more sudden storms on the river and wild fluctuations in the water level from one day to the next. Several of her colleagues are away on a field trip downriver in a small boat from Vidin as part of a project to track the numbers of two endangered birds, the sand martin and the little ringed plover, down the whole length of the Danube. We climb up into the observation tower. An olive green military van of the Bulgarian prison service drives a batch of new prisoners over a small bridge on to the island. Everything is green here, even the prison vehicles.

The Danube flows past Belene like a solid mass, a moving carpet. 'Its impossible to say exactly how many islands there are,' says Stela. 'Some disappear one day, others appear the next.'

The Danube shore on the right, southern bank is steep, a cliff rising vertically from the water, while the left bank on the Romanian shore is low marshland. The road from Belene descends to the plain of Nikopol, the old Nikopolis. The ruins of the west wall of the Roman fort, built by the emperor Marcus Aurelius in AD 169, crumble gently into oblivion. It was a Roman victory, *nike*, over the Dacians, forgotten by all except the school-children and tourists in little Danubian museums. A thermal power station on the far bank hisses and roars, periodically releasing an accumulation of steam like a wrestler between rounds. From another chimney, a thin trail of yellow smoke rises, like urine – the shoreline industries of the Romanian town of Turnu Măgurele. The sky is restless, and great rolls of black cloud, black as the tarred hulls of fishing boats, swoop down from the Carpathians, though the sun still shines on the Bulgarian shore. A Romanian barge, moored to the dock with its bow upstream, waits for a load of gravel that passes through a long contraption of conveyor belts and chutes. The Danube is strangely calm, reflecting it all. Images of Romanian factories alternate black and white in the colourless river.

By naming his new town after a particular battle, Marcus Aurelius seems to have set the scene for a spate of decisive battles in the history of the place. On the plains of Nikopolis, the flower of British, French, Dutch, Hungarian and Spanish youth met their doom in 1396 in the last, disastrous crusade, against a disciplined army of Turks and Serbs.[8] By all accounts, they rather deserved it. The crusaders, led by King Sigismund of Hungary, were stung into action by the daring raids of the forces of the Turkish sultan, Bayezid the Thunderbolt, from his fortresses at Nikopolis, Lom and Vidin on the Danube. Sigismund and his allies gathered at Buda in May 1386, and ignoring Sigismund's advice, provided on account of knowledge gleaned from his own long rivalry with the Ottomans, took the offensive, marching down the valley of the Danube as far as Nikopolis, looting, pillaging and raping each Christian, Jewish or Muslim community in their path. Fortified by the excellent wines they found on the shores of the Morava river in Serbia, they camped in front of Nikopolis, preparing to annihilate the small Turkish garrison at their leisure. 'The Western knights, with no enemy to fight, treated the whole operation in the spirit of a picnic,' writes Patrick Kinross. When Bayezid finally arrived to do battle in November, with a force at least as large as their own, – twice as large according to some accounts – the French troops were so keen to prove themselves in battle, to justify their resentment that the expedition had been placed under Hungarian command, that they charged the enemy against the express orders of the ever-cautious Sigismund. The best report of what happened next comes from a French survivor, Jean Froissart. At the head of the French troops, Philippe d'Elu called to his standard-bearer, 'Forward banner, in the name of God and Saint George, for they will see me today a good chevalier!' Seven hundred French cavalry charged uphill, scattering the weak auxiliary troops of the Ottomans. Just beyond the brow of the hill, however, the full force of Bayezid's troops lay in wait. 'The crusaders were still, by the standards of the time, essentially amateur soldiers, fighting in the past and in a romantic spirit. They had learned nothing of the professional art of war as it progressed through the centuries, none of the military skills of the Turks, with their superior discipline, training, briefing and tactics, and above all the mobility of their light-armoured forces and archers on horseback,' writes Kinross.[9] The men of the last crusade were massacred. After several hours, the remnants of the army split, some fleeing to their boats to sail back up the Danube, others beginning a long march home beside the river and across the Carpathians, where survivors from the villages they had torched on the way took revenge on them. The day after the battle, Bayezid had all ten thousand prisoners

executed, except for the Count of Nevers and his entourage who were
forced to witness the beheading of their men, one by one, roped together
like cattle.

I meet Vasile Popov by the shore in modern Nikopol, watching the
approach of a storm from the north. He's a handsome man in the camou-
flage jacket favoured by all Balkan men who keep their old leather one for
special occasions and whose denim jackets of their youth are now too
threadbare, too small, or have been purloined by granddaughters. He also
has a fine moustache, slightly reminiscent of Joseph Stalin, but a much
kinder smile. His first Danube story is just hearsay, a tale fondly told in the
town, of how in the bitter winter of 1956, a logjam of ice threatened to
destroy Nikopol, forming a solid wall and forcing the river to flood its
banks. The Romanian army opened fire with mortars, shattering the ice-
flows, which then obediently resumed their passage downriver. The town
was saved. Exactly half a century later, during the floods of April 2006,
Vasile personally took the President of Bulgaria, Petar Stoyanov, on his
boat through the flooded town, to show him the damage and to press the
locals' claims for compensation. That same spring, he took his two daughters to the school graduation ball by boat through the still-flooded streets.
The girls stepped elegantly ashore in their long dresses.

Vasile works for the town council; 'there's no other work here . . . apart
from the factory making electricity metres, which has already closed.' Even
the foundations of the old factory have been stripped to the bone by the
Gypsies, he says, in their hunger for scrap metal. He used to fish from his
own boat, and his best catch was a female sturgeon weighing ninety-five
kilos, with twenty-two kilos of caviar. The caviar he sold for three hundred
dollars a kilo, keeping only a small plateful for himself and his family to
taste – 'fishermen always sell what they can, and keep the worst bits for
themselves . . . I managed to pay for my daughters to finish their education,
in mathematics and foreign languages, with that fish,' he says proudly. But
the story has an unhappy ending. The same year, he caught hepatitis from
a dirty needle used by the dentist who was fixing his teeth, and spent the
rest of the money getting the treatment he needed to combat the illness. He
has still not got back his strength. 'I used to be so strong I could change car
tyres by lifting the whole car up with one hand, and replacing the wheel

with the other.' Now he can't even go out fishing any more, has sold his boat, and lives on his two hundred dollars a month salary from the town council. He loves talking about fishing. There was a lake to the west of the town, where large fish, catfish and amur, got trapped by the changes in the level of the river. Men would beat on the water with sticks, while others would wait with nets across the mouth of the narrow channel, which led the water back to the Danube. 'They jumped like dolphins – straight into our nets,' he laughs. He also used to catch amur, a big carp-like fish imported into Europe from the Far East, using cherry tomatoes as bait.

Just as Nikopol witnessed the start of Ottoman domination of the Balkans, events here beside the Danube were also central to its end. In 1812 at the Treaty of Bucharest, the border between the Russian and Ottoman empires was established along the Prut river. Four hundred and twenty years after the Turks first occupied wide swathes of south-eastern Europe, their political and military strength lay in ruins. Historians have long debated how exactly the Ottomans, so effective in the fourteenth, fifteenth and sixteenth centuries, lost their grip. A Turkish historian, Mehmed Genç, argues that the failure of the Turkish authorities to supply their armies with weapons, tents and food properly, especially from 1750 onwards, was the main problem.[10] One reason for this was that the army refused to pay the market price for their goods, and depended on several large suppliers. Their supplies, however, were exhausted and they were pushed to the brink of bankruptcy by the delays, or even the complete failure, of the state to pay. Research by the Hungarian historian Gábor Ágoston has added further reasons – the fact that many of the supplies came not from the Turkish motherland, but rather from Bosnia, involving a long journey first through the mountains, then up the Danube.[11] Yet another cause of the defeats in the age of gunpowder was the very variable technical quality of both firearms and ammunition.

The collapse of the Ottoman empire would tax the minds and budgets, and stimulate the ambitions, of European statesmen for the next hundred years. The essence of what came to be known as the 'Eastern Question' was whether, as the German statesman Count Metternich put it, the Sick Man of Europe (Turkey) 'be sent to the doctor, or to his heirs' – that is, the many states still under Ottoman control, all straining for independence.[12] The River Danube was to play a crucial role in the strategic diplomacy, wars and skirmishes that followed. By 1852, a third of all shipping on the Danube was British. The first steamships had appeared on the river in the 1830s.[13] The industrial revolution in Britain needed raw materials and foods from the Near East, and markets to sell its rapidly expanding range of manufactured products. The route up and down the Danube, across the Black Sea to Constantinople then across central Asia to India, was a third shorter than round the Cape of Good Hope. 'If in a political point of view the independence of Turkey is of great importance, in a commercial sense it is of no less importance to this country,' Lord Palmerston told the House of Commons in 1849.[14] And for that trade to flourish, the survival and stability of the Ottoman empire appeared the best guarantee. Madder root needed by British industries to dye textiles, valonia to tan leather, wheat and corn to feed Britain's fast-growing population, raw silk and raisins, all came from the Ottoman empire. The grain grew on the rich farmlands of the Danubian plain.

Britain intervened on the Ottoman side in the Crimean War, from 1853 to 1856, to prevent Russian encroachments that threatened her trade routes from the north. The ships carrying letters home from British soldiers travelled up the Danube, alongside other ships carrying grain to feed their wives and sweethearts.[15] Each ship issued its own postmark on envelopes, and they are now much prized by collectors. Meanwhile Russia was pressing ever closer to the Danubian principalities of Wallachia and Moldavia, on the northern banks of the river, and to what would later become Bulgaria on the southern shore. The tsars presented themselves as the champions of the Balkan Christians. From the 1850s, France also became a supporter of the national independence movements against the Ottomans.

In 1848 Habsburg Austria crushed the revolution and war of independence in Hungary with Russian help, and more than four thousand Hungarians and Poles fled to safety on Ottoman territory. When Vienna and St Petersburg demanded their extradition to face almost certain execution, the British and French sent their fleets to the Dardanelles to protect the Turks from a possible Russian attack. Public sympathy in Britain was firmly on the side of Hungary and her Turkish friends, and against the 'bullying' tactics of Austria and Russia. 'By an ironic twist of history,' wrote L.S. Stavrianos, 'Turkey now stood out in the public mind as the champion of European liberty against the brutal despotism of the two emperors.'[16] The peoples of the Balkans, on the other hand, saw Russia as a useful ally to break the Turkish grip on their countries once and for all. In December 1877, Vasile Popov tells me proudly, a threat by the Russian and Bulgarian besiegers to flood the city of Pleven, the modern Plevna just to the south-west of Nikopol, finally forced its Turkish defenders to surrender after a five-month siege.[17]

While Bulgaria was shaking itself loose of Constantinople, and into conflict with its neighbours about just how big an independent Bulgaria should be, the Romanian-Danubian principalities of Wallachia and Moldavia finally managed to unite, first of all under a home-grown prince, Alexander Cuza, in 1861, then under a foreign one, Charles of Hohenzollern-Sigmaringen, in 1866. Cuza, though unpopular with the Romanian liberals who had set their hearts on a foreign prince, pushed through an important land reform in 1864 that stripped the monasteries, which owned 11 per cent of all arable land, of their holdings. He also liberated the large, semi-nomadic Roma population from slavery.[18]

A clock strikes twelve on the wall in Milan Nikolov's office. We stop talking to let it finish. Twelve strokes can take such a long time. The waiting seems appropriate, as we are talking about his own history and that of his people. Both his grandfather and his father were born in Ruse. His family are Calderash Gypsies, coppersmiths, whose work has been sought after for centuries throughout eastern and central Europe. The Calderash are one of the proudest and most traditionally-minded of the Roma tribes.[19] Milan is the sixth of seven children, four boys and three girls. Part of his community has assimilated, he says; some have become Muslims or Christians, and many have lost their roots. He still speaks the Roma language and works in the city council to improve his people's lot. He studied agriculture at university, an unusual subject for a man from a community that has been traditionally landless, but has been increasingly drawn to social work since he finished his degree – to deal with the age-old problem of how better to integrate the Roma into society and politics. He was elected as a councillor for the Union of Democratic Forces, a centre-right party that won the 1997 elections, but has largely disintegrated at national level. Rain starts falling heavily outside as we speak, battering the panes, followed by peals of thunder. The city beyond his windows goes dark, the roofs lit up by brilliant flashes of lightning. I imagine the storm sweeping down through the whole Danubian plain, conducted by the river.

Mesere is the Roma word for justice, and some Bulgarian Roma still maintain the Roma court system, overseen by the elders of the community, just as they do in Romania. He describes it as a way open to Roma families to solve conflicts between them, without resorting to the state justice system. Divorce is one area in point, in a community where the young usually marry very young. Aged forty-four he has three children of his own, five grandchildren and one great granddaughter. Another use of traditional justice is in disputes over property. When one family starts building on land which another claims, they can turn to the *mesere*. Theft can also be dealt with – there have been cases when a father was held responsible, and fined, for the burglaries of his son. The whole point of it is not to 'do justice', but to restore peace within the Roma community.[20] As the rain eases, we talk about weddings. Better-off Roma like himself are expected to contribute to other Roma weddings, though some money comes back when his own children or grandchildren marry. Weddings function as a bank within the community. Those who contribute to the wedding of your children expect your contribution when their turn comes round.

I find Pastor Iliya leaning on the fence in front of his church, a little balder, a little thinner in the face than when I first met him, here in the Humata suburb of Lom four years earlier. He has a fine moustache, a freshly ironed pin-striped shirt which he wears outside his black trousers, and a tiredness, almost a desperation, in his eyes that was not there before.

Lom is, or was, a success story for Bulgaria's half a million Roma, a town where few Roma pupils drop out of school, where nearly half the Roma children win a place at university, and where top officials in the town administration – the deputy mayor, the director of social services, and a good number of doctors, police officers and engineers – are Roma. The skills of local Roma community leaders in raising funds for the town, combined with a protestant work-ethic that men like Pastor Iliya have instilled into the community, helped the fourteen thousand Roma in this town of twenty-eight thousand pick themselves up by their own bootlaces.[21] Then the 2008 economic crisis hit and settled in for the duration.

North-west Bulgaria is the poorest region in the poorest country in the European Union. Central funding was cut for Lom's many social and educational programmes on which the Roma had built their progress. As an EU member from 2007, the community also found it much harder to tap EU funds than when the country was a candidate, knocking at the gate. 'When you were last here, we were feeding twenty-six children every day,' Iliya reminds me. They were mainly children whose mothers were working abroad, or whose fathers were in prison. The soup-kitchen was staffed by volunteers from the community and funded by donations from the congregation of his Pentecostalist church – all Roma. But, as more and more adults came begging at the church door, the pastor took the hard decision to stop feeding the children. There were too few coins in the box to feed very many.

He's especially weighed down with the problems of the world, because he is just back from a gathering of all the Roma pastors of Bulgaria, where unemployment, homelessness and poverty were the main themes. And debt. 'My people know no boundaries!' he laughs, bitterly. 'They find it very hard to resist something which catches their eye. Like a plasma TV. So they borrow money. Then when they cannot pay the money back, the lender comes and takes their house.' The problem is all the more entrenched, because these are cases of Roma exploiting Roma. Usury is illegal, but victims are reluctant to report their follow Roma to the police, however cruelly they are treated by them, partly from loyalty, partly out of fear. Interest rates are 100 per cent a month. Some Roma get rich by exploiting the weakness and poverty of their fellow Roma, who lose even the little they had in the process. And the sight of Roma fighting Roma is the subject of mockery from the wider, non-Roma, society – the salt rubbed into the wound. 'I tell my congregation – do not borrow money if you cannot pay it back! Stay away from those who charge you such interest rates. If you need money, go out and work for it in an honest way!' But there never was much work here, even in the boom years in Bulgaria, let alone now in the depression.

So Father Iliya is going to restart the free meals for children – the congregation will be encouraged to bring a little rice, or flour or oil, or vegetables – anything they have to spare except money. He has also set up a room with computers, next to the church, where users must pay a pittance, except between two and four each afternoon, the hours reserved for those children who cannot afford even the lowest denomination coins. The upstairs of the church – built by his own congregation – is lined with mattresses for the homeless. All of this is taking its toll on Iliya. He has a kind of flu, speaks thickly though his nose, his eyes have lost some, but not all, their sparkle. I say goodbye to him on the porch of his yellow church. There are flowers in all the windows. As I drive away I look back to see him supporting himself between two black gate-posts.

Niki Kirilov is also much less optimistic than when I last met him. We sit at a table outside a restaurant overlooking the main street in Lom, with his friend Svetlin Raykov. I eat catfish from the river, and drink excellent beer from the Almus brewery in Lom – Almus being the old name of the town. My hosts sip soft drinks. There's a graduation ball going on, and the streets are thronged with girls in mini-skirts and boys with ties thrown loosely round their necks. Each bar and restaurant pumps music into the early summer evening. 'Listen – the *gadzos* (Roma slang for non-Roma) have even stolen our music!' Niki jokes, but it is the only joke of the evening. 'There's a fundamental difference between being poor in a poor country, and poor in a rich country,' he says. Many Roma have gone abroad to work, to Italy and Spain in particular. There's even a joke in Bulgaria that there are only two ways to leave the country – Terminal 1 and Terminal 2 at Sofia airport. 'As a Roma you are marginal, without rights here or there . . . but at least those who come back have learnt to put rubbish in the bin! . . . For years I've been pushing young Roma to study. To go to university, even when their families can't support them. Now they finish university and there are no jobs for them. And they come back to Lom and say to me, "You lied to us. You cheated us. You said it would be better if we had an education, and its not." What this means is that we are losing the tools to change the Roma, to help them.'

Niki is one of the leading Roma intellectuals of Bulgaria. His sister is at the Sorbonne in Paris. His voice is respected in Roma and non-Roma circles. 'Fifteen years ago we had a dream. I don't want to imitate Martin Luther King, but they have taken that dream away from us.' What had impressed me most about him at our first meeting was his total lack of self-pity or complaint. His was not a litany of words such as 'discrimination' and 'prejudice' – words 'devalued by over-use' he had told me then – but rather a list of individual and collective successes. But this time he is worried by the growing desperation of the Roma, and the increasing hostility between them and the majority, white population. 'The gap between the Roma and non-Roma is getting bigger and bigger, and if that process is not stopped, sooner or later there will be clashes, ethnic clashes here.' He also worries about the retreat of the state from the Roma ghettoes in Plovdiv, Bulgaria's second largest city, where teachers no longer bother to teach Roma kids, and where what he sees as the 'Islamisation' of young Muslim Roma is going from strength to strength.

The Ministry of Education in Sofia has cut funding for one of his programmes in Lom because he included non-Roma children in it, although the money was for a Roma project. He wrings his hands – 'but the whole point of it was to integrate the Roma with the non-Roma!' His voice lifts, almost shouting over the roar of a car that is backing precariously towards our table. 'So what can you do?' I shout back. The car's engine is switched off. We can talk normally again. 'We fight, of course, but we have fewer and fewer tools . . .' Niki Kirilov expresses both admiration and frustration about Livia Jaróka, a Hungarian member of the European Parliament, and the most prominent Roma in the whole of Europe.[22] She told me recently that she had spent her first five years in Brussels learning the system – of political influence, and access to funds, and how she feels that she is in the European capital for all Roma, not just for her own centre-right Hungarian party, Fidesz. He agrees that you have to know the system; that has been the key to his own success and that of Lom in Bulgaria. But, he adds, 'if she wants to represent us, she should tour the Roma communities of eastern Europe, listening to our problems, and telling us what she is doing on our behalf – then she would have a real mandate to speak for us in the corridors of power!' Otherwise, she is in danger of being 'a lone Roma monkey,' he says. 'Because everyone likes to laugh at Roma monkeys! They add colour . . .'

On Saturday morning I go with Niki's friend Milenko to Lom market. The first of the local spring vegetables are for sale, spring onions and leafy vegetables from the greenhouses. The Roma don't have land, so I'm more interested in the stalls on the edge of the market where they are selling their wares. Spasska sits behind a pile of small, white haricot beans, and is introduced to me as a fortune teller. She's a grandmother figure of indeterminate age, who speaks in a great stream of Bulgarian intermingled with words from the Romani tongue. I go round the back of her stall for her to read my fate in her beans. First she takes my hand, places it over the big pile of beans, places her hand over mine, and asks my name. Then she starts dividing the beans swiftly into nine piles, with between one and four beans in each. It all happens so fast, and she keeps talking throughout, I do not notice the moment that she shifts from exchanging pleasantries with Milenko to the incantation with which she begins to read my destiny. Milenko stumbles over his simultaneous translation, such is the speed of her delivery. I will have a very good exit, she says – does she mean death? I ask him – 'I don't know! She used the word for "exit"' he mumbles. 'You have a big fight with the woman you love. You are desperate, in ill health,' Spasska continues, her hands racing between the beans, adding and subtracting all the time, the piles rising and falling. 'You want to start a new job in a new place – that would be good for you. Everything will be all right if you go to your new job.' She pauses, looking at me to say 'this is your pile, and this is your woman's . . . you have thoughts to live with or without her, but she is ready for you, you call her, she is ready to live with you . . . if you call her, everything will be all right, and your exit will be excellent.' She stops in mid flow, and it is all over. 'I think this is the moment when you should give her some money,' Milenko suggests. I ask her how much it should be. 'There is no fixed price,' she says. 'Pay what you want. I have no food. Give from your heart.' I give her a ten leva note – five Euros – and she seems content, if not very impressed. 'How did she learn to read the beans?' I ask. 'A priest taught me,' she says, rather surprisingly. 'I had no money to buy nappies for my grandchildren, so I was begging outside a church. The man came up to me and offered me a whole bag of money. I looked into it and took out a ten leva note. That is all I need I told him, though I could have taken it all. "Did you go into the church?" the priest asked me. "When the shepherd loses just one sheep, he leaves all the others to go and find the one that is lost," he said. "From now on, that will be your role in life."'

We thank her and stand up to go, turning down a chance to buy some holy water. Milenko walks me through Lom and points out shops which are owned by the better-off Roma families. One selling fancy clothes for special occasions, another selling children's toys and bicycles – one family alone owns six or seven shops in the centre, and employs twenty people. We're on our way to a café with a Roma waitress, to meet Mladenka, a twenty-three-year-old Roma girl who is studying at medical university in Sofia. She's sitting there already when we arrive, a mass of lush, dark hair framing a pretty face, with black earrings, and deep brown eyes. She's wearing a Snob Cat T-shirt, and is a little bleary from the previous evening's revelry – a night dancing with her friends and relatives, celebrating her younger sister Pavlinka's graduation. She only finished school herself aged twenty, because the whole family went to the Czech Republic for several years to work in an air-conditioning factory. There she saved enough money to pay for her first year at university in Sofia. For the second year, she won a scholarship for students of Roma origin, from the Roma Education Fund in Budapest. She wants to come back to Lom when she finishes her course, to work in the hospital – to help her people, she says. Most of all, she would love to become a doctor, but does not know if she will be good enough, or will be able to find the money and time to study. Her words suggest that it is high time she started contributing to the family coffers. Her parents were aghast when she first mentioned she had won a place at university, but have slowly come round to the idea. She has never had a problem at school or university because of her ethnicity and is proud of her Roma identity. She does not hide it as many do when they start to make progress away from the ghetto. All her classmates from high school are already married with children, but her younger sister is following in her footsteps – sort of. She wants to study bakery and cake-making at the University of Plovdiv. Her older sister is in Lom, aged twenty-seven and married with two children. As for Mladenka, she will have her hands full with local health problems. There is something known as 'Lom disease', a kind of muscular dystrophy of the arms and legs, caused by a missing chromosome that affects the Roma in particular.[23] 'And the Danube?' I ask. 'I can't swim!' she confesses, though she likes to walk beside it with her friends when she comes home from her long sojourns in the capital.

On Saturday afternoon I sit with Milenko to watch the famous Karbovski show. It's one of the most popular on Bulgarian television, almost a national institution, and an example of the mockery, according to Roma leaders, of the everyday racism which they feel the Roma are exposed to. 'Karbovski carefully chooses the most ridiculous, the most awful cases, and thus

reinforces this stereotype of the Roma as weird, lazy, parasites.' Martin
Karbovski looks the ideal TV chat show host: neatly ironed blue shirt,
braces, short-cropped hair, intellectual-looking glasses and a little neat, carefully cultivated beard on his chin. His show is so popular, Milenko explains,
because he asks direct questions – unlike most Bulgarian journalists. This
week's Roma theme is a Romeo and Juliet story, a love affair between a
Roma boy and a non-Roma girl – Danielle. The non-Roma family reacts
violently to their daughter going out with a Roma. 'Why did you hit your
own daughter?' Martin Karbovski asks her father. 'I don't have a daughter,'
he replies, pointedly – in other words, no girl of mine would ever go out
with one of 'them'. 'We're honest, working people,' the father concludes –
making clear that no Roma, in his estimation, could be like that.

Milenko puts on a recorded copy of an earlier show, about Roma trans-
vestites working as prostitutes. The triple strangeness – of Roma, trans-
gender, and paid sex – are the perfect ingredients for a Karbovski
interview. 'We don't need millions, we just need a normal life,' says a man
dressed as a woman, his dark face fragile and hurt above his large breasts.
'I just want to be a healthy person . . . and help other people.'

'Oh come off it!' says the host. 'You – help other people?'

'I cannot eat if someone else is hungry and looks me in the eyes,' says
Tonsu the Roma.

'Do you know that we live in the European Union?' asks Karbovski.

'Yes. That's why every Bulgarian goes abroad to work.'

'Would you leave?' asks the host – in a way that suggests he would like
him to.

'Yes. If I find a way.'

'And would you work abroad as a prostitute?'

'Maybe. But I can do other things . . .'

'What is the Roma word for prostitute?'

'*Hangeli.*'

'Do you feel ashamed of what you do?'

'I can't be ashamed of myself. We are how God creates us. If God had
given me horns on my head, then I would have to live with them too,
wouldn't I?'

'Do you vote in elections?' Karbovski asks – this is his style, to ask totally
unrelated, provocative questions, to keep his viewers glued to the screen.

'I vote for the party I'm paid to vote for. They give us twenty, thirty leva . . .'

'What's the matter with your mouth?' Tonsu is grimacing, painfully.

'My tooth hurts.'

'Why don't you go to the dentist?'

'Because the dentist would charge me twenty-five leva, and then I wouldn't have any money left to feed my children. It's cheaper to take a painkiller. That only costs two leva.'

'Do you feel happy?' Karbovski asks, finally.

'Just look at me. Do you think I look like a happy person?'

The gravel beach at Lom is the scene of a short story by the contemporary Bulgarian author Emil Andreev. In 'The Return of Teddy Braun'[24] a small boy listens entranced to the drunkard Teddy Braun, whose real name is possibly Todor, but might even be Mladen, as he spins a yarn about his origins. He's the son of a Red Indian father and an Irish mother, born on the shore of the Mississippi, he says – a river that makes the wide Danube at Lom look more like a stream. The child drinks up every word, and drinks down each lemonade Teddy buys him, while the man's drinking partners mock and insult him at every turn. Eventually Teddy sets out to fulfil his boast to swim the Danube, right across to the Romanian shore. The reader is left with the impression that he probably drowns. Many years later the boy, now grown up, finds himself in Lom again and wanders down to the shore. The Seagull restaurant they sat in together has been burgled and smashed up, the sandstone wall is broken and the beach a wasteland. Suddenly he hears a voice in English behind him. 'Come on, Ted, we'll miss the ferry. Granny Ramona is too old to wait . . .'

The drunkard, it seems, was telling the truth, or a part of the truth, after all.

Half an hour's drive from Lom, a steep road leads down into the city of Vidin, the regional capital. For only the second time on my journey, on this Saturday afternoon there are prostitutes lining the main road. The big, empty office blocks beside the road have signs in the windows – 'Office space to rent, 23 Euros a cubic metre.' This is the town where Momi does not like to bring his travelling circus. Poised on the south-westward shore of a great zig-zag in the river, Vidin is like a guard post, a citadel at the top of the Danubian plain.

I check into the Hotel Bononia, against the better advice of my guide-book, and wander down on to the promenade along the Danube shore. A park of shady trees, playgrounds and ice-cream stalls stretches all the way to the Baba Vidin fortress. A young woman in a long, flamingo pink dress has just got married and stands beside her elegant bridegroom for a photo-graph before rejoining the guests at the restaurant behind her. Each large Bulgarian city seems blessed with one particular kind of tree. In Silistra and in Ruse it was the horse chestnut; in Vidin it is the sweet-scented acacia. There is also a constant drift of white cotton on the breeze from the hybrid poplar, Stalin's favourite tree. In addition there are Islamic tomb-stones, laid out in the grass with beautifully carved grapes and pomegran-ates. And a black-rimmed poster mourning the death of an angler. 'To mark the passing of forty days without our beloved Tsvetan Iliev Tsokov – Fisherman', reads the text, and there is a black-and-white photo-graph of the man himself, sat quietly beside his rods in a little harbour. The poster has already been fixed here for three months, and Tsvetan himself has almost faded from the picture, while the black outline of the boats is as strong as ever. The magic figure of forty has lingered on in the popular culture of south-eastern Europe longer than elsewhere on the continent. 'In the religious lore of both Christian and Mohammedan the same number constantly recurs,' wrote R. W. Hasluck.[25] 'The great fasts of the Christians are of forty days, dervishes of the Khalveti order likewise prac-tise fasting and mortification for periods of forty days . . . there are forty traditions of Mohammed . . . forty ogres, forty jinns and numerous groups of forty saints.'

That evening I eat fish on the deck of a restaurant moored to the shore and watch the river traffic as darkness falls. The *Mercur 307*, of the TTS line, its decks painted red, white and yellow, pushes a long barge of black coal upriver from Galaţi. There are two Romanian tricolours and a blue European Union flag, and the mounds of coal piled high on its decks look like a model of the peaks of the distant Carpathians. Along the railings of my restaurant, bulbous yellow lamps shine against the darkening sky like blobs of caviar. In the far distance, the half-completed Vidin to Calafat bridge is lit up across the river. Closer to hand, a fisherman struggles to start his outboard motor as his small blue boat, the *Gloria*, floats gloriously downstream. Then a huge Ukrainian ship, the *Ruse*, its name written in both Latin and Cyrillic script, roars downstream pushing no less than three barges, each the length of a football pitch – the biggest single craft I have seen on the river. The ship is black, with a square bow, and sailors in blue overalls walk along a dark-green deck. In the pitch darkness of the May night, as I pick over the bones of my supper, a Bulgarian ship registered in Lom, the *Phoenix*, pulls slowly upriver, looking for a berth for the night.

I get up early the next morning to watch the sunrise, and make a small driftwood fire on the shore. I have watched the sun sink into the Danube many times on this journey, but this is the first time I watch it emerge out of waters upriver, a scarlet ball leaking red paint into the whole landscape. After breakfast that morning, in the village of Pokraina near Vidin I track down a family of Calderash Gypsies I met in the marketplace in Lom who make copper stills in which to distill *rakia*, plum brandy. Tseko Natovi is the grandfather. He sits and rests on a bench with cushions in the corner of the yard, and oversees the work with a critical eye. His sons Sasho and Eulogi do most of the work, while his third son, Mitko, translates for me. He is the only one of the family to try his hand at something different – he's studying to be an accountant in Bucharest. There is also a smaller boy, also called Tseko, aged about ten. The women flit through the yard like swallows – mothers, daughters and grandmothers – cleaning fish, hanging out washing, and smiling shyly while their men do the talking. One is Mitko's wife. They are only just married. Most of the work with the copper takes place under an old walnut tree in the yard. Sasho sits cross-legged on a piece of cardboard in the dust and takes a ring of copper, while his brother Eulogi prepares another circle of copper for the base, swiftly going round the edge with a pair of pliers, cutting and bending up little tabs in the soft metal. The base is then attached to the body of the vessel with the help of a strip of copper wire which goes between them as the tabs are each hammered down one by one. This is one of their smaller stills, designed for 150 litres of *rakia*. The largest they do is for five hundred litres. Despite the beauty of the piece, I cannot convince myself that it would get much use in my Budapest flat, so I opt instead for two copper bowls with big looped handles, like Gypsy earrings.

Mitko's mother sets to work immediately, to melt a metal bar to coat the inside. There is a hearth built into the soil beneath the walnut tree. Mitko makes a fire in it with wood, then brings pieces of coal, while one of his brothers brings a vacuum cleaner, in which the flow of air has been reversed to turn it into an electric bellows. The fire blazes, and my copper pots, one at a time, are heated over the furnace by Mitko's mother, holding them in a pair of tongs as she squats in the dust. Apart from the hoover, it might be a scene of copper-smelting from any time in the past seven thousand years. The bar of zinc and lead – a modern luxury – is melted in the pot until molten silver drops fall from it, first green then bright translucent silver. When the whole inside of the pot has been coated, it is left to cool. Then the copper is re-polished.

The men have finished the still and *rakia* is brought. Only the men drink, while the women clean the fish. Mitko's wife shyly puts on the gold, Austro-Hungarian sovereign, which she wears on a chain round her neck. On one side of the coin is the emperor Franz Josef, who sports a Bohemian beard and pony tail, though it may just be a head band, tied in a ribbon at the back, and the words FRANC IOS IDG AUSTRIAE IMPERATOR. On the front is the imperial double-headed eagle, with the Habsburg crest, and the words HUNGAR. BOHEM. GAL – for Hungary, Bohemia and Galicia, three of the Austrian realms, and the date 1915.[26] She wears it outside an equally astonishing shirt depicting a long-haired, long-legged girl sitting back in a rather sultry style in a red chair. Her own single ponytail hangs dark over her shoulder. Standing next to Mitko, framed by the dense green foliage of the trees, the couple might have been married that morning.

CHAPTER 7

River of Dreams

It is not birds I sculpt, it is flight
CONSTANTIN BRĂNCUȘI[1]

'Did you ever see the fairies yourself?'
'Just once,' he affirms, 'in a dream. They were dancing round and
round in an opening in the forest. And do you know what?'
He pauses for effect.
'They were all wearing beautiful blue dresses – like Gypsy girls!'
MOMIR PLAVI, *MIROČ*[2]

AHMED ENGUR was born on the island of Ada Kaleh, in the middle of the
snakelike zig-zag the river performs after breaking through the confines of
the Iron Gates. He fell in love and was married there in 1967 to an island
girl, the year before the island was destroyed. His father came from Bosnia.

'Ada Kaleh was a beautiful place. I remember the fruits best of all . . . and
the floods; the streets were often under water in spring . . . Even now I dream
I go to the island by boat, set foot on it, and walk there. The memories come
back, walking up and down the island, just as it was, in my mind.'

We talk in the yard of his house, while his wife Mioara makes Turkish
coffee. The family are Turks, like almost all the former inhabitants of the
island. Only the baker was Romanian. Ada Kaleh was a time bubble, with
its mosque and minaret, its old fortress – the name means 'the island of
the fortress' – and its protected status between the Ottoman and the

Austro-Hungarian empires. Less than two kilometres long, and three to four hundred metres wide, it was in Turkish hands from the fourteenth to the twentieth centuries for all but the twenty years from 1718 to 1739. That was long enough for the Austrians to rebuild and reinforce the handsome brick fortress, probably on the foundations of a Roman one, which allowed the Turkish garrison to control the river traffic in both directions. At the Congress of Berlin in 1878, when Serbia won her independence, Bulgaria was prevented from emerging as a major Balkan state, Romania received northern Dobrogea, and the island was so tiny it was completely forgotten.[3] It remained under Turkish rule even when the left bank returned to Romanian control. Eventually Romania took it over, but the island remained always special, with its own micro-climate, its figs and pomegranates. Trips there were especially popular with children for the pistachio-flavoured ice cream. Action films were made – Ahmed remembers having a brandy with one of the famous actors. 'I drank one to his three.' His task was to stand guard over the camera equipment while they were filming. 'I was even paid!'[4]

Ahmed attended primary school on the island till he was aged eleven, then went to boarding school in Orşova, just across the straits. When his father died, the family could no longer afford the cost of boarding; he tried another school, then left. 'If you can't study, you'd better learn to row, because there will always be work on an island for those who can row,' they told him. So that was his first job, rowing the children to the school he no longer attended in the mornings, and back home in the afternoons. 'It took about ten minutes – more when the water was high. The key was to stay as close as possible to the bank, then cross at the shortest point.' With his friend the son of the imam, he converted a rowing boat into the island's first sailing boat – just for fun. 'We travelled between the island and the shore, or just up and down the Romanian side, because of the border guards.' Yugoslavia was on uneasy terms with the rest of the socialist bloc, and freedom to move was severely restricted. 'We were guarded like in a camp, so that we wouldn't try to leave Romania,' Mioara remembers. They had to be back on the island by eight o'clock in the evening. She remembers barbed wire along the shore and soldiers with guns. Each time they crossed to the island, they had to write down their names in the register of the border police.

When Ahmed finished his schooling in Turnu Severin, his first serious job was in the cigarette factory on Ada Kaleh. 'My job was to take the tobacco from one part of the factory to the other. The tobacco came from the mainland. There was no space on the island to grow tobacco!' 'We used to roll them by hand at first. Then we got a machine. "Musilmane" they were called – terrible cigarettes – with no filter!'

'The "Nationale" were even worse!' Mioara chimes in. 'We made them with the leftover tobacco! That was when I started to smoke . . .' she adds. In the book of photographs of Ada Kaleh, recently published in Bucharest, there are pictures of the tins in which the cigarettes were sold – proudly proclaiming where they were made. 'The sweets, the Turkish delight, and the fig jam were the best,' she remembers. She shuffles off and returns with a jar of her own fig jam from the fruit in her yard. It is sweet as treacle, and the seeds have a pleasant crunching sensation between the teeth. 'You peel the figs, and stand them in limestone water for half a day. Then you add sugar and water, and boil them all together for two or three hours on a small flame. You should put them in jars while the mixture is still hot.' There was also a refreshing, almost non-alcoholic drink, called *bragă* in Romanian, and made from hops. It is still sold in the marketplace in Turnu Severin.

The destruction of the island was long in the planning and quick in the execution. Ahmed worked in the mid-1960s as a waiter in Turnu Severin. He remembers a meeting of top Romanian and Yugoslav communist officials, and how, just as he was bringing them their after-lunch coffee, one of the Yugoslav comrades asked what would happen if the people refused to move from the island. 'Then we will just flood it anyway, and they will run like rats,' said the Romanian minister, gleefully. He managed to go back to the island only once, on a military boat on which the soldiers travelled, to lay dynamite around the buildings. He was on the shore in Orşova drinking brandy when they lit the fuse. 'It was as though they declared war on the island. On nature itself.' The minaret fell only half way, and stayed at an angle of forty-five degrees. Two beautiful, tall thin cypresses from the graveyard were chopped down. One by one the old buildings were blown up or bulldozed. Local people were promised that once the dam was built they would enjoy free electricity. In fact, forty years after it was built, there are still frequent power shortages. On the street in front of Ahmed's house is a great pile of logs, waiting to be split – mostly beech from the mountains nearby. 'We always heat with wood, its cheaper, and more reliable.'

Mioara worked in a bank in Turnu Severin. The original plan was for the inhabitants to move to the island of Simian. When they refused they were given a choice – to leave for Turkey or to go somewhere else in Romania. 'Many went to Turkey, but most soon came back . . . they didn't like the climate, or the conditions,' she says. The Sultan's carpet, fifteen metres long and nine metres wide, which once covered the floor of the mosque, was split. Half is in the Iron Gates museum in Turnu Severin, the other half is on the floor of the main mosque in Constanţa, on the Black Sea coast. In Babadag, the woman who showed me round the tomb of Sari Saltuq[5] was born and raised on Ada Kaleh.

Down by the harbour in Orşova, with Ahmed's help I track down Erwin Osman, his best friend's son and the grandson of the imam. Erwin is repainting the hull of his boat for the tourist season. He takes groups up and down the river all summer, but never across. Romania has been in the European Union since 2007; Serbia might join if lucky in 2020. Borders divide people, but in borderlands people can wander, and meet. Both have been present in the fate of the Danube – yesterday's barbarians are today's or tomorrow's allies.

Every now and then, Erwin takes a visitor out who used to live on Ada Kaleh. They travel into midstream and cut the engines in the exact place where the island once stood. 'Do they throw flowers?' I ask.

'I've never seen that . . .' he admits. 'Mostly they just lean quietly over the railings, gazing down into the water.'

On the shore there's a statue of a woman throwing a wreath of flowers into the waters, in memory of the island.

Erwin's grandfather was the imam of Ada Kaleh, and spent thirteen years in prison. He was convicted as a spy and enemy of the communist state on the sole evidence of possession of a Romanian-English dictionary. When he came back from prison, Ahmed remembers, 'he was always the first to proclaim "Long Live the Socialist Republic of Romania" at public meetings. What they must have done to him in prison to make him do that!' His wife shudders.

The first Iron Gates dam, between Orşova and Turnu Severin, was completed in 1971. Éva Hajdú remembers passing the island in the early summer of that year, on a cruise to Ruse on a ship which belonged to the Hungarian Interior Ministry. 'On the way back, the island had completely vanished beneath the waters. It was so sad,' she told me, overlooking the shore of Lake Balaton, Hungary's inland sea.[6] During those same weeks, there was an attempt at resistance by some of the older inhabitants of Orşova, who sat on their beds and refused to leave their homes. They were dragged out by police and soldiers.

Erwin and I study my book about Ada Kaleh which includes many photographs from his own collection. One, from 1945, shows the imam and two priests, one Orthodox and one Catholic, blessing the Romanian troops in front of the main theatre in Turnu Severin as they set out to occupy Transylvania.[7] There is no Jewish rabbi present, Erwin points out, for obvious reasons. His maternal grandfather, he tells me, was not a critic of the regime but a victim of it. He was made into a scapegoat at a time when the authorities needed scapegoats. After he was released from prison he was chosen as a representative of minorities in parliament in Bucharest, and took part in delegations to the Arab world when Ceauşescu was cultivating such friendships. His paternal grandfather was a sweet-seller on both the island and the mainland. 'I am a Muslim but I don't go to the mosque, as the nearest one is 350 kilometres away in Bucharest. I have a copy of the Koran. A tiny one, in my wallet, and another one at home. I can't read it, though, as it's in Arabic. My sister has my grandfather's copy. My mother died five years ago. She's buried in Istanbul. These photographs were very important for her.'

Professor Constantin Juan lives in a long housing estate down near the shore-line, in one of the blocks of flats built for those rehoused from old Orşova. Aged ninety-three he still lives alone, but is looked after by his children and grandchildren. He remembers Ada Kaleh well from his many visits, and from his later work as an ethnographer. 'The first time – I must have only been four or five – I was struck by the fact that everyone still dressed in the oriental fashion.' Bloomers for the women, fezes for the men. I move him gently on to some of the yawning gaps in my research on the island, especially the legendary figure of Miskin Baba, a Muslim saint whose house and tomb were on the island. 'Miskin Baba was the king of Bukhara in central Asia. One night he dreamt of an island in the middle of a river where the people needed him. So he travelled and travelled, asking all the way where such an island might be found, until he reached Belgrade. There he found an island, but he knew that was not the place. So he asked a group of fishermen, "Where could you find a lot of fish – as many as Jesus Christ found?" because he knew the fishermen were Christians. And they told him the way to Ada Kaleh. He lived there for many years, and helped the people a lot, just as he had dreamt. And when he died he was buried there. Even after his death he continued to defend the island . . . Once a young man dreamt that he should tidy up his grave, because if he did so, another man would come and help the islanders. That was in 1931, and he obeyed the dream. A year later the King of Romania, Carol II, visited the island, and did much for the people.' A society was established to help the poor, run by a local businessman called Ali Kadri who married a Jewish woman from Orşova. But in 1940 he left for Istanbul.' Without his wife, the story goes. Professor Juan has other stories of the more eccentric inhabitants on the eve of the Second World War. A Hungarian called Bicsárdi, for example, a naturist who refused to wear clothes.[8]

Local people did not believe that everything would be destroyed. It was very hard for them. He remembers in particular the two, massive cypress trees in the Turkish graveyard, cut down when the mosque was destroyed. Even Miskin Baba could not withstand the final attack by the combined comrades of Yugoslavia and Romania. His tomb was moved, like the others, to Simian Island. But no one knows where it is any more. 'Many times I have dreamt that the Danube went back, and I walked through the streets of Old Orşova, looking for the place where my house was, that I could go back inside and live there again. I dreamt that many times.'

Târgu Jiu lies in the hills, an hour's drive north of Turnu Severin. It seems a long way from the Danube, but it is not hard to justify the detour. Ever since I came to live in eastern Europe, half a lifetime ago, I have wanted to see the birthplace of Constantin Brâncuşi.

The Table of Silence stands in the town park, near the Jiu river. Twelve symmetrical stools, like half melons, surround a simple, round stone table. Like all of Brâncuşi's work, there is something both ancient and radically modern about it. The number twelve, the distance of the stools from the table, and the name of the work invite contemplation. It's already summer in the park: the buzz of the birds and the chatter of the townsfolk are loud. I photograph a young couple sitting on one of the stools, the girl in the boy's lap. He wears sunglasses and a green T-shirt; she has shoulder-length, dark-brown hair, turns her face away from the camera, and cups his chin in her hand. As I study the photograph later, I notice both have identical bracelets, giving the impression that they are actually one person with four hands. Brâncuşi would have liked this. A policeman stands guard in the background, in a light blue shirt in the summer heat, arms folded. Then an older woman arrives, on high-heeled shoes, from her body language the boy's mother, rather than the girl's. They sit on three stools, the mother in the middle. The table radiates silence. Beyond are a line of willows, and steps that lead up to the embankment of the River Jiu.

Down an alleyway of trees stands the Gate of the Kiss. The kiss, highly stylised, represents that between a soldier and his sweetheart, and the soldier and his child as he sets out to war, and was intended as a war memorial to the Romanian defenders of the city in a battle with German troops in the First World War.

'Here are my pictures of the Temple du Baiser,' Brâncuşi wrote in a letter to Doina Tătărescu, the wife of the Romanian Prime Minister Gheorghe Tătărescu.[9]

'Through this doorway one will enter a garden . . . Do you recognize the patterns on the stone? . . . these columns are the result of years of searching. First came this group of two, interlaced, seated figures in stone . . . then the symbol of the egg, then the thought grew into this gateway to a beyond . . .' The patterns he refers to resemble the wooden tiles on the roofs of peasant houses. The 'egg' on each side of the top of the columns is split down the middle, in the centre of another ring of stone. There are no features on the two faces, but the intimacy lost by the absence of lips and eyes and chins is regained by the sheer proximity of the two halves of the stone. The whole face rubs against the other for the last time before they part forever. The circle of stone around them is the cocoon of their love. And the world beyond the gate, as Brâncuşi writes, is the other world where they will be reunited. 'Don't you see these eyes? The outlines of the two eyes? These hemispheres represent love. What is left in memory after one's death? The remembrance of the eyes, of the gaze which voiced one's love for people, for mankind.'[10]

Hobiţa, the village where Brâncuşi was born and grew up, tending his father's sheep, is half an hour's drive from Târgu Jiu. His own birth-house burned down, but another wooden house built by his father, a carpenter, was put in its place, and is said to closely resemble the original. The wooden tiles on the steeply sloping roof are individually carved – just like the vertical shapes on the Gate of the Kiss. The house is made of big, solid beams, and has just three rooms and a long front porch. The whole structure is raised from the ground, with geraniums in a tray along the terrace. The room on the right has a dirt floor, a hearth with earthenware and iron pots and pans and cooking implements arranged around it, and a small spinning wheel. In the far room on the left is a writing desk, with flowers on the table and black-and-white pictures of Brâncuşi at work in his atelier in Paris. The picture from 1935 – when Brâncuşi was forty-eight – shows a vigorous, bearded, determined-looking man, his hair still dark but his beard already grey, with a cigarette between his fingers and his arms resting on his knees. In the picture from 1938 he looks awkward in a suit and tie, presumably at the opening of an exhibition, but his big hands rest on top of each other, as though impatient to get back to work. In the picture from 1946 he has aged a lot, seems exhausted with the world, leans back with his eyes shut, a peculiar domed hat on his head, though there is still a sculptor's mallet in his hand. There are simple, painted icons on the whitewashed walls, and a story printed out above his desk.

'Long, long ago there lived a master carver, whose skill was beyond anything known in the world . . .' the story begins. Commissioned by the gods to build a stairway to heaven, the master obliges, and the stairway becomes the wonder of the world. 'When his last hour arrived, the master mounted the stairway and climbed to heaven, where he has been watching over his heritage on the earth ever since.'

The years passed and evil people came, and began demolishing his stairway, and locked it away in a place where no light could penetrate, and set about building a different one of their own.

'The anger of the gods was so great, they wept tears of fire, and set fire to the whole earth. Heaven and Earth mourned for a long time, until the gods granted grace to new masters.

'Early one fine autumn morning, the masters broke the locks on the old stairway, and set it in its old place, now covered with golden tears. When the sun rose, the gods and the people saw the staircase, and marvelled at its beauty.

'Nobody knows the masters' names or saw their faces; they disappeared as mysteriously as they appeared. They silently returned to the work from which they were interrupted by the gods.

'According to the legend, fire will burn any evil man who tries to lay hands on the staircase, and will light the way of the good man.'

'I was told this story by an old man, seated on a bench, close to the staircase of the gods, on a moonlit night. People who go to see the staircase meet the man and listen to his story. Could it be that the man is the Master himself?'

Brâncuși's garden is as tranquil as one of his sculptures, but wild and abundant in a different way. The small red and yellow plums are just ripe, overhanging a wooden outhouse lined with farming tools. The wooden columns are carved in upward spirals. Brâncuși learnt to carve wood with a sharp knife as he tended the sheep. The stone walls are overgrown with lichen, the well is deep and cool, and I haul up a wooden bucketful of water to parch my thirst and wash my face.

In the graveyard up the road, resting peacefully in the summer shade, his parents' graves are marked by a simple wooden cross: Nicolae Radu Brâncuși, 1831–1884, and Maria Brâncuși 1851–1919. The cross has a little roof, and the graves have a small fence around them, each fence post topped by a carved wooden star. The whole graveyard is deep in purple clover. In the last years of Constantin's life in his Parisian exile, he immersed himself once again in his own language and culture, and made several efforts to come home to Romania, or at least to bequeath his work to his home country. But the communist authorities perceived him to be a decadent artist, and wanted nothing to do with him, so he became a French citizen, and instead gave his work to France. His workshop is still preserved in the Pompidou centre in Paris, and he is buried in the Montparnasse cemetery where a version of his monumental sculpture 'the Kiss' stands on the grave of his friend Tania Rachevskaia.[11] This kiss is undoubtedly one exchanged between lovers. The lips, arms and feet meet and merge hungrily with one another.

Brâncuși never married.

On the road back from his village to Târgu Jiu, I stop to drink homemade lemonade with Ovidiu Popescu, the man in charge of Brâncuși's work in the county. He remembers the change in the attitude of the communist authorities. 'It all began when they rebuilt the memorial house to him in Hobiṭa . . . in 1967.' Ironically, the same regime that carried out the death sentence on Ada Kaleh, Old Orşova and other settlements along the river, began at the same time to rehabilitate one of Romania's greatest sons. But the story is not so strange – communism survived so long through its flexibility, the cruelty but also the generosity of its protagonists; by giving with one hand and taking away with the other. Only when it became brittle, and incapable of subtlety, did it collapse. 'Should Brâncuşi's remains be exhumed from Montparnasse and brought home to be buried beside his family in Hobiṭa, as some Romanians would like?' I ask Ovidiu. 'I think he was deeply sad in his heart, as he lay dying in France. But I don't think he would like to be buried in Romania. He accepted that fact, he bought his grave there . . .' In a park on the northern edge of Târgu Jiu, the third and most remarkable of Brâncuşi's works in his hometown points to the sky. The Endless Column ends rather abruptly – sixteen and a half hollow rhomboid shapes, made of laminated steel, painted with ship's varnish, like the hulls of the barges on the Danube, to protect them from the wind and water, the sun and ice. Inspired by the carved pillars which held up the porches of his childhood village, and the tree at the centre of the world of dreams and fairy-tales, it was also inspired by the turning of a simple screw. It contains 'little material and much thought', as a Croatian architect once said to me about the fifteenth-century bridge in Mostar.[12]

Brâncuşi grappled all his life with the problem of how to approach and express the infinite. The column, to be endless, cannot be too tall. 'If it was too big, it would resemble the Tower of Babel.' It has no base or capital, so it has no beginning, and no end.[13] 'Nature creates plants that grow up straight and strong from the ground,' Brâncuşi wrote, on the eve of the inauguration of the column in the park in Târgu Jiu. 'Here is my column. It is in the garden of a friend in Romania. Its forms are the same from the ground to the top. It has no need of pedestal or base to support it, the wind will not destroy it, it stands by its own strength . . . It is thirty metres high, and you know that my friend there once told me that he had never been aware of the great beauty of his garden until he had placed my column there. It had opened his eyes.'[14]

I stand beside it in the park, and its long shadow of rhomboid shapes
stretches out across fresh mown grass, past a short policeman.

The Danube at Eselniţa at dawn is calm as a millpond. This is more lake
than river, and at thirty metres deep it is the inverse of Brâncuşi's tower.
There are no coincidences in engineering, or in nature.

Doru Oniga's little hotel is built partly on the shore, partly on the river
itself, with a floating landing stage. I lower myself slowly into the water of
the Danube for the first time on this journey. It is summer now, but the
water is cool. Swallows flit over my head, so close to the water their wings
almost break the surface. And I swim slowly upstream, towards the Iron
Gates. Wooded hills slope steeply down to the river, which narrows all the
way to the gorge where the slopes turn to cliffs. There's a little church at the
base, like the churches of Meteora in Greece, but at the base, not the top of
a pinnacle of rock. The water reflects the clouds and only a thin line sepa-
rates the identical halves. There are two smudged suns; the whole morning
is like an egg, sculpted by Brâncuşi, with a double yoke. Back in my room
I open a slim copy of the poems of George Seferis at the following verse:

> we thought we knew
> there were beautiful islands
> somewhere round here
> close by
> perhaps here
> or a little further on
> no – just here
> where we are groping.[15]

After breakfast, Doru's son Nicolae takes me upriver by boat. We pass
the church, built in the 1990s to replace 'the church under the water', lost
when the dam was constructed. According to my *Guide to the Romanian
Orthodox Monastic Establishments*, the original church was dedicated to the
Prophet Elijah.[16] 'Throughout its long-lasting history, the monastery
suffered years of appalling hardships: ravages inflicted by a host of invaders,
obsequious offerings required by dire circumstances, foreign autocratic
domination, and, in the long run, the hostility of nature itself (it was

flooded by the waters of the Danube River).' A perfect recipe, then, for a life devoted to prayer. Several winters' supply of firewood is stacked high as a wall beneath the church, and an icon is painted on the white wall facing the river, of Christ in a golden cloud blessing his disciples as he rises to heaven from a landscape of spruce trees. These give a rather Balkan, rather than Middle Eastern, flavour to the picture. Above the words 'Manastirea Mracuna', Romanian and European Union flags, divided by a large cross, are painted on the wall. The octagonal dome and the pointed roof, less than twenty years old, are already rusting. Hanging baskets of red, white and pink flowers line the terrace outside the monks' quarters. Perched at the end of the narrow straits of the Danube, the church blesses travellers on their way.

Upstream from the church, the bulbous features of Decebal, moustachioed and wide-eyed, have been carved into the rock face, forty metres high and twenty-five wide. The ancient Dacian leader stares across the river at the opposite cliff. The words *Decebalus Rex, Dragan Fecit* (Decebal the king, Dragan made it) are carved into the rock beneath his face.[17] The cliff rising above his head into the wooded slope provides him with the illusion of a huge forehead, or a pointed wizard's hat. The Romanian businessman who commissioned the work in the early twentieth century, Iosif Constantin Dragan, tried to persuade the Serbs to sculpt the face of Hadrian, facing Decebal across the river, but the Serbs refused – they have their own, more recent heroes, and do not share that identification with Decebal which many Romanians profess. Even Decebal is unfinished – Iosif Dragan ran out of money.

Navigation through this stretch of the Danube was once the most treacherous on the whole river. As the Danube forced its way through these mountains over tens of thousands of years, it lined its bed with the jagged rocks it tore from the limestone cliffs in its path. The Danube falls by several metres over a short stretch of only a hundred kilometres, and the combined effect on the water of the rocks on the bed and the sharp gradient of the river came to be known as 'the boilers'. If the journey downriver by boat was a helter-skelter race to dodge the rocks beneath and along the shore, the journey upriver was even more dangerous.[18] Hadrian solved the problem by building a road, carved deep into the cliff face, to bring his legions from Rome to confront the Dacians. The road was dug by slave labour, like Gheorgiu-Dej's canal to the Black Sea from Cernavodă. The road was used from the seventeenth century onwards by teams of horses, to pull ships loaded with salt or grain upriver – the first towpath on the Danube. Only with the advent of steam ships and paddle steamers in the 1830s could larger ships manoeuvre upriver with ease. How the *Argo* must have struggled through here, the men at the row-locks, worshipping and simultaneously hating Medea and Jason, the lovers in the bow, as they strained upriver, the golden fleece draped around the mast, the sails pulled down to prevent the sudden, strange winds of the gorge tugging the ship to its doom.

Nicolae steers his motorboat under a cluster of acacia trees overhanging the water, and we step tentatively ashore, into the Veterans cave. The rock vaults overhead like the gateway of a cathedral, such as Salisbury or Cologne. A glorious ray of sunlight bursts like a spotlight through the roof. I sit on my dusty throne in brilliant sunlight, in the epicentre of the velvet darkness. It feels like the end of a journey. I could stay here forever. The cave got its name from the Austrian soldiers who set up camp here in the dying decades of the Ottoman empire in the nineteenth century, to harry passing Ottoman ships – western pirates, attacking the galleys of the Empire of the East. A little further upriver is the Ponicova cave. There is a treacherous footpath down to this one from the road on the other side of the mountain. The Danube is only two hundred metres wide at this point, to Serbia on the far shore. In Ceauşescu's time this was famous as an escape route from communist Romania. So many men and women attempted the treacherous crossing that the Romanian authorities posted border guards permanently in the cave. Some escapees were shot as they swam; others were caught by Yugoslav border guards when they made it to the far shore and returned to Romania to receive their punishment – several years' hard labour. Yet others escaped detection, or were fortunate with the border guard they encountered, who let them quietly pass. Yugoslavia was a much more open country than Romania, and there was a good chance they could continue their journey to the West from there, especially if they had friends to help them. I met the owner of a pizzeria in Constanţa once, who had escaped Romania from here in the early 1980s. He made his way to New York, and worked his way up from dish-washer to restaurant owner. After the revolution he returned to Constanţa and now has his own business empire.[19] The *Tui Mozart* passenger cruiser, registered in Valletta, Malta, roars by downriver. I hope they have someone on board to tell the passengers the story of these caves.

The Iron Gates might actually be better named the Iron Gateway – there is no gate to block the way, just the sixty-kilometre passage from the plains of the Lower Danube behind me to those of Serbia, Croatia and Hungary ahead. Travelling through the gates, by road or boat, I have the sense of an umbilical cord. The river is very deep here – as deep as the ledges off the Black Sea coast at the Danube mouth. It is exhilarating to be trapped between cliffs, with so much water below and sky above. The richly wooded undergrowth of the slopes on either side of the river provides a special climate for all kinds of plants, and wildlife, especially for snakes, the most ancient symbol of the Danube.

On the pontoon of Doru's Danube Star Hotel, a former chief engineer in the Romanian merchant navy, Gabriel Florescu, a guest of the hotel, talks about his years at sea. Now he's the head of the harbour in Constanţa, but often comes to Eselniţa. He used to take cargoes of timber to Britain in the early 1990s when the forests of the Carpathians were being decimated for export. The propeller of his ship broke once, off Plymouth, on a wreck left from the Second World War. They limped all the way up the coast to North Shields to get it repaired. The *Meanogorsk*, flying a Ukrainian blue and yellow flag, goes upstream towards the boilers. Carrying grain, Gabriel says, or steel. The cargo is buried deep in the hold, and the hull is deep in the water as we watch through our binoculars. It slows at the approach to the 'small boilers', then takes the narrow channel close to the left bank. 'It can rain in Orşova, but we don't feel a drop here,' Doru says. 'The wind blasts through the Gates, deflecting the rain up to Băile Herculane – the Baths of Hercules.' It suddenly gets cool, at eight in the evening. It is hard to believe, sitting here watching it, that such a huge river can squeeze through such a narrow gap. Beneath the pontoon, the large head of a catfish hangs as a trophy. The fish was more than a hundred kilos in weight and nearly three metres long when Doru trapped it in the shallows beneath his hotel. He drives me up the valley to Băile Herculane. From here, there are daily trains to my home in Budapest. The town got its name from a myth relating to the Greek god Hercules, who slew a dragon in a cave nearby. The domed roof of the railway station is decorated with enormous frescoes of the man in action. It was not an easy fight, even for a god, and Hercules was badly wounded in the encounter.[20] Fortunately there were healing springs to hand. And that may be the main point of the story – not how Hercules slew the dragon, but how he was healed of his wounds. The thermal springs were also tapped by the Roman armies to heal their sore feet after their long march from Rome. The water pours out of the rock at 54 degrees Celsius, and has to be cooled to 37 degrees to be used. Like Karlovy Vary in Bohemia and Héviz in Hungary, the town developed as a fashionable holiday resort in the nineteenth century, made possible by the opening of the railway line through the mountains to Timişoara in 1878. The Cerna river flows steeply down through a thickly forested valley. The name means 'black' but the colour of the water is red, because of all the iron in the rocks. The forests, and the woods on either side of the Danube, are especially famous not only for their snakes but also for their turtles. 'Poor turtles,' wrote Brâncuşi, 'they crawl along so close to the devil, but whenever they put their heads out of their shells, they risk being trodden on by God.'[21]

On the Danube shore, I talk to a man herding a few cows along the road. Aleksa Jorsa is sixty-five and used to drive sixteen tonne trucks, carrying coal down to the harbour in Tisoviţa, now lost beneath the waves. 'I was born by the Danube, but we were not allowed to swim in it because of the border. The shore was like a no-man's-land; we could see it, but not get close to it.' The river often froze over before the dam was built, but not any more. In the old days, the army blew up the ice to get the floes running again, as at Nikopol. He misses Ada Kaleh, which he used to admire across the water, but only went there once, when he was aged nine or ten, on a school trip. He remembers the candies best, the nuts and sweets. Everyone was sorry when the island was destroyed, along with grazing land his family owned beside the river. Nonetheless he is nostalgic for the communist years because everyone had work. Now he supports his daughter and her two children on his pension alone. This is a beautiful place, he agrees, but all the youngsters leave because there is little chance of finding work.

Electricity pylons, painted yellow and black, cluster near the Iron Gates dam like football supporters, impatient to get into the stadium before the match. A group of German bikers queues to have their photographs taken in front of a 'no photography' sign, and are moved on by angry policemen, incensed by ridicule of the power of the state. The dam itself has twelve gates, flanked by massive concrete walls. It is a structure of which the Romans would have been proud, and reminds me that I am a barbarian at heart. There is little traffic over the top. The Serbian customs post on the far side is decorated with two 'Wanted' posters – the grinning, clean-shaven features of the Bosnian Serb military commander Ratko Mladić and the bearded, brooding face of Goran Hadžić, indicted for the killing of 271 hospital inmates in Vukovar in 1991.[22]

The Ottoman fortress of Fetislam lies right on the Danube shore, a little outside Kladovo. Several fishermen have spread their nets and their ragged shirts to dry between the crumbling arches. They have unrolled mattresses in what must once have been the guardrooms and live like Gypsies for months at a time, selling their catch, and saving money to take home. Lime trees and mulberry bushes push up between the ruins. From the battlements of the fortress I can just make out the ruins of Trajan's bridge on the far side.[23] What was once the most important and imposing structure of the whole region is now dwarfed by giant grain silos, cranes, cruiseboats, and the ragged skyline of Turnu Severin. 'How sad,' wrote the German traveller Helmuth von Moltke in the 1830s, 'that the Roman bridges have not survived. I believe that below Regensburg, not a single stone bridge crosses the river, below Vienna no strong bridge, and beneath Peterwardein (Novi Sad) not a single bridge of any description. This bridge (at Kladovo) would have been the only permanent crossing point for three hundred miles, if it had not been destroyed by those who built it, to protect themselves from the Goths.'[24]

The museum at Kladovo is divided into two sections: Roman and Prehistoric. There are chunky, hexagonal floor bricks, the rusting blades of Roman and barbarian swords, a frieze of Trajan and his men on the Danube shore in front of their fine bridge, and an image of the god Mithras in white marble, with a cruel mouth and what looks like shaving foam bubbling out of his head. There is also a frieze of the ritual slaughter of a bull – part of the initiation rites of the followers of Mithras.[25] The other half of the museum contains replicas of the astonishing fish-gods or goddesses of Lepenski Vir, forty kilometres upriver. When the decision was taken to build the dam, archaeologists were given three years to find what they could before the precious sites along the banks disappeared beneath the flood waters. From 1965 to 1969, the Serbian archaeologist Dragoslav Srejović excavated several Mesolithic settlements. His most amazing discoveries were at Lepenski Vir.[26] Fifty-four huge, egg-shaped stones, with half-human, half fish-like faces were found on terraces above the river. Most were placed among the foundations of trapezoid dwellings – guardians of the hearth, facing the doorway and the river. The floors of the houses were made of violet-red stone, fragmented into triangular tiles. Each of the heads has a stern face, their mouth turned down at the edges, as though by the strain of the current of the river, and large, bulbous eyes. Srejović named them Danubius, the Family Founder, the Forefather, the Fairyman. Marija Gimbutas saw in the symbols engraved around the faces, the zig-zags, chevrons and labyrinths, evidence of goddesses rather than of gods, of fish-women and ancestresses.[27] Others have non-human features – 'the Deer in the Wood', 'Last Sight' and 'Chronos'.

Whoever the people who once lived here were, the settlement shows little sign of attack or defence. The same village seems to have existed here for three thousand years, its inhabitants living peacefully on fish and game. A huge cliff face, known as the Big Rock, faces it across the Danube. Only at the very end, around 3500 BC, are there signs of destruction by fire. There are other peculiarities. The bodies of newborn children were buried beneath the floors of the houses. Adults were buried with their bodies oriented to the flow of the Danube, their heads pointing downstream. Srejović's fellow archaeologist Ljubinka Babović describes Lepenski Vir as a place of worship, divided into night and day sanctuaries, a Stonehenge of the Danube.[28]

A northerly wind blows off the Danube, making the mid-summer heat in Kladovo more bearable. Boys run down to the water with the huge, inflated inner tubes of tractor tyres, and plunge into the water after them – diving platforms, or bouncy castles. Their older brothers keep their distance, waist deep in the water, concentrating on the more serious business of catching fish, their long lines cast far out into the stream. Just down from the dam, this is the last place on my journey where sturgeon can still be found in the river. The former caviar factory in Kladovo is defunct. There are actually two dams, Iron Gates I and II. Kladovo is near the top of the storage lake created by Iron Gates II, which opened in 1984 – an eighty-kilometre long stretch of near-stagnant water, except when the great locks are opened at either end. My son Matthew has joined me for this stretch of the journey, and I try out his skateboard on the walkway beside the river. The wheels make a loud noise on the tarmac. At least I can now add the humble skateboard to the list of means of transport I have used, travelling up along the shoulders of the old Danube.

On the shore at Kladovo is a simple stone monument to Jewish refugees from central Europe, to whom the town offered shelter in the spring of 1940. 'In this place from January to September 1940 the only safe harbour existed for one thousand Austrian and Central European Jews, on their way to the Holy Land – all victims of the Nazis,' reads a bronze plaque. They had set out from Bratislava on boats down the Danube, trying to reach the Black Sea, then cross through the Bosphorus and the eastern Mediterranean to Palestine. When the authorities prevented them from continuing their journey, the Federation of Jewish Communities found extra boats for them to stay in, moored to the shore in Kladovo. Eventually 207 immigration certificates were issued for Palestine, for young people aged fifteen to seventeen. They were able to continue their journey by train, through Yugoslavia, Greece, Turkey, Syria and Lebanon, in March 1941.[29] The following month the Germans occupied Yugoslavia, and all the others were killed in, or on the way to, concentration camps. There was just one survivor. In the autumn of 1944, as the Soviet Black Sea fleet sailed up the Danube, the retreating Germans sank all 130 of their naval ships in lines across the Danube, to slow the Soviet advance.[30] Most were removed, but one appeared from the depths in the summer of 2003, during the same drought which caused such problems at the Cernavodă nuclear power station in Romania.[31]

On the car radio, the Serbian singer Djordje Balašević is singing a ballad about the break-up of Yugoslavia. 'We don't look each other in the eyes any more,' he croons, 'we just look at one another's car registration-plates.'[32] The letters displayed used to indicate exactly where the car was registered, and as republic after republic slipped into war in the 1990s, this information could be a matter of life and death, letting you know if those coming at speed towards you were likely to be friend or foe. The post-war number plates in Bosnia were carefully designed to be neutral so that it was impossible to guess where the vehicle came from.

In Mosna, a tiny hamlet on the creek where the Porečka flows into the Danube, Vitomir Marković tells the story of how one famous local veteran of the partisan struggle in the Second World War refused to leave his home as the waters rose after the building of the dam. He climbed on to his roof with his twelve children and raised the Yugoslav flag. The problem was all the more delicate for the authorities as Marshal Tito himself had been his *kum*, the best man at his wedding. 'After two days, they persuaded them all to come down, into a boat,' Vitomir remembers. 'They were given a big new house in Donji Milanovac. Nothing was too much for them.' Vitomir came to the area in 1962 as town clerk, and has stayed ever since. He has an album of black-and-white photographs, including one of himself in the early 1960s, with six other men and four children, posing with a huge beluga sturgeon, as long as a man, on the grass in front of them.

The Danube is silver green here, almost velvet in texture, and the wooded slopes reach right down to the water. Early the next morning as I swim in the Porečka a fairy mist hovers just over the surface. Smoke rises from the woods – the sign of charcoal burners at work. A German yacht, nine metres long with a family on board, is moored in the creek, its mast stepped. They are long-distance travellers like myself, and there's a bicycle secured in the bow. We drive up a road of zig-zag bends to Miroč, high on the hill overlooking the Danube. On the far bank there are glimpses of the two surviving towers of Cetății Tricole standing out of the water. Pink dog roses and bright yellow rattle decorate the roadsides. The road plunges deeper into dense forests, and it is hard to believe that it will ever reach the village. But at last it does, and we sit down to drink coffee in the main square. It's Saturday morning, and what looks like a wedding tent is being put up behind the village restaurant. It is no wedding, however, but the rare visit of one of the sons of the village who has made good in the wide world and is now staging a gathering of all his friends and family from far and wide.

I wanted to come to Miroč to hear the story of the legendary Serbian hero Marko Kraljević. Casual questioning of the people milling around the square leads me to Momir Plavi, a forest worker. He knows the story best. We stand in the shade of the 'wedding tent' and he begins his tale.

'Marko Kraljević and Miloš Obilić were good friends, and were drinking together one night here in the village inn. Now Miloš liked to drink a lot of wine, and when he began to drink he always began to sing. "Don't sing so loud," Marko said to Miloš, "because the fairies will hear you and they will get angry." But Miloš wouldn't listen, and, soon enough, the furious fairies arrived and struck Miloš dead. Marko saw what happened, and jumped on his legendary horse, Sarac – meaning dappled – to chase after the fairy who had killed his friend. At long last he caught her, and forced her to gather mountain herbs and make a concoction to heal his friend's wounds. And that is how Marko Kraljević brought Miloš back to life.' According to another version of the same story, Marko talks Miloš into singing as they ride their horses over Miroč mountain, against his better judgement – he well knows the *Vila* (fairy) Ravijojla will be jealous of his beautiful voice. But Marko persuades him, Miloš starts singing, then Marko falls asleep in the saddle and the fairy starts singing along with him – and kills him out of jealousy. Both versions end in the same way with Miloš restored to life.[33] 'Do you know what herbs she used?' I ask Momir. He lists four or five, but the only name I recognise and can find later in my *Dictionary of Weeds of Eastern Europe*, is *kantarion*, common St John's wort.[34] The others names include words which sound like *itricaz* and *podubica*.

'Are there still fairies in these hills?' I ask Momir.

'No! The real fairies have all gone, only fake ones remain.'

'Why did they leave?'

'Long ago they lived here and ruled this part of the land. No one knows why one day they went away.' Afterwards he adds in hushed tones – as the square is filling up, ready for the afternoon's festivities – that they 'may still be here somewhere, but they don't show themselves any more'.

'Did you ever see them yourself?'

'Just once,' he affirms, 'in a dream. They were dancing round and round in an opening in the forest. And do you know what?' He pauses for effect. 'They were all wearing beautiful blue dresses – just like Gypsy girls!'

On our way down the labyrinthine slope we visit the brick hives of the charcoal-burners. I've seen them before, in Greece and in Hungary, where the beechwood pile is designed to burn right through. Here they have permanent structures of brick, in the same, beehive shape. The charcoal-burners themselves are absent, but an enormous ferocious dog appears from nowhere and starts bounding towards us, as if in slow motion. At the last moment the rope tied to his collar pulls him back.

Fifteen kilometres from the mouth of the Porečka, the Lepenski Vir site has been recreated above the water level, under a huge steel and glass hangar. The dome overhead gives it a slightly Disneyland feeling, but the walk there is pleasant, across a meadow ringed by beautifully restored whitewashed houses and through a wood. The houses were moved here from their original site on Poreč Island, which, like Ada Kaleh, was lost under the waters of the dam. 'What was special about Lepenski Vir was that people lived here without interruption for two thousand years,' says Dragan Provolović, the man in charge. Their view across the Danube must have been similar to the one today, of the remarkable outcrop of stone opposite, known as the Big Rock. While the people in most prehistoric societies lived in houses of the same size, with no apparent social difference, here some houses stand out from the others. Young men work barefoot and shirtless on the site in the heat, carefully placing each stone exactly as it was found. As an attempt to make archaeology accessible to mass tourism, it is bold. But I would rather look at the photographs in the books, gaze on the faces of the fish-gods in the museum, and walk along the shore to get back into the mind of those who once lived here. 'Danubius' himself, his yellow sandstone head contrasting with the reddish-grey stone of the earth where he now rests, looks out over the whole site. Even his mouth seems to be drooping more than usual.

Far below on the river, the Osijek barge from Croatia pushes its rusting brown load downstream. One stone not on display here, the most interesting find of all, is wrapped in tissue in the vaults of the Serbian National Bank in Belgrade, pending the completion of more than a decade of renovation. A brownish, spherical stone, with holes drilled at either end, it is inscribed with letters resembling Ks, Xs, Vs and Ys. According to the Italian archaeologist Marco Merlini, 'the possible usage of this object includes use in divination or for keeping records relating to important cyclical events. If the signs inscribed on the stone from Lepenski Vir were used for divination, they are perhaps the oldest example of writing used for this purpose.'[35] Merlini's database for the Danube script contains over four thousand signs, taken from more than eight hundred objects

– figurines, clay pots, utensils and stones. The area where they were found covers parts of eleven modern countries, from Hungary to Greece. All appear to have been produced between six and eight thousand years ago. Whether or not they constitute a writing system is bitterly disputed by experts, and no one has yet advanced an attempt at translation. This leaves everyone who comes into contact with them the space to dream. And Marija Gimbutas's dream is the boldest so far – the mythical city of Atlantis, an advanced civilisation that slipped away without trace into the ocean, might instead refer to the civilisation of the Lower Danube. If so the remarkable Minoan culture found on the island of Crete was actually an outpost of Danubian civilisation.[36]

CHAPTER 8

River of Fire

The Ottomans were reputedly astonished at the appearance of a
Russian fleet in the Dardanelles in 1770, and made a formal protest to
the Venetians for allowing the Russians to sail from the Baltic
to the Adriatic Sea, alluding to a channel connecting the two,
sometimes represented on medieval maps but, of course, non-existent.
The Muslim Discovery of Europe, BERNARD LEWIS[1]

THE MUSCULAR fortress of Golubac squats on the Danube shore, the pride
of kings and sultans, its ten towers crumbling into oblivion. The castles
at Golubac, Ram and Smederevo are like studs on the soldier's belt of the
Danube below Belgrade. In wealthier, better organised countries, these would
be jewels to which domestic and foreign tourists would flock for a taste of
worlds gone by. Instead, the Danube shore in Serbia is neglected, the glory of
ageing anglers, kids swimming in their underpants, and locals who either
cannot afford to follow the caravan to the Adriatic coast each summer – or
who have fallen so deeply in love with the secret folds and fronds of this
inland river that they cannot imagine a day or night away from her. There are
exceptions: the annual catfish competition in Tekija, the sailing regatta each
August on the Danube at Golubac, and the handsome site of Viminacium
above the river, where the Roman forces massed to march through the
Danube gorge to defeat Decebal in the year AD 101, all draw the crowds.

Golubac gets its name from the Serbian word *golub* or the Hungarian
galamb, meaning 'dove'. 'Dove-house' is an unexpectedly peaceful name for

a town with such a martial history. The association with doves goes back to the very beginnings, in the sixth century AD when the Byzantine emperors rebuilt a Roman stronghold to protect themselves from the raids of the Huns and Goths.[2] Most of the ten towers of the main fortress are square, built before the age of firearms made rounded towers necessary. The lower, octagonal tower, the most recent, was built by the Turks in 1480, against the Hungarian armies, which developed a habit of re-taking their own castles. The tower appears low because most of it is underwater – the river level here is raised by the Iron Gates dam. The Babakaj rock protrudes from the mid-stream of the river. Medieval garrisons used to tie a heavy chain from the ramparts to Babakaj both to prevent hostile ships passing and to extract customs duties from friendly ones.

The main road beside the Danube passes through a tunnel drilled in the sheer rock, in at the southern end and out again at the north. A family with lots of children is shepherded through, girls in hot pants pose for photographs on the rough walls, and Zawisza Czarny – the Black Knight – oversees the fountain dedicated to his memory at the far end. A Polish soldier and diplomat, he first served King Władysław II, then King Sigismund of Hungary, and his name became a byword for bravery and reliability. The 'Black' in his name comes from his long black hair and black armour, neither of which is done justice by his bronze plaque, which shows him in profile, instead emphasising the fine jut of his beard and the ornate plumes sprouting from his helmet.[3] After a glorious career winning tournaments against the most renowned knights of Europe, he was killed in battle against the Turks at Golubac, protecting the retreat of Sigismund's forces by boat across the Danube when he ignored the king's order to save himself. 'In Golubac, his life was taken by the Turks in 1428, the famous Polish knight,' reads the inscription, in Polish and Serbian, 'the symbol of courage and honour, Zawisza the Black. Glory to the hero!' In her own humorous way, Nature pays tribute to him, raining a constant supply of juicy black mulberries onto the monument. The water from the spring is cool and metallic on the tongue. We fill our bottles and carry them down for a picnic on the shore. The Black Knight's armour is still preserved at the Jasna Góra monastery in Poland, where the Black Madonna of Częstochowa, her face scarred, bestows blessings on her pilgrims.

We sleep in a rudimentary campsite on the Danube shore near Brnjica. Sitting under a willow in the early morning, the wind suddenly picks up; sending dark cat's-paws spinning across the water. At seven in the morning the *Mercur 306* barge heads downstream, bound for Galați. A boy comes down to fish in the river while his girlfriend washes her hair with shampoo in the shallows. He speaks slowly, patiently to her, as though he is explaining the ancient art of fishing. I shut my eyes to hear the wind in the willows, the fizz of his line snaking through the air, the spin of his spool and the splash of the weight hitting the water, far out in the river. He opens a can of beer. She ties up her hair. Birds call to each other across the water. Even the patches on the Danube here look like a script.

I have two interpreters on this leg of the journey. Lola, a Bosnian Serb from Sarajevo, in whose battered, Bosnian registered car we are travelling, and Lacka, a Hungarian from Subotica, a maker and mender of violins, guitars and flutes. Silhouetted against the water, smoking his pipe, Lacka looks very much like Zawisza the Black – without the helmet.

One evening in a fish restaurant, Lola takes two sticks down from the wall and demonstrates how they are used to catch catfish. 'You beat on the surface of the water like this . . .' he says, drumming on the table and making the wine glasses and plates jump. The Hungarians have a special word for this stick, the *putyagató*, while the Serbs call it a *buchka*. The sound it makes in the water is an imitation of what large catfish do with their tails, to call to others to come and eat.

Both men were caught up in the Yugoslav wars of the 1990s, in rather different roles. By candlelight, sipping white wine, Lacka tells his story. 'My grandfather taught me to repair fishing nets as a child, with a big needle. He lived in a little thatched house with an earth floor, with no electricity, just petroleum lamps. I remember going up into the attic of that house in July, in the heat. The dust rose slowly, through the shafts of sunlight. You had to tread carefully, as if you were on the bottom of the sea. I can still smell that attic, the dust, the dry wood, the wooden basins to wash clothes in, or mix bread. And the boxes with bars that we used to put into the river, like cages, to catch the fish. I can remember the creak of each of the wooden stairs . . . My grandfather married a girl from Zenta, on the Tisza [a tributary of the Danube that joins the river north of Belgrade] . . . My master, Lajos Dudás, was very strict, well educated, very aware of his Hungarian national culture,

1 Mile or Kilometre Zero, from which the length of the Danube is measured: the lighthouse at Sulina.

2 Leaving Sulina with Adrian Oprisan, towards Crisan and Karaorman.

3 In the heart of the Danube delta, on the way to harvest reeds near Crisan – from Adrian Oprisan's boat.

4 Aunty Nicolina was not at home, but Uncle Simion was. 'I never could stand fish.' Outside their house in Sulina.

5 The Glykon in the National History and Archaeology Museum at Constanţa: the head of a lamb, the ears of a man, body of a serpent, and the tail of a lion – like the Danube.

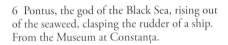

6 Pontus, the god of the Black Sea, rising out of the seaweed, clasping the rudder of a ship. From the Museum at Constanţa.

7 The Kneeling Oak at Karaorman: keeping the Turks safely in the ground – or a place for donkeys to scratch their backs.

8 Alexander's grandmother in Karaorman: preparing a bucketful of carp to last Alexander a week at university in Tulcea.

9 The sweet waters of the Danube mingle with the Black Sea at the southern mouth of the Danube near Sfântu Gheorghe.

10 Babadag – Recep Lupu's wife and mother-in-law. 'In the Pentecostalist church, you can marry who you wish!'

11 Gypsy girl in Babadag. 'And anyway,' Regina adds, 'if we stayed at school, the boys would steal us.'

12 Mitya Alexi, fisherman in Ghindăreşti: 'In my household, money is like the Danube. It flows through our fingers!'

13 Nikita Ivan, fisherman in Ghindăreşti: unravelling a net the colour of his full beard.

14 Momi Kolev and a camel called Emir, Koloseum Circus, Ruse, Bulgaria. 'In Bulgaria…we enjoy life!'

15 Air pollution on the Romanian shore. A storm gathers over Nikopol in Bulgaria, site of the defeat of the last Crusade in 1386.

16 The Iron Gates from the water, looking upstream towards the Church Above the Water, which replaced the Church Beneath the Water.

17 Danube dawn at Eselniţa, looking downstream towards the lost island of Ada Kaleh, across the storage lake formed by the Iron Gates dam.

18 Siege damage on the water tower at Vukovar: The doves of peace have taken over Vukovar's war monument.

19 Wetlands at Kopački Rit. 'They [hunters] have to realise that now they have to move over, and make way for the nature conservers': Tibor Mikuska.

20 The monument to the Soviet liberators at Batina, Croatia. The Red Army crosses the Danube in November 1944, under the onslaught of German artillery.

21 'The best flood protection is a wide floodplain, to absorb the rising waters': snails waiting for the all-clear, after the floodwaters fell, Kopački Rit.

22 'The flood waters are already climbing the steps of the Hungarian Parliament, and are expected to peak in the capital on Sunday night.' Budapest, June 2013.

23 The Danube bend in Hungary from the stern of the *Tatabánya*, March 2010. Just seven months later, she was wrecked off the Turkish coast.

24 At the helm of the *Tatabánya*, heading upriver with the mainland on the left, Szentendre Island on the right.

25 'The best job in the world.' Hermann Spannraft at the wheel of the cable ferry, Ottensheim, Austria.

26 'I haven't eaten salmon for ten years' Josef Fischer and his fish, Rossatz, Austria. A love affair with a threatened species.

27 'I would like to look after people,' says Hava, 'because I have been through so much myself. I know how much help people need.' The Atsaeva family in Grein, Austria.

28 Hi-tech from the nineteenth century. The cable ferry at Ottensheim, one of only four left on the Danube. The ferry uses no power other than the current of the river.

29 The Inn and the Danube meet at Passau. The 'white gold' of salt was exchanged for the yellow-orange gold of wheat.

30 The tailor of Ulm: The Danube dilutes his homesickness. 'I'm glad that I live so close to a river which flows all the way to the Black Sea.'

31 The youth of Ulm. Geraldine, Erdem and Theresa. Three kids, just starting out. An image of a harmonious, modern Germany.

32 Mother Baar shows the young Danube the way to the Black Sea. The Baar is a plateau in south-western Germany, bordering the Black Forest.

and he taught me to make musical instruments. On his deathbed I sat beside him. He opened his eyes, held my hand, and said, "Son, in you my thoughts will live on." Those were his last words to me . . . I remember my first visits to the Danube as a child, at Bezdan, near Apatin. It was so huge, so wide, for me it was more impressive than the sea.'

In May 1991 when the troubles began in Croatia, Lacka, married by then, with a four-year-old daughter, was teaching at a school in Subotica. His call-up papers to report for duty as a reservist in the Yugoslav army arrived, but he just ignored them. 'The thought of war was so remote, so impossible. But then the brother of a friend came back from Croatia, badly wounded. He said Hungarians were fighting other Hungarians – on the Croatian side. Only then did I start to get frightened. Then I heard other stories, that our own army killed those of its own soldiers who didn't want to fight . . . I was happy when I watched the big demonstrations in Bosnia, against war. The people of Bosnia were the most peaceful in the whole of Yugoslavia. Then another letter came, a reminder. I was just coming down the stairs at the school where I taught one day, when I saw two military police in uniforms with white bands round them. I heard voices and my name mentioned, and the secretary of the school saying I had gone. I climbed out of a ground floor window and got away. I didn't tell anyone, not even my wife and daughter. I packed my tools and a few clothes, and started cycling towards the Hungarian border. The green border seemed a bad idea, and so did the nearest crossing, Tompa, because it was too quiet. So I cycled to Röszke, about thirty kilometres away. That was good because I knew there was not a big distance between the Yugoslav and Hungarian border posts, unlike at Tompa – in case they tried to shoot me. Then I got lucky. I handed my passport to the border guard, through a little window. He started searching to see if my name was on the list of those called up who were banned from leaving the country. Just at that moment another policeman came into the office, and they got into a big argument with each other. So they didn't see me put my hand through the window, take back my passport, and start cycling for dear life towards Hungary, until it was too late [to stop me].' Apart from his tools, he carried two books, the Bible and *Lord of the Rings*. He cycled all the way to Budapest and bought himself a map with the last of his money in Tobacco Street, behind the big synagogue. Within a few days he found work with a violin maker.

That evening we sleep on the balcony of a guesthouse in Vinci, opposite the island of Moldova Veche. The Danube flows directly from north to
south here. The house is in a pinewood at the end of a sandy road. The
smell of the pines, their scent melting in the summer night, is the smell of
the south, but the sight of the trees is of the north, a foretaste of the pines
of the Black Forest at the end of my journey.

Before Veliko Gradište the Danube bends again, to flow from west to east.
The road runs along an embankment, built for flood protection. I stop to
talk to an old woman, sitting on a stool in a little shelter built of branches,
keeping a watchful eye on a herd of black-and-white cows grazing on the
floodplain. She has a blue and grey headscarf, a face so brown and wrin-
kled I'm not sure if her eyes are open or not, and wears an old green jumper
despite the July heat. The man who owned the cows has died, she says,
in a matter-of-fact way. His funeral is taking place that very day. She
volunteered to look after his cows until the family decides what to do
with them.

A barge passes upstream with a load of new cars from the Dacia-Renault
factory at Piteşti near Bucharest. Black cormorants sit hook-necked on the
wrecks of whole trees left bald by the Danube floods, or flap their heavy
wings, flying in straight lines low over the water. Beside them even the
seagulls seem small and peaceful. In Hungarian the word for cormorant is
kárókatona. *Katona* means soldier, and *káró* may come from the Turkish
word for black, as in Karaorman, the village in the Danube delta, or
Karadeniz, the Black Sea. The Serbian bank here is flat, but the last corner
of Romania, on the far side of the Danube, is rich with light green hills,
dotted with dark patches of trees.

Radislav Stokić has been working on the Danube for fifty-five years, and
he's not yet finished. He wears a straw hat with a green rim and a green
band, and a chequered shirt with a black collar. The boat he has just bought
sits silently in the harbour at Ram. It's a barge with a black hull, dark blue
amidships, a bridge bristling with aerials, speakers and spotlights, and bright
white cabins in the stern, and no name. She is eighty-five metres long and
ten metres across. In his seventieth year, Radislav is starting a new line: a gas
station, for ships up and down the river between Zemun and Borča. 'This is
the biggest boat I've ever bought. All she needs now is a name, and some

fuel tanks.' He's found a niche in the river fuel market, he reckons. 'We'll
have a crew of three or four, moor her on the side of the river, and get down
to business. At the moment there are only three places to fill up on the
whole 240 kilometre Serbian stretch of the river, at Belgrade, Novi Sad and
Kladovo. His boat is going to fill that niche. He has worked all his life on
barges, going up and down river, except for three years in Libya. First with
his father, then alone. He knows everything about machinery, about stone
quarrying, and about boats. He can't imagine any other life. When the Iron
Gates dam was being built, he used to ship stone for it from the quarry at
Golubac. 'We carried the stone for the roads on the shore, and for the dam.
We built everything . . .' he says. Didn't the dam do a lot of damage? It did,
he admits. Especially on the far shore, at Stara Palanka. The river level used
to be six metres lower here. A lot of good agricultural land was lost. He and
his son are involved in bridge repairs and building now. After NATO
bombed the Serbian bridges in the spring of 1999, he got a lot of work
rebuilding them. He has two boats with cranes that he hires out, 'the biggest
in Serbia,' he says proudly. One is 419 tonnes, and especially designed for
building bridges. 'Now we look to the Chinese. Just yesterday I signed a
contract with them, for the new terminal in Kostolac.' The Chinese also
have a plan to build a new bridge, right over the Danube. Another firm is
bidding for the same work, but he's confident he can win the contract.

We sit drinking coffee together in a bar in Ram harbour, until the ferry
arrives from Palanka – the *Javor*, a little tug boat, pulling a metal platform
across the river with just four or five cars and trucks, and a cluster of
passengers. Up on the hill above Ram, the old Ottoman fortress is tucked
away behind a row of private houses, with square towers like those at
Golubac, but smaller, a hilltop fortress rather than one guarding the shoreline. Some of the windows are fluted, with beautiful brickwork around the
inside in the Turkish medieval style. One window opens onto the vast
flooded Danube like a keyhole I peep through. The river turns silver in the
afternoon sunlight. The barge pushing upriver is a small, black scratch on
the all-silver surface. The inside of the fortress is overgrown with grass and
wild flowers. The Turks took the key to the keyhole with them, and the
Serbs seem unsure what to do with their heritage. On the way back to our
guest house in Vinci, I spot the old lady we met on our way, driving the
cows down river, up to their bellies in the water.

The wedding at Smederevo is just getting under way when we walk into Saint George's square. The bride floats across the paving stones, radiant in her white dress, her blonde hair frothing like wheat beer, a tight bodice emphasising her slim figure. Her train is held by three tiny bridesmaids, each prettier than the next. She carries a bouquet of red and white flowers. I'm less sure of the bridegroom. Something about his dark red tie mounted with a brooch, the cut of his suit, the angle of his shoes, and the dark glasses which hide his eyes, makes me feel that this is not a man I would like to buy a used car from. But fortunately I don't have to, and can enjoy his wedding day instead. A gorgeous dark red open-top Jaguar stands ready to sweep the happy couple to their perfect honeymoon. A girl who resembles the bride enough to be her younger sister, her long blonde hair falling over her salmon pink frock, dances to the five-piece Gypsy band. The Gypsies are perfectly turned out in black ironed trousers and matching mauve shirts – a drummer, two horns, and two trumpets. The music is rollicking, like a small boat on a big sea in an Emir Kusturica movie.[4] Even one of the pageboys, no more than five years old, is wearing dark glasses. A beggar, his bare feet exposed to reveal toes twisted cruelly upside down, hobbles among the elegant guests, seeking alms. In the doorway of his church, the young priest waits, smiling at first, but increasingly nervous for the pagan revels to end and the service to begin. He fingers a large bronze cross of the sort that used to be thrown into the Danube for the kids to dive for on feast days and win humble prizes. The sun beats down on the square and the Gypsies offer one last rousing chorus, to usher the congregation through the doorway.

To reach the fortress of Smederevo from the town, you walk towards the river, and cross a maze of rusting railway tracks. My first impression of the fortress is of a row of teeth, from which the middle ones have been knocked out by a powerful blow. That blow came in June 1941, when a vast store of munitions brought in by the German army exploded. Not just the fortress but the whole town was devastated. Shrapnel from the explosion landed up to ten kilometres away, and 2,500 people were killed. The fortress withstood the many sieges of its history better than it withstood the many marriages. The Serbs fought against the Turks at the battle of the Field of Blackbirds in Kosovo in 1389, but with the Turks against the Hungarians at the first battle of Nikopolis seven years later, in 1396. This is conveniently forgotten by Serbian historians, who interpret the Kosovo battle as the beginning of 'five centuries under the Turkish yoke'. In fact, Serbs, Romanians, Bulgarians and Hungarians fought as often with as against the Turks, as the Ottoman empire expanded into south-eastern Europe. Excellent soldiers, the Turks were initially valued as temporary allies in east European power struggles.[5]

Serbia in the early fifteenth century was a buffer state between the powerful Hungarian kingdom to the north and the growing Turkish dominions to the south and east. Smederevo, Ram and Golubac were right on the frontier. In 1403 the Serbian despot Stefan Lazarević became a vassal of the Hungarian king, and received Belgrade from the Hungarians as a reward. In 1426 his successor, Durad Branković, had to hand the city back to the Hungarians, and began to build his new capital at Smederevo. The borders of Serbia have wandered considerably, sometimes as far south as Macedonia, but only since 1918 as far north as Vojvodina, traditionally under Hungarian rule. The fortress was finished in 1439, all twenty-five towers, twenty-five metres high, in a triangular shape at the confluence of the Jezava and Danube.

Branković's younger daughter Katarina was married to Ulrich II of Celje, a close ally of the Hungarians, at a ceremony within the fortress walls in 1434. A letter from Sultan Murad II arrived soon afterwards, asking for the hand of his elder daughter Mara. It would have been churlish, and probably unwise, to have refused. She set out for Bursa, the then Ottoman capital, the same autumn. That marriage won the Serbs five years of peace. In June 1439 a massive Turkish army, 130,000 strong, attacked Smederevo. But Branković had wasted no efforts in preparation for his sons-in-law, and his fortress initially withstood the attack, despite a Hungarian refusal to come to relieve the siege. However, in August hunger drove the fortress commanders, Branković's sons Grgur and Stefan, to surrender. They were sent to Anatolia and blinded, despite their sister's attempts to save them. The fortress and the two blind princes were returned to Serbia under the terms of the Treaty of Szeged. In 1449 Branković imprisoned the Hungarian regent János Hunyadi in the dungeons of Smederevo, until his countrymen paid a heavy ransom. Seven years later, Hunyadi came to the aid of the Serbs, and raised the siege of Belgrade from the Turks. Just to keep a foot in all camps, Hunyadi married his own daughter to Mehmed the Conqueror. Marko Kraljević, the Serbian champion of the weak and downtrodden, died in 1395, fighting on the Ottoman side against the Wallachians at the battle of Rovine. The church bells in Hungarian Catholic churches are still rung at noon each day to commemorate Hunyadi's victory (though not his daughter's marriage), at the suggestion of the Pope, who believed Christian Europe had been saved from the Muslim peril. It would be interesting to read a history of this period written from the perspective of these Hungarian and Serb princesses.

In 1453 Mehmed conquered Constantinople, the last Byzantine bastion. Edirne, to the west, became a centre of drum manufacture for the Ottoman armies marching north to capture the Balkans and eventually Hungary.[6]

In 1459 Smederevo fell to the Turks for the last time. A city grew within the three-metre-thick walls, and beyond, and became a major port and centre of trade and intrigue throughout nearly five hundred years of Ottoman rule.

Down on the shore a young man dressed only in swimming trunks turns his back on the past to angle for catfish and perch – *smudj* in Serbian – in the broad Danube. He used to work in the steel factory in Smederevo, which employed tens of thousands in communist times, but is now reduced to a few hundred employees. He finds it hard to believe in the latest plans to build an oil refinery here – in competition with Pančevo, just upstream. There's a sense of waiting in the town, and of weddings. The other product for which Smederevo is famous is its grapes. The *smederevka* grape produces a drinkable wine in its own right, and helped fuel the defeat of the French and Hungarian knights at Nikopolis. But its greatest glory is an indirect one. The ever-busy Durad Branković transplanted vine stock from the gentle slopes above the Danube here to his estates in Tokaj, in eastern Hungary. There they flourished on the volcanic soil to produce the sweet, world famous Tokaj *aszú* wines, 'the wine of kings', which are strongly recommended for wedding nights.[7]

The sandstone cliffs at Vinča, between Smederevo and Belgrade, betray little of their importance in European prehistory. Travelling by boat upriver, or on a weekend excursion out of Belgrade, one might be excused for thinking the cliff is mainly there for the use of sand martins. I climb up a path to the side, over a low fence, into a grassy rectangle with two solid wooden huts. The doors are locked, but through the windows I can just make out fading posters on the wall, a cardboard box on the table. Hammering on the doors and windows elicits the barking of all the dogs of the neighbourhood, but nothing else. I will have to carry on to Belgrade to find an archaeologist who can turn the key in the locked door of the mysteries of Vinča. 'The people of Vinča appeared so suddenly in the late Neolithic, around 6000 BC, it was as if they stepped off a plane,' jokes Andrej Starović. 'And when they left, nearly two thousand years later, it was as if they just got back on that plane, and left without a trace.' Wherever they came from, they brought the magic art of metalworking with them – certainly of copper, according to the available evidence, but also possibly of gold. 'In the 1950s, the old professors who discovered Vinča and Lepenski Vir laughed out loud when a young archaeologist, Boris Jovanović, claimed he had found evidence of copper mining at Majdanpek, in eastern Serbia. Fox-holes, they called them.' But the younger man has been proved correct.

The Vinča culture also produced magnificent pots, with anthropomorphic lids and shapes, and delicate and sensual figurines. The ceramic figures wear human or animal masks. The eyes are almond-shaped, with protruding noses, and usually no mouth. Some have lines incised on their bodies, suggesting clothing. 'Fox-like, with raised, elongated, almond-shaped eyes surrounded by incised lines, an exaggerated chin line ending in a pointed snout,' reads the internet catalogue entry for one figure, 'and two thick cylindrical horns or ears at the top of the head that have incised cross-bands. A diamond is incised into the brow. A rare type.'[8] Some have flattened, spade-shaped heads, with dramatic lines above and below the eyes. There are clay snakes and snake forms inside bowls. Fifteen hundred Vinča settlements have so far been identified, with a population ranging from one hundred to eight hundred in each. Taking an average of two hundred, that would make a total population of 300,000. If the average were four hundred, then the Vinča population was 600,000.[9]

Andrej Starović and I sit together in the restaurant of the Travelling Actor guest house in Skadarska, a steep cobbled street which is the nearest Belgrade gets to the smells and tastes of Sarajevo, the Ottoman gift to the Balkans. Andrej looks young for an archaeologist, with his hair tied back in a pony tail, and shoulders that suggest physical strength rather than bookish knowledge. The pots produced by the Vinča people had lids in the form of human and animal faces, with the ears of cats, the eyes of owls, and human noses.

'When Professor Miloš Vasić excavated Vinča in the 1930s, he assumed that it was a successor civilisation to the Starčevo, on the far bank of the Danube,' Andrej explains, 'but in fact they were just neighbours. Vinča's leaders or rulers were the Bill Gates's of their time, because they introduced a completely new technology – metalworking.' In the early years of the century, Miloš Vasić found so much zinnober, or zinobarite – an ore of mercury – at Vinča, he concluded that it was the centre of a cosmetics industry – that the red was rubbed onto the bodies of the people, onto their clay pots and figurines, and placed in the graves of their dead to symbolise blood, for the afterlife. He also uncovered many ovens, but unlike the ones used to bake bread, or fire pots, these had their floor sloping towards the mouth, and ridges built into the floor, to keep the objects heated inside in place. On Mount Avala, just above Smederevo, Vasić also discovered the seam of zinobarite which the Vinča people must have tapped. Some archaeologists concluded that the extraction of the red powder was not the purpose of the process, but the by-product. What the craftsmen were really after was mercury. And what the mercury was good for was extracting gold. This was dangerous work, because mercury when it evaporates is extremely poisonous. A Croatian archaeologist called Alexander Durrman explained the fact that all representations of people, including the figurines found at Vinča, invariably wear animal masks, and always without mouths. According to Durrman, these were not masks for elaborate religious ceremonies, but for the – equally magical – task of smelting gold. This could also explain the sites of Vinča settlements on the shores of rivers. The tributaries of the Danube, since time immemorial, have run with fine flakes of gold. Almost all Vinča settlements are on the banks of great rivers – not only the Danube but also the Sava, the Tisza and the Morava. This helps explain another of the enigmas of Vinča culture, the almost complete absence of graves. As these were rivers that flooded regularly, forming and eroding islands all the time, most of their graves, with all the grave goods buried within them, must simply have been washed away.

If gold was the luxury item which the masters of the Vinča people excelled at producing, their everyday metallurgy was the extraction of, and work with, copper. There are several important seams of copper in the mountains of eastern Serbia, notably at Bor, and at Prokuplje. My *Atlas of Central Europe*[10] shows the largest known copper reserves in the whole of eastern Europe in a square of territory that begins just to the east of

Belgrade at Ram, stretching all the way through the Iron Gates to Vidin, and to the south as far as the city of Niš. The Copper Age, as the Late Neolithic is known, centred on the main copper seams along the Middle and Lower Danube. While the issue of gold production is still an open question, all experts agree that the Vinča people produced large amounts of copper objects. Not simply in the form of pendants, rings and necklaces, but also as knives, axes and many practical objects. Pločnik, just south-west of Belgrade, appears to have been the main copper workshop of the Vinča culture. The latest laboratory techniques help not only to date objects but also to discover where the minerals used in their manufacture came from. One of the surprises with copper goods from Vinča is that the copper came not from the mountains near Bor, but rather from Mount Kopaonik in southern Serbia, on the border with Kosovo.

The other important product of the Vinča culture is salt. The salt mine near Tuzla in Bosnia is two hundred kilometres to the west of Vinča. Salt from there may have been brought overland, but was most likely transported on dug-out boats down the Sava river. This is the only edible salt in the whole of the eastern Balkans, the evaporated remains of a lake left behind when the Pannonian Sea receded, sixty million years ago. Another Vinča anomaly is directly connected to salt. 'From the beginning of the Neolithic in nearly every culture, there is a steady fall in the amount of hunted animals in the people's diet, as the proportion of meat from domesticated animals – pigs, sheep and cattle – rises. But in Vinča, exactly the opposite happens!' said Andrej. Studies of the bones found in Vinča settlements suggest that the proportion of game, red deer in particular, increased over time. One study shows that a single settlement at Petnica, west of Belgrade, with eight to ten houses supporting around forty to fifty people, produced an astonishing seventeen tonnes of game in one year – far more than they would have needed for their own use. A lot of salt is necessary to preserve meat, although the salt can be reused several times. With the help of the salt from Tuzla, the meat was traded hundreds of kilometres up and down the Danube, Sava, Morava, and Tisza rivers. Pločnik covered 120 hectares, and supported a population of up to five thousand – one of the biggest settlements in the whole of Europe at that time. The north of the area was completely given over to copper-smelting ovens – like an industrial estate on the edge of a modern city. The technology used to hunt and kill the deer is easily traced. There were three main sources of obsidian flint in Europe in the Copper Age: the island of Milos in the Aegean, the hill at Tokaj in Hungary and the island of Lipari off Sicily.[11] Modern dating techniques study the strontium particles in flint, which vary in the natural rock in each of the three sites. Each obsidian arrowhead can now be traced back, at the laboratory of nuclear physics in the Buda hills in Hungary, to one of those three sites. And the Vinča arrowheads studied so far all came from Tokaj in Hungary, four hundred kilometres away, first down the Tisza, then the Danube. Salted red deer killed in the hills overlooking the Danube were traded for more obsidian flint, to hunt more deer.

The question of possible literacy is the hardest of the many Vinča nuts to crack. 'However fragile the documentary bridge may seem today between the decay of writing in the Danube civilization and the earliest documentation of Linear A signs in Minoan Crete around 2500 BC, the time gap is not so dramatic as to exclude a historical relationship by means of cultural memory between these two traditions of script use,' wrote Harald Haarmann, of the Institute of Archaeomythology in California.[12]

Andrej himself is not completely convinced. 'I'm pretty sure that the Vinča system of signs was a kind of very structured and strict written communication. But whether we can call it an actual "script" or not is less important.' If one accepts that these are written signs, what might they have been meant to communicate, and to whom? 'My research as an archaeologist shows clearly that almost 90 per cent of the objects with signs found so far came from the context of everyday domestic life, from the interior of houses. From garbage pits, and not from graves, or from sanctuaries, or from ritual places. That is not so easy to explain.' Why the great Danubian civilisations of the Copper Age died out is as big and as enigmatic a question as how they arose, and from whence. Once again, modern research is turning some of the old theories on their heads. 'The way our teachers explained the end of Vinča was the following. Vinča as the capital started to decline, so all the other settlements inevitably followed. We now believe that the Vinča settlement near Tuzla, and the salt mines that were so central to their ability to export meat, were destroyed *first.*' The loss of salt may have been the killer blow for the Vinča people. 'The attackers came from the north, from the Hungarian plain. For the first time in my research on Vinča, I saw real evidence of battle, of destruction in war. A lot of arrow heads, burnt houses, even a skeleton, left where the body fell. Then, nearby, evidence of a settlement of a completely different people – the victors.'

Skadarska Street intersects with Francuska Street in Belgrade, home to the Serbian Writers's Union and a restaurant with traditional Serbian food. The nineteenth-century villa is a well-established nest of nationalists and communists. You reach the entrance down the side of the building. In March 1999 I came here one evening with some fellow reporters. Entering the hallway, a staircase spirals down into a murky restaurant in which the brightest objects are the perfectly starched, almost fluorescent white shirts of the waiters, floating between the tables like fireflies. The gloom allows those who have been sitting here for hours a chance to survey each new arrival at their leisure, before they are identified themselves. As we reached the bottom of the steps, an elderly woman shrieked across the room: 'Simpson is here, war is . . inevitable.' The tall man at my side, the easily recognisable figure of the BBC's chief foreign affairs correspondent John Simpson, froze in mid-step as if he had been hit by a sniper's bullet.

'Who is that woman?' John asked me.

In the ebbing darkness, I recognised the fragile figure of Dessa Trevisan, the doyenne of the foreign press corps in Belgrade and a long-serving correspondent for the London *Times*.[13] I whispered her name.

'Oh, Dessa, how are you?' he asked, and went and sat on the arm of her chair. The broken fabric of the hubbub rapidly healed. Plates of fiery red paprika baked in olive oil and stuffed with sheep's cheese bounced from the tables, hurled down by waiters who identified us as the enemy, but who were determined to maintain the tradition of Serbian hospitality to the bitter end. During the war in Bosnia, if you failed to drink enough plum brandy with the gun-toting thugs on the roadblocks, you could be killed on the spot for that reason alone. Serbia is a nation of Boy Scouts. If there's no fire, no alcohol, no meat roasting on the spit, the men get bored very easily.

Dessa Trevisan was right. A few evenings later we watched NATO missiles rain down on Batajnica, the base of the Yugoslav Air Force just outside Belgrade, and on the bridges over the Danube. The waiters of the Writers' Union, like many of their compatriots, spat fire and fury that their Second World War allies had turned against them so cruelly, so incomprehensibly.

And we were holed up in the luxury of the Hyatt Hotel, just across the Sava river in New Belgrade, being bombed by our own airforce.

The strategic importance of Belgrade, at the confluence of the Sava and the Danube, is best appreciated from Kalemegdan, the fortress on the headland overlooking both rivers. In November 1990 I came to Belgrade for the first time, hoping for an interview with President Slobodan Milošević. Vladimir Stambuk, one of his minions in the Socialist Party of Serbia, met me instead. We drank freshly squeezed orange juice in the socialist headquarters in the same drab skyscraper across the river which would later be the target of NATO airstrikes. Milošević was in no way responsible for the impending collapse of Yugoslavia, the suave Stambuk explained – the leaders of the other republics, of Croatia, Slovenia, Bosnia-Hercegovina and Macedonia, were to blame.

Josip Broz Tito, the partisan leader who had defeated German forces in numerous skirmishes in the Second World War and became president of the new Yugoslavia in 1945, died of old age in 1980. He kept this disparate empire of feuding nationalities and interest groups together for so long by skilfully playing each off against the others. Without Tito there to pull the strings, every nationality set off in its own direction. Milošević offered to restore to the Serbs, as the largest nation in Yugoslavia, what many felt – especially members of the nationalistically minded Writers' Union – was their rightful position as 'first nation'. This kindled the desire of other peoples, reluctant to live under Serbian domination, to leave the federation. First Slovenia and Croatia in 1991, then Macedonia and Bosnia in 1992, Montenegro in 2005 and Kosovo in 2008 jumped ship with varying degrees of bloodshed.[14]

In 1915, another foreign correspondent, John Reed of the *New York Times*, found himself crawling over Kalemegdan, to get a better view of Austrian positions. 'From the edge there was a magnificent view of the muddy Danube in flood, inundated islands sticking tufts of tree tops above the water, and the wide plains of Hungary drowned in a yellow sea to the horizon. Two miles away, across the Sava, the Austrian town of Semlin (Zemun) slept in radiant sunlight. On that low height to the west and south were planted the invisible threatening cannon. And beyond, following southwest the winding Sava as far as the eye could see, the blue mountains of Bosnia piled up against the pale sky. Almost immediately below us lay the broken steel spans of the international rail bridge which used to link Constantinople to western Europe – plunging prodigiously from their massive piers into the turbid yellow water. And up-stream still was the half sunken island of Tzigalnia, where the Serbian advance-guards lay in their trenches and sniped the enemy on another island four hundred yards away across the water. The captain pointed to several black dots lying miles away up the Danube, behind the shoulder of Semlin.

"Those are Austrian monitors," he said. "And that low black launch that lies close in to shore down there to the east, she is the English gunboat. Last night she stole up the river and torpedoed an Austrian monitor. We expect the city to be bombarded any moment now. The Austrians usually take it out on Belgrade."[15]

The military museum on Kalemegdan is defended from the elements by a line of obsolete pieces of Serbian, German and Russian artillery. The first room is lined with the spears and helmets of Thracians, Celts and Illyrians, from 1000 to 400 BC.[16] There is a good selection of Turkish weaponry from the sixteenth century, including a bow of Tatar maple, the tree much favoured by Ottoman bow-makers over the European yew. There is a muzzle-loading Austrian regimental gun, with the inscription 'I was cast by Balthasar Heroldt in Vienna, 1655'. And a display case with the title 'Weapons of the unequal opponents', with the pick axes and scythes of the Serbian peasants used during their first uprising against Ottoman rule in 1806, arrayed beside the cold, carved steel of their Turkish oppressors. Room 16 is given over entirely to 'Battles against the Turks in the seventeenth and eighteenth centuries', including a German-language map entitled 'Victorien der Christen über den Erbfeind', which translates as 'Victories of the Christians against the eternal enemy'.

In another room, the haunted features of Gavrilo Princip gaze down from the wall, the assassin of the Archduke Ferdinand and his wife in June 1914 in Sarajevo, whose shots sparked the First World War. The subsequent Austrian ultimatum to Serbia arrived at the Moskva Hotel, the smartest place in town, because the Serbian government did not yet have a telegraph machine of its own. The machine still sits proudly in a case behind the reception desk. In the museum, next to the photograph of Princip and his fellow conspirators, is an official telegram from Sarajevo – 'Execution of the verdict in the assassination case of Veljko Čubrilović, Misko Jovanović and Danilo Ilić accomplished without mishap this morning between 9 and 10.' There are also items from the two aerial bombardments of Belgrade, in the spring of 1941 by the Germans and the spring of 1999 by NATO. There are fragments in the Cyrillic script from books burnt when an incendiary bomb hit the National Library. Beside this is a photograph of the *Drava Monitor*, a ship of the Yugoslav navy, in action on the Danube near Bezdan against the invading Germans in April 1941.

From more recent wars, there's a laptop captured from the Kosovo Liberation Army on Mount Pastrik in Kosovo in December 1998, and the cheerfully yellow shells of two cluster bombs, banned under international law, dropped on the city of Niš by NATO planes in May 1999, which killed sixteen and wounded twenty-seven civilians, according to the caption. And finally the combat fatigues of a US airforce pilot named Carpenter, whose F-16 plane was shot down the same month.

Overloaded by so many mementoes of war, I stumble out into the Kalemegdan sunshine – to yet more war monuments. Ivo Meštrović's giant sculpture nurses a falcon on his left hand and a sword in his right, and gazes down on the Sava river from roughly the spot where John Reed must have crawled in 1915. Beyond the red maple trees, perhaps the descendants of those planted by the Turks, there's a stone to commemorate the feat of arms of János Hunyadi in saving Belgrade in July 1456, decorated with a fresh wreath from a primary school in Hungary. And on the far side of the hill overlooking the Danube stands a statue to the Despot Stefan Lazarević, my old friend from Golubac.

At one time the hills of cities such as Belgrade and Buda were thick with Turkish gravestones. So few remain today in either city one wonders what these particular men did to deserve the honour of their enemies, or whether it was just their good fortune, and the efforts of the Turkish authorities in later years to restore occasional reminders that their rule was not as bad as it is depicted in local history books.

One of the most interesting buildings on Kalemegdan is the hexagonal tomb of Damat Ali Pasha the martyr, killed during the battle for Petrovaradin fortress opposite Novi Sad in August 1716. There are little red ribbons tied by the Muslim faithful on the bars across the windows of the tomb against the admonitions of the imams, just as they are on the bushes around Koyun Baba's tomb at Babadag. The sunlight bursts through the bars, and gives a fleeting impression that the green-decked tomb radiates light. The Serbs won the battle for Petrovaradin, and the Turks continued their long retreat across the Balkans.

A stumpy ship called the *Dunav*, carrying what looks like fuel, pushes purposefully down the Sava, then carves a wide loop to head upriver on the Danube towards Zemun, past Great War Island. The Danube north of Belgrade is broad and sluggish, especially in summer, moving self-confidently south-eastwards, not a river to be trifled with. In Zemun, a suburb of Belgrade, a friend takes me to his favourite restaurant, right on the shore, to drink walnut brandy and white wine, and eat catfish basted with garlic, and watch the world go by. There's a canoe pulled up on the bank, belonging to a Frenchman in his seventies on his way to the delta. But the paddler himself is nowhere to be seen – stocking up on provisions in town perhaps.

Mustafa Zade, also known as Köprülü the Virtuous, was one of the better Turkish Grand Viziers of the seventeenth century, and it looked for a while as though he might reverse the decline of the Ottoman empire's fortunes. The siege of Vienna had failed utterly in 1683; Buda was lost in 1686. In 1690 Köprülü advanced at the head of a large Ottoman army and retook Niš and Belgrade. In the summer of 1691 he marched north beside the Danube from Belgrade to meet the Austrian Prince Ludwig, who came south from Petrovaradin. They met at Slankomen. Turkish superiority on the river failed to compensate for the better armed, better commanded Austrian army on dry land. A deadly barrage of musket fire met each successive Turkish charge.'When defeat appeared imminent Köprülü himself, hoping in the last resort to save the day, led a desperate charge. Calling upon Allah, he cleared his way with a drawn sword, flanked by his guards, through the ranks of the Austrians. The heroic gesture was in vain. Their ranks stood firm. He was hit in the forehead and killed by a bullet. His guards saw him fall, lost courage, and fled. His commanders, who might for a while have concealed the news of his death from the troops, broke into lamentations and allowed it to spread, thus undermining morale and creating a general panic,' wrote Patrick Kinross.[17] 'For the Ottomans, the death in battle of their last shining hope . . . was a crucial disaster. Hungary was lost to them. So . . . was Transylvania.'

Stari Slankomen shimmers in the summer haze, a clutter of red-roofed houses along the shore, and a tall church on the higher ground. Just opposite, the blond Tisza, known higher up as the black and the white Tisza, high in the Carpathians in Ukraine, flows into the Danube. The Tisza was poisoned by a spill of mercury from the gold mine at Baia Mare in Romania in January 2000. Almost all fish life along five hundred kilometres was destroyed. Some heavy metals flowed into the Danube, but the main damage was to the Tisza.[18]

In May 2011, as I travelled up the Danube, the Bosnian Serb military leader Ratko Mladić was arrested in Serbia after sixteen years in hiding. I had seen his handiwork in Bosnia and well knew the fear the families of his victims had of him, and of the adulation of his former soldiers. Unusual among officers, he always personally led his troops into battle. That meant that whenever atrocities were committed, he was never far away. In July of that year I am invited to the house where he was caught, in the little village of Lazarevo, not far from the Tisza and Danube rivers. Branko, Mladić's second cousin, sits in the shade under a mulberry tree. There's plum brandy on the table, and fizzy juice for the driver. Branko's neighbour, Nenad, is the first to speak. 'It was five o'clock in the morning. I'd just walked over to Branko's garden to water my peppers, the big red ones which we call "elephant's ears". When I looked up, there were policemen everywhere – in uniform and plain clothes. "What's up?" I asked. "Did someone die? Or are you here to buy a pig or a lamb? – Branko has both."

Neither, they replied. "We need you as a witness, for a house-search."'

Ratko Mladić was well known and well liked in Lazarevo. Many simple, rural Serbs regard him as a man who won battles, and who was on the run for sixteen years, not from justice, but from anti-Serb sentiment in the world. Atrocities like the three-year siege of Sarajevo, the shelling of civilians, and the cold-blooded killing of thousands of non-combatants at Srebrenica, tend to be either disbelieved, or quickly glossed over in such company. The more so since Mladić has many relatives in Lazarevo and, as it turns out, was a regular visitor both in his army years and since, when he was the world's most wanted man after Osama Bin Laden. In the early 2000s, Mladić even kept bees in the village. At that time, armed bodyguards stood close by, to discourage any attempt to seize him. 'Your gun is showing,' Nenad, ever the joker, told one of them at that time. 'It's meant to be showing,' the man told him, pointedly. Interestingly, the Serbian police never showed any interest in the village, fuelling theories that the state security organs knew very well where he was all those years, but chose to leave him in peace. A week before his arrest, Mladić's son Darko visited Lazarevo for the feast day of Saint George. The general was ill, his supporters had run out of money, and he was tiring of a life in hiding. The absence of commandos, and the peaceful, almost routine, nature of the whole operation, give the distinct impression that it was all arranged in advance, with Mladić's agreement.

'I am the man you are looking for,' he announced, as the police walked into his room. Seated in his track-suit, one arm limp from a stroke, the general was sarcastic, but polite to them, who seemed amazed to find their quarry here. 'Which one of you is the American?' he asked. 'Who is the one who killed my daughter?'

The suicide of his twenty-three-year-old daughter Ana in 1994 may have tipped the scales in Mladić's mind and turned him from a rational, ruthless soldier into an irrational military leader, capable of mass murder.

They found two pistols in the cupboard, American made. When the police inspector asked him about them, Mladić said one was a gift from a volunteer in the war. Mladić tried to reassure the police that he had no thought of escape or of violence. 'If I had wanted to, I could have killed ten of you, because you were just one metre from my window. But I didn't want to, because you are young people, and you are just doing your job.'

By nine that morning, Mladič was sitting in a black jeep, being driven to the War Crimes court in Belgrade. Within a year, he was on trial for genocide and other crimes against humanity at the International Tribunal in the Hague.

The police stayed on in the village, and Nenad with them. 'This all looked to me a little bit like a circus. When I see the thief caught on television, with a couple of cartons of cigarettes, there are the special police with their long-barrels, breaking down the doors and everything. But here there was none of that, I told them. But they just smiled at me. "No comment" was all they would say.'

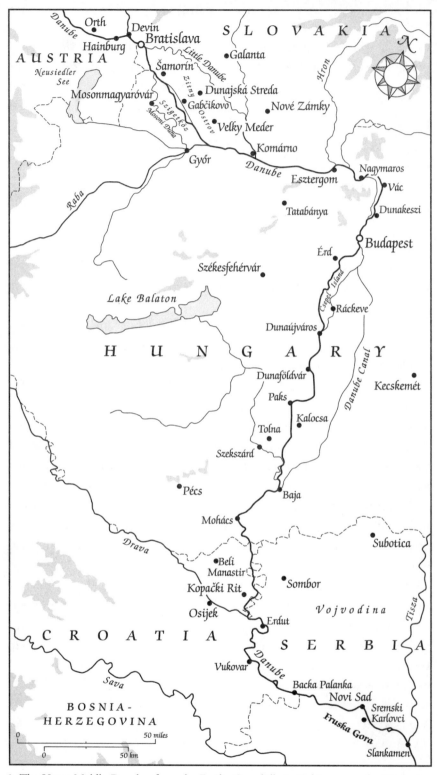

3. The Upper-Middle Danube, from the Fruška Gora hills in Serbia, across the Hungarian plains to the foot of the Carpathians in Slovakia.

CHAPTER 9

The Black Army

One fortunate morning, when the edge of the sky was tinted by the pink
of dawn's blood, when the moon turned its flag around, and the black
army rose; when the dawn showed its pink face, and a wound appeared
on it like the cut of a sword . . .

KEMAL PASHA ZADE, poet in the court of SULEIMAN the Magnificent[1]

THE CLOCK tower in the castle at Petrovaradin, the fortress on the right
bank of the Danube in Novi Sad, has four wide faces, so that those on
ships passing on the river below can always tell the time. The Danube cuts
a long, pensive meander through the city, as though uncertain whether to
stop for the night or move on. The little tower reminds me of the lighthouse in Sulina at the start of my journey. The big hand has three white
grapes, the little hand two, against the black of the clock. There's a golden
globe on the top with a weather vane, but no wind this July day to take the
edge off the summer heat. The hands hardly leave a shadow on the faces of
the clock.

The fortress on its rocky outcrop was home to the first known settlement, by a Celtic tribe. They were displaced by the Romans, who valued
the defensive possibilities of the place. The 'Petro' in the name comes from
a Byzantine bishop called Peter. In 1526 Suleiman the Magnificent
marched with his army to the decisive battle with the Hungarians at
Mohács. Taking the town, he told his Grand Vizier Ibrahim, would be
'like a snack to keep him going before breakfast in Vienna'.[2] In fact it was

not quite so easy, but when the Turkish soldiers blasted two holes in the walls by attaching mines, resistance crumbled. Five hundred of the defenders were beheaded and three hundred taken into slavery. The criteria for deciding their fate is not known. The Serbs had to wait till 1716 for their revenge, when Damat Ali Pasha was defeated by Prince Eugen of Savoy. He tried to rally his forces with a charge straight into the Austrian ranks. His reckless bravery and death were much like those of Mehmed Köprülü at the battle of Slankomen. Damat Ali did not die on the spot, however, and was carried, mortally wounded, on horseback by his troops to Karlowitz – Sremski Karlovci – and died there. In the garden of the Church of the Lower Town in Sremski Karlovci an enormous white plane tree stands, one of the oldest in Europe, planted exactly three hundred years ago when the church was built. Perhaps Damat Ali the Dauntless breathed his last in its teenage shade. Not to be outdone, the Orthodox seminary nearby boasts a magnificent yew of similar girth and vintage – the plane almost white with age, the yew dark and green and brooding.

Novi Sad is Serbia's second city, proud of edging ahead of Niš in the south, and proud above all of its position, straddling the Danube, a rich modern city, the Birmingham of the Balkans. The heat of summer, the cheap ice-cream and beer, make it lighter and brighter than Belgrade, and the agricultural wealth of the province of Vojvodina makes it the most prosperous in Serbia. In the 1960s and 1970s it became a mecca for the pop-starved youth of eastern Europe. The denim-clad teenagers of Yugoslavia had an easier time of it than those kids of Ruse who had to watch their priceless vinyl records being smashed to pieces by border guards. 'Yugoslavia became the most powerful rock'n'roll country in the region,' wrote Vladimir Nedeljković in his book *The Danube Girls and Boys*.[3] Radio Novi Sad had a powerful transmitter that reached across the satellite states of eastern Europe and deep into the Soviet Union. It broadcast first jazz, then beat music. 1964 was the turning point. 'All over Europe that year, the Baby Boom generation started to build a new world on the ruins of the history and politics of the Second World War, personified by Joseph Stalin in the East and Sir Winston Churchill in the West . . . The standard of living was high, the country was open, foreign rock magazines were available everywhere . . . So much lucidity, wisdom and goodness take place only once in a hundred years.'[4] By the end of the 1970s, the hippy culture was turning to punk, and Novi Sad had its own band, Pekinska Patka. 'Nobody had thought like that before them. No one had played like that before them. Nobody had looked like that before them.'

The dreams of the 1960s and the rude rebellion of the 1970s turned sour in the 1990s. Young men fled into exile rather than fight Slobodan Milošević's wars. Many who stayed were killed or wounded on the battle-fields of Croatia, Bosnia and Kosovo. The crowning disaster of the decade came in 1999, when Novi Sad received special attention from NATO. Three bridges over the Danube, the oil refinery and many electricity trans-formers were hit. The Varadin Bridge, constructed by German prisoners of war in 1946, was the first to fall, just before dawn on 1 April 1999, the seventh day of the air-strikes. Liberty Bridge, the most modern, completed only in 1981, was hit by three missiles on the evening of 3 April. The Žeželj bridge, built in 1961 and named after its architect Branko Žeželj, proved the most resilient. The first missile struck on the night of 20 April, but it needed another direct hit, on the night of the 25th, to knock the last twisted metal supports into the swirling Danube. There is a seventeen-second black-and-white video, posted on YouTube, of the final blow, filmed from a camera in the nose of the missile. The final frame explodes in a fuzz of black-and-white particles. One of the jokes circulating in the city immediately after the bombing was that Novi Sad was the only city in Europe where the river flows *over* three bridges.

The task of rebuilding began even before the war ended in June 1999. The Serbs wanted the West to pay for the damage, as compensation for 'the aggression'. The European Bank for Reconstruction and Development put up some of the money. Slobodan Milošević arrived at the opening ceremony on the Beska motorway bridge over the Danube. 'Dear citizens of Novi Sad, dear citizens of Vojvodina, dear bridge builders! The worst eleven weeks since World War II are behind us, in which the most brutal aggression was carried out by the largest military machinery ever created in the world.' The Beška bridge would be rebuilt within forty days, Milošević promised – the magic forty again – because its building blocks were prepared 'even while the bombs were still falling'.[5] Thirty-nine days later, traffic was rolling over Beška once again. The three bridges in Novi Sad took longer. I sat in a small motor boat filming the ruins of Liberty Bridge a few months after the war. The pilot grew increasingly nervous. The huge chunks of concrete that had fallen into the water created unpredictable whirlpools as the Danube swept over them. We had to cut the engine for me to speak into the camera. Each time I had to repeat my words the danger increased.

Up and down the river, shipping companies fumed about the unexpected interruption to their trade. The United Nations-imposed sanctions against Yugoslavia in the early 1990s had been bad enough, with sudden searches of barges by international monitors looking for oil or weapons. But now the Danube was impassable, at first because of the dangerous debris, and then on account of the temporary pontoon bridge the city authorities threw across the river to reconnect the two halves of their town. For ships to pass, this had to be opened up completely. Once a fortnight, at first, when a long queue of barges had built up, then once a week. The wine exporters of the Ruse region were just one of the injured parties. Sending their wines to their favourite markets in Britain and Scandinavia, by road or rail as opposed to ship, was adding about 20 per cent to the retail price, Danail Nedjelkov, the Bulgarian member of the Danube Commission, told me at the time. That extra cost destroyed the place they had won in the market, which they were never to win back. Wines from Chile, South Africa and California poured into the breach created by cruise missiles.

In 2001, ten years after the Serb–Croat war, I found the whole museum collection from Vukovar in the basement of the Petrovaradin museum. From shards of Neolithic pots to elegant turn-of-the-century oil paintings from the Bauer collection, they became the subject of a bitter dispute between the two countries. The Serbs said the collection had been removed for safekeeping after the siege. The Croats said the items had been looted by Serb soldiers and irregulars when they captured the town and shot the remaining population. Eventually the items were returned.

The Petrovaradin fortress has many treasures of its own: the ossified remains of a wooden Danube long-boat; ancient maps of the Danube which show the wriggling course of the river, rich in islands, before regulation straightened its back and disciplined its elbows in the nineteenth and twentieth centuries. Each successive map seems to have less islands. Evocative names such as 'war island' and 'snail island' fade from the maps, and from memory. There's an etching of Suleiman the Magnificent in

1526, on his way to victory at the battle of Mohács, and a black-and-white photograph of the *Baross* paddle steamer.

The twentieth-century history that the new generation wanted to shrug off was particularly heavy in Novi Sad. In January 1942, Hungarian soldiers and police carried out their worst atrocity of the Second World War. In an attempt to discourage partisan activity and scare the local population, several thousand Jews, Serbs and some left-wing Hungarians were rounded up and taken down to the Danube and shot. Their bodies were dumped through holes cut into the ice. When the partisans captured Novi Sad in 1944, they wrought a terrible revenge on the Hungarian population of the city and the surrounding countryside, rounding up and killing several times as many Hungarian civilians. The sad story of both massacres is told in two novels by the Hungarian author Tibor Cseres, both published in the 1960s.[6] In June 2013 the presidents of both countries met in the village of Čurug, and apologised for the autrocities of their own countrymen.

The Danube reopened fully to shipping only in 2005, six years after the bridges were destroyed.

Just to the west of Sremski Karlovci, and to the south and west of Novi Sad, the Fruška Gora hills stretch in a thin, sandy-soiled line along the Danube. In any other landscape they might draw little attention, as the highest peaks reach only five hundred metres. But in the broad plains of Vojvodina, Fruška Gora rises like Table Mountain, visible from all directions. I remember crossing the border from Hungary by car, on my way to report on the war in Bosnia, and the relief to the eyes of those hills. A host of monasteries were built here from the sixteenth to the eighteenth centuries, initially with the blessing of the Turks, then with their indifference as they lost more and more of their Balkan possessions. Since Serbia lost Kosovo, with its far more ancient and imposing monasteries, the importance of Fruška Gora as the main, accessible stronghold of the Serbian Orthodox Church has increased.

At Grgeteg monastery, I buy thick, dark honey from hives kept by the monks, and walk into the morning service. A choir of nuns sing like angels, like the young nuns I have heard at Gračanica monastery in Kosovo, and Trebinje in Hercegovina, both places scarred by war. After the morning service, I sit under the cloisters to talk to the aptly named Father

Gregor – Grgeteg is from the Serbian form of his name. The church was blessed, he says, in communist times by the relatively benign attitude of the authorities. The monastery nearby, at Vučedol, was used as a prison camp by the Nazis in the Second World War, which helped anchor the church on the side of the anti-fascists, unlike in most other countries of eastern Europe. The Croatian archbishop of Zagreb, Alojzije Stepinac, initially supported the coming to power of the Ustashe, the Croatian fascists, and offered only muted criticism of their crimes during the war.[7] He was eventually tried by the communist authorities and sentenced to sixteen years imprisonment. The Vatican responded by making him a cardinal, to Tito's fury. Gregor describes the loss of Kosovo in 2008 as 'temporary' – as impossible to bear for the Serbs as the loss of London might be for the English. I drive away from his peaceful oasis of Christian love through fields of tall sunflowers.

The following day, I turn on the radio to discover that the last of the Serbian war criminals on the run, the bearded Goran Hadžić, wanted for his role in the killings in Vukovar, was discovered, hiding just five kilometres from where we sat talking, near the monastery of Krušedol. Hadžić is accused of taking part in the cold-blooded murder of 261 patients and staff from the hospital in Vukovar, who survived the autumn 1991 siege.[8]

We stop in Ilok for coffee, to reconnect with the green waters of the river. At a café right on the shore, I befriend a young German-Croatian couple, Christian and Daria, who are cycling downriver from Vienna to Belgrade. They have the same bicycle map as mine, and assume we are cyclists too. We compare notes, and in no time my friend and companion on this stretch of the journey Lola (whose real name is Milorad Batinić) persuades them to leave the Danube at Novi Sad, put their bikes in the back of his car, and drive with him to the Adriatic coast. The two cyclists are so happy, so much in love, that they cannot keep their secret for long. A few hours earlier, on the shore of the river, Christian had proposed to Daria. She said yes.

A left turn off the main road to Vukovar, five kilometres before the city, leads past tall trees and outbuildings to Ovčara farm. The farm seems to be prospering. The sheds are packed with grain and the lower buildings filled with pigs. There are vines basking in the heat, and sunflowers and maize growing tall. This is where those taken from Vukovar hospital were killed. Many were patients from the hospital. They included a radio journalist,

Siniša Glavašević, whose reports from Vukovar chronicled the siege.[9] Some were bludgeoned to death in the hangars; the rest were taken out to a ditch by the road and shot on 20 November 1991. One of the Serb commanding officers, Viktor Šljivančanin, was sentenced to five years in prison by the War Crimes Tribunal. Goran Hadžić was a simple farm worker, accused of taking part in the killings. The white marble sculpture that stands in front of the farm building shows a jumble of body parts and bones. Inside, the floor is made of bullet cases. Photographs of the victims are displayed along the walls in the dark, with lights coming on suddenly to show their faces. There are personal items too – glasses, cigarettes, identity papers. In the centre of the room their names are projected in green light, spiralling downwards, out of sight.

The water tower of Vukovar sprouts over the town, like a tubular mushroom, growing wider at the top. It is my first water tower since Sulina, and while the one serves as the reminder of the kindness of strangers, this one is a symbol of the cruelty of neighbours. And like an old mushroom, bits are falling off it. The tower provided target practice for Serbian gunners besieging the city. It was so large, it was hard not to miss, but their guns and mortars proved incapable of anything more than chewing away at the masonry. The building has been left as a war monument, of a very different kind to the carefully crafted, pinpointed memories of Ovčara farm. It is a monument to the sheer stupidity of war. The door is locked and bolted, but, as I listen at the base, I can hear all the sounds of Vukovar – the passing buses, a child crying, boys playing football, a door slamming. The tower is an echo chamber. Then I distinguish another sound: pigeons cooing, and the sudden beat and flurry of their wings as they circle the dark interior. The doves of peace have taken over Vukovar's war monument.

The city hospital still functions as a hospital, but in the basement there is a museum devoted to its work during the siege. There are bunk beds made up, wax models of nurses, and Siniša Glavašević's young, nervous voice broadcasting the day's news. Screens have been set up with short films about the siege. There is also a hall of mirrors, with glass cases in which candles burn continually. Twelve candles become twelve hundred. My face distorts horribly in the mirror. The effect is powerful, and disturbing. But there is a flavour of war propaganda. I want to know what the Serb soldiers felt, bombing this town. I want to know if they felt any remorse. Who they were, where they went to school, if they knew the people they were attacking. And what they are doing now.

When I hear of Hadžić's arrest, I ring Kristijan Drobina, the man in charge of the memorial site at Ovčara farm. 'Probably the Serbian government felt it was the right moment to arrest him – there must be a political reason, to do so now,' he says. 'I'm pleased but I don't know how this will end. Šljivančanin was released on good behaviour after three years. That means he served just eight days in prison for each person who was killed here. They constantly try to minimise what happened at Vukovar, to turn it into a local dispute. But what happened there was ordered by the Serbian government . . .'

In January 1999 I came to Vukovar on a trip arranged by the Organisation for Security and Cooperation in Europe (OSCE). The OSCE were trying to help implement the terms of the Treaty of Erdut, which confirmed Croatian control over the whole region of Eastern Slavonia, seized by the Serbs in 1991. A key provision of Erdut, as with the accords which ended the Bosnian war in 1995, was that everyone had the right to return to their homes – Croats who had fled in 1991, and Serbs who had occupied those houses. The atmosphere was very tense – the remaining Serbs feared they would all be treated as war criminals.[10]

Jovan Njegić was collecting waste paper to sell. He earnt about eighty-seven dinars – twenty-five Deutschmarks a month – just enough to live on. He used to have a house and two shops. 'Before the war, we didn't know who was a Serb, who was a Croat here. Fifty per cent of the marriages were mixed.' He was living with his eighty-nine-year-old mother. He wept as he described taking her down into the cellar to escape the shelling. His wife and daughter went to Zagreb. All he wanted was for them to come back. He took me for a walk down the road, to see his old house. 'That was it,' he says, pointing to a gutted ruin, overgrown with bushes. 'They brought petrol and set fire to it. Look up there – you can see the bathroom! I had a shoe shop here, and a bakery. All built from good materials – just look at these bricks.' Another man wandered over to where we stood, on the edge of an open air market. It was a man with a beard, which suggested he was a Serb. 'This is the last Serb territory in Croatia – where shall we go now?' A Croat in a nearby village, Ivan Prilavić, said he stayed through the war because he couldn't bear to leave his house. What does he think of the

Serbs now, I asked. 'Some were human beings, some were not.' Wasn't he afraid for his life? 'The bullet which is meant for me hasn't been made yet,' he laughed.

Vladimir Stanimirović was the elected leader of the local Serbs in 1999. He was anxious to underline that the Croats started the war, with their mistreatment of his people. 'At the beginning of 1991, the Serbs here were arrested, maltreated and some disappeared and their homes were blown up. Serbian officials were fired on the basis of decrees passed in Zagreb. I was a psychiatrist in a hospital, and I was arrested too, and only released when decent Croats intervened. My only crime was to be Serb . . . We recognise that there were war criminals on both sides. And we support the idea of arresting them. We support the work of the Hague Tribunal.'

Jacques Klein, an American General with a French-German name who acted as governor of the region under the UNTAES (United Nations Transitional Administration for Eastern Slavonia) administration, is a big man with a big voice. He speaks in very short sentences, like a military telegram. 'Our role as the UN mission is the peaceful reintegration of the region into Croatia. Our aim is to keep the multi-ethnic character of the region. To create an atmosphere of confidence. To allow the return of refugees.' He described what happened when the phone lines were restored after the war. 'In the first 48 hours, 25,000 calls were made. The dialogue was re-established. There were also hate-calls. That's to be expected . . . People come back in buses we lay on, to see their old homes. If the situation is calm, they get off the bus, and chat with their old neighbours. Quite often what you hear is the question, "How did this happen to us? We didn't start the war. How can we have turned on each other?" An amnesty is the key. You cannot demilitarise a region without psychologically demilitarising the people. If people don't return, we're going to have a big game reserve in the centre of Europe. The mothers here deserve it. There are women walking round here with pictures of their missing sons. I want closure on this issue. We have no alternative but to help them . . . We have to stop playing the game that this is some other place. This is Croatia. These are your choices now. Negotiate with the Croatian government. Get the best possible package you can.' To finish, he gave an example from the American Civil War. 'It went on for five years. There were 600,000 casualties. At the end Lincoln said "It's over". And he was killed for it. But fortunately his policies held. Did it end the war? It didn't. But it changed the venue to an academic war, which is still fought today – the media, the flag, Alabama, Dixie . . . but its not being fought with guns. That's what they have to do here. Get over the killing part of it. Then you can keep arguing.'

Vukovar is much improved since that visit. Many houses have been repaired; you can even walk down some streets and forget there was a war here. In one of the houses near the shore, still in ruins, purple flowers burst from the frame of an upstairs window. Just after the end of hostilities, down on the Danube shore, I saw the Croatian chequerboard flag disintegrating, strand by strand in a strong wind, beating against its own flagpole. Now the Croatian flag droops beside the flags of other nations, unstirred by any patriotic wind. I sit at the table of a smart restaurant on the shore to write my report on the Hadžić arrest. Waiters scurry to and fro with a spring in their step. Yugoslav waiters could once be found all over the world – as ubiquitous and as good at their work as Albanian bakers. The style and elegance, the speed of service, and the dignity with which even the smallest tip is received, go back generations. The cranes stand blue and yellow in Vukovar port. The church towers have been repaired. Vukovar, the castle of a man known as *vuk*, meaning 'wolf', has come out of the tunnel of war. Jacques Klein's recipe for peace is being tried out in the kitchens.

The climax of the trip to Vukovar in January 1999 was a flight in a military helicopter over the region, including the Kopački Rit wetland forest. I remember the cold, the roar of the engines, the experiments I made, shouting into my microphone, to try to record something in broadcast quality, and the view – the vast expanse of frozen forest, brown and black on the white frost and ice.

In June 2012 I travelled through Kopački Rit again, a little closer to the water this time, paddling a canoe, on a trip organised by the Worldwide Fund for Nature (WWF). For the first and only time on this journey upriver, I allowed myself to be carried downriver on the current.[11] On the WWF flood-plain map, thick yellow, brown and blue lines have been drawn on a satellite map of the Hungarian, Croatian and Serbian borderland area, through which the broad Danube and its tributary the Drava river flow. The yellow lines either side of the river show the historical floodplains, 211,000 hectares wide, and include the Serbian town of Apatin, and parts of Mohács and Baja in Hungary. The area between the brown lines is like a strip either side of the Danube, much narrower than the first – the areas affected by recent floods – down to 53,000 hectares. The dark blue line indicates the meandering course of the Danube itself, and the shape of the Kopački Rit wetlands, like the outline of a seated goddess. The Croatian and Serbian governments plan to regulate another 115 kilometres of the Danube and the Drava rivers, reinforcing the banks with stones and cutting off the remaining meanders to guarantee a sufficient depth for shipping all year round. The WWF and local environmental groups argue that the ships should be adapted to the river, not the river to the ships, and that with the benefit of modern communications technology it should be possible to keep the relatively small volume of traffic on the Danube flowing, without recourse to more dams or more river regulations.

The monument to the Soviet liberators on the outcrop of rock over-looking the Danube at Batina is thirty-five metres high – a woman cast in bronze, holding in her outstretched left arm a red star. If you stand far enough away, you can see that the star is made of thick red glass. Around the base of the monument are dramatic frescoes portraying the desperate attempt of Ukrainian soldiers to cross the Danube by boat in November 1944, under constant fire from the German unit dug in on this hilltop. The Red Army had just captured Belgrade and was pushing north towards Hungary. In one frieze, a Soviet soldier is swimming alongside a landing craft in the icy waves, while his comrades stand upright firing their machine guns. With huge loss of life – at least two thousand dead – the Ukrainians succeeded in establishing a bridgehead in the wine cellars at the foot of the hill. The German defenders were only overcome when the Soviets brought up their own heavy artillery and delayed their river crossing for twenty-four hours while they pounded the hilltop. There's a recent wreath at the foot of the monument, in the blue and yellow colours of the Ukrainian flag. In the base of the monument 1,287 Red Army soldiers are buried. The Danube banks are thickly wooded on either side. On the far bank is Serbia, on the nearside, the red roofs of Batina. A red steel bridge connects the two countries. A German barge, the *Panther*, registered in Hamburg, passes, low in the water. Through binoculars, I watch the man in the bow, busy coiling a long, green rope. He doesn't look up. Coming upriver, a passenger cruiser, the *A'Rosa Riva*, has an enormous red rose painted on her white hull. I can see the outline of people, stretched out in their deck-chairs, getting used to the slow pace of river life.

Ten thousand years ago the main stream of the Danube was further east, down where the Tisza now flows. In the seventeenth century, all the land between the Drava confluence with the Danube and Mohács in southern Hungary was owned by Prince Eugen of Savoy – given him by the grateful Habsburg emperors for his military successes against the Turks. The forests became game reserves, rich in wild boar and deer, jealously guarded by their aristocratic owners, and after the Second World War by the new communist elite. Tito himself came here to hunt with his friends. At that time the forests were administered by the Forestry and Hunting authorities of the regional councils, strictly under Communist Party control. Since the return of democracy, environmental pressure groups and the national park authority compete with the hunters and foresters. 'They have to realise,' said Tibor Mikuska, of the Croatian Society for the Protection of Birds and Nature, 'that now they have to move over, and make way for the nature conservers.'[12]

The border itself is a new problem. As Croatia joins the European Union in 2013, while Serbia stays out for a few more years, it will be Croatia's task to reinforce this section of the twenty-eight-member bloc's new external border. The obvious technical solution would be to beef up both banks. 'That would be a disaster,' says Tibor. The more ecologically friendly solution, he suggests, would be for the border to be managed jointly by Serbs and Croats, and the Danube allowed to continue to peacefully meander between them, sometimes higher, sometimes lower, but not tied into a straitjacket which would have fatal consequences for the fish and for the rare birds that nest along this pristine section.

The next morning we drive along fragile, dusty embankments to reach the shore, just downriver from Batina. I share a canoe with Arno Mohl, a conservation expert of WWF Austria. At the core of the dispute he says, as we paddle idly downstream close to the Croatian bank, is a clash between two philosophies of flood management. 'It is widely accepted in western Europe that the best flood protection is a wide floodplain, to absorb the rising waters, as still happens in Kopački Rit. Croatian and Serbian engineers still believe that the only way to deal with floods is to build up both banks with vast quantities of rock.'

A white eagle, one of only twelve pairs surviving in Kopački Rit, arches majestically over the Danube. Its wing span is so great, its head and even its white tail seem minuscule in flight, like afterthoughts to a design focused only on perfecting the wings. The upper branches of the poplars we pass are bare, killed off by the droppings from the cormorants that perch there preening themselves, watching out for fish in the waters below. The sandy island in midstream we planned to picnic on is nowhere to be seen – just the tops of the bushes which grow on it. So we paddle on through the afternoon. The *Panther*, the German-registered boat we saw the previous day from Batina, passes downstream – she must have moored below Batina for the night. Willow trees can last three hundred days in a flooded forest, oaks barely sixty. The banks are thick with willows, with the water rising well up their trunks. There is also a mix of other, non-indigenous species: Canadian poplars and maples. On the far side a barge, the *Sveti Dimitar*, registered at Lom in Bulgaria, passes downstream, its engine rumbling and rattling into the distance, drowning out the roar of birdsong.

Arno and I compare the fate of the countries beside the Danube. Austria owed much of her economic prosperity after the Second World War to her damming of rivers for hydro-power, I suggest. Are you not now trying to deny Croatians and Serbs the prosperity you in Austria enjoy?

'We deeply question the economic benefits of these massive interventions. The floodplain forest is suitable for sustainable forestry. Beneath it there is a huge ground water resource full of valuable drinking water. There is a wealth of fish species, so important for those living from fish, and this is also an important area for eco-tourism. People come here from all over the world to see a place which escaped the destruction of forests elsewhere in Europe. The question is: will this unique area be turned into a man-made landscape, or will it be preserved as a jewel to be used in an economical, sustainable way?'

After several hours paddling we turn right, off the main Danube, into a side arm which feeds the wetland forest. The water flows more slowly here, and there is a different atmosphere to the main stream. Everything is more secretive, as if nature is listening to her own body, with its giggles and gurgles. A kingfisher flies along the shore, a vivid flash of turquoise blue. Tiny snails have climbed the stalks of grass and reeds to escape the rising water. By now it is receding, but they have not yet been informed. There are shadowy recesses under the willows which bend low over the river bank. The journey is only fifteen kilometres, but feels longer in the heat.

At four-thirty the next morning I set out with Tibor and two German colleagues to photograph birds. Willows dot the wide, flooded plain. Purple herons stand sentinel on top of cylinders of newly bailed hay. Two white-tailed eagles watch from the top branches – the female bird higher and larger than the male. Two families of wild boar swim through the marshes, followed by a lone, nervous red deer. Yellow flowers grow out of the marshland, brilliant against the dark trunks of the willows. Reeds form a green carpet, swaying in the breeze. Clumps of yellow-green mistletoe stand out against the darker green foliage. In the distance, through binoculars, I watch a black stork, rarer and shyer than the white storks that make their nests on poles and chimneys in the villages. The southern part of Kopački Rit has been a protected area since 1967. 'The wettest period is usually in May, and the driest in September and October, before the autumn rains,' says Tibor, who grew up in the nearby village of Kopačevo. 'About 70 per cent of the floodplain area here was lost to agriculture or construction, but there has been no major forestry here since 1967, and no hunting since 1991 . . . The lucky thing is that humans are spoilt! It is either too humid, too hot or too cold. Or there are too many mosquitoes. We bring visitors to experience the wilderness, but after an hour they usually want to return to civilisation!' So the wilderness is not overloaded with eco-tourists.

There are discreet wooden platforms and guided boat trips out on to the lakes. We turn off the dyke to visit a colony of grey herons, high in the poplars. The air is full of the impatient clacking of the chicks in the nests, and the loud squawks of their parents, gliding gracefully over the trees, bringing them food. The shadows of the birds pass over the leaves, before the great birds themselves appear. A single white feather from an egret floats slowly down from a nest, twisting in the early sunlight. This is the largest grey heron colony in Croatia – 770 pairs. 'I know because I counted them!' says Tibor. The female birds lay four to six eggs, out of which two to three fledglings hatch. In a bad year, when it rains during hatching time, only one chick survives, because the eggs get chilled, or the chicks catch cold. The grey heron population is growing in Europe, nevertheless, and the birds are getting bolder. Traditionally they ate mostly fish, but now they eat rodents as well, and like seagulls feed more and more on rubbish dumps. 'It is the fate of all wetlands to dry out, as part of the natural silting up process. In two to three thousand years, this will become a forest. What the regulation work would do is to accelerate that process into a few decades.' Golden orioles call sweetly from the undergrowth, where reed warblers and green finches reside. As the sun rises higher in the yardarm of the trees the mutter of frogs turns into a roar, and we flee the wilderness in search of breakfast.

The road to the site of the battle of Mohács leads down avenues of horse chestnuts. A domed hall with its exhibition of posters is just being completed. The monument itself is simple and touching compared to the martial glories of the Romans and Serbs further downstream. The centre-piece is a low, circular mound containing the remains of the eighteen thousand Hungarian soldiers who died that day. 'The greatest defeat since Mohács,' a glum taxi-driver once told me, when the Soviet Union beat Hungary 6-1 in the opening match of the 1986 World Cup. Mohács haunts the Hungarian imagination, just as Trianon does, the 1920 treaty that divided the country up, after its defeat, with Austria and Germany, in the First World War.

The mound is laid out with bushes with blood-red leaves. All around are Hungarian *kopjafák*, carved wooden posts traditionally placed on the graves of Hungarians to symbolise the personal characteristics of the dead person. At Mohács the posts are adorned with spirals and curves. All are beautiful in their way, and recall Brâncuşi's Endless Column. But while the Romanian artist was seeking to reach the heavens, these are designed to ground the memory of the warriors in the earth. Suleiman himself, carved at the entrance, has a red diamond mounted on the crest of his turban, and dangling metal earrings. For a moment it seems a rather sympathetic portrayal of the arch-enemy of the Hungarians, until I notice the bag of wooden heads, dangling from a net around the base of the statue. Opposite him, the youthful Lajos II, the twenty-year-old Hungarian king, stands defiant, in brown tunic and blue belt, holding a small shield in his right hand. Pál Tömöri is there too, Archbishop of Kalocsa, further up the Danube, the commander of the Hungarian troops in southern Hungary, a grave figure with a long beard, and a blue eagle mounted on his yellow belt. Lola, a former Bosnian Serb soldier, is moved by the scene. As a former fighter against the Muslims, he feels at home on the battlefield.

The final message of the exhibition is reconciliation, in the words of the Hungarian poet, Attila József.

> Remembrance absolves into peace
> The war fought by our forefathers.

After the defeat at Mohács, King Lajos drowned in the Csele stream nearby, weighed down by his armour after being thrown from his horse. Suleiman stayed with his troops on the battlefield for several days, expecting the arrival of the main Hungarian army. He could not believe that this once great nation, the main foe of his empire, could put so few armed men into the field. At that time Hungary was divided, with a third under Ottoman occupation, a third held by the Habsburgs, led by Ferdinand, their candidate for the now vacant throne, and a third, Transylvania, a vassal state of the Ottomans, but enjoying considerable freedom. For the next 150 years, Hungary became an almost constant battleground between the Habsburgs and the Ottomans. The country has never regained its greatness, though it has often tried. The blue, rather chubby, features of King Mátthias, Lajos's grandfather and the last great king of Hungary who died in 1490, gaze up from the one thousand forint Hungarian banknote. His own 'black army', the *Fekete Sereg* was disbanded by the country's nobles after the king's death, as an obstacle to their own greed.[13]

CHAPTER 10

Smoke, Ash and a Tale or Two

Constantly bring to thy recollection those who have complained greatly
about anything, those who have been most conspicuous by the greatest
fame or misfortunes or enmities or fortunes of any kind: then think
where are they all now? Smoke and ash and a tale, or not even a tale.
MARCUS AURELIUS, *Meditations*, Book XII[1]

THE 07:56 intercity train from Budapest reaches Pécs in the south of the
country, close to the Croatian border, at 10.32. Then there are two short
hops, first to Villány, famous for its red wines, then to Mohács, arriving at
12.15. It's September, and my journey up the Danube has arrived at an
interesting stage. I've reached the country which has been my home for
half my lifetime: Hungary. I've decided to travel this leg of the journey by
bicycle, to get a new perspective on a country whose language I speak and
which I think I know well.

Sheep all face the same way in a meadow, watched over by a lone shepherd. No fields in an English sense, with hedges, gates and a stile, exist in
eastern Europe. In Hungary and Romania, Bulgaria and Serbia, there is
always a shepherd with the sheep, guiding them to the best grass, and
home again at the end of the day. The sheep face the same way, into the
wind, because they like the feel of the breeze on their faces. They remind
me of boats at their moorings in a sheltered harbour, swinging head to
wind. The early morning sunlight catches their wool from behind, as
though each has a halo.

There are only a few passengers on the red, two-wagon train that carries me into Mohács – Gypsy lads and old ladies – the story of the Hungarian countryside. The young people leave for work in the cities. The men die young, worn out by a life in the fields and by a diet of pork and brandy. The Roma scrape a living, mostly on welfare, dying ten years earlier than their fellow Hungarian citizens. The post office has shut down. The village school closed long ago. The old ladies, kept alive by their love of flowers and comforted in their loneliness by the constant buzz of the television, share the villages with the Roma. The poorest of the poor, Roma or non-Roma alike, sometimes steal to survive. The village shop, if there still is one, sells white bread, sugar, oil, flour, cigarettes, sour cream, twelve different kinds of salami and some rather sad looking potatoes. My chosen country in the twenty-first century. But everyone has a story to tell. Much has happened since the battle of Mohács.

The town of Mohács is five or six kilometres from the site of the battle. A woman in the town museum lets me leave my bicycle, laden with panniers, inside the building. Mohács seems to be a city of kind women. The museum is named after Dorottya Kanizsai, who set out for the battle-field in search of her stepson, the young bishop Ferenc Perényi, after the disaster of 1526, and with the help of local priests and several hundred peasants, buried him and thousands of other fallen Hungarian soldiers in a mass grave – the mound at the centre of the monument today.[2] In a painting of the scene from 1860 by Sóma Orlai Petrics, Dorottya is portrayed cradling the head of the dead man in her arms, amid the desolation of the battlefield.[3] The silver Danube snakes away into the distance, under a thunderous sky.

There are black ceramic pots on display, the speciality of local Slovenes. These were once taken down the Danube from here and across the sea to Constantinople – black pots across the Black Sea. Hungarian potters made brown pots flecked with yellow, yellow with green. The Croats were the wood-carvers. There are also blouses and skirts from the traditional costumes of the various nations of southern Hungary – Slovenes and Bosniaks (Bosnian Muslims), Serbs and Croats. On show is a sleeveless leather jacket of the Šokac people, who live on the border with Croatia, decorated with yellow, blue, black, purple, red and pink flowers with a red leather binding round the edges. The Bosniak woman's waistcoat beside it is less crowded with flowers, but equally fine. There are zigzags of lace, and lines of yellow and red, embroidered on a brown background. In addition, the museum sports tablecloths of fine woven hemp, bedding and embroidered cushions, and magnificent chests, one painted deep blue and decorated with flowers, another of hewn wood, decorated with black waves, moons and stars. Painted furniture became popular in the mid-nineteenth century. In the graveyards, the stone or cross betrays the age and gender of the dead. A young girl's grave was decorated with two headscarves when she was first buried. These were later given as gifts to the priest.

The ferry across the river goes every half hour. I eat fish soup at the Révkapu (Ferry Gate) restaurant, which is run by a Roma man and his son. The soup swims with fat chunks of carp, its skin, fishbone and fish-eggs, but the flavour is good, and the paprika in the soup gives it colour and edge. There's a September feeling in the air; the other diners on the terrace bask in the last heat of summer. I feel sleepy after my meal, but the journey ahead is long and I'm on my own. On the way across the water, the ferryman rebuffs my attempts at conversation – he's a taciturn fellow. Apart from the defeat of 1526, and a revenge victory in the return battle in 1687, Mohács is famous for its annual Busó festival. People dress up in sheepskins and wooden masks with animal horns – *busós* – and parade through the streets. The festival commemorates a raid across the Danube by masked locals, which scared the living daylights out of the Turkish garrison. They fled, according to the story, leaving the town in Hungarian hands.

I reach the far bank and strike out upriver, along the dyke. The bicycle path is part of European Route 6, which crosses Europe all the way from St Nazaire at the mouth of the Loire to Tulcea in the Danube delta, following the Loire, the Rhine and the Danube.[4] It's already three o'clock in the afternoon. I'm constantly distracted by the river, wheeling my bike down on to the shore, to paddle or skim stones. I've travelled much of the route so far on the right, southern bank of the river. But I want to travel as far as Budapest on the left, the eastern bank – among the 'barbarians'. Long-distance cyclists pass, always downstream. Sometimes we stop and talk: a Swiss couple from Zurich, going as far as Osijek; a British couple heading all the way from St Malo on the Normandy coast to Constanţa, nearly three thousand kilometres. They brought too much gear, and have just posted their tent back to Britain. They're full of the dreams of an Indian summer, twenty kilos lighter. How dangerous are the stray dogs in Romania? Is it true they attack cyclists without warning? Is there somewhere good to stay in Vukovar?

There is no obvious gradient, but I feel I'm cycling uphill all the way. The prevailing north-westerly wind blows in my face. I'm cycling on an old city bike, at least thirty years old, the gift of a German neighbour. I'm afraid the thin, narrow tyres will puncture on the sharp gravel, but at least I've brought mercifully little luggage. I want to cover the 220 kilometres to Budapest in five days.

The defeat of its army in 1526 was a disaster for Hungary, but a blessing for Austria. The Crown of Saint Stephen, which had been presented to the Hungarian king in the year 1000 by Pope Sylvester when the country converted en masse to Christianity, now passed to the Habsburg dynasty, which took over Hungary's role as 'the last bastion of Christian Europe'. But Ferdinand, the Habsburg claimant to the throne, was challenged by János Szapolyai, who arrived too late at Mohács to save King Lajos. Szapolyai was now recognised by the Ottomans as the rightful king. Both were crowned by their respective patrons, and the scene was set for 150 years of wars and skirmishes between the two empires on Hungarian territory, which laid waste the countryside.[5]

This period is depicted in most Hungarian textbooks as one of uninterrupted exploitation by the Turks, which is largely the legacy of nineteenth-century, fiercely anti-Turkish, historians such as Gyula Szekfű. 'We may search in vain for the positive effects of Turkish rule. We are talking about two opposing cultures, whose natural relationship is one of conflict,' Szekfű wrote. 'The Turkish slave state seized victory while the traces of Hungarian European civilization were wiped out.'[6]

The real picture is more nuanced, according to Géza Dávid of the University of Budapest, working from his own research and that of another historian, Gábor Ágoston.[7] The sudden fall in the population of one parish was often matched by the sudden increase in the population of another. The main threat to life, he argues, was not Turkish oppression, but disease, especially the plague. And when people fled, they rarely crossed from Turkish into Austrian-occupied Hungary, although they could easily have done so as the borders were blurred and porous. Those in Turkish-occupied Hungary may have been more comfortable than those in the Austrian occupied part. The deforestation of the country was caused as much by the building needs of Christian as of Muslim armies. The positives include the many steam baths, and the introduction of paprika and various other vegetables, as well as tree varieties such as the sweet chestnut, the seeds of which were brought up the Danube.

At Dunafalva I talk to a lady waiting for the little passenger ferry with a big basket of freshly gathered tomatoes. She lives in Dunaszekcső on the far side, and comes over each day to water and pick her vegetables. She also owns vines on the far side, in the sandy, loess soil near the old Roman camp, and produces white wine, which I should come and savour if ever I'm passing on the other bank, she says. I'm tempted to cross on the ferry with her, but then I will not reach Baja by nightfall. A group of six schoolchildren, weighed down with satchels, wait for the ferry beside her. Not a bad journey to school and back each day, across the river. The *Armaris*, a Dutch barge, passes upstream, close in to the far bank, the compulsory car parked on the stern.

Dunaszekcső is famous for a handsome bronze bust of the Roman emperor Marcus Aurelius unearthed here. On display in the museum in Pécs it shows the emperor well-bearded and curly-haired, less the philosopher king than the military commander, called away from Rome to face the first attacks by Germanic tribes across the Danube. The bust was probably made in his honour, just before his visit, on the warpath. He spent the years from AD 167 until his death in Vindobona (Vienna) in AD 180, driving back a succession of invasions by the Marcomanni, the Quadi, the Iazygians and other tribes. These were the first waves of a tribal tide that would eventually wear down and overwhelm the Roman empire. But for another two hundred years the Romans held their own along the *Limes* frontier, reinforced their fortresses along the river, and extracted a high price for the burning of their forts and the killing of their men. The *Meditations*, for which the Stoic emperor is most admired, were begun in 167, as Marcus Aurelius reluctantly gave up his sedentary life, resolving the quarrels of his fellow citizens, to confront their fiercest foes. 'Time is like a river made up of the events which happen, and a violent stream; for as soon as a thing has been seen, it is carried away, and another comes in its place, and this will be carried away too.'[8] His stoicism, his single-minded sense of duty and purpose, are tinged with the melancholy of a man far from home. Only four of the thirteen children his wife Faustina gave birth to survived beyond childhood. I imagine him high on a wooden tower, being hastily reinforced with stone, gazing down into the brown-grey Danube.

Just before the village of Szeremle I hear the sheep before I see them – all five hundred of them, clanking their bells as they shuffle between the dyke and the wooded shores of the river. It's easy to stop on a bike, travelling long distance, to waylay people I like the look of. Sanyi the shepherd lives on his own in a house tucked away in the elbow of the dyke. The sheep are owned by a man in Szeremle who has a farm – the white buildings we can see on the horizon. The farmer split up with his wife, Sanyi tells me, and lost everything – he used to have more than two thousand sheep, worth seventy US dollars each, but these are all he has left. The shepherd sighs, full of sympathy for his master's plight. We offer each other water, and he offers me his hand rolled cigarettes. Then he tells me his life story.

'You can live well here from your own produce – a few pigs, egg-laying hens, and vegetables from your own garden.' He tried living in a town once, he says, but couldn't stand it – 'you can't raise animals in the city; someone would report you!' His wife was killed by a train in 1995. His children are grown up and live in Pécs. He visits them, and likes to see his grandchildren, but is always glad to get home. His face is dark from the sun and the rain. He might be Roma, but it doesn't seem important to ask. He's interested in my journey, impressed that someone would bother to cycle all the way to the capital. 'I've walked my own share of long distances,' he says. 'When I broke up with a girlfriend once, I set out on foot from Harkány, and walked all the way to Pécs' – a hundred kilometres or so. He remembers a 'foreign couple', who pitched their tent between the dyke and a field of corn. 'I came over the ridge in the early morning, with all my sheep. They were shouting, I was shouting, but the sheep couldn't help it – they trampled right through them!' He shakes with laughter as he tells the story. 'There are fewer mosquitoes this year, and that's a blessing. Some years they are terrible. But we need rain desperately. The sheep have nothing to feed on! Just look at them!' I watch his animals, nosing around in the yellow grass. I have the impression that I am the first person who has spoken to him for weeks.

In Szeremle there's a pond where the croaking of the frogs sounds like thunder. Wild apples grow from trees along the way. Another shepherd, Jóska, tends seventy sheep of his own. He worries about the weather, too. 'It hasn't rained here for six weeks.' He sells the lambs to the Italians at two to three weeks old, weighing twenty kilos. They are transported live to Italy for slaughter.

In Baja I find a small hotel for the night, proud of my progress. Only thirty-two kilometres from Mohács, my legs and back ache, and my eyes are dazzled by the sun and wind. After a shower, I walk gingerly through the town to Petőfi Island in search of supper. From the terrace of the Vizafogó (Sturgeon Catcher's) restaurant, overlooking the Sugovica, I watch the orange lights of the town come on, and the stars grow brighter over the Danube. Through the glass window, on television, Hungary is playing Moldova at soccer. The waiter brings regular reports of the score, with each glass of wine or plate. The final tally is 2–0 to Hungary, a great victory.

The hero of Baja is István Türr, just as the heroine of Mohács was Dorottya Kanizsai. Down on the Danube shore, the István Türr lookout tower boasts a plaque at the entrance. 'This stone is dedicated to István Türr; the Austrian army officer sentenced to death; commander of the Hungarian Piedmont legion; the volunteer in the Baden, Turkish and scout wars; one of the immortal one thousand of Marsalai; Garibaldi's general; the general of the governor of Naples Victor Emmanuel; the brave soldier in every battle. Who fought on foreign fields, under foreign flags, for the honour of the Hungarian sword, and for the glory of the town of his birth.' A second stone table extols Türr's other peacetime virtues: the initiator of the Ferenc József and Baja canals, 'champion of the idea of the Panama canal, champion of public education, and of peace between nations'. Something of an all-rounder, then. At the top of the tower, hundreds of padlocks, engraved with the names of lovers and sometimes whole families, have been attached to the railings, and their keys thrown into the Danube. Valerie and Ludovic, Márti and Laci, Fernanda and Tamás, all linked with hand-carved hearts. The bottom of the river here must be thick with keys, the sediment of love.

The next morning Éva Kis shows me round the István Türr museum, which is dedicated to fishing and other Danube-based pursuits. The nets are fine and delicate, like the lingerie of a river goddess. As nubile as Danubia? Why did the Romans insist on the whiskery Danubius?

The *csontos kece* is a three-part net ringed with cow bones, designed to be hauled along the riverbed. The bones are just right for this purpose, strong, yet light enough to bounce over the obstacles and scrape through the gravel on the bottom of the river without getting heavy and water-logged, like wood. There are mirror nets, now banned for animal rights reasons as the fish suffer so much in them when they are caught; huge nets resembling women skirts, requiring great strength and skill to throw out into the water. And a black-and-white photograph of a young man doing so, watched with uninhibited interest by three girls who have paused from their task of cleaning fish. A large beluga sturgeon, about three metres long and preserved in a case, is in a place of honour near the entrance, its four huge whiskers poking down from below its nose like skewers, its face viewed from the side strangely human, like a caricature of a whiskery man with a carnival nose. On the wall is a medieval illustration explaining how sturgeon were caught – not with the *garda*, the fences of the Lower Danube, but with a stout rope, held right across the river bed, from bank to bank, with wicked-looking hooks dangling from it, each weighed down with a lead ball. As the sturgeon migrated upriver, staying close to the bottom, these hooks would catch in their sides and, when the rope was hauled up, the fish could be caught and eventually landed. In this picture, the fish is several times longer than the boat. 'When the children see this one,' says my guide, pointing to the great preserved fish, 'they think it's a shark.' Big barbed hooks are displayed along the wall, and there's a price list from 1746: twelve forints for sturgeon, two forints for catfish, one and a half for carp. The sturgeon catch for six parishes in the Kalocsa bishopric is listed for the same year: 10,000 kilos in the spring, 11,000 kilos in the autumn.

Another part of the exhibition deals with the traditional water mills on the Danube. Baja was especially favoured because of the strong current, close to six kilometres per hour. There are scale models and drawings of the mills, which were made from two boats, moored together like the hulls of a catamaran, one substantially larger than the other. Between the two, a large water wheel with paddles is suspended that was turned by the current where the boat was moored, to turn the mill in the larger of the two boats. There are also models of the grain boats that were pulled upriver along the tow path by teams of horses, to take grain to the mill-boats. Each is decorated with bowsprits, which resemble neither the goddesses of the Greeks nor the dragons of the Chinese, but the head of the chello of the Hungarians – ever a musical nation.

Unlike in Mohács, where I ate fish soup waiting for the ferry, dunked with big chunks of crusty white bread, the tradition in Baja is to cook pasta in the soup. Éva explains why. By law, the millers were obliged to feed their employees. Fish were classified by the church as 'fasting-food', suitable to be eaten on Fridays and during Lent. As a result, the millers' boys complained that fish soup was not 'real food', and that the millers were not treating them properly. The millers' wives solved the problem by mixing home-made noodles, made from the plentiful flour and eggs, into the soup, to make it more substantial, and so satisfy both the hard-working lads' hunger and the stipulations of the law.

According to a cookbook published in 1622 by István Galgóczi, there are nineteen ways to prepare sturgeon. According to another, published in Kolozsvár-Cluj in 1695, 'Salt the fish and leave to stand for a little. Then cook it in wine with white bread. Add pepper, saffron, ginger, honey and vinegar and cook well. Serve hot.'[9]

There is also a tall wooden statue of St John Nepomuk, the patron saint of millers and sailors. As confessor to the family of the King of Bohemia, friction arose between him and the monarch. When John maintained the secrecy of the confessional, and refused to disclose to the king what the queen had told him in confidence, the king had him tortured, his hands chopped off, and he was thrown from the Charles Bridge in Prague into the River Vltava. As he hit the water, the story goes, the surface rose, full of stars, and bore him to safety. Each year on 15 May the people of Baja carry his statue by boat down the Sugovica branch of the Danube and parade it through the town. A large barrel of wine is broached for the occasion, and the townspeople can drink their fill in honour of their saint's miraculous survival.

The final exhibit in the museum is a closed wooden boat drilled with holes. This was for the fishermen to load their catch into and pull behind their boats like a submarine, all the way back to the town to sell the still fresh fish. The wealthier fishermen pinned a gold fish over their gates, while the poorer ones lived with their families in shacks on the shore from spring to autumn. Each poor family owned a single copper cauldron and ate their fish soup from spoons made from river shells. A seventeenth-century map on the wall, from Count Marsigli's famous guide to the Danube published in Amsterdam in 1726, shows the river as an unruly dragon, curling and curving across the landscape, before it was tamed and straightened into its present straitjacket in the nineteenth and twentieth centuries.[10]

> Oh Fiery River
> Flow out over the land.
> Men have destroyed the roads of wonder,
> And their cities squat like black toads
> In the orchards of life.[11]

Cycling upriver from Baja, I take a detour into the city river port. In Marsigli's day, even to reach the port I would have had to cross one or two meanders of the river, but now the path is smooth, out through the suburbs, past schools, houses and István Türr's tower in the unseasonal heat. The docks are a sparse clutter of tall cranes and railway tracks, grain silos with German-sounding names, and trucks turning.

László Nagy is director of the port, which is still owned by the state. Nine barges can moor at one time here and pay for the privilege. It's one of the busiest ports in Hungary, he says, handling 600,000 to 900,000 tonnes of goods a year, about a tenth of all the freight that passes through Hungary on the river, and which actually touches the shore. Later, I check in my *Statistical Handbook of Hungarian Shipping 1945–1968* for the corresponding figure from the communist era.[12] Just a little lower for Baja – 500,000 tonnes that year. Stone and gravel were the single biggest items then, followed by mineral oil, iron and manganese ore, coal and coke, fertiliser, timber, and finally grain. 'Soya comes upstream, mostly from Brazil. Boats load local wheat, barley, sunflower seed, maize and oilseed rape for the Austrian market. This year trade has been weak.'

The blockage of the Danube from 1999 to 2003 still casts a strong shadow over business, which has never recovered, László says. Low levels of water are a constant problem, with ships forced to unload goods and send them on, more expensively, by train. The general state of Hungarian agriculture is another theme. 'This used to be a country of ten million pigs – now there are less than three million!' In the summer of 2012, Prime Minister Viktor Orbán promised to double that number to six million. There are also positive sides to László Nagy's tale – a new brand name has just been launched – Kincses Bácska – the Treasures of Bácska County – to advertise local produce. 'Its success depends on three things: the persistence and willpower of the people, the good example of investors, and the good will of the state.'

Before I get back on my bike and cycle past his giant cranes, the conversation strays inevitably to recipes for fish soup. 'One kilo of fish, ideally carp,' he suggests, 'a litre of water, a head of onion, and a spoonful of paprika, and cook together for three to four hours.' On the second weekend of July, at the annual Baja fish-soup festival, up to two thousand cauldrons of soup compete for the prize – 'and no two soups are ever the same!' Wine must be drunk with the soup, he insists, because according to a local saying, 'fish must never swim three times in water – once in the river and once in the pot is enough – there shouldn't be water in the stomach as well!'

Sustained by such advice and more, I wobble back up the dyke. Under the bridge over the Danube, a black plaque with gold lettering is mounted by a small road. 'At this point on 1st November 1921, Charles IV the rightful King of Hungary boarded ship and left the country to escape his enemies. In remembrance of this, Hungarians, learn to love your country better than you hate one another.'[13] It is a brusque but important message for a people always generous to strangers but rough on one another.

In the shade of a forest to the right of the dyke, one of István Magony's five hundred sheep has just given birth. We approach very slowly and stop at a good distance so as not to disturb the ewe, who is peacefully nibbling at the green weeds among the dry, yellow grass, while her little black and white lamb, already standing unsteadily, tugs anxiously at her udders. István lives alone in a shack further up the dyke, 'across the stream, between two sets of bee-hives'. His wife left him, unable to bear the loneliness of a shepherd's life. Another lamb was born last night. He needed to help with that one, but this ewe managed all on her own. His boss, the owner of the sheep, will drive out in his Mercedes to take the mother and lamb away from the flock for a while. István earns 30,000 forints a month in cash – about 150 dollars, with all his food and tobacco paid for. He knows other shepherds who earn 80,000 forints, but have to pay for their own keep, and he's happy with this arrangement as it is – he could easily spend a thousand forints a month on cigarettes, two packets a day. The sheep graze on the *parlagfü*, a weed with gentle green fronds that has spread widely across central Europe and is blamed for hay fever and all the school and workdays lost each September. The sheep love it, he says, and proves it by hunting for a stem of the weed to show me, where the sheep have been grazing since this morning. We have trouble finding a single leaf. He gets up at five-thirty each morning and sets out at six. He walks with his flock till ten, then rests with his sheep in the shade till three, then sets out back, about ten to twenty kilometres a day. He gets home at seven, and it is dark, at this time of year, by eight.

I feel I'm just beginning to uncover the secrets of a countryside I have passed through for years. Just further on up the dyke, Tibor cares for forty-two cows and a bull – 'Look at him, poor bloke, he can hardly walk, with so many women to please!' He lives in a caravan further upriver, and, like everyone else, grumbles about the drought and the scarcity of grass for his animals. As the maize is cut and harvested, the farmers allow him to take the cows into the fields to taste the leftovers – 'but not for long, too much is not good for them'.

I stop for a *fröcs*, the Hungarian name for a drink of half wine and half carbonated water, then get chased by dogs as I come down to the ferry crossing to Gerjen. I pedal like the wind, thinking of my fellow English folk already exposed to the horrors of the Romanian hounds I had dismissed so lightly. I attribute my own miraculous escape to the timely intercession of a painting of a blue-cloaked Madonna, baring her breast to reveal a heart struck through with a dagger. In her right hand she holds a white flower. 'Roadside Mary, Pray for us we beg' reads the inscription, and the date 1947, a year when Hungary, that lost so much in the war, was being twisted to fit the iron grip of the Communist Party and its Russian masters.

Down by the water I watch a party of tourists coming ashore from one of the huge, gleaming Danube passenger ships, the *River Adagio*. They're all Americans, and as open and friendly to a stray English cyclist as if I had shown up on their own porch on the Mississippi. We sit drinking beer from plastic mugs in the shade of a little bar set up by some enterprising Hungarian who must have a copy of the ships' timetables. As my luck would have it, they're retired nuclear submariners who served for years under the polar icecaps, waiting to push the button to wipe out the Soviet Union and start the Third World War. The tattoo on the forearm of one man shows a wide expanse with a rocket soaring up through the ice, and the slogan – 'North Pole, August 1960'. I was six months old then. If the war had broken out, I would not have had much of a life, irradiated in the cellar of the house I was born in by the River Medway, just south of the incinerated remains of London.

My drinking partners and their wives are full of the joys of their cruise. They flew to Bucharest and took a bus to Ruse, where they boarded ship. They can't tell me which was the best place they visited, but the organisers have clearly gone to some lengths to give them a taste of local life. A Serbian man and his wife gave them an excellent dinner near Osijek – 'very critical of the government,' one man remembers. In Vukovar they praise the excellent meal cooked for them by a Croatian family. Wasn't it strange to be travelling above water after so many years? Far from it! they chortle in chorus. Some of them have known each other for fifty years. 'The worse times under the ocean, in the nuclear submarines, were the first week, and the last,' says one man, whose record was eighty-three days under water. 'And what of the dangers of the job?' I ask. They look at each other a little sheepishly, to check that none of their wives are listening. 'The girls in the ports,' one explains. 'We were lucky that those were the years before AIDS. But there would be mornings . . .' he pauses for effect, 'when you woke to see whose head lay on your arm on the pillow, and you wanted to gnaw your arm off!'

I've had a few drinks by this time and the sun is sinking fast above the far bank. I abandon my plan of sleeping in Kalocsa and start to enquire among the small cluster of houses if there's anywhere I can find a bed for the night. Tamás Klopcsek is caretaker for several buildings belonging to the local council and finds me a comfortable bed in one of them. He had a thriving car-repair garage in Kalocsa during the communist era, repairing Western makes of cars such as Rovers and Fords. He needed good contacts in western Europe to buy parts, which drew him to the attention of the authorities. As a suspected spy, the state took everything from him, though he was not sent to prison. Instead, he got a job as a long-distance truck driver, and did that for twenty-three years. As we talk, his large alsatian, Nero, takes a particular interest in the tyres of my bike, no doubt detecting traces of the mongrels who tried to bite through them. From the mobile home in which he sleeps, Tamás produces a certificate which shows his two million miles without an accident, printed in Geneva. Now he enjoys a semi-retirement, growing and bottling fruit. The council has plans to restart the ferry service, which will bring more visitors.

I eat alone at sunset in the restaurant on the shore, and taste the white wine of Szekszárd – a region best known for its red wines, but which clearly has something more to offer. I wake soon after midnight, to hear the engines of the *River Adagio* churning the water – casting off to get my submariner friends to Budapest in time for breakfast. In the early morning, I swim upriver in the chilly green waters, barely making any progress against the flow. Somewhere upstream, not far away, is the nuclear power station at Paks, which cools its turbines with river water and pumps it back out much warmer, like the power station at Cernavodă. But I cannot travel the Danube without getting my chin wet. And I nearly survived the Third World War, after all.

The Paprika Museum in Kalocsa is the only one of its kind in the world, and as I come through the door I understand why – the magnificent smell of the scarlet red powder hurts my eyes and burns my nostrils. The Turks brought paprika to Hungary after the battle of Mohács, and it has turned into the national spice, livening up dishes from goulash to paprika mush-rooms, and the ubiquitous fish soup. I have seen Hungarians put paprika on scrambled eggs, and use it to control greenfly on roses. Known first as 'Indian pepper' or 'Turkish pepper' in the great medieval herbals, Kalocsa and Szeged emerged in the eighteenth century as the best paprika-growing districts. There are black-and-white pictures of paprika in great sacks in 1956, at the time of the great flood in Baja. Part of the museum is dedi-cated to the work of the Hungarian Nobel Prize winner for chemistry Albert Szent-Györgyi and his discovery of ascorbic acid, later known as Vitamin C. This he first extracted, not from citrus fruits, which have rela-tively small amounts, but from paprika. 'For some unknown reason nature has made the Hungarian red paprika the most miraculous storage for ascorbic acid,' he wrote in 1937, well on his way to his discovery.[14]

For the first time since Mohács the day is overcast when I set out and the clouds make cycling easier. I cut inland from the dyke, and the road takes me through field after field of glorious red paprika, contrasting with the dark green of the stem and leaves. Keen to uncover some of the secrets of this miraculous plant, I hail a line of women harvesting it. The headgear of each is different – a straw hat, a headscarf, a baseball cap.

I ask for just five minutes of their time, and they tease me that they can only spare three. '*Nem győztem az angolokat várni, várni, bekellet a, bekellet a TSZCS-be állni . . .*' sings Eszter Boldizsár, when she finds out my nationality. 'I couldn't wait any more for the English, so I had to join the Co-operative . . .' – a song from the end of the Second World War, when the dreams that British and American troops would rescue Hungary from communism evaporated. I apologise for the delay, on behalf of the entire British people. The paprika look red and rude, erect on the plants or curled up in the white buckets. The sound of them landing in the buckets as the women throw them from nearby is like the patter of rain at the start of a summer shower. How can one tell if the paprika is ripe? 'Just from the colour; those over there aren't ready yet. We call them smoky . . . They grow best here because there's more sunshine. That means the colour is better, and there's more vitamin C in them.' Eszter has grown paprika and tended them all her life. The plants require a lot of input, 'precise work – the hoeing, spraying, watering, picking, the tying into strings, the grinding into powder'. And what does she like most about the work? 'The work itself! Whoever likes to work finds their pleasure in it. Those who don't like labour won't find pleasure in anything, anyway!' Its seasonal labour, and the women pick through the year – poppy seed, maize, peas, beans, whatever they're paid for.

'Paprika is a plant with a memory,' says another woman, Irén. 'If you start watering it at the beginning, when it's small, you have to water it all the way through. Its roots go downwards. If they find enough water, they feed from their smaller roots, near the surface, and never grow a strong, central root. Look at these ones here – they've never really been watered, and look how beautiful they are! It's going to be a good year.' The previous year it rained all through August, and the paprika harvest was worthless.

'The sun is the god of the paprika plant!' And how do you tell which are sweet and which are spicy? 'You must never plant the two kinds near one another, because then you get plants which are both at the same time. And you can't sell them,' says Irén. She used to decorate plates by hand at the porcelain factory in Kalocsa, but the workforce has dropped from a hundred and twenty, to just four. 'That's how I became a peasant!'

My three minutes are up, though the women didn't stop working for a moment as we talked, and they each present me with a paprika, to dry at home and plant out for my own crop next spring.

At Ordas I stop to read the plaque on the massive, pollarded trunk of an oak. 'Here the bloody flag of freedom flew,' reads the text. 'Ferenc Rákóczi II camped under this tree from 30th April to 26th May 1704.' Soon after the Austrian Habsburgs drove the Turks from Buda and the third of the country they had ruled for 160 years, a new conflict broke out between the Hungarian nobility, which had mostly converted to Protestantism during the Reformation, and the Austrians who were determined to reimpose Catholicism on their new dominions. Starvation and oppression in the countryside provoked the peasants to join the rebellion led by Rákóczi, in the hope of an end to serfdom. For once, noble and peasant marched under the same 'bloody banner of freedom'. The armies of Charles VI defeated the Hungarians in the field, but the Austrian emperor thought it wise in the Treaty of Szatmár in 1711 to confirm the privileges of the nobles and grant them autonomy. The peasants got nothing.

Near Dunapataj, another shepherd in this country of shepherds, János, walks two hundred sheep towards me along the dyke, a bleating wave, thickening and thinning at the edges, cream-grey on green. János has a flat hat and a curved staff and an equally curvy moustache. The profession of shepherding survives, he says, thanks to the hunger of Italians for lamb. Few are eaten in Hungary, but 'if you have more than five hundred, its worth milking them for their cheese'.

I cross the green iron bridge to Dunaföldvár at four thirty in the afternoon, my first visit to the right bank of the river since Mohács. The town's name means 'Danube hill fort', and after booking into a room overlooking the shore I climb the hill to explore the castle. The museum is shut, but in a shop nearby a woman called Eszter sells her pottery. We chat until her partner arrives. Imre hitchhiked to England for the legendary Isle of Wight rock festival in August 1970. It took him a whole week to get there, and a week to get back, but he said it was all worthwhile. It was the last time Jimi Hendrix played – he died two weeks after the festival. Imre and I walk down to the lower town to eat a fish soup together in a restaurant. Eszter meets us there, and they walk me back to my room. She talks about the birth of her child, how she nearly died in childbirth, and how scary it was 'on the other side'. A full moon hangs over the sandy cliffs above my temporary home. I sometimes find myself invited deeper into people's lives than either I or they expect.

I get up very early and cycle up the hill to see the cliff-top that gave this town its name – earth fort – and to listen to the seven o'clock bells. Inside a wine cellar at the end of a cobbled street an elderly man turns the big metal wheel on a green-painted wine press. He offers me a glass of fresh must, which I am glad to accept for my breakfast. Then I help him crush his grapes, while he drops armfuls of them into the centre from a loaded wheelbarrow. Uncle Feri has two kinds of grapes – *ezerjó* and another one I can't quite understand. But it doesn't matter. The grape juice is pinky-orange in the early September morning light, and sweeter than wine.

On a rock in the castle grounds is a bronze statue of László Magyar, one of Hungary's greatest explorers, emerging through the shape of Africa, his hat tied on his back, a parchment map unrolled in his hands.[15] The illegitimate son of a big landowner, he went to elementary school in Dunaföldvár, enrolled as a cadet in the Austrian merchant navy, and served on the slave boats between Madagascar and the Caribbean. He stayed in touch with his homeland and applied for a research grant from the Hungarian Academy of Sciences to explore South America. When this was turned down he tried his luck in Africa instead. In May 1848, as his fellow countrymen embarked on their war of liberation from Habsburg Austria, he discovered the source of the Congo river, sailing the last stretch upriver with six Cabindan sailors from Angola. In his diaries, he describes the arrival of the river in the Atlantic: 'This huge river, six nautical miles wide at the mouth, flows with great force from east to west, pouring its yellow, troubled waters into the ocean with such awesome power, that the yellow colour of its waters, and their sweet taste, can still be experienced, three nautical miles out to sea.' He took the name Enganna Komo and settled down in the coastal town of

Benguela with his many wives, including the fourteen-year-old Ina-Kullu-Ozoro, the daughter of a local chieftain. When he closed his eyes at night, with the sound of the Atlantic Ocean resounding along the shore, did he ever dream of the Danube at Dunaföldvár?

In the grounds of the castle there is a massive millstone, worn down not by the wheat but by the golden grains of the sun and the silver rain. I bought an old iron wood-burning stove in this town once, made in the town of Nadrág, meaning 'trousers', in Transylvania.

I cycle back across the bridge and take a detour down to the gravel works, in search of recent treasures dredged up from the river. But the men are busy and none too helpful. The roar of the machinery drowns out my attempts at conversation, so I turn my bicycle and wobble away northwards. Some lads stay at home, watching the gravel of the Danube flow through their fingers. Other strike out for foreign parts.

Dunaegyháza, Apostag, Dunavecse, Szalkszentmárton . . . I cycle like the wind upriver, like a hound now with the smell of home, Budapest, in my nostrils. I make sandwiches near the dyke at Tass, then miss the left turn across the dam on to Csepel Island. So I keep up along the Soroksári branch of the Danube, the junior branch of the river. The main shipping lane continues further west, on the far side of Csepel Island. This is an angler's world. The weekend cottages are crowded with fishermen perched, big-bellied on little pontoons, or dozing in rowing boats awash with empty beer bottles. The mottled afternoon light sharpens the edges, the fronds of the water, half reed, half willow, a mosaic of deep shade and blinding sunlight. There are bars with a few chairs outside and a jug of wine on the table, replenished from a barrel in the cellar.

In Ráckeve I cross a small bridge over the Soroksári Danube branch to climb the fireman's tower with the librarian from the children's library, whose other job is to take strangers out onto her perch, overlooking the river. The view is magnificent in all directions. I can see the hills of Buda, still forty kilometres away, in the far distance. Down on the Danube shore at Ráckeve I see my first Danubian water mill, lovingly restored. Before 1950, there were six of them on the main river here. Each spring they were pulled by hand by the men along the towpath, on 15 March, the national holiday, all the way down the Soroksári branch to the main river, then up the other side of Csepel Island. Then back again each autumn, on 30 November, unless the ice and cold on the main river forced them back beforehand. The mill can grind more than a hundred kilos of flour an hour. There's a label on each bag declaring it to be 'unfit for human consumption', which is not true, I'm told, but the mill cannot get official approval according to European Union requirements. I would buy a bag and taste it myself, but there's enough ballast in my saddlebags already. The men running the museum ply me with apples, and recommend 'the last miller', eighty-two-year-old Márton Reimer, who lives just along the towpath.

'I was nine when I started work on my father's mill,' says Márton. He's pleased to have a visitor, even though he's told his story a thousand times. His wife slips away discreetly to make fresh lemonade. We sit in the garden. He wears no shirt, and his hairy chest is white in the sun. 'My job was to carry sacks of flour, forty to fifty kilos, on to the boats, then row them across to the mill, with my father's apprentice. Sometimes I rowed, some-times I steered.' He worked all through the summer holidays, till ten in the evening, while his father was away at the front, and then when he came back as well. By the end of the war, Márton had grown into a tall, muscular lad, he tells me proudly, and weighed seventy-two kilos. But the commu-nists didn't like men such as his father, who owned two water mills. 'Kulaks' they were called, and their property was confiscated by the state. At first the young Márton got work at a nationalised mill at Adony, close to where his father used to moor the family mill, just offshore where the Danube current is strongest. Then in 1950 the authorities decided to smash up the last four remaining water mills that had survived the war and the fighting on the Danube between the Red Army and the Germans. Why did they destroy the mills? 'That was the point of communism – to take away everything from everybody, and destroy it,' the man on the restored mill told me at Ráckeve. Through the creaking of the planks on the water, I heard Karl Marx turn in his watery grave.

Márton Reimer is surprisingly unnostalgic about those days. 'The life we had then will never come back. It was very hard work. By the end I was carrying sacks of grain and flour weighing up to a hundred kilos. Then I got a job in the car factory in Csepel. Working in a factory with a screwdriver, a hammer and a spanner in my hand was child's play after that!' His other great passion is angling. 'Turn that thing off,' he gesticulates at my tape recorder, and leads me by the elbow inside his house to see his trophy case. It looks like the collection of an old soldier – a forest of medals. Large silver coins with images of lone fishermen or lone fish, and ribbons in the national colours. What does it take to be a good angler? 'Good hands, good eyes, and a bit of biology, to know the temperament of the fish.' But there are fewer fish in the river than there were. In the individual championships, he used to catch ten to fourteen kilos in the competition time of three hours. Now people are happy if they catch five to six kilos.

His first memory of the Danube is of being out with his uncle. 'I must have been five or six. "Look, Uncle, look!" I shouted. There was an empty canoe, floating down on the current. We caught it. There was no one in it, just a bamboo rod, a real beauty. Well, we took it to the shore, looked after it, and told the gendarmerie, of course. It was several weeks before anyone came to claim it. Unfortunately, they took away that bamboo rod as well. I was catching so many fish with it!' Before and after the rod he used to make his own from sticks and fishing line, buy hooks for two fillers (the smallest unit of the forint currency), catch crickets, strip their wings off, and pierce the hook through their bodies. 'That was our youth – now life is different. They spend millions on equipment for a competition. Angling is becoming a sport for the rich.' He remembers two big spills of phenol from the Csepel paper factory: in 1954 and 1964. Almost all the fish in the Soroksári Danube were wiped out, and not a few in the main river. 'One of the accidents happened in winter. The phenol got under the ice and killed all the best fish. The corpses they collected filled eighteen wagons – pikeperch, carp, catfish.' Even the cyanide spill in the Tisza in January 2000, which wiped out most fish life for several hundred kilometres, was not as bad as these, he says.

We drink homemade lemonade. He puts his shirt on for a photograph, and the waves of a passing ship laps peacefully against the towpath, all overgrown.

Coming out of Ráckeve, there's a poem by János Arany, the nineteenth-century Hungarian poet and translator of Shakespeare, engraved on the wall of a building.[16]

Duna vizén lefele viszik a ladik, a ladik . . .

The Danube carries a young woman downstream in a rowing boat from Szentendre with a load of red apples to sell in the market in Kevi. How many lovers that red face deserves, beneath that tight headscarf! The poet ponders. Then the plot thickens. Jovan (John) is waiting in the market in Kevi with a bloodied knife. And there are worms in the red apples the young woman carries.

From Ráckeve, it is just eleven kilometres to Tököl, on a fast, straight road, past a young offenders' prison. Csepel Island is flat, rural at the southern end, heavily industrialised in the north, with communist-era housing estates, factories and docks. An Irish friend, Donal, cycles out to meet me with his daughters, a welcoming committee.

The next morning I leave at six thirty, pass the old military airport which the British bombed in the Second World War, and am in the suburbs of Csepel by eight.[17] Only five kilometres till home. My bicycle map offers few clues as to how to navigate the busy, rush hour traffic, so I stop to ask a man for the least congested street. He suggests one, and I set out slowly down it, hemmed in by the first heavy traffic since I left Mohács.

Suddenly a car swings round from my left, to enter the side street I am just passing in front of. I start to shout but there's no time to get out of his way. He sees me at the last moment, just as his bonnet smashes into my side, and brakes hard. I go flying through the air and, as I fly, I instinctively curl up in a ball, landing on my lower back in the road. He jumps out to apologise. '. . . No harm done? I'm so sorry . . . where do you live? I'll drive you home . . .' The traffic stops. Everyone stares. I half stand up, but there's a dull pain in my back, getting worse all the time. Two passers-by help me into the recovery position on the dry grass on the kerb. I hear sirens. The police arrive and breathalyse first me, then the driver. The most important question seems to be if either of us has been drinking, rather than my physical condition. Then the ambulance pulls up. I'm put into a vacuum mattress and gently placed in the back. I'm thinking all the time: *just a bruise, can't be anything worse.* Then I overhear the medics talking. 'Where shall we take him?' 'Spine injury, looks bad. Lets take him to the Merényi.' I have never heard of it, and mistake the word 'merényi' for 'merénylet' – assassination attempt. In the midst of the pain I almost laugh. Surely they don't think the driver was trying to kill me?

I'm wheeled into casualty, overtaking all the hopeless cases who have to queue. The X-ray machine breaks down while I'm lying on it. The driver of the car, Károly, a professor of Homeland Security, has followed me in his car, with my twisted bike in the back, and all my possessions. He comes in to check on me so often the nurses assume that he is my relative. Eventually the X-ray machine is fixed. I'm curled up in the waiting area on a trolley. A young doctor comes over, waving the X-ray and some papers. 'Bad news I'm afraid. You've got a broken vertebra.' Visions of a life in a wheelchair swim before me. I want to ring my wife, want to see my children, want them to know, want them not to know, want to have taken another road, want to have got up earlier, want to have left the house in Tököl later, anything, anything but this.

CHAPTER 11

The Wind in the Willows

Contrary to our expectations, the wind did not go down with the sun. It
seemed to increase with the darkness, howling overhead and shaking the
willows round us like straws. Curious sounds accompanied it sometimes,
like the explosion of heavy guns, and it fell upon the water and the island
in great flat blows of immense power. It made me think of the sounds a
planet must make, could we only hear it, driving along through space.

ALGERNON BLACKWOOD, 'The Willows'[1]

MY BACK takes a long time to heal. My daydream of finishing the journey
by bicycle all the way to Donaueschingen has to be abandoned. All the
men in my hospital ward have back injuries, and are in a much worse
condition than I am. Three were in bike accidents, one fell off a ladder.
Each day we hear the helicopter, bringing spinal injury cases from all over
the country. Every evening the nurses bring our painkillers. It's a Darwinist
democracy – the most able man in each ward gets to hobble out, and plead
with the nurses on behalf of a fellow-victim. The best and worst moment
each day is the 'big visit', when the top doctors and their acolytes tour the
wards. They alone have the information which we, the patients, need: the
latest analysis of our condition, the experts' opinion on our future lives.

On the third day 'the white-haired one' as the nurses have dubbed him,
as his name is unpronounceable, appears beaming at my bedside. 'Where's
the American?' I hear him say – and hope he is better at biology than geography. 'Good news!' he booms. The crack in my vertebra could be better

described as a fracture. It will probably heal completely in three months. I can go home that evening! I feel hot tears of gratitude, of laughter, rolling down my cheeks.

The winter is a long one. Three months turn into six months. I can walk, stand, even sit a little, but not very much. I cannot run, or cycle, or play football with my youngest sons. Early each morning I travel one stop on the tram with the boys, to set them on their way to school. Other men wave at trains. I alone wave at trams, until the number 41 or number 19 to Batthyány Square turns the bend, out of sight.

Count Lajos Batthyány was Hungary's first prime minister, in office for less than two hundred days, and was executed by the Austrians for his part in the failed revolution of 1848.[2] He was born by the Danube, in Bratislava or, as the Hungarians have always known it, Pozsony, in 1807. One of his less well-known achievements was to plant fifty thousand mulberry trees on the estate of his manor house in Ikervár by the Rába river, a tributary of the Danube in western Hungary.[3] The plan, hatched with fellow reformers such as István Széchenyi and Lajos Kossuth, was to build up a Hungarian silk industry. The trees still flourish in the grounds. For much of the twentieth century the house functioned as a children's home and the fruit was a consolation for orphans.

Once my children are safely on their way to school, I walk along the Danube shore. Freedom Bridge crosses to Pest at this point. I walk down one stairway, cross a busy road, then climb another set of steep steps down to the water. In late January, as temperatures brush minus 20 Celsius, a procession of ice-floes appears in the waters, messengers from upriver. The level of the water is low, so I can walk along the narrow shore in the early morning gloom. I am rarely completely alone. A man called László in his early seventies discharged himself from hospital with a life-threatening condition. He comes and sits by the river to fish. Either the river will heal him or the cold will finish him off, but he's not going back to that hospital, he says. Another man, Imre, in a rather expensive overcoat and good shoes, who carries his possessions in two large plastic bags, has been homeless for ten years since he returned from teaching in Cairo. He has a long-running court case against the person who occupied his flat while he was away, and although he could rent another place, this would lessen the pressure on the court to rule in his favour. I don't know how much of his story is true. I see him for several days in a row, eating his breakfast in a little park opposite the Gellért Hotel. His mind wanders as we speak, between the articles he reads voraciously in discarded newspapers, his memories of Egypt and Greece, his sense of injustice, and knowledge culled from a lifetime of reading and thinking. Our last conversation is about British princesses. Then he disappears.

There is a place where waste water from the thermal springs beneath the Gellért Hotel flows out into the Danube. In the snow and ice, this becomes a favourite haunt of ducks, coots and seagulls. The seagulls fly to and fro through the rising steam, relishing the damp heat on their wings, then settle on the rocks close by. The ducks bathe and flutter importantly in the warm waters, like pashas in a Turkish bath. The colder the morning, the bigger the crowd of birds. They are nervous of my presence, but grow used to it after a while, the stranger with the walking stick, and a black box which clicks but does not flash. When the river is high, the steam outflow disappears beneath the swollen waters. Unable to go far, I get to know the river in one place, day after day. I notice how swiftly the level changes, in a matter of days or even in hours. I witness the constant changing of its colour, of its surface, and the skyline along the Pest bank, the churches and water towers, the strange whale-like structure over the old warehouses and marketplace, and I explore the half kilometre between the Danube and my home off Béla Bartok Street, and the people who frequent it. There is the young street-sweeper with a pony-tail, pushing a giant pram loaded with leaves, beer cans and old newspapers. After Christmas he plants a sprig of evergreen in the front left corner of his cart, his very own Christmas tree, bristling like his moustache. There are the women in the bakery that sells four different kinds of rye bread, and buttery French croissants if I am not there too early. Hungary is a nation of the *kifli*, a crescent-shaped white bread roll presumably inspired by the crescent moon on the mosques during the Turkish occupation. This particular bakery also boasts a long, straight salty 'beer' *kifli* – presumably to prove a Hungarian genius for taking the best from Ottoman times and bending it to their will. Just outside the bakery there is always a big man in a suit that fits awkwardly beneath his big anorak, with a small moustache perched like a cockroach on his upper lip, of which he seems inordinately proud. His black shoes are

polished to a high gloss, and, like the street sweeper, there is always a cigarette in his left hand. While more fortunate peoples turn their backs on
this ugly habit, the Hungarians still love their cigarettes. They wear them
on their hands like medals from lost wars.

Closer to Mészöly Street, I encounter the dog-walkers. Little clusters of
smiley women with small, yapping dogs who walk over Gellért Hill at first
light, and congregate on the street for a good chat while their dogs sniff
each other. We greet one another warmly, with a nod or a grin, but never
once stopping to go beyond appearances.

One morning in January, the children and I make a miniature snowman
on top of the green litter bin at the tram stop from three small snowballs.
The end result bears an uncanny resemblance to the Venus of Willendorf.[4]
The rim of his cap is a gleaming Hungarian five forint piece. When I come
back, twenty minutes later, he has already gone – stolen for his cheap cap,
knocked down by some fun-hating fellow perhaps, or taken carefully away
and set up again on some glorious windowsill.

Twelve warm springs flow beneath Gellért Hill.[5] In the Ottoman era
this was known as Gerz Elias Hill, after a Bosnian hero, killed when he
paused to pray in the midst of battle. The Turks called the springs the
atchik ilidja – the 'bath of the virgins', and built a structure over it to keep
the virgins suitably discreet and entertained during their ablutions.[6] This
was destroyed during the Austrian siege in 1686, and rebuilt piece by piece
over the following centuries. When the dust had settled, the virgins
returned, if we can believe the canvases of those fortunate nineteenth-
century artists allowed in to paint them. The Hungarians more prosaically
called it 'the muddy baths'.

In the 1920s and 1930s, the hotel above grew ever more magnificent,
with porcelain tiles from the Zsolnay workshop around the baths and
scenes from János Arany's 'Death of Prince Buda' up the main stairs of the
hotel.[7] The sixth canto of the poem tells the story of a hunting expedition
by Hunor and Magyar, which begins on the shore of the Caspian Sea in
pursuit of a miraculous stag. It ends on the shore of the Sea of Azov, where
the two heroes settle on an island and carry off two local maidens. Their
offspring become the founders of the Huns and the Magyars. The closed
area of the baths lies beneath the main road leading to Freedom Bridge.
Stairs lead down off a long damp corridor to an octagonal pool where the

warm water disappears into the rocks. Invisible trams rumble overhead. The temperature is 30 degrees Celsius, but the humidity is close to 100 per cent. I climb a ladder into an overhanging cave to see the source of one of the springs, hewn deep in the reddish-grey rock.

Thermal waters are Hungary's hidden treasure. The earth's crust is thinner here, so the waters are closer to the surface than in most countries. The baths are famed for their healing powers, and for the sheer pleasure of immersing your body in them. They are situated in a gradual curve, starting at Gellért Hill, curling north-west from Buda through the Pilis Hills and finally to Hévíz – which means 'warm water' – 160 kilometres from Budapest. The warm waters must have been a decisive factor in encouraging first the Celts, then the Romans, then the Hungarian tribes to stay here, and no doubt made the Turks reluctant to go home as well.

In the early 1990s I began to research the fate of the springs of Budapest, alarmed by newspaper reports that suggested the water levels were falling dramatically. The opening of one new bath after another, especially on the Pest side of the river, the bottling of more and more spring water to be sold as mineral water, and the wastefulness of the bauxite and coal mines in Tatabánya, which poured first class water down the drain, day and night, all took their toll. If the thermal waters fall below a certain level in Budapest, the Danube will flow in and destroy them. From 1965 to 1975 alone, 292 thermal wells were drilled in Hungary. 'We are on a knife-edge,' István Sárvári of the Water Resources Research Centre told me, 'and you cannot live on a knife-edge for long.'[8] A team led by him drew up a plan to save the waters. The mines, thermal baths and mineral water bottlers were asked to limit their consumption. Swimming pools were told to clean and reuse their water, and leave the healing waters for the special establishments. The plan was largely followed. By 2012 there were two dozen bathing houses and thirty-six specialised baths in the Hungarian capital, tapping 118 thermal springs and consuming seventy million cubic metres of water a day. As far as I could find out, the danger has passed – for now. To put the numbers in perspective, the Danube flows through Budapest at an average rate of two thousand cubic metres a second. In the whole country there are close to 1,300 thermal baths.

During the late 1980s and early 1990s, Mihály Dresch and his Jazz Quartet played nearly every Friday in Kinizsi Street, on the far side of the

Danube from where I live. The venue was a spacious, rather dingy, students' bar, improved by the candles on each table, cheap beer, the haze of cigarette smoke, but above all by the music. Mihály Dresch himself, a tall willow of a saxophone player, silent as a bass player, could make a twig sound melodious.[9] Over the years we move cautiously from a smile of recognition to brief exchanges of greetings. He rarely sings at his concerts, too busy with his flutes and clarinets and saxophones, but when he does his voice is haunting. My favourite is his rendition of a Transylvanian love song:

> Maros partján elaludtam, jaj de szomorút álmodtam
> Azt álmodtam azt az egyet hogy a babám mást is szeret.
> Szeress, szeress csak nézd akit,
> Mert a szerelem megvakit . . .

> I fell asleep on the banks of the Maros, and there I had the saddest dream,
> I dreamt my darling has another lover besides me.
> Love then, love, but watch out who,
> Because love can blind you, love can blind you . . .

The Maros, or Mures river in Romanian, flows for 760 kilometres through Romania, to finally reach the Tisza in Hungary at Szeged, which in turn flows into the Danube near Slankomen. That's a lot of shoreline, to walk with one's sweetheart, and fall asleep and dream the sweetest as well as the most bitter dreams.

Another version of the same song has a man fall asleep beside the Tisza, not the Maros. He dreams the saddest dream, that 'I will never be yours, my darling'. He wakes to see nine gendarmes standing over him. 'Where are your papers?' they ask. 'I'll show you my papers,' he says, and pulls out a pistol from the inner pocket of his jacket, and shoots down two or three of them. 'Oh God, what shall I do now? Should I flee or should I stay?'

In my wardrobe at home I have a bright blue T-shirt, embroidered with both the Turkish crescent and Hungarian tricolour, a gift from the President of Turkey Sultan Demirel when he visited Budapest in 1997. The year is embossed on the shirt, just beneath the flags, with the name Gül Baba. The shirt is so well made, it looks as good as new sixteen years later. Gül means rose in Turkish, and Gül Baba is the father of the roses, just as Babadag in Romania near the start of my journey was the mountain of the father. Gül Baba was a Bektashi monk who arrived in Buda after the battle of Mohács in 1526, already advanced in years.[10] He died in 1541 during the first Friday prayers to celebrate the Ottoman occupation of the city by Suleiman the Magnificent, in what is now Saint Mátyás church. Janissaries were soldiers of the Ottoman armies, abducted by Turkish press-gangs from Christian families in their youth, then trained as soldiers or administrators of the Ottoman empire. Many were Bektashis.[11] It is the only one of the mystic Sufi orders that permits the consumption of wine – for religious purposes. This clearly endeared them to the wine-loving Hungarians, as did Gül Baba's work on the ground. He established a soup kitchen for the poor on what has been named Rose Hill ever since, in his honour.

An octagonal tomb or *türbe* was erected over his grave by the Turks. This was one of the few Ottoman buildings which the Hungarians and Austrians did not demolish after the Turks were expelled in 1686. For a brief period in the eighteenth century it was converted into a Christian chapel dedicated to Saint Joseph, but since then the tomb's Muslim character has been respected by the Hungarians. In the mid-1990s it was carefully restored with Turkish state funds. A rather fanciful bronze statue of Gül Baba now stands at the start of a little promontory, with an excellent view along the Danube. There is a rose garden, with roses brought from Turkey as well as local, Hungarian varieties, a fountain and an art gallery. Outside the site, old horse chestnut trees bow their heads over the tomb. Inside, the coffin is draped in emerald green embossed with gold, and the Bektashi mitre, the symbolic turban of the sheikh, stands at the raised end. It is the quietest and one of the most beautiful places in the whole city. It is also the northernmost place of Islamic pilgrimage in the world. On the eve of the First World War, in an early flurry of Hungarian–Turkish friendship, a joint commission of archaeologists excavated the tomb.[12] Beneath the floor they found the skeleton of an elderly man, corresponding in stature and date to the sparse descriptions of Gül Baba, as well as the remains of two other men, one a soldier, killed in battle, probably during

the siege in 1686. My 1907 edition of Béla Tóth's *Gül Baba* portrays a
white-turbaned, white-bearded fellow on the cover, leaning on a walking
stick, surrounded by pink roses. 'The scent has long gone . . .' the tale
concludes, 'the grandchildren have died, but the memory of the good Gül
Baba lives on, a saint even if he performed no miracles, a poet even if he
wrote no verses, and a man who loved roses, even if he sometimes wasted
a few.'[13]

In March 2010 I took an underground train to the docks at Újpest to
board the *Tatabánya*, a handsome riverboat, built at Balatonfüred on the
shore of Lake Balaton fifty years earlier. Forty-nine metres long and seven
metres wide at her broadest point, she had a 1,200 horsepower diesel
engine, and could reach twenty kilometres per hour in quiet waters. Boat
enthusiasts devoted their free time for several years to lovingly restoring
her. The month before my journey, she was involved in the rescue of two
German registered barges, the *Würzburg* and the *Bavaria 53*, which struck
an infamous ledge of rocks on the riverbed near Dömös, in unseasonably
low water on the Danube. On that March day her crew were commissioned to deliver the shell of a floating restaurant to a customer beyond
Esztergom, about six hours steady haul upstream from Budapest. There's a
crew of five, including Gábor Jáki, president of the Hungarian Shipping
Association, and László Vasanics, the captain. The cold of the March
morning soon evaporates on the bridge, as we head out under the railway
bridge and leave the noise of the city far behind. The sun comes out and
the water is as clear as a mirror, reflecting perfect cumulus clouds. The
wheel of the *Tatabánya* is enormous, and the ship only responds to a strong
spin in one direction or the other. All the crew sail for the pleasure of it
now – most are ex-employees of the state shipping company Mahart.

'In communist times,' one of the older crew tells me, 'the best thing
about working for Mahart was the smuggling.' Travelling once a month
up the Danube to Regensburg in Germany, the crew would hide caviar
and champagne behind the panels on the journey upriver, and fill the
same cavities with French perfumes and jeans – unavailable in the eastern
bloc – on the way back. In 2004 Mahart was privatised and lost all its
river-going goods ships, though it continues as Mahart Passnave with some
passenger traffic. The privatisation was the final blow in a long decline in

the fortunes of Hungarian river transport since the glory days of the late nineteenth century when Orşova was still a Hungarian port, and when Hungarian ships dominated the middle and lower sections of the river. The rot began when Hungary lost the First World War on the German side, and lost not only two thirds of its territory but had to pay reparations. These included the pride of the Hungarian river fleet. This was painstakingly rebuilt in the 1920s and 1930s, only to be decimated again in the last years of the Second World War, sunk by Russian air raids and mines laid in the river, during the terrible four-month siege of Budapest in the winter of 1944. The fleet was restored under the communists, and between 1945 and 1995, 'three million passengers and two million tonnes of cargo a year were transported on the Danube,' the Mahart website proclaims proudly.[14]

In 2004 the Hungarian cargo fleet was bought by the Austrian Danube Steamship Company DDSG. Then it was sold to the Swiss firm Ferrexpo in 2010, which ships iron ore pellets on the Danube. The pellets are produced at the company's vast open-cast mines in central Ukraine, on the left bank of the Dnieper river. The iron, which feeds the steel plants of Europe, is quarried from beneath lands which once fed one of Europe's first civilisations: the Tripol'ye-Cucuteni.[15]

The engine room of the *Tatabánya* is an orchestra of grey-, green- and red-painted pumps and pistons. It is also the warmest place on the boat. The paint is peeling, however, and the ship is losing money, and may have to be sold. The sun disappears behind the clouds. We pass Vác, with its famous prison right on the shore of the river. This was once home to the Hungarian train bomber Szilveszter Matuska, who escaped in the chaos after the Second World War and was never seen again.[16] The Danube is silver now, painted with black and white clouds. We pass Szentendre, a pretty town of yellow churches, where Serbs fleeing the Turks took refuge. In 1720 nearly 90 per cent of the population were south Slavs. We take advantage of the high Danube, leave Szentendre Island to starboard, and come out on to the wide Danube bend at Visegrád. The sandbanks on the northern tip of the island are invisible beneath the swirling waters. When the river is low, this has always been a favourite place to bring my children, to build fires from driftwood, caught high and dry in the tall willows on the shore.

Opposite Visegrád, on the left bank of the Danube, is Nagymaros, where the final section of the Gabčikovo-Nagymaros hydroelectric project was nearly constructed.[17] The avant-garde jazz pianist György Szabados brought his grand piano down on to the shore of the river, to play against the dam. The Danube Circle, led by the biologist János Vargha, was formed to oppose it. When I came to Hungary in the mid 1980s, my first reports were about the Danube Circle. At that time you could be arrested or beaten up by police for even wearing their badge – a winding blue line, split by white. Austrian Parliamentary deputies came to Budapest in 1986 to help the campaign, and were detained in Batthyány Square at the entrance to the metro. When I tried to take photographs of the arrest, I was detained with them. We spent three hours locked in a classroom as embarrassed policemen and their political masters tried to decide what to do with us. Eventually we were released with a warning. Illegal demonstrations up to twenty thousand strong marched on parliament to demand that the project be scrapped. The first democratically elected government, under József Antall, unilaterally cancelled construction. The Slovaks pushed on regardless, and twenty years later, the two countries are still arguing over the division of the waters. László Vasanics explains why the question of the Nagymaros dam is still a painful one for Hungary. The site at Nagymaros is the only place it could have been built, he explains, because of a cliff beneath the waters close to the village of Dömös, a few kilometres upstream from Visegrád, and because of the Szentendre Island which we have just passed. Also, it happens to be one of the most beautiful places in the whole country, since the loss of the mountains of Upper Hungary (Slovakia) and of Transylvania, to Romania, after the First World War. The Pilis mountains on our left, and the Börzsöny mountains on the right, hide their heads behind hands of low cloud.

Then we pass Helemba Island, 1,713 kilometres from the lighthouse at Sulina and the mouth of the Vah river on the Slovak bank. The island, like most islands, was a burial ground before the Magyars occupied Hungary. First mentioned in church records in the thirteenth century, it became famous for its apricot trees. Now it is uninhabited, a great bush of willows, just turning green. Grey heron watch our ship pass, feigning interest in anything other than the wash of our bow wave on their gravel bank. Travelling the other way the Dutch-registered *Novalis* from St Annaland sweeps downriver. We pass under the green Mária Valéria Bridge that links Esztergom, the seat of the Hungarian Roman Catholic Church, to Štúrovo on the Slovak bank. This was destroyed in the Second World War, and its ruins stood for decades as a denial of the official myth of Hungarian–Slovak reconciliation, under the careful control of socialist internationalism. It was finally rebuilt in 2001, and has since been much prized by Slovaks as a way to get to work in Hungary, where unemployment is much lower, and for Hungarians to stroll over to the thermal baths in a town they still call by its pre-war name, Párkány, and taste some proper beer.

We deliver the boatel to its owners in a small bay overhung with willows. There are strange huts, poised above the water on sturdy concrete bases, on a superstructure of steel. The new restaurant looks small once we have cast her off, the red hull and bright white upper decks shrink into the shore. In the distance stand the blocks of flats on the outskirts of Esztergom.

This was one of the last trips of the *Tatabánya*. Burdened by the cost of her upkeep, her owners reluctantly sold her to a Greek shipping company soon after my journey. Renamed the *Anya*, and sailing under the convenience flag of Panama, she motored away down the Danube, bound for Istanbul in September 2010. It has never been particularly lucky to rename boats, and this was no exception. On 5 December 2010 the *Anya* foundered in heavy seas with the two barges she was pushing, just off the Black Sea beach of Kilyos, north of Istanbul. One of the barges broke in two and sank. Listing heavily and taking on water, the Bangladeshi crew managed to steer the *Anya* and the other barge onto the sandy beach of a popular holiday resort. Nothing more is known of her. Her former Hungarian fans believe she was taken to the scrapyard.[18]

In July 2012 I visited Szentendre again to meet the Slovene geomancer Marko Pogačnik. Originally an avant-garde artist and sculptor, he became an adept at the ancient art of geomancy – divining from the earth – and developed what he calls lithopuncture.[19] Tall, carved stones are placed carefully at strategic places on the crust of the earth, to heal the damage done by human violence. One area of conflict where he has placed stones in the past is either side of the border between the Republic of Ireland and Northern Ireland.

Pogačnik's own country took him seriously enough to choose his design for a new coat of arms for Slovenia, newly independent of Yugoslavia. Like the old coat of arms, the centrepiece is the triple-peaked Mount Triglav,

Slovenia's sacred mountain. New features include a two-lined river running across its base, instead of the old three-lined river, and an inverted triangle of silver stars representing democracy poised on a dark blue sky above the mountain. It is a fine symbol, even a powerful one, and Slovenia has prospered under its blessing since independence more than most countries in eastern Europe.

We sit drinking late harvested white wine from Balatonakali in a friend's garden. He has just finished a three-day course of lectures, teaching people to read and communicate with nature, with trees in particular. The earth, he believes, is going through a massive transformation and needs our cooperation to succeed. If we refuse, or fail to do what is needed of us, he fears the end result will be chaos.

In Lotti and Kata's garden in Szentendre I wanted to talk to him about the Danube. Especially about the harm done to it by human intervention, the vast regulation works of the past hundred and fifty years, the straitjacket into which the river is forced, the dams and dykes. For all its lingering beauty, at dawn or sunset, what happens to a river when people treat it as a motorway for ships, or a flush toilet to take away their waste? 'Ecologists, as people with rational minds, always look in a segmented way at a central point, while for me what is important is this aspect of the river that is whole in every place. This means that if a river has enough space and time to enjoy its young days, and places in-between to regenerate, then the river is capable of overcoming these problems . . . There is a limit, nevertheless, to how much a river can take. So this is not an excuse for what humans do. It is optimistic, but it is also demanding, to be more conscious . . .'

A lot of Marko's recent work has been in cities. In Paris, he had a vision of the Seine holding a plate up out of the waters, with a snake curled up on it, representing the whole course of the river. 'We think of relationships being always between human beings, but the river is also somebody, is a being, is an individual, is somebody in our vicinity. It is not enough just to enjoy a walk along the river. There should also be at least two minutes dedicated to the river – diving with one's sensitivity, so to say, into the river. Feeling it, sending an impulse from the heart. If we could learn again to relate to rivers – this would be a great help to these beings . . . I was working east of Basel, at Rheinfelden. There is a big plan by the German and Swiss governments to make a gigantic dam on the Rhine. And while I was working there I had a vision that the Rhine showed itself as a dry channel, completely dry, and the snake was not coiled but in knots. It was a sense of the great alarm of the river. The Rhine was making me aware of what problems the river would have to overcome such an obstacle – to stay one, to stay interconnected.'

He tells me one story of the Danube in Budapest. 'When I was trying to sense the presence of the river, I was very surprised that at the Gellért – which is like a natural dam – the river starts to flow backwards. Not physically, but as if the essence of the river would turn back to the height of Margit Island, and, let us say, circling and spiralling this whole area. It is as though something important is taking place in its history, like an initiation. As though it is gathering its energy before this great outflow into the Hungarian plain.'

Upstream from the city of Győr, the Szigetköz and Csallóköz (Žitný Ostrov) region of the Danube between Hungary and Slovakia spreads like a fan of islands, of floods and shallows, and was once the main breeding ground of the sturgeon and all the sixty or so fish species in the river. When Algernon Blackwood wrote about it, at the start of the twentieth century, this stretch was still largely intact, a mysterious and often frightening stretch of river, where the spirit of the Danube turned suddenly serious, haunting and awe-inspiring.

The 1977 state contract between Czechoslovakia and Hungary foresaw a massive intervention along a two hundred-kilometre section of the river, from the Danube bend at Nagymaros to the uppermost tip of the new storage lake in Slovakia. The stated aims were to win 880 Megawatts from the river, to eradicate flooding and improve navigation. The end result, according to the preamble of the treaty, 'will further strengthen the fraternal relations of the two States and significantly contribute to bringing about the socialist integration . . .'[20] Instead, the project has poisoned relations between the two countries, destroyed precious wetland forests, and threatened the long-term water supply of millions of people. The only mention of the environmental impact in the original treaty was Article 19. 'The Contracting Parties shall, through the means specified in the joint contractual plan, ensure compliance with the obligations for the protection of nature arising in connection with the construction and operation of the System of Locks'.[21]

On the positive side, the Gabčikovo dam provides 8 per cent of Slovakia's electricity supply, according to official estimates, and a large water-sports facility on the storage lake near Čunovo.

The centrepiece of the project was the diversion of the waters of the Danube into a vast above-ground canal, thirty kilometres long inside Slovakia, to generate electricity at Gabčikovo. Another dam was to be built, 120 kilometres downstream at Nagymaros in Hungary, to generate more power and to limit fluctuations in the water level. The plan was for the two countries to build the scheme together and share the electricity. Even some of the tame government scientists who studied the project were appalled by the implications. They feared the impact on the immediate area, on the vast underwater aquifer that had taken tens of thousands of years to build up, filtered through the gravel and washed down from the Alps. They worried about the impact on the flora and fauna on the banks of the Danube, both in the areas of construction, in those covered by the sixty-square kilometre storage lake and along the section of the river between the two power stations. When the Hungarian radio journalist János Betlen put some of these questions to a senior Hungarian engineer in 1983, the answers were so weak that he was ordered to go back and do the interview again, this time with carefully vetted, soft questions and reassuring answers. He suggested they send a technician instead, not a journalist, if they already knew the answers they wanted. He was suspended for six months.[22]

The protests on the Hungarian side that stopped the Nagymaros dam in the early 1990s were hardly mirrored on the Slovak side. Work was almost 80 per cent completed in Slovakia when communism collapsed and Slovakia was building up to independence from the Czechs on 1 January 1993. Instead of recognising it as a white elephant, the dam at Gabčikovo, and all the canal and construction projects which went with it, became a prestige project for the nationalist prime minister Vladimir Mečiar. The fact that most of the inhabitants of the area affected were ethnic Hungarians made it even more painful for Hungarians – and sweeter for the Slovak government. Just as for the Romanian and Serbian governments when the island of Ada Kaleh was destroyed by the Iron Gates dam, the local inhabitants were seen as collateral damage. When Hungary washed its hands of the project, Slovak engineers put an alternative version, the 'C-variant', into operation. In October 1992 they diverted the Danube a few kilometres further upstream than originally planned, at Čunovo rather than at Dunakiliti. There, both banks of the river are on Slovak soil, and the Hungarians were powerless to stop them – except by military force, which was never contemplated. In a matter of days, the great bed of the Danube, or rather the labyrinth of beds through which it flowed, on both the Hungarian and the Slovak side, dried up. Algernon Blackwood's wilderness, where rebels once lured unsuspecting conquerors to their doom, was drained. I spent the last six months before the diversion filming in the forests and creeks, and in the villages on both sides of the river. The people were bitter, but resigned to what was about to happen. 'Our throat will be cut,' said Ferenc Tamás, a fisherman on the Hungarian side.[23]

On the Slovak side of the Danube at Csallóközaranyos, Ferenc Zsemlovics took us down to the huge gravel beach where he used to wash gold with his father, and set up his apparatus one more time. A watery sun rose over the willows as he poured gravel through a wooden contraption that looked like a raised hen hatch, turning every grain, not just the gold flakes, to burnished gold. Ferenc's father bought his first car with the little ingot of gold he and his son washed from the river. They took it into the bank, exchanged it for cash, and took the money straight to the Skoda salesroom, sometime in the mid 1970s. There was so much gold in the Danube then, if you knew where and how to pan for it, Ferenc said, even his village was named after the metal: *Arany* in Hungarian means gold. When the people weren't washing gold from the river, they were fishing. He remembers from his childhood that a Jewish merchant called Mr Weiss used to buy their fish from them, and take it on his horse and cart to the market in Bratislava. His father was also taught to wash gold by an elderly Jew in the village. Almost all the eighty thousand Jews of Slovakia were killed in the Holocaust.

Béla Marcell arrived from the museum he directed in Dunajská Streda, Dunaszerdahely, to be interviewed on the banks of the river just before it was diverted. He was well versed in the rich folk stories of the region. 'Among the people of Csallóköz there are many legends about supernatural beings, about the storm wizard, whom people think of as a student. With his eleven companions, he studied the art of storm-bringing in a cave. And when he had completed his studies he set out to visit the villages in a ragged gown. When he arrived in a village, he always asked for something to eat and drink. Whatever he was offered had to be whole – a whole loaf of bread, from which he cut himself a slice, or a whole jug of water from which he poured himself a drink. And when he was given what he had asked for, he blessed that village, and the next harvest was always good. But when he did not receive what he'd asked for, he cursed it, and storm or fire followed his visit, blowing away the roofs or destroying the crops. That was his punishment.[24] . . . The storm wizard is said to have had a book from which only he could read. You or I might have studied it in vain, and have attended university, but we would never have understood a word. Now, once I was talking to a group of people in the village of Bős [Gabčikovo], and an old man piped up and said he knew where the wizard's book was – buried under an old tree on the Danube shore. So I suggested to him that we should go together, at midnight, and dig it up. "Are you mad?" he retorted. "We would be torn apart by the witches . . ." So we couldn't dig the book out. And it seems to have been buried beneath that monster' – he emphasised the last word with venom, and nodded his head towards the hydroelectric dam – 'which has made the whole place so hideous.'

Twenty years later, in the spring of 2012, I return to see the hydroelectric turbines, the canal, the storage lake, and meet some of those I interviewed in 1992. Béla Marcell had died two years earlier, but in Csallóköznádasd I meet Elenóra, the daughter of Sándor Bölcs. Sándor was a self-taught thatcher who thatched and repaired most of the houses in his village from the 1950s to the early 1990s. I remember him well, sitting astride his roof, speaking of his pride that he has handed his skill on to his sons and sons-in-law, so that they will still be thatching – he paused to grin, and point with his elbow, 'when I am on the other side'. I followed his gaze, down the steep-sloping far side of the roof, and into the world of the dead. Elenóra is living in a more modern house now, built in front of the old thatched house where her father brought up the family. Just beyond it is the huge, outward sloping wall of the canal, eighteen metres high. If it were ever to break, hers is one of the first houses that would be swept away. Sándor crossed to the other side at the age of seventy, with prostate cancer, just a couple of years after I met him. 'Even in the hospital in Bratislava, he was still making little models of the stall in Bethlehem – thatched of course,' his daughter remembers. 'It was certainly the hard work that got him,' his son-in-law adds. 'He would work in all weathers in the reeds, in the snow and cold and damp.' He would stuff newspapers inside his rubber boots, and set out.

There's not much thatching done in the village any more – the roofs are tiled, and thatch is seen as a luxury. The four of them can still thatch, but only get to practise their craft three or four times a year, normally to repair a roof. They make a living from building and fencing now, instead.

To get to the three villages on the far side of the canal, Vojka, Doborgaz and Bodíky, a ferry crosses twice an hour, but is often stopped by high winds. There is almost always a strong wind now, they say, whereas before they were protected by the forests that were chopped down to make way for the dam and the canal. The villagers have been told that if the wind speed ever gets up to a hundred kilometres per hour, the dam could collapse.

The majority in the villages are now second-home owners. The dam and all the roads that were built with it completely opened up the closed world of villages and water, regular floods and islands, to the outside world. There are fewer and fewer Hungarians and more Slovaks, though the two peoples have always got on well, on a local, if not political, level. The storage lake beyond Čunovo, and all the other little recreation lakes into which the old wetlands have been channelled, are lined with weekend houses. Some of them are even thatched – 'and some are really beautiful,' Elenóra admits, readily. As we speak, she bounces her daughter Zsófi on her knee, and we sip red wine from the Izabella grapes Sándor planted in the garden. One thing that hasn't changed, they say, are the mosquitoes, barely a nuisance some summers, unbearable in others. Local people like to climb the walls of the canal, and watch the barges and passenger ships pass in summer. In winter, when the lakes freeze, the children skate as they always have, and Elenóra wishes her father had lived long enough to see his grandchildren skate. We bid each other fond farewells, and I drive down the road to Gabčikovo. On the top I park the car and watch the waves breaking along the huge mass of concrete and steel.

I drive towards Bratislava to see the ferry crossing, but crossings for the rest of the day have just been cancelled because the wind has reached sixteen kilometres an hour – and regulations say they should stop the ferry if it crosses the twelve kilometres an hour threshold. There are two ferries, but only one is in working condition. As well as the captain, several of the other crew gather round the table, to drink tea and chat about the old times. 'What I miss most,' says the captain, 'is the kindergartens and schools. In Bodíky both have closed down, together with the post office. There's just a bar left – three bars in fact!' The men laugh. A doctor visits the villages once a week: 'you have to get ill on the right day!' they laugh again. The villages have been connected to the mains water supply and to the sewage system. They drink water from the tap, not from the wells any more. And the soil is still good for their vegetables – for maize, wheat and sugarbeet.

I stop on the shore near Čunovo, to visit the Danubiana modern art gallery, on an exposed promontory.[25] There are white waves on the grey green waters of the storage lake, and sculptures around the gallery, of strange blue, white and green figures, of rakish golf players, of a peculiar Napoleon head, by the Dutch-born sculptor Hans Van de Bovencamp, somehow add to the bleakness of the place on a cold day. 'In creating large sculptures, he focuses on their interaction with the surrounding environment,' reads the blurb. Two giant twisted metal hens or cockerels alone seem to do justice to the tortured former wilderness of the place. Out of the water huge piles of rocks protrude, and the lake is lined with concrete embankments.

At last, to my relief, a great V-shaped formation of geese flies high overhead, a reminder of the awesome symmetry of nature. I long for William Blake in this plastic playground.

> In what distant deeps or skies
> Burnt the fire of thine eyes?
> On what wings dare he aspire?
> What the hand dare seize the fire?[26]

The road into Bratislava from the Danube villages and Šamorín is quiet, compared to the brash motorways that approach the Slovak capital from other directions. I've chosen a boatel moored on the Danube bank to stay in, just beneath the white castle. One hundred and seventy-two kilometres of the Danube's length flow through Slovakia, and Bratislava, like Budapest and Belgrade, and to a lesser extent Vienna, owes much of its glory to the river.

Pulling my small suitcase down the plank, I'm assailed by a wonderful smell of Indian curry – there's an Indian restaurant on board. Over breakfast the next morning the manager tells me that the boat used to be busy as a floating brothel, downriver in Budapest, before he found a better use for it in Bratislava. He gives me a little brass cabin number from those times, number 301. I sleep like a log both nights on his sturdy craft, lulled into my dream world by river waves and seagulls.

Jaromír Šibl leans slightly forward over the table as we talk in his office, a tram's ride from the city centre, between the Botanical Gardens and the Waterworks Museum. He's a tall, bearded man with a Santa Claus twinkle in his eye, who looks as though he was born with a rucksack on his back. I first met him in the late 1980s and early 1990s, as he was one of the few brave Slovaks who opposed the construction of Gabčikovo. Now he runs an environmental organisation called Broz.[27] 'The main victim is nature. The point is that normally this was a floodplain area which was regularly flooded several times a year, the whole area, the islands, the meadows and the forests. You could only travel through the forest by boat. The whole ecosystem was based on this simple fact of regular floods.' One pleasant surprise has been the lack of damage, so far at least, to the huge underground aquifer, beneath layers of gravel which are in places several hundred metres deep. There is a lack of research, he adds, but the research published so far by Slovak scientists is reassuring.

The fall in the ground water-level, on both sides of the river, but especially the Slovak side, is much more alarming. Hungarian engineers and policy-makers faced up to the fait accompli of the Slovak diversion of the river early on, he said. The only agreement ever reached between Hungary and Slovakia about the Danube was the construction of an underwater weir in the old bed of the Danube near Dunakiliti. This allows a small lake to build up from the remaining waters in the river, which is then carefully redistributed through the region via a system of natural and man-made streams and canals. This helps to keep the water level up, and prevents the complete drying out of the area which the diversion would otherwise have caused. On the Slovak side the situation is much worse, according to

Jaromír, because the Slovak authorities refuse to do anything at all about the problem. 'The official policy of Slovakia is that the 1977 treaty is still valid, and we should behave accordingly. This means that we should use whatever means we have to force the Hungarians to complete not only this part of the original project, but also to complete Nagymaros. So if we take any steps that were not envisaged in the original project, we would be implicitly agreeing that the Hungarians were right when they stepped out of the treaty. And this would weaken our position in an eventual future legal dispute. This is the main political problem which we have not overcome for the past twenty years.'

In 1997, the Court of Justice in Luxembourg found both countries guilty of breaking the 1977 treaty, Hungary for stepping out of it unilaterally and Slovakia for pressing ahead with the C-variant.[28] It ordered both to reach agreement over the division of the Danube waters, of which Slovakia now takes 80 per cent. No agreement has been reached and none seems likely.

In Bratislava, the level of the Danube has risen half a metre as a result of the storage lake, adding to the flood threat during periods of high water. No studies have ever been published comparing the cost of construction and maintenance of the dams and managing the vast sediments in the storage lake with the value of electricity gained. Broz focuses its efforts on smaller projects, to improve or restore the natural balance of the river and the lands beside it: on Petržalka, the part of the city on the right bank of the river, dominated by vast housing estates, and on restoring traditional animal grazing on the banks near Bratislava and downstream at Komárno. Before the communists took over, the willow forests along the shore of the Slovak Danube were pruned by local people for firewood and grazed by their animals. After fifty years of neglect the Broz project enabled people to gather firewood again, and their animals drove back the many invasive species that had harmed the willows.

Before leaving Slovakia, I drive northwards to visit the castle and cliffs at Devin, overlooking the Danube. This is where the Carpathian Mountains start, and where the Old Europe of Marija Gimbutas ends – the westernmost point that the Copper Age civilisations reached. The castle stands on a steep cliff, overlooking the point where the Morava river flows into the Danube. The Romans dislodged the Celts from here, as from castle hill overlooking Bratislava. Devin is named after *deva*, the Slavic word for maiden. It was an important fortress on the corner of the Greater Moravian empire, as well as for the Hungarians. Following their defeat at the battle of Mohács in 1526, Hungarian kings were crowned in St Stephen's Church in Bratislava from 1536 onwards. In the mid-nineteenth century, the Slovak poet Lud'ovit Stur, after whom the town of Štúrovo, opposite Esztergom, is named, gathered his friends together to plot the birth of the Slovak nation, attracted by the rugged beauty and historic importance of the place. That was only forty years after Napoleon's retreating forces blew large parts of it up – the ruins made it even more attractive to the Romantic imagination.

At the foot of the cliffs beside the river, a concrete arch stands riddled with bullet holes, a memorial to all those who died trying to swim the Morava river to the Austrian side to escape Czechoslovakia. On the back are the names of more than a hundred people who met that fate on this heavily guarded section of the border.

Georg Frank comes out of his castle to welcome me. He's younger than I expect, too young to have taken part in the 1984 protest movement against the Hainburg dam, which made this park and his job possible. As manager of the Donauauen national park, he oversees the water levels, the trees and beavers, the fish and owls and frogs and little creeks of this stretch of woodland.[29] He drives me down half overgrown tracks in a red park-authority jeep into the restricted area of the woodlands. Then we walk for a while together, two grown men in a sea of snowdrops. I pick a handful to sniff. They do have a faint scent, but nothing like the full-blooded linen of Babadag. These ones are made to delight the eyes, not the nose. Next time we stop the car we hear the woodpeckers straightaway. Each plays a different, rattling note on the tree, depending on the hollowness of the wood, the hardness of the trunk, and the power of its beak. Georg lists all the woodpeckers of this wood. The Balkan, black, white and red, the greater-spotted, green and, more elegant, the lesser-spotted, the rarer of the three, and several others; closer, or further away – turning the wood into an echo chamber, a carpenter's workshop.

He takes me to see one tree in particular, with all the reverence of a visit to the queen of the forest. The black poplar only grows on land that is regularly flooded. It gets its name from the darkness of its trunk, which it keeps even in the brightest sunlight. The trunk of this one is surrounded by fallen wood, and there is a lighter brown wound in the back – the work of beavers. The beavers diligently make a ring around the trunk, then saw deeper and deeper with their teeth until the tree falls. There's no danger of that happening with this one, Georg says, though he is impressed by their boldness – attacking one of the oldest trees of this forest. 'It's too far from the water – they have easier prey along the banks.' We wander down to the shore of a wide creek and scare two young boar, who crash away through the undergrowth. Since this became a national park, there has been no forestry here – but there are signs of the old forestry in every hybrid poplar, growing tall and thin and disappointing in their uniformity, compared to all the other kinds of poplars. The park authority has decided not to chop down the planted poplars in this section, but to allow the beavers to do the job themselves. And on the far shore, it's clear they are fulfilling their ecological duty with a passion – five or six tall poplars, their bark all gone, on the brink of falling.

Then we go down to the Uferhaus, the River Bank-house, an old restaurant on the shore. The Danube seems male again here, manly, a weight-lifter. The flow is swift – swift enough to attract the dam-builders thirty years ago – and the barges labour upstream, groaning and whispering and grumbling against the current. We choose a table outside and order pikeperch fillets with a pat of garlic butter on each. Not from the Danube, Georg sighs. From ponds in Hungary or Slovakia. There's not enough fish in the main river.

Georg calls Josef, the chief forester. He turns down all offers of food and drink to tell his story. 'I was born in December 1944. My father was a Sudeten German, my mother a local girl. When the Russians came, he was expelled. My mother and I stayed here. We were very poor. My mother got work looking after the cows for a local landowner, on the far shore, at Haslau. We had a couple of goats of our own, so we could always drink goat's milk. I remember as a child, how much I longed for cow's milk. Now I find out that goat's milk is better for you anyway! . . . The Russian soldiers used to come down to the shore to catch fish. They were always very kind to us, even shared their bread with us. I remember it was black, very different to ours, and had a funny taste. They had a very crude way of catching fish. They would throw a couple of hand-grenades into the water, and the explosions killed lots of fish and brought them floating to the surface. Then they would gather them in big boxes, load them into the back of their trucks, and drive away again. What the Russians didn't realise was that the bigger fish, that were just stunned by the explosions, only floated to the surface an hour or so later. So we children would take those home. Or take them to the restaurants to sell!'

His first income, at seven years old, was from selling fish to the restaurant outside which we now sat. Then he got a job in forestry, on the same estate as before, which in the meantime had been nationalised. 'As a forester?' I ask. 'A wood-hacker, rather!' he grins – the lowest of the low. He learnt to plant fast-growing trees in straight lines, and was even sent to Novi Sad and the forestry school in Osijek, to learn how to grow trees even faster, even straighter. 'The speed was all that mattered. Plant them, watch them grow, bulldoze them all down, plant new ones.'

When the protests against the planned Hainburg dam broke out in the early 1980s, and the Austrian prime minister granted a ten years' pause for reflection, Josef was suddenly out of work. He and his colleagues would have had the job of clearing all the forests on both sides of the river, to make way for construction – the same trees which the young Austrian environmentalists were climbing and chaining themselves to, to stop the bulldozers. So Josef started commuting to Vienna, where he got a job in a bread factory. In the meantime at Orth, 110,000 people pooled their savings to buy the forest to create the national park. One day Josef got a phone call from the director. Would he meet him for a drink? Over a cup of coffee, in middle age he was offered the task of undoing his life's work, of helping the forest return to something like its natural state, of overseeing the removal of artificial barriers, the natural reflooding of the forest and the destruction of the straight lines of his youth. The one thing he, as forestry manager, was no longer allowed to do, was to plant or cut down trees. 'It was strange at first, very strange. You have to look at trees in a very different way . . . letting them grow by themselves, fall by themselves, slowly rot into the forest floor. And the most amazing thing was, as we let this happen, how all the wildlife re-appeared in the forest.'

Another man cycles by and Georg calls him over. Martin has long hair, partly hidden in a woolly hat. He's on his way home after a hard day's work, but spares us some minutes. Martin and his wife have just finished restoring a water mill, now moored on a creek a few kilometres upstream. How had they done it? With passion, he says. And madness!

While we talk, Georg is feverishly tapping the keyboard of his mobile phone. 'She says yes!' he suddenly announces, excitedly. He has just arranged for me to go owl-spotting with the girls tonight. So as darkness falls I find myself in the pleasant but rather unexpected company of Christina, who is writing her PhD on owl behaviour, and a Latvian student on work experience, bouncing down a dark track, ever deeper into the forest. At one point a whole herd of deer – I count at least eight – is scattered by our approach, leaping lightly away down the sides of the grassy dyke, some to the left, some the right. We stop, watch them regroup cautiously, then walk peacefully away into the forest. A little while later we take a right turn, down into the forest again, until we reach a clearing which Christina reconnoitred earlier. There she sets up her own recording and broadcasting equipment. The plan is to play the calls of different kinds of owl, so that real owls living in the wood will assume their territory has been infringed upon and will come to examine the intruders. It's a starry night, but only a small pool of stars is visible above the ring of trees. First Christina plays the sound of a male tawny owl. The cry is long and mournful, the recording one of her own. It echoes through the forest, like ripples in water. I imagine the ears of the entire forest twitching in response, including fellow owls and their prey. But there is no reply. Next she tries the call of an eagle owl, a bigger, fiercer bird. Almost immediately, a long, low hoot comes in response – but of a different note. 'It's a tawny!' she whispers. Now she turns on the recording equipment, which looks like a small, curving satellite dish. Soon it is calling, closer and closer to us, though its wing beats are completely silent. As it approaches, we hear the higher pitch of a female tawny, following the male through the forest. Then the two of them settle, effortlessly, in the tree next to us. We can see them clearly outlined against the starry sky. A few nights earlier, on a similar expedition, an eagle owl flew so close over her head she had to duck down, she says.

Every owl, not just every kind of owl, has its own voice, and she has trained her ear to recognise individual birds, Christina explains. She makes careful notes in a log book, complete with GPS coordinates, and the sounds which attracted each owl in turn, with the light of a spotlight attached to her forehead. A thin, pretty girl, humorous . . . birdlike. We make some more owl sounds, record some more. While waiting for the owls, our eyes peeled on the heavens, we identify the constellations. The tawnies we saw were just under Gemini, twin stars blinking in the darkness. The girls will stay out all night in the forest, going from place to place, but I should press on, to Vienna. They drive me back to my car in the village of Stopfenreuth. 'How did you get interested in owls?' I ask. 'I am an owl,' Christina says simply, with only a trace of a smile around her mouth. 'I don't need to sleep at all at night; I like to sleep till midday . . .

We bid one another birdlike farewells; the girls go back to their dark wood and their birds of prey, and I plunge across the Danube bridge towards the highway and the bright lights of the Austrian capital.

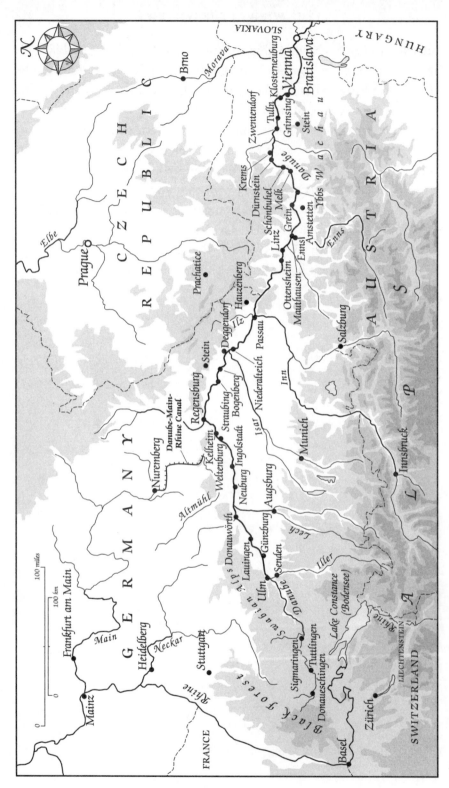

4. The Upper Danube from the castle at Devin to the source of the river in the Black Forest.

CHAPTER 12

Danube Fairytales

'Man, a god when he dreams, barely more than a beggar when he thinks.'
FRIEDRICH HÖLDERLIN[1]

THE NASCH market in Vienna is a double line of stalls, like the floats of a fisherman's net, but the net itself is lost in the depths of the River Wien which gave the city its name, then disappeared beneath its streets. There's the Theater an der Wien on the corner, to remind market-goers that they are walking on water. The market, like most of Vienna, is far from the Danube, which bypasses the city like a cruise ship in the night. It was named after the ash wood containers in which the milk once sold here was stored. It boasts an elegant fish market, though none of the fish here actually come from the river. The Wien river survives, just about, in its concrete tunnel, and funnels out into the Danube canal.

Each fish on display carries a neat tag with its country or region of origin, like a Miss World contest. There are *Saibling* – char – from Mariazell, carp bits for fish soup from the Gut Dornau in Lower Austria, *Hecht* – pike – from the Neusiedler lake on the border with Hungary and trout from Salzburg. Everything else is imported from other seas: salted cod and Coquilles St Jaques and Venus mussels from the north-east Atlantic, eight different kinds of caviar, including sturgeon eggs from the Caspian, and even deep-frozen pikeperch – an authentic Danube fish – from Kazakhstan. At the downmarket end of the fish-stalls, a young man from Negotin in eastern Serbia stands over a green tub in which six muddy and rather lost-looking carp swim to and fro – from the Czech Republic, he says, as though that explains their demeanour. Negotin is a town not far from Miroč, to which Marko Kraljević pursued the fairy who killed his friend Miloš. The man has been in Vienna for twenty-three years, which must mean he was almost born here – his parents wisely got out of Serbia soon after Slobodan Milošević came to power. A pointy-faced man with blue eyes and an unshaven chin sells *Wanderbrot* – Dick Whittington food – delicious, compacted dried fruit, ideal for long journeys. I buy a big chunk for the road. 'I'm from the Soviet Union,' the man announces, a country which, according to my calculations, has not existed for more than twenty years. When I gently point this out, he confesses that his homeland is actually Uzbekistan – 'but no one here has ever heard of it.' If I came from the legendary city of Samarkand, I tease him, I would proudly tell the whole world about it at every opportunity, and thereby win extra custom for my stall.

An elderly Austrian man sells red wine from Montenegro and white wine from Mostar, where the River Neretva flows deep and turquoise beneath the single arch of the repaired bridge, even when the sky is the dullest shade of grey. The stall has been in the family since his father bought it in 1965. And how's business? He frowns. 'Euro-teuro . . .' – a mocking reference to the European currency which has made everything more *teurig* (expensive). He grumbles about the gentrification of the market, the little cafés springing up everywhere. Just above his head I spot *chai tou vounou* – Greek mountain tea, in its traditional plastic bag – and snap up a couple of packets. I used to buy it by the armful in the marketplace in Istiea in northern Euboea, but apart from rare finds like this, it remains one of Greece's best kept secrets, or worst-marketed treasures.

Then along the Franz Lehár alleyway to the Café Sperl.[2] The ghost of Franz Lehár sits at a table near the entrance, putting the final touches to the score for the 'Merry Widow', fated to become one of Hitler's favourite light operas, to its composer's misfortune. What did the German dictator think as he sat listening in the dark of the concert hall; what passed behind his closed eyes? Lehár was born on the north bank of the Danube in what is now Komárno in Slovakia. In 1902 he became conductor at the Theater an der Wien, and the Sperl was the nearest place to retire for a quiet drink to compose his next work. His wife Sophie was of Jewish origin; she converted to Catholicism but nonetheless drew the hostility of the Nazis. Hitler is said to have intervened personally to end the machinations of those who wanted her deported to the death camps, because he was so fond of her husband's music. Another ghost at the Sperl tables is Lehár's fellow Hungarian Emmerich – or Imre – Kálmán. A talented pianist and composer, he worked closely with Lehár, then escaped the Nazis in 1938, first to Paris, then the United States. Hungary has furnished western Europe with so many exiles.

Miklós Gímes, a Hungarian journalist and son of the 1956 revolutionary of the same name, once told me how he fled Budapest in November 1956 as a child of seven with his mother, leaving his father behind as the Soviet troops re-invaded the country. And how his mother took him to a smart Viennese café like this one, and spent the last of the coins the Austrian Red Cross had given them at the border on cakes. As they sat there, in their long, unfashionable coats, clutching all their possessions in a single suitcase, the Viennese middle class studied them like creatures from another planet, then one by one came to their table and gave them money.

The Sperl, with its old wooden tables, and rather brusque and beautiful waitresses, is definitely conducive to writing. Between slices of cake I trade limericks with a friend:

'The national game of the Czechs,/is not what a person expects./This peculiar nation,/thinks defenestration,/is far more exciting than sex.'

'An ancient fish is the pike,/his long faces are never alike./When I slept in Vienna,/I awoke in a terror,/that a pike might alight with my bike!'

The military museum is a sturdy red brick fort five stops on the metro from the Nasch market.[3] The first floor is lined with exhibits from the two Ottoman sieges of Vienna, in 1529 and 1683, and from the mopping up operations which followed: the capture of Párkány and Buda. The arrow that lodged beneath Count Guidobald von Stahremberg's shoulder during the siege of Buda is preserved at the centre of a glass monstrance, above the figure of a turbaned Turk who kneels in heavy chains with three dogs snapping at his heels. There is an accompanying verse: 'Ein Pfeil, so zwanzig Jahr in Fleisch und Bein gesteckt, und tausend-fachen Schmerz dem Helden Leib erweckt, wird durch des Künstlers hand von seinem Sitz

gebogen, und nach gemachten Schnitt noch glücklich ausgezogen.' ('This
arrow lodged for twenty years in a hero's flesh and bone. It tortured him
much, but was happily cast out by a surgeon's skilful craft.') Guido was the
cousin of the commander of Vienna's defences, Ernst von Stahremberg,
and distinguished himself by his bravery, leading sorties out from the walls
to attack the besieging Turks. He was seriously injured during a desperate
attempt to stop the Turks storming the city after blasting a hole in the city
wall. When he was struck by that arrow at Buda, just three years later, he
must have thought his final hour had come.

The Grand Vizier, Kara Mustafa – Mustafa the Black – reached Vienna
with his army on 13 July 1683. The message he sent, asking for the uncon-
ditional surrender of the city, the conversion of its inhabitants to Islam, or
their departure with guarantees that they would not be attacked, received
no response from Ernst von Stahremberg. The city had only twelve thousand defenders under his command. King John Sobieski and his Polish-
German troops were still several days' march away. By all accounts, Kara
Mustafa was a poor general compared to some of his shrewd and battle-
hardened predecessors in the Ottoman military. Ibrahim, the elderly pasha
of Buda, advised him to postpone his attack and first secure control of the
frontier. 'In support of his argument the pasha recounted the fable of a
king who placed a pile of gold in the centre of a carpet, then offered it to
any man who could take it without treading on the carpet. The winner was
the one who rolled up the carpet from the edge, until he reached and was
able to grab the prize,' in Patrick Kinross's words.[4] However, Ibrahim's
advice was rudely dismissed, and Black Mustafa marched straight to
Vienna. Without heavy artillery, so far from his base camp, he had to rely
on mining the walls. For this to be done, trenches were dug by prisoners of
war, right up to the city walls. On 4 September, more than two weeks into
the siege, the greatest breach was made in the walls, and Turkish troops
entered the city for the first and only time. But after hours of bitter, hand-
to-hand fighting, they were ejected. That was the nearest Turkish soldiers
ever came to taking Vienna, and the turning point in the siege. The same
day came news that John Sobieski had crossed the Danube at Tulln with a
bridge of boats, and had met up with the forces of Lorraine, Bavaria and
Saxony. The three armies marched together for three days to reach the
Kahlenberg ridge of the Wienerwald, the highlands overlooking Vienna to

the west, which the arrogant Mustafa had left undefended. The Turks, although outnumbering the Christian armies, were now caught between the city walls and the relief army looking down on them from the heights. On 12 September 1683, a Sunday, bright and sunny after the rain of the past few days, John Sobieski personally led the attack. His soldiers seemed to the Turks like 'a flood of black pitch coming down the mountain consuming everything it touched.' By six in the evening, Kara Mustafa and the remains of his army had fled. Twenty-five thousand Turkish tents and their rich contents were seized that day, but the one on display in the museum was taken during the siege of Petrovaradin in 1716. It is richly decorated with carpets, and, rather incongruously, with oil paintings of the heroes of the battle on the Austrian side. In front of it is a massive cannon, the 'Morser', used in the siege of Belgrade in August 1717. A single cannonball killed 3,000 Turks when it struck their munitions store high on the Kalemegdan – a predecessor of the explosion at Smederevo in July 1941.

The museum seems almost deserted, until I spot a woman in a head-scarf, walking arm-in-arm with a man with a moustache, and a younger man who is clearly their son, showing them around. Suleiman is a law student at the University of Vienna, and has lived in the city for eleven years. It's his third visit to the museum, he says, and he has arranged this excursion 'to show his parents things related to the Ottomans'. We agree to meet again later, to discuss his experience of being a Turk in Vienna.

'My father was more affected by it emotionally than I was,' he tells me, when we meet at the Café Stein. His parents came out from Istanbul to help him and his wife with their new-born baby, Kerem. 'Many Turks live in Austria, but they have no idea that this museum exists.' 'What about the way Turks are presented, as the eternal enemy . . . kneeling in chains under the Habsburg rulers?' I ask. 'Before I came to Austria, my uncle on my mother's side told me about a statue, of a Christian priest in St Stephan's Square, standing over a Turk. So I went to see it when I arrived. There's not so much material from the siege here. Sobieski took most of what he captured with him to Cracow, which was the Polish capital then, and it's on display in the museum there.[5] I think a lot of images of Turks were made by people who never actually met one. There were all the wars at the time between the Ottoman and Habsburg empires, so it was necessary to portray the Turks as some kind of monsters. But there were also many other contacts – we were neighbours, after all. All the foreign ambassadors and travellers who spent time in Istanbul paint a very different picture. I think the Austrians used the encounter with the Ottomans, with the Turks, much more wisely than the Spanish did. The Spanish just threw the Muslims out of their country. Here, the Austrians learnt many things from them. Like coffee-drinking, and visits to the bath-house!'

He enjoys living in Austria, and says the people are kind to him on the whole, but most of his friends are fellow foreigners: Turks, Albanians, Bosnians, Arabs. 'I don't know why that is. Maybe because we are all strangers here, and that draws us to one another. There is also prejudice towards us, but I do also have Austrian friends.' Suleiman comes from Constantinople, and his wife is from the city of Yozgat in central Anatolia. When they have both finished their doctorates they plan to go back to Turkey to work. He plans an academic career. With a qualification from a European university his job prospects will be better in his own country. He attends a Turkish mosque close to his flat regularly, and sometimes goes to other mosques and *meschid* – prayer halls – in the city, if he is passing. Muslims tend to stick to their own national groups, he says, Turks with Turks, Saudis with Saudis. But when they pray together, in the mosque attached to the Islamic Cultural Centre on the banks of the Danube, he is always careful not to offend his fellow Muslims from Arab countries by doing things in a way that they find hard to accept. He cites one particular ritual prayer, the *hesbat*, which Turkish Muslims say aloud in a group, but which Arabs recite silently and alone. He does it in their style when they are at the same prayers, out of respect for their feelings.

'What if Kara Mustafa had taken Vienna?' I ask before we leave the café. The street is loud all around us, the hubbub of any western capital, the laughter of the women in the café, the sirens of police cars, the bells of the churches. 'The sultans were already weak at that time, in the seventeenth century. As far as I know, Kara Mustafa had plans to set up a state of his own in central Europe. He might have ended up at war with the sultans himself. In any case, what makes a state strong is if justice reigns. In the latter Ottoman empire, there was less justice, and more corruption. In my view, that is why it fell apart. What makes Europe strong today is that it is just. It was God's will that the Turks did not capture Vienna.

Would it look different if they had? For sure . . . the streets would not be so straight!'

Downstairs, on the way out of the museum, stands the car in which the Archduke Franz Ferdinand and his wife Sophie were riding when they were assassinated by Gavrilo Princip and the Black Hand gang beside the Miljačka river in Sarajevo in June 1914. The car is painted dark green and has the name 'Graf & Stift' on the bonnet. The archduke's eggshell-blue tunic is stained with blood, and one side is cut open in an L-shape, presumably by physicians trying to save his life. But Princip could hardly miss his target at such close range. Ferdinand's bodyguards that day, if he had any, must have been masters of incompetence. Also on display are three of the Browning-Colt pistols used by the assassins, which match the fourth I saw in the Military Museum in Belgrade. There's a poignant photograph of Ferdinand, Sophie and their sons and daughter. The peculiar green-plumed feather hat the archduke was wearing that day is also on display. I try to imagine the moment when the children were told of the death of both their parents. The assassins would later express regret over the death of their mother. 'We did not know that the late Franz Ferdinand was a father,' one of the conspirators told the court. 'We were greatly touched by the words he addressed to his wife, "Sophie, stay alive for our children." We are anything you want – except criminals. In my name and in the name of my comrades, I ask the children of the late successor to the throne to forgive us. As for you, punish us according to your understanding. We are not criminals. We are honest people, animated by noble sentiments; we are idealists; we wanted to do good; we have loved our people; and we shall die for our ideals.'[6] A portrait of Sophie, in oil pastels and chalk, and looking rather shy, stands on an easel next to the car. The way the reflection of the overhead light falls on the glass front of the picture gives the impression that she is wearing a golden crown. Her husband incurred the wrath of almost the entire Habsburg court for marrying 'beneath himself' – poor Sophie was a 'mere Bohemian countess'. While the coffins containing their bodies were accorded full military honours by the army on their sad journey home by train to the coast, and thence by battleship to Trieste, followed by train to the South Station in Vienna, they were disposed of with a minimum of ceremony at Klein-Pöchlarn beside the Danube. 'One can hardly grasp the enormity of it,' begins the front page article of the *Reichspost* for Monday 29 June 1914, beneath the headline 'Heir to the Throne and his Wife Murdered', 'our archprince and heir to the throne, the man in whom the peoples of the Habsburg empire entrusted all their hopes, indeed their whole future, is no more.'

The Viennese Police Academy is in Marokkanerstrasse (Moroccan street). I've arranged to meet Omar Al-Rawi, a Social Democratic deputy on the city council, who was born in Iraq, to watch the swearing in of 350 new police officers. A handful of them are Muslims, and several dozen are from national or religious minorities in Austria. Travelling from east to west on this river, I'm especially curious about the fate of 'easterners' when they reach western Europe.

Lana Sehić stands at attention in her dark-blue uniform, her cap with red band and gold braid, silver stripes down the sides of her trousers, and the double-headed eagle on her left shoulder. She has deep brown eyes and red lips, and she's glowing with pride and happiness. Beside her thinner-necked, blonder, mostly blue-eyed colleagues, one might guess that she was not born in this corner of central Europe, but who would guess that she comes from Bosnia? 'I was ten years old when the war broke out in Sarajevo. My father was killed in the first month – as a civilian, not a soldier. Soon after that we escaped in a convoy, with my mother. We went to Germany first, because my mother had relatives there. Then we came for a month to Austria to visit a family. They helped us stay here.' She and her mother were among the 90,000 people from Bosnia who found temporary refuge in Austria in 1992. Now she feels more Austrian than Bosnian. She goes back once a year on the anniversary of her father's death, to see her grandmother – her last relative in Sarajevo. She was attracted to the police force by a friend's stories. There are a hundred thousand immigrants from the former Yugoslavia living in Vienna, and the fact she can speak their language makes her job as a policewoman easier. Looking down the list of names, there are several others from the former Yugoslavia. She is not a practising Muslim. 'There are Serbs, Catholics and Bosniaks in our family, so my parents thought it would be better if we were brought up without religion.'

As one of the most prominent members of the Muslim community in Austria, Omar Al-Rawi has a broad overview of both its diversity and its unity. 'The first and most important experience for most Muslims when they come to Vienna is that they see their own religion in all its variety. Muslims can be very tolerant of Jewish and Christian people, but when it comes to their own community . . .' he chuckles, 'they have a lot of struggles with each other.' Many confuse their ethnic and traditional ways of living with their faith, he says. Shi'ites and Sunnis from Iraq, Wahhabis from Saudi Arabia, staunch Sunnis from Turkey . . . 'when they meet, a big discussion begins. They have to learn to be tolerant of each other.' About half the Muslims in Austria are of Turkish origin, then comes a group from the former Yugoslavia, such as Lana. After them the Arabs, the Pakistanis, the Afghans and Iranians. 'We also have a new, Russian-speaking Muslim community here – the Chechens. So we had to get hold of Korans in Russian translation.' While the parents have often lost their religion, their children return to it, he has noticed. Since the terrorist attacks on the Twin Towers and the Pentagon in September 2001, and the bomb attacks in London and Madrid, state surveillance of the community has also visibly increased. 'Muslims in western Europe have freedom of thought and of speech, and the imam can say anything he wants at Friday prayers, without fear that the security police will imprison him.' But the attacks have led to what he sees as a state backlash. 'They should differentiate more between being liberal in their faith, and radical in political ways. You can have strong feelings about the war in Iraq, or the situation of the Palestinians, without preaching hatred or intolerance . . . It would be interesting to compare this situation with that of Liberation Theology in Latin America. There were priests and preachers there who were very liberal in their theology, even going against the Pope and the Vatican, but at the same time very left wing. More attention should be paid to the same nuances in Islam in Europe. When Muslims here gather, and sing their songs, or quote verses from their poets, Austrians stare at them and wonder what is going on.' Austrians use double standards towards Muslims, but Muslims are guilty of double standards towards one another, he says. He sees no contradiction between being a Social Democrat and a Muslim – the two ways of thinking fit very nicely together. And besides, 'it's much safer to be a politician here than in my own country,' he laughs.

A month after my visit, Austria was finally due to open its labour markets to fellow European Union nationals from eastern Europe. 'This is

not going to be a dramatic topic . . . Because the East is already here,' said
Labour Minister Rudolf Hundstorfer. There were already 29,000
Hungarians, 17,000 Romanians and 16,000 Poles in Austria, he stated. He
expected at most 25,000 more to arrive after 1 May 2012, looking for
work. Those figures were disputed by Heinz-Christian Strache, the leader
of the far-right Freedom Party, who feared hundreds of thousands rather
than just tens of thousands more people would arrive.

The road out of Vienna to the north-west follows the tram tracks, out
through the city towards the village of Nussdorf. It was here in September
1683 that the first clashes between the Saxon and Imperial Dragoons on
the Austrian side and the Ottoman defenders took place. By nine in the
morning the Austrians had taken Nussdorf. Meeting nothing more frightening than trams and buses, I head out of the city with the Danube clearly
visible on my right, and down to the shore at Klosterneuburg. Legend has
it that Duke Leopold III (1351–86) was walking in the vicinity with his
wife when the wind off the river caught her veil and blew it into a tree.

Looking up into the branches the emperor had a vision of the Virgin
Mary, and ordered a monastery to be built on the spot. The town has
grown up around it. A later story of Klosterneuburg concerns a certain
rat-catcher – a slightly different version to that of the better known Pied
Piper of Hamelin.[7] Here, too, a reward was offered by the city authorities
to anyone who could rid the city of a plague of rats. Here, too, a piper
appeared and led the rats out of the city, down to the river to drown. When
the mayor refused to pay the agreed fee the piper refused the pittance in
the purse thrown down at his feet. When he returned, some weeks later, he
played a different tune, and all the children of Klosterneuburg followed
him down to the Danube. There they boarded a strange, brightly painted,
ship. They sailed away downstream and were never seen again – except for
two children: one because he was deaf and had not heard the wonderful
music; the other because she had gone back home to change her skirt.

Looking back towards Vienna the Danube here is silver, and black trees
bend low over it as if in blessing. There's a row of tables and benches on the
shore outside the Uferhaus café with a sign chalked up on a blackboard –
'Sorry [in English] – opens circa end March.' Across the road are three
brightly painted Tibetan prayer-wheels, oil drums mounted on their ends

that one can spin as one prays, and a line of prayer-flags, blue, white, red, green and yellow, brightening trees still in their winter greys. 'Dear visitors,' reads the sign, 'please take care of yourselves and your children when you enter this prayer-construction. We are not responsible for your safety! May all sentient beings be happy. Thank you for your visit.'[8] The road reaches a ridge, overlooking the dam and power station at Greifenstein, a concrete wall across the river, and just one of the forty-nine dams that block the Danube in Austria.

Caesar Augustus (23 BC to AD 13) was the first Roman emperor to send soldiers across the Danube, as part of his plan to enlarge the Roman empire as far as the River Elbe. When that proved too ambitious, the Danube became the naturally defensible frontier. Hostile tribes gathered on the far shore, and the Danube became a war zone. Grateful archaeologists are still reaping the benefits – a row of excellent museums has replaced the Roman fortresses all along the river in Austria.[9]

In Tulln, a statue of Marcus Aurelius on horseback stands on the riverbank. In the first years of his reign, the Langobards crossed the Danube in the north, and the Sarmatians further south, to attack the Roman empire. Roman troops, many of them seasoned veterans of the Persian wars, drove them back successfully across the river. A pattern was established that would last until the Romans finally retreated under a rain of blows two hundred years later. The tribes across the Danube alternately fought and struck deals with the Romans, and the Romans incorporated the tribesmen and their weapons into their own ranks.[10] Ballomar, the king of the Marcomanni, was temporarily at peace with the Romans, and acted as a mediator between the empire and other tribes. But by the late AD 160s, the empire had been severely weakened by the plague which Roman soldiers had brought back with them from Persia. Seeing their chance, the Marcomanni and other German tribes based in Bohemia massed for a new assault. Marcus Aurelius spent almost the entire last thirteen years of his reign fighting the Germans. On his horse on the shore at Tulln, Aurelius looks more certain of victory than in the bust found at Dunaszekcső. Or perhaps the sculptor of the latter was more interested in the philosopher king, and the former in the war-seasoned commander of the imperial army. Around the year 170, Ballomar led a huge German force across the Danube, defeated a Roman army twenty thousand strong at Carnuntum, (near the modern Hainburg) and pressed on towards Aquileia near the Adriatic coast in northern Italy. Marcus Aurelius led the counter-attack in person, Aquileia was relieved, a new command was established in northern Italy, and the Roman Danube fleet was reinforced. By 171, the Marcommani had been thrown back across the Danube, Marcus Aurelius had added the title Germanica to his collection, and coins were minted to celebrate the victory in 172, with the inscription '*Germanica capta*' – subjugated Germania. With the Marcommani at a safer distance, the emperor moved the Legio II Italica up to the Danube, based first at Albing (Krems) then at Lauriacum (Enns). The history of this period is one of constant probing by the tribes on the northern bank of the Roman defences on the southern bank. In the summer of AD 173 the Quadi attacked across the river from the territory of modern Slovakia. The Legio XII Fulminata was ambushed by a larger Quadi force and appeared to be on the verge of disastrous defeat when a sudden downpour of rain reinvigorated the Roman troops, who had run out of drinking water. At the same time, according to two contemporary accounts, lightning struck the Quadi. According to Tertullian, the 'miracle of the rain' was due to the prayers of Christian soldiers in the Roman ranks; according to the rival account of Cassius Dio, to the prayers of an Egyptian magician to the god Mercury.[11]

The story illustrates the gradual penetration of Christianity into the Roman army, brought back by the regular movement of Roman soldiers between the different borders of the empire in East and West. Traders and troops also brought with them other gods and cults. At the museum in Tulln is a fine marble relief of Mithras ritually spearing a bull, while a scorpion attacks its testicles. At the top of the image are Cautes and Cautopates, the torch-bearers of Mithras, and the sun and moon shine down. The Romans took care not to displace the gods of the tribes they conquered, but rather to co-opt them and dress them in Roman tunics. Mars, the Roman god of war, was identified among the Latobici tribe as Mars Latobius; the Celtic goddess of light Epona and the tribal goddess Noreia with Minerva, or perhaps with Fortuna. Many of the first Christian martyrs were Roman soldiers. The only known Christian martyr of the Roman province of Noricum was the Holy Florianus, who was tortured then thrown into the Enns river, near its confluence with the Danube at Krems on 4 May 304.[12] Poor Florianus, had he survived only a few more years, could have taken advantage of the decision of Constantine I (AD 306–37) to tolerate Christianity. The Christians helped soften the blows which rained down during the last years of the empire in the fifth century as it buckled under renewed tribal attacks.

Attila the Hun was the most successful of the Hunnish kings. He ruled from 438 until his death in 453, allegedly as a result of a nosebleed on his marriage bed, in the arms of his new wife, Ildikó. At its greatest extent, his empire reached as far west as the Rhine.[13] According to the Hungarian writer Mihály Hoppál, he was buried in three coffins, one gold, one silver and one iron, was because a shaman said he should be buried 'in a ray of sunlight, in a ray of moonlight, and in the dead of night'.[14] According to legend, his grave was dug at a point where the River Tisza was diverted. Horses then rode to and fro over the place to conceal it. The river was then allowed to flow back over the place. All those who had taken part in the burial were killed. Mihály Hoppál traces the legend through Hungarian history, all the way to the present day. When Sándor Petőfi, a poet and young leader of the 1848 war of independence against the Austrians, died on the battlefield, his grave was similarly disguised by the passage of horses' hooves. The commander asked which of the hussars could remember where it was. The two men who said they could were immediately shot. In June 1958, Prime Minister Imre Nagy was executed by the Hungarian puppet government of János Kádár, installed by the Soviet Union after the Red Army crushed the Hungarian revolution. Buried face downwards, wrapped in tar-paper, in Plot 301 of the Rákoskeresztúr cemetery on the outskirts of Budapest, his grave and those of others executed after the revolution were trampled on by police horses. Relatives bribed the grave-diggers to tell them who was buried where, and in 1989 the bodies were exhumed and the martyrs reburied with dignity.

Severinus, whose name means 'from the north', was originally a hermit who arrived in the region at about the time of the death of Attila. By then, the small- and medium-sized towns along the Danube were under constant attack from the tribes. Severinus hurried between them, gathering donations of food and clothing further inland and transporting them to Roman outposts such as Comagena (Tulln). He maintained good relations with the tribal leaders – to ensure safe passage for his charity work. Severinus died in 482, and when the Roman garrison finally withdrew in 488, never to return, they took Severinus's remains with them.[15] He was finally laid to rest at Frattomagiore, north of Naples. He would have appreciated the inscription, taken from Book VI of Marcus Aurelius's *Meditations*, on the plinth of his statue: 'Life is short, with but a single fruit: a pious disposition, and social acts.'

The river front in Tulln smells powerfully of pine woods, but there are no pines to be seen. I track the scent to the bark arranged thickly by diligent gardeners around the flower beds that dot the lawns. A statue of the artist Egon Schiele, born in Tulln in 1890, stands in front of a museum dedicated to his work, his fingertips just touching. The sculptor has portrayed him as a brooding, somewhat dissolute youth, mindful of his nude portrayals of young girls, and his time in prison on charges, never proved, of laying those same hands on them. Today, the young girls of Tulln walk past in jeans and trainers, more interested in the mobile phones in their hands than in their bronze alleged pornographer. They pass the floating Danube stage, moored just offshore for summer performances of rock bands and theatre groups, and the last stone Roman tower, which once oversaw the western gate of the town. In the Middle Ages it was used as a store for weapons and gunpowder, and in the nineteenth century for salt. Local people still know it as the Salt Tower, not the Roman or Powder tower. A Dutch registered barge, the *Regenboog* (Rainbow) from Landsmeet passes downstream in the sunshine. The Danube is a rare blue.

I pause briefly at Zwentendorf, to see the nuclear power station the Austrians built then stopped, heroically, by popular demand, when it was almost ready to go on line.[16] Two white flags fly outside, as if signalling the surrender of the nuclear lobby. Everything is clean and tidy, with hardly a car in sight, like a child's scale model. A single chimney has bands of red, white and red around the top, the colours of the Austrian flag. Birds perch along the railings where steam was supposed to gush out. A long goods train passes, carrying cereals to the city.

I drive inland for a while, to explore the hills sloping down towards the river, turn a sharp corner and stop suddenly at the sight of a single column with a globe on the top. 'From 15th April to 8th May 1945,' reads the inscription, 'this was the front-line between German and Soviet troops. In this place the Second World War ended, on 8th May 1945. Twenty-eight German soldiers and eleven civilians lost their lives here'. Could they not just have laid down their arms? Didn't they know the war was already lost?

What motivates men to fight to the bitter end? A little tower, almost like a minaret, but with an over-proportioned tiled roof like a pixie's hat, surmounted by a cross, stands beside the track. The vines are freshly pruned, and the early spring paints the valley in browns and greys and ochre. The marble ball on the top of the column is inscribed in Gothic script with the words *Freiheit in Frieden* – Freedom in Peace. No one can argue with that. 'The Austrian Association of Comrades wishes you a pleasant rest,' reads the plaque on the bench next to the monument.

In Stein I find another war memorial. So long after the Romans, such a short time after the great conflagration of the Second World War, this is still a martial landscape. Up a steep stairway from the river, a whole church is dedicated to the dead of both wars. 'The Tears of the Homeland, and the Mercy of God, for our fallen comrades from Lower Austria at Stalingrad, 1942/3.' In the Minorite church in Stein, a different installation is on display rather than the ritual flowers and crosses of Christian remembrance. Sixteen loudspeakers are mounted with magnets on nine square steel plates on the floor of a side-chapel in the cloisters, beneath Gothic windows, arched in prayer. Hans Peter Kuhn's sound installation 'Out of the Depths' features a large industrial-sized halogen lamp suspended over the bass speakers.[17] The sound emitted from them is almost too deep for the human ear, so the viewer sees rather than hears the trembling of the membranes of the speakers, like the skins of drums. 'On and off, little sounds become audible, yet in principle, the installation is silent. Since each of the membranes vibrates independently and unpredictably, the impression of a strange, autonomous entity is created.' The Minorite church was built in the thirteenth century and dedicated to St Ulrich. When the monastery was closed in the 1790s, the church became a storeroom for tobacco, another of the gifts, such as coffee, which the Turks first brought up the Danube. Since 2004 the church has been used for exhibitions and concerts. On the night of my visit, a concert by the Ethiopian harpist Alemu Aga and the Saint Yared Choir is taking place as part of a series dedicated to the Image of God.[18] The vibrant silence of Hans Peter Kuhn's exhibit clears my mind for the rich tones of the *beguena*, the tall Ethiopian harp that King David played in the Old Testament when he wearied of dancing. The voices of the choir coil among the pillars and the harp strings cast their own light in this ancient church.

'The wolf also shall dwell with the lamb, and the leopard shall lie down with the kid, and the calf and the young lion and the fatling together; and a little child shall lead them. . . . They shall not hurt nor destroy in all my Holy Mountain.' In the catalogue of the concert, there is a quote from Psalm 31. 'To the chief Musician, a Psalm of David. In thee, O Lord, do I put my trust . . . for thou art my rock and my fortress.'

After the concert I eat wild garlic soup – bear onion, they call it in German and Hungarian – softened with sour cream, in the Salthaus restaurant off the Minorite Square. Through a low window off the cobbled street I glimpse broad-shouldered lads in white aprons in the warm orange light, rolling up their sleeves to start work on the next day's loaves. I sleep in my room under the cragged lip of King Richard's castle at Dürnstein. In the early morning I climb the steep path up to the fortress. Two men are already at work, rebuilding a stone terrace to prevent the erosion of the precious soil down the steep hillside. One wears a sweatshirt with a picture of an eagle. The very first apricot blossom is out in the orchards below me as I climb. This is the Wachau region of Austria, which owes its name to the guards who watched for invasion, but its fame and glory to the deep orange of its apricots. It is too early for the new crop, but last year's fruit is proudly displayed in every shop and stall along the little cobbled street in Dürnstein. Orange – the colour the bourgeoisie allegedly fear most. And here I am in middle-class Austria, where apricots paint the valleys with their fantastic hues.

Richard the Lionheart was imprisoned in the castle of Dürnstein for four months in the winter of 1192 by Duke Leopold V of Bavaria, with whom he had set out on the Third Crusade. Despite his capture of Acre and other coastal cities, Richard failed to take Jerusalem, the main prize of the crusade. The Muslim leader Saladin magnanimously allowed unarmed Christian soldiers into Jerusalem to pray before they left, but the proud Richard did not join them. Like Vienna for Suleiman, Jerusalem proved one stop too far for the English king. He set out back from the Holy Land in August 1192 towards England, impatient to be home, but was caught by Leopold, who demanded a hefty ransom.[19] The tiled roofs of the village below look orange in the morning light, like the dark, burnished orange of apricots that have been cooked long and have begun to pick up the colour of the heavy iron pot in which the jam is made. The hills of the Wachau rise out of the Danube, their villages still drowsy in the mist. The tower of the monastery church is painted white and blue, with a clock face with Latin numerals and four angels looking out for the welfare of passing sailors. The top is crowded with little baroque cherubs carrying spears, bows and arrows. The gold cross has a cockerel on the top like a weather vane. The path winds upwards to the ruined castle, on its pinnacle of rock, and there are humorous descriptions, in English, of the main characters in the story of the Lionheart. There's even a poem, allegedly written by the king himself:

> No man who's hailed can tell his purpose well,
> adroitly, as if he could feel no pain;
> but to console himself, he can write a song . . .

His rival, Leopold, is assigned this text:

> I was unfortunately not able to enjoy spending the ransom money for long. Excommunicated by the Pope as punishment for taking Richard the Crusader captive, I fell from a horse and died unexpectedly.

The story of how Richard was tracked down by his concerned people is also told. The bard Blondel roamed the Danube, singing Richard's favourite ballad. When he reached Dürnstein, and began the verse 'No nymph my heart can wound, when her favour she shares, and bestows her smile on all . . .' he heard Richard's voice continue, from his dungeon, 'Hate I would prefer to bear, than with others love to share.'[20]

The fortress was only conquered once in its long history, by the Swedes towards the end of the Thirty Years' War in 1645. That war left the Danube valley and Bohemia at the mercy of famine and disease. Just as Habsburg–Ottoman rivalry turned Hungary into first a battleground, then a waste ground, this series of disputes between the houses of Bourbon and Habsburg devastated central Europe. The castle at Dürnstein was never rebuilt, though it was briefly reinforced in the 1660s as a forward chink in what remained of the chain of defences of Christian Europe, in case the Ottomans managed to capture Vienna.

From the top of the citadel, I watch climbers with ropes, scaling a cliff. The castle is 324 metres above sea level. Have I travelled two thousand kilometres, and climbed so little? A Dutch barge passes ponderously below, the *Johanna-M*, registered in Werkendam, with three cars on the stern. Then a cruise ship, the *Viking Legend*, its decks bare, the passengers just visible through the windows below.

Opposite Dürnstein, Josef Fischer works among his fish tanks. A large, jovial fellow, his main work was in his vineyard, until he began fish farming as a hobby. Now his son has taken over the wine-making, to allow him to concentrate on salmon. The *Huchen* (Danube salmon) is the most prized fish of all on the Danube upstream of Vienna, and one of the rarest. Josef has at least ten thousand in his garden. His is the most successful breeding project for the salmon in Austria, and I've arrived on the day of the annual fertilisation of the eggs. First he drains the pond where the largest female fish, nearly two metres long, is swimming slowly, as if in anticipation. Then he catches her in a big sheet and carries her gently in his arms over to a green tub. There, a chemical has been mixed into the water to make her drowsy. Then he carefully runs his hands along the whole length of her body, to squeeze out the eggs he knows are there. But the preparation period was too short. This year he missed out several important steps as an experiment. The experiment fails. No eggs. Josef takes it in his large stride. 'I have enough, more than enough salmon here,' he says, carrying the salmon back to the pond, which is slowly refilling with water.

The fish are divided by age – the youngest a year old, then three years, then five. There are small windows on the tanks, and you can watch the fish swimming past, like visitors to the opera. Ten years have passed since he last ate one, Josef confesses. He can't bring himself to eat them any more; he loves his fish so much. Each year he puts several hundred, sometimes several thousand, back into the Danube. As he works we sip first his white wines, then his rosé. If Leopold the Virtuous had treated Richard the Lionheart like this, he might never even have wanted to return to beery, blustery Albion.

Hermann Miedler is a fisherman on the left bank of the Danube. You can't miss his house – he's built a red model lighthouse in his garden – 'so I can find it when I come home late!' he jokes. And he jokes a lot. The lighthouse is surrounded by large, polished rocks he has dragged from the Danube – 'my wife complains that there are so many stones here, there's no room left for flowers . . . I've been living by the Danube for fifty-seven years, and fishing for all but the first seven. As children we were always down by the water. In those days you could say to your parents, "I'm just going down to catch a fish", and you did. You can't say that any more – though I'm a better angler than I was then, and have better equipment. It has become a real achievement to catch a single fish in this great river.' He welcomes the work of ecologists and local councils in the Wachau to restore the lost meanders of the river. One project has been completed at Rossatz, close to Josef Fischer's salmon breeding garden. A new one is underway at Grimsing, just upriver.

Hannes Seehofer walks me over a rocky path, past bulldozers digging out, rather than filling in, an oxbow. It's a deconstruction, rather than a construction site. As at Orth, before Vienna, a tough deal has been struck with local landowners to allow the Danube a little more elbow room, to benefit fish and wildlife. The Count of Schönbühel, who lives in a castle opposite and owns the land, insisted that if his island was to be allowed to flood, he wanted a bridge at least, to be able to reach it at lower water. Half the project is already completed, and the Danube flows through a meander to which it was denied access for a hundred years. Nearly forty fish species were noted in the water here within six weeks of the reopening – including carp and *Nase,* two fish on which the salmon feed. Danube salmon enter the river from the tributaries, but a much longer migration route upriver would need to be restored for them to become a sustainable population in the river again.[21] Work is now almost complete on another meander, just upriver from the first. 'When they built the big hydroelectric dam upriver at Melk, the river fell two metres, so it could no longer enter the meander. The willows suffered, and other trees, hardwoods took their place – beech and ash.'

We stop to examine a black poplar – not quite as big as the one I visited with Georg Frank in Orth, but just as tall and craggy. There are just forty or fifty left in the whole Wachau. Biologists have discovered a rare red beetle living in this tree – long thought to be extinct in this part of Austria. Out in mid-stream, between the island and the Schönbühel castle, two rocks protrude from the water, known affectionately by locals as the cow and her calf. These are the bane of many ships' captains lives – especially those travelling upstream.

This is the narrowest stretch of the Danube in the Wachau. When the river is in full flood, in early summer, it can reach as deep as ten metres. In periods of drought it can be as low as one and a half – preventing all large shipping for several weeks. 'Between the dams here, we have only thirty-five kilometres of running water,' says Hannes. 'The next power station is another twenty kilometres further on, but its storage lake stretches back at least twenty kilometres upstream. The fish need sheltered places, like the new meander we are making, in which to breed. One of the main problems for them in the main stream is the ships, especially the cruise liners, which are in more of a hurry. Their bow-wave washes away any eggs that the fish have managed to lay along the gravelly shores.' Two ways exist to create new habitats for fish-spawning: opening meanders and putting down new gravel banks beyond the main shipping lane, to give the fish places to shelter behind. He points out piles of gravel, dredged from the shipping lane, then carefully put back into the river closer to the banks. These look like ungainly heaps, but the next high water will flatten them out. Their ecological value is enormous. Not only can fish spawn behind them but birds like the little tern like to lay their eggs in the gravel.

Melk Abbey stands powerfully orange and white above the confluence of the Melk river and the Danube, like an apricot ripple ice cream. The green dome and twin towers of the baroque church of St Peter rise out of the largest courtyard.

In the year 1012, Colomann, an Irish – by other accounts Scottish – pilgrim on his way to the Holy Land, was caught by local people who mistook him for a spy and, as the poor man could not explain himself in any language they could understand, hanged him on a barren elder tree. The body failed to decompose, to the wonder of his tormentors. A year and a half after his death, according to the account of Matthaeus Merian the Elder, one Rumaldos hacked a piece off the body to treat his sick son. When he did so, fresh blood flowed from the corpse, and the barren tree grew fresh leaves – final proof of a miracle. Even his son felt better. The body was taken down and given a decent burial in the church in nearby Stockerau, and when the following year the Danube burst its banks and flooded the whole countryside, the river steadfastly refused to pour into this particular church. Poor Colomann's mortal remains were finally reinterred in St Peter's church at Melk when the Benedictines founded their monastery on a steep cliff top overlooking the confluence of the Melk and the Danube. The monastery also boasts a splinter of the cross on which Christ was crucified, and a lance which belonged to the martyr Mauritius. The wealth of the monastery is partly thanks to the Babenberg family which owned it for many centuries, and were one of the first ruling families of Austria, and partly to the frequent visits of members of the aristocracy, who never paid for their accommodation, but brought gifts instead.

Some of the nine hundred pupils who attend the school in the monastery cross the Danube each day by ferry. I walk through great hallways with baroque frescoes on the ceilings, where ladies have taken out the windows to clean them. In the famous monastery library there are books in fifteen languages, including a Navaho–English dictionary and two huge globes by the famous Venetian astrologer Vincenzo Coronelli: one of the earth and one of the heavens.[22] Built in 1693, he used the forty-eight 'constellations' identified by Ptolemy, and supplemented them with knowledge brought back from the southern hemisphere by European seafarers. The ancient Greek version included the constellation Argo, named after Jason's ship. If the mythological story is true, the *Argo* must have sailed past this very spot, long before the monastery was built on the hill. The constellations are depicted concave rather than convex. I would dearly love to gently spin the globe, but have to content myself with the vision of Aquarius the water-carrier, lugging his giant frame and dressed in an animal skin, around the sky.

A more recent miracle runs parallel to the huge hydroelectric dam that blocks the Danube just upriver from the town. A fast flowing stream – *melk* actually means 'slow-moving stream' in Old Slavic – meanders through the woods on the left bank of the river, carefully dug to allow fish to migrate upstream. The meanders are there to slow the flow down and give the fish more chance to succeed. Regular monitoring proves that it is much used. The water level upstream of the dam is ten metres higher than downstream, so the design had to accommodate that difference. A similar stream is being built at the next dam at Ybbs, but construction has been slowed by the rocks on either side of the river. One day, if every Austrian dam has such a fish bypass, the salmon will be able to migrate long-distances up river again. Then Josef Fischer can cheerfully go back to his vines.

The town of Grein on the left bank of the Danube is the place where ships tied up and took on river pilots before attempting the treacherous onward river journey. By a hotel on the river front I ask a woman cleaning windows the way up to the castle, and note from her accent that she is as much a stranger as I am. She's from Chechnya, she says, a refugee with her husband and small child, recently granted asylum. Could she tell me her story? She hesitates, and asks her husband. No way! He is polite but firm. There is another family of Chechens, however, a little up the valley. Maybe they will talk.

I follow their directions, and find a courtyard awash with clothes on pegs, and children – from Somalia and Afghanistan. The Chechens live upstairs. Seda Atsaeva is eighteen and speaks the best German. She lives in two rooms, with her father Umar, mother Hava, two younger brothers and a sister. They fled Grozny in 2004, because of the war, she says. They got as far as Poland overland, through Russia and Belarus, spent ten weeks in a refugee camp, then decided to move on – on foot. They walked into Germany carrying rucksacks – her mother pregnant with Adam. Seda was ten, her brother Djochar six, and her sister Rayana four. They walked at night, at 2 a.m., through a river, the water up to her father's chest, as he carried the children across one by one on his shoulders. Then they walked through a forest, and finally reached Austria. 'My husband has a very good sense of direction,' Hava says proudly. 'When I was a child at school in Grozny,' she explains, 'I had one lesson of German a week. So when we decided to flee Chechnya, I decided we should come to either Germany or Austria.' Hava has already passed one German language exam, and has started on the higher level. Seda is in her first year at business school and wants to work in a bank. The other children are at school in Grein. The six of them live on 720 Euros a month, and anything their Austrian friends give them. 'I can hardly believe how kind people have been to us . . . They help us so much,' says Hava. But their existence balances on a knife-edge. After seven years of paperwork, their application to stay in Austria was finally turned down, and it looked as though they would have to leave. 'But how can we go back to Chechnya? Our house was destroyed, and my children don't speak Russian – they don't even know the alphabet!'

Within two months of our meeting, they expect to hear the result of their appeal. Apart from the uncertainty, life is not easy for the Chechens, even beside this idyllic river. 'Three months ago, my sister sent me a text message that our father had died. I had not seen him for eight years, since we set out. That was very hard. I went down to the banks of the Danube and cried. After a while, the river took away my sadness. My heart felt lighter after that.' Each evening the family walks beside the river. As a treat, they occasionally take the ferry to the other side and back. Her hope is to work as a teacher, in a kindergarten, or as a carer in an old people's home. Umar, who was a policeman in Grozny, could work in construction she says – but they will only be allowed to work if they get their papers. 'I would like to look after people,' says Hava, 'because I have been through so much myself. I know how much help people need in their lives.'

In the early morning, 6 a.m. at Ottensheim, the first sign of life on the old cable ferry is a thin column of smoke from a chimney as the church bells peal out across the river. Then I see movement on the bridge of the boat.

Captain Hermann Spannraft speaks stylish, almost aristocratic, English, and loves his job, shepherding his ferry to and fro across the Danube. He's been doing it for twelve years. The cable ferry has been in operation at Ottensheim since 1871, and the first model lasted a modest ninety-one years, until 1962. The 'new' one was built in the shipyards in nearby Linz, and has been in service since 1963. It uses no external power, just the force of the current in both directions. 'Not quite in all weather conditions – but almost,' says the captain, puffing on a freshly stoked pipe, and spinning the huge polished wheel through his hands. 'The steering of the ferry depends on the height of the water – the more water there is, the faster the ferry, and it's a little problem when the water is low . . .' On the rare occasions when there is not enough strength in the Danube, he has a small, ninety-horsepower outboard motor to push the ferry the last stretch towards the right – Wilhering – bank. The current is stronger on the Wilhering side, and that can also cause problems if the wind is blowing from the west. Once or twice the ferry has been blown on to the bank when the outboard motor was not enough. Then the ferry had to be pulled off by another boat, though no harm was done.

Crossing on a Sunday morning, with only a couple of cars and cyclists, our progress across the Danube is almost completely silent. I lower the window on the bridge in search of sound. Just the distant chimes of the

Sunday churches, and the lapping of the water against the steel hull. 'There used to be more cable ferries of this type, in the days when there was not a single bridge between Linz and Krems. Now just four are left, at Ottensheim, Spitz, Weissenberg and Korneuburg.' Each weighs ninety tonnes, and can carry twelve normal-sized cars. It might look quiet now, he says, but on a busy weekday they can hardly satisfy demand, as drivers try to dodge the morning rush-hour traffic on the way into or out of Linz and schoolchildren queue to get to and from school. 'Very occasionally, we have to admit that Nature – the water and the wind – is stronger than the technology and the knowledge of the captain, and then we have to suspend the ferry for a while,' says the captain. He steers, while his mate Refik keeps an eye on the passengers, ties up the ferry, and lets the cars and passengers on and off the boat. Refik is tall, with big hands and wrinkles of laughter round his eyes. He was a soldier on the Bosniak side at the start of the Bosnian war, and came as a refugee to Austria in October 1992. 'We must think positively, and just look forwards, not back now,' he says. 'This job is very peaceful and beautiful. It's the best job in the world!'

I notice a small blue and yellow Bosnian flag on the bridge, and a copper pot for brewing Turkish coffee, beside the stack of firewood – the source of the smoke I saw rising from the chimney in the early morning. Thanks to Refik and his family's presence here, Ottensheim and Vinac, near Jajce in central Bosnia where they come from, have become twinned towns, with numerous visits between the two. Hermann himself is just back from a trip there.

By this time we have crossed back to the Ottensheim side of the river, and a frequent traveller, Julia, comes up on the bridge to see her old friends. She used to cross on the ferry every day to the gymnasium on the other side. Today she has just been across for extra maths tuition. 'We make so many friends among the regular passengers,' says the captain. A rather smart woman with four little girls comes aboard, and her daughters rush excitedly from side to side in their Sunday frocks. The captain blows the ship's horn in farewell, and Refik stands with Julia on the deck, waving goodbye.

CHAPTER 13

Oh Germany, Pale Mother

Somewhere within me, dearest, you abide forever – still, motionless,
mute, like an angel stunned to silence by death or a beetle inhabiting the
heart of a rotting tree.
MIKLÓS RADNÓTI, Postcard 1, 1944[1]

I HAVE to reach the concentration camp before it closes at five, and as
I drive up the road from the Danube past the granite quarries, I realise I'm
not going to make it. The irony is not easily dismissed; I'm rushing to get
to a place which 200,000 people would have given anything to get out of.
I want to see Mauthausen in Austria before I reach Germany.

Digging through the past or present of any people is like sifting through
the garden of a house in a small provincial town. One finds jagged edges of
glass and concrete, fragments of bone, traces of lives destroyed and loves
lost. Each newspaper I buy in each country I travel through is full of tales
of perverse adults and abused children, corrupt politicians and gruesome
traffic accidents, of human stupidity and cruelty. Nevertheless, after the
beauties of the Wachau valley, after the tentative buds of the apricot
blossom and the garish glory of last year's fruit, after the solemn dignity of
the war memorials to Austrian and German soldiers, it is hard to grasp the
enormity of Mauthausen.[2]

In Budapest I have met Hungarian Jews who survived the forced
marches to Mauthausen in the dying months of the Second World War.
The Hungarian poet Miklós Radnóti was on a death march from a

concentration camp in Bor in Serbia, the site of the copper deposits which
gave birth to the Vinča culture, towards Mauthausen. Some of his saddest
poems were found in the sweat-stained pocket of his jacket after he was
shot in November 1944, unable to keep up. He has contributed – in
German – one of the most memorable lines of Hungarian poetry, '*Der
springt noch auf*' – 'That one will get up again' – a line used about him by
a German guard, as he lay, three-quarters dead from exhaustion, in a ditch
by the roadside just inside Hungary after three months on the road.

> I dropped alongside him, his body rolling over,
> already tightening, a cord about to snap.
> Shot in the neck. You'll be finished off like this –
> I muttered to myself – so just lie still.
> Patience flowers into death now.
> *Der springt noch auf,* spoken over me.
> Mud and blood drying on my ear.[3]

He did 'spring up', as it turned out, but not for long. He died, shot in the
head, at Abda, near Győr, three days later. There's a small monument to him,
and the twenty-one others who died in the same ditch beside the Rábca river.

It's too late to tour the camp, but a friendly girl lets me into the bookshop and gives me time to buy a map and a booklet. There is even a sense
of relief, that I don't have to visit the gas chambers, the crematoria, or look
at photographs of the gas van that travelled between Mauthausen and the
satellite camp at Gusen, killing people as it went along; that I don't have to
ask what happened in the inmates' brothel, or what card games the SS
guards played in their pleasant guardrooms. It will be enough to listen to
the wind whistling through the hedge which grows where the ashes from
the crematoria were dumped. I will not be able to see the two surviving
ovens, where people, not figurines, were baked. The March twilight seems
an appropriate time to visit a place where time has stopped. I look down at
my watch. Only the second hand moves, round and round.

Mauthausen opened as a concentration camp in August 1938, just five
months after Austria was annexed by Germany. Walking above the granite
quarries, I take refuge in my mind in the worn, granite hills of Dobrogea,
two thousand kilometres downstream. There is no railway here. None

could have achieved the stiff climb up into the hills above the Danube. Images of railway tracks and cattle wagons, packed to the roof with human beings, are so closely linked to Auschwitz and its particular machinery of death that Mauthausen seems appalling in a different way. That inmates were marched here on foot, one by one, under the watchful eyes of gun-toting guards. Or driven in trucks, each with a driver who knew what he was taking his prisoners to. The hardness of the human heart that made Mauthausen possible seems harder than any ancient rock, chipped away by human hands. They could have brought granite for the 1972 Munich Olympic Games from here, presumably. But granite from Dobrogea, from a different, albeit still active dictatorship, was safer.

The bored, intelligent expression of Adolf Eichmann looks up at me from the shelves through his ungainly spectacles in the concentration camp bookshop. It is a photograph taken at his trial in Jerusalem in 1961, from an exhibition on display at the County Court in Linz. The designer of the brochure has drawn a red square on the black and white picture around Eichmann. Oak-man. One hundred and ninety five thousand people were sent to Mauthausen over a seven year period. One hundred and five thousand of them died, worked to death in the quarries, in the armaments factories, or at satellite camps set up throughout upper Austria. Half of those who died did so in the last months of the war, crushed by the death-throes of the German war machine. Hundreds more died after liberation by US soldiers on 5 May 1945, three days before the last German soldiers and civilians died, fighting the Red Army near the town of Stein.

'*O Deutschland, bleiche Mutter,*' reads the final verse of a poem by Bertolt Brecht, engraved on the wall of remembrance outside the concentration camp:

O Germany, Pale Mother!
How have your sons arrayed you
That you sit among the peoples
A thing of scorn and fear![4]

The poem was written in 1933, the year Adolf Hitler came to power.

The forty countries whose nationals were killed at Mauthausen each have their own memorials. The statues from eastern Europe, erected in the

1950s, display the same lock-jawed brutality that State Socialism and National Socialism had in common. But Germany's statue is shockingly tender – sculptor Fritz Cremer's portrayal in bronze of Brecht's 'Pale Mother Germany'. A seated, more than life-size figure, her breasts barely distinguishable beneath a crumpled shawl, her hair short, her head straight, her right hand in her lap, her left hand dangling beside her, as she half turns on her bench. Someone has placed a small red carnation between the fingers of her large right hand. Her chin is raised. It is the position a mother might take at a kitchen table when one of her grown-up sons appears unexpectedly in the doorway. Two copies of the statue exist, one on the grass next to the Berlin Cathedral, another at the cemetery in Magdeburg in eastern Germany at the site of more victims of fascism. Below the road and the memorials is a tall, weeping willow tree, beneath which the ashes of Russian inmates are scattered. The tree is magnificent in its late March colours, turning from grey to green. Its wands absorb the last light. It must have stood here when Mauthausen was a prison camp. The German-speaking peoples always understood trees.

I drive down through the valley in the gathering gloom, back to my comforting river. Hungarian Jews on their way here must have wondered how the same river could flow beneath the fine bridges of Budapest, past their homes, and so close to their doom. Did old Mr Weiss, the fish-merchant who travelled up and down beside the Danube each day in his cart and bought the fish the Zsemlovics family caught to sell in the market in Bratislava, die here?

The River Ilz is black in aerial photographs of Passau as it flows into the Danube and the Inn. Passau is the city where the three rivers meet and their waters jostle for position. Though it looks slightly narrower than the Inn here, the Danube wins, as it always does, but the others lose none of their power and prestige in the process. It is as if they continue to flow, independently and unmixed, like hidden garments beneath the Danube's heavy overcoat.

I find a room in a small hotel overlooking the Ilz. Elderly gentlemen and their spouses from the Kameradenbund, the Association of Former Soldiers, are drinking beer in the restaurant downstairs, and devouring great plates of meat, pickles and potatoes. I join them at a long table. Hilda tells me how she married an American soldier, stationed in Germany after the war, and how she went back to live with him in the US for thirty years. Her American accent is perfect. When her husband died, she returned to her own people. She hands round small, black-and-white photographs of herself as a child, and of her husband. She is accepted by the company as a soldier's wife, and therefore one of them. The lines between rival armies, between victors and vanquished, occupiers and occupied, dissolve on the banks of the Black Ilz so many years after the Second World War.

The rampant red wolf of Passau bares its claws on the city's coat of arms.[5] As a major production centre of swords throughout the Middle Ages, a simplified version of the wolf was engraved on every blade, to give the warriors who wielded them the courage and invincibility of a wolf. In the museums of Belgrade and Novi Sad, of Budapest and Vienna, I have studied Passau swords marooned in glass display cases, their dull blades itching for the taste of blood. The sword-makers at Solingen, the rival sword-producer in Germany in the Middle Ages, began putting wolves on their own blades when they realised how popular they were with fighting men.

In 1803 Passau lost its much prized independence and was incorporated into the State of Bavaria. In 1847 the last German wolf was killed in Bavaria, perhaps in the forests near the source of the Ilz on the border with Bohemia.[6] There are no known wolves left in Austria, less than fifty in Hungary, three to four hundred in Slovakia, a thousand in the former Yugoslavia, while Romania – high in the horseshoe-shaped Carpathians – has two thousand five hundred, according to a study commissioned by the Council of Europe. 'Animals were considered admirable according to the extent to which they accepted human domination, and those considered rebels such as the tiger or wolf were often demonized. This led to a moral crusade for the extermination of wolves and other large predators . . .' wrote Boria Sax of the Victorian Age. But their rehabilitation was at hand.[7] 'The Nazis were constantly invoking dogs and wolves as models for the qualities they wanted to cultivate: loyalty, hierarchy, fierceness, courage, obedience, and sometimes even cruelty. Hitler's code name was "the wolf".' He was also fond of telling people how his name stemmed from the Old High German words – *adal* – meaning 'noble', and *wolf*. Baby Adolf was born in a pub, the Gasthof zum Pommer, in the hamlet of Ranshofen near Braunau on the Inn river, just upstream from Passau, in April 1889. He moved with his family to Passau at the age of three, then to Linz at five, so his formative years were spent near the Danube. There is little doubt that the symbolic wolf of Passau made its mark on the young boy's imagination. 'For the cult of the wolf seemed to offer the Nazis a promise of the discipline sometimes associated with "civilisation" without its accompanying decadence. Of nature without anarchy. As an animal which had been extinct within Germany for almost a century yet lived on in figures of speech, folk tales and iconography, the wolf suggested a sort of primeval vitality that had been lost.'[8]

In 1934 Germany became the first nation in modern times to place the wolf under protection. This was a symbolic act, a nod in the direction of an extinct beast, since there were actually none left to protect. But there were dogs. King Michael of Romania, whom I interviewed on his ninetieth birthday in October 2011, told me that while playing with his favourite dog as a teenager, he discovered that its former, Nazi owners had tattooed the letters 'SS' inside its ear.[9] Hitler's admiration for the wolf did not encourage him to share its diet – he was a committed vegetarian. A plaque set up outside his birthplace in Ranshofen in 1989 was made, fittingly, from dark Mauthausen granite.

After its swords and its wolf, the other product for which Passau is famous is salt. The salt was mined in the Austrian Alps in Salzburg, and in Hallstein, Hallstatt, Reichenhall, Bad Ischl and Altausee.[10] *Hall* was the Celtic word for salt, and can be found in many places associated with the salt trade. Like the Vinča and kindred people along the Lower and Middle Danube five thousand years earlier, the Germans grew rich on salt. Batava – the Celtic name for the settlement – changed over the ages to Passave, and then to Passau. Salt was brought down the Inn to Passau, where it was kept in warehouses for at least three days, by law. It was then either loaded onto ships to take it up, or down, the Danube – upriver the ships were pulled by horses – or loaded on to carriers and their pack animals for the long trek up the banks of the Ilz into Bohemia, and all the way to Prague. This route became known as the *Goldene Steig* (Golden Steps), because of the wealth of goods that flowed along it through the eastern Bavarian woods. The 'white gold' of salt, quarried from beneath the earth, was exchanged for the yellow-orange gold of wheat that grew on its crust. On their journey north from Passau, the first major town the *Säumer* (carriers) reached in Bohemia was

Prachatitz, now Prachatice in the Czech Republic. In the other direction, many Bohemian goods, especially grain, grown in the rolling hills of south Bohemia, were carried back to Passau, stored, then shipped on.

The Veste Oberhaus is a fortress on a hill overlooking the confluence of the three rivers. Built in 1219, it was the seat for most of its existence of the Bishop of Passau, who owned the lands far and wide, and controlled the trade. A lithograph from 1830 shows the banks of the Ilz, close to my hotel. In the foreground is a ship-building workshop and two completed *Zille*, the standard transport boat on the rivers. The shores of the River Ilz, before it reached the Inn and Danube, were ideal for ship-builders. Fifteen workshops were registered at the mouth of the Ilz in the late sixteenth century. The journeys took their toll on the boats – a single boat was expected to survive thirty return journeys to Hallein. The museum has a rich collection of ship-builders' tools, their picks and chisels, and chests used to carry and store the salt. One of darkened wood is painted with the date 1540 above the Passau wolf, who is prancing in the same direction as a worker, bowed under the weight of the sack of salt on his shoulder. He's carrying it towards a warehouse where other sacks are neatly stacked. The salt trade in Passau suffered several disasters over the centuries. In 1594 Prince Maximilian established a monopoly of the trade in salt at Hallein and redirected it downstream to Linz. The powerful kingdoms of Bavaria and Austria took it over and Passau was sidelined. Salt and the goods it was exchanged for still passed in large volumes through Passau, but the wealth that went with it flowed like salt through the fingers of the citizens. Passau never quite recovered, and sank from being a capital to a provincial city. A feather pen-and-ink drawing from the late eighteenth century shows a convoy of salt-laden ships being pulled upriver from Passau to Regensburg. According to the text, the convoy comprised thirty-nine horses and their riders, six main ships, and eight smaller boats, twenty-eight riders, eight servants and twenty-one ship's crew. One of the captain's tasks was to regularly measure the depth of the river with his stick.

In another room of the museum is a sketch for a wall painting to celebrate the wedding of Emperor Leopold I to his third wife Eleonora Magdalena von Pfalz-Neuburg in December 1676. His previous wife, Claudia Felicitas, had died in April of the same year, and it was felt inappropriate to celebrate his new nuptials in the same city, Vienna. An opera was staged downriver in

Linz for the wedding with the title 'The immortal Hercules', in the hope that the house of Habsburg would be blessed at last by offspring to continue the family's already three-hundred-year grip on power. The opera succeeded, and the family kept the throne for another three hundred years.

The old city of Passau feels like an island, an illusion created by the confluence of the Inn and the Danube. At the very tip is a small park, with a labyrinth, a playground, and a large anchor, fixed to a rock with an inscription: 'Dedicated to the martyrs of the Danube' all those who died, by accident or design, in its dark waters. It was erected by 'The Friends of the Rivers and the Seas' in 1971. On the iron handle of the anchor someone has left a handwritten clue to a treasure-hunt: 'You are still far from the goal. You must go next to a small art gallery, and fulfil a task. Tip: the gallery is near a Greek restaurant.'

Young girls chase each other round the labyrinth. Fathers push their sons self-consciously on the swings. Nearby on the wall of a church I find a plaque in Hungarian, engraved in stone. 'Within the walls of this church rests the Blessed Gizella, Princess of Bavaria, wife of Saint Stephen, first Hungarian queen, and nun of the Niedernburg convent.' King Stephen converted the Hungarians to Christianity in the year 1000, and was rewarded for his efforts with a crown from Pope Sylvester in Rome. The crown was lost and found many times, rescued by American soldiers at the end of the Second World War,[11] and finally returned to Hungary by US President Jimmy Carter in 1977. When I first moved to Hungary in 1986, I used to visit it in the National Museum. Power and the right to property in Hungary lay not with the monarch but with the crown. Hungary was known historically as 'the lands of the crown of St Stephen'. On 1 January 2000, the Fidesz government moved the crown, with a lavish ceremony, from the museum to the parliament, where it has stood in a glass case ever since, exactly beneath the main dome. Beautifully decorated with Byzantine kings and saints, it has a peculiar, sloping cross. For many Hungarians it is the symbol of their country's dogged survival through the centuries, against the odds. For others, it should have stayed in the museum – of no more consequence, as one liberal philosopher commented, than 'a Swiss cap'.

The Blessed Gizella married her prince at the age of eleven in the year 996, and anchored the Hungarian kingdom firmly in Europe. Until that time the country had been seen by west Europeans as a wasp's nest of dangerous central Asian nomads. The coronation of Stephen as king in 1001 completed the process. Five hundred and fifty years after the death of Attila the Hun, the Hungarians presented themselves as allies of the West, of the Holy Roman Empire; Gizella's older brother was Henry II, the Holy Roman Emperor. As the king credited with converting the Hungarians to Christianity, Stephen and his wife toured their dominions, founding new churches. When he died in 1038, Gizella quarrelled with his court and took refuge as a nun at Niedernburg, where she died in 1045. Her tomb in the quiet church is wrapped in the tricolour emblems of Hungary. There is an exhibition of photographs showing two nuns carefully cleaning the skull of Gizella after it was exhumed. In a little side-chapel of the church dedicated to her, the tomb is on display, at knee height. The skull inside is clearly visible and is mounted with a golden crown, while her bones are wrapped in costly silks and pearls. Prayers and pleas to Gizella, in Hungarian and German, are carefully recorded in a visitor's book:

'Dear Gizella, grant our family the strength to hold together, look after our two daughters, accompany them on the ways of their lives, strong in faith, and prepare us for the world to come.'

'Dear God, make my grandma well again – Your Victoria.'

'My Dear Gisella, please, please help me to be happy once again in my life. And to be healthy again. I love you. Angela.'

'Dear Gisella, I'm here again. I beg of you, listen to me. Please help my son, in his great troubles. Maria.'

Down on the Danube bank, the big passenger ships have warning signs in English on their steps. 'Attention. Stairs slippery because of ground frost.' The *Kilian*, a barge flying the German flag, pushes upstream. In silhouette against the bright sunlight on the wall behind, I can distinguish the short beard and glasses of the helmsman, motionless on the bridge.

Volker Enseler has come a long way from the Biblis nuclear power plant where he worked for forty years of his life. I bump into him by the Danube

at Hofkirchen, on a less than picturesque stretch where bulldozers are
working to improve flood defences. His long, easy gait, and the small rucksack on his back, mark him out as a fellow long-distance traveller, coming
the wrong way, as usual, down the Danube towards me. He is a tall man
with a sun-tanned face etched with the determination of the post-war
generation in Germany. He wears a bright red raincoat, despite the warmth
of the day, and matching baseball cap, a yellow scarf at the neck, and has a
good laugh, which softens his rather stern, punctual demeanour. Before he
retired, he explains, he noticed a sign near his home in Flensburg, on
Germany's northern border: 'Genoa 2,700 km'. He determined to walk it,
and did so, in ten stages over about six years. He walks about thirty kilometres a day – just before his seventieth birthday. How much does his rucksack weigh? 'Six point nine kilos,' he replies, so precisely that we both laugh.
'But I bought two tangerines this morning, and I've drunk my half litre of
water, so it's probably up to about seven!' He walks for the joy of it, and the
sense of freedom it gives him. He thought once that he would like to make
the pilgrimage to Santiago de Compostela – the Way of Saint James. When
he heard that one million people walk it each year, he chose this walk
instead – 'where there's just me – and a few old people with dogs.' He
always asks to stroke them. Sometimes they let him, sometimes they don't.
When he got to Genoa, he bought a bottle of red wine, sat down in the
main square, and wrote forty-five postcards. Then he walked to the railway
station and took the train home to Flensburg. On this trip, he set out from
the Weltenburg monastery near Kelheim and has been on the road for
seven days so far. He appreciates the modest prices, compared to places he
has walked in northern Germany, especially on the Lower Rhine.

His mention of the Rhine reminds me how close I now am to the end
of my own journey. It is as though, as one reaches the source of the Danube,
the Rhine comes closer, and the two rivers compete for every word, as well
as every stream. 'I was rather lazy,' Volker Enseler says, 'and never changed
jobs in my life – which gave me a rather good pension.' He calculates he
needs about a hundred Euros a day for his walk, for accommodation, food
and wine. Forty to sixty for a room for the night, twenty to thirty for a
good evening meal, and the rest on his lunch, entry tickets for museums
– 'or a second glass of wine or beer in the evenings – after sweating all day!'
His job at the nuclear power station was safety – workers' safety, plant

safety, nuclear safety – 'to make sure the whole thing didn't fly up into the air!' Given that it still appears firmly fixed to the ground, he regards his work as a success. He thinks he'll make it to Budapest in four or five years' time, at this rate. We trade addresses. A few days later, I get an elegant, humorous email from him: he's had to cut short his journey. His feet were giving him grief. But not to worry; his journey downstream will continue.

The Danube winds upstream through the lowlands of Bavaria, or so it seems to me, with so many mountains at my back. The landscape is over-crowded with houses, with roads, with progress. This is small-town Germany. I pause in Niederalteich, in search of girls in short skirts. According to my cyclists' travel guide, a church commission to investigate why so many chil-dren – one in six – were born out of wedlock here, concluded that it was because the local women wore such short skirts; the men could not restrain themselves.[12] I spot only some Turkish girls, wearing decent long dresses and pretty headscarves. No doubt the bishops would be much relieved.

In Bogenberg, on the left bank of the Danube – the right-hand side on my journey – I find a hill at last, and drive up to the Maria Himmelfahrt pilgrimage church. I prefer the German word *Himmelfahrt* ('sky-journey') to the English 'Ascension'. It reminds me of the Prophet Mohammed's 'Night Journey' from Mecca to Jerusalem, and from Jerusalem to Heaven, on his famous mount Buraq. This, in turn, reminds me of Marko Kraljević's journey on his famous horse Sarac ('dappled'). The pilgrimage church has a fine octagonal tower, but feels dark and oppressive inside. I soon find what I'm looking for: the statue of Mary. In 1104 a statue of Mary was found on the Danube shore at the foot of the hill, rather like the crosses all the way downstream at Dervent in Romania. The local villagers took this as a sign of grace, and when the local lord installed the statue in a chapel in his castle a steady flow of pilgrims arrived to see the miraculous Madonna. In 1679 Father Balthasar Regler had the statue undressed 'for scientific purposes' and discovered that it depicted a pregnant Mary. From then on, women hoping to conceive, or praying for a safe pregnancy, flocked to the Bogenberg.[13] During the Thirty Years' War, when Swedish troops swept through Bavaria, they targeted all 'Catholic' objects in their Protestant reli-gious zeal, and the poor pregnant Mary was hurled back down the steep hill into the Danube below. Here the stories diverge. According to one version, the statue was caught on the branches of trees – a completely logical conclusion, even for a blond, strong-armed Swede – and returned to the church. But the statue just inside the doorway to the right, according to my guidebook, is not the original. Loyal Catholics have done everything they can to make it seem so. A rather chubby-faced, sad Mary, wearing an elaborate crown, rests her hands on her distended belly, which has a window in it through which one can see an embryonic Jesus. If this is not the original statue, where is that now? Might the Swedish throw have been effective after all? Might the Madonna still be making her watery way down the river, fertilising the fields and maidens on her way?

As statues go, I prefer the little wooden musical box, a model of a village church at the back of the building, with the inscription: *'Beim Kirchlein wirf ein Zehnerl ein, dann wird's Dir Aug' und Ohr erfreun'* – 'throw ten pfennigs into this little chapel, to make your ears and eyes delight . . .' A fifty-pfennig coin would bring the same pleasure, the text continues, while those who are 'strong in sacrifice' are invited to put a whole German Deutschmark in (someone has kindly changed this to 'Euro') – 'for this you will be amazed by the sweetness of the song, and the glory of the light!' Such an invitation is hard to refuse. After a few seconds of clunking and whirring, a simple tune begins and the doors of the church swing open. A little priest comes out, smiling, looks around, and goes back inside.

The sun sets into the Danube at exactly ten minutes past seven. I still have an hour's drive ahead to reach Regensburg in the dark.

Regensburg is the northernmost point of the Danube, arching up all the way from Passau, then down again through Ulm towards Donaueschingen and its mysterious source. The hotel I have chosen proves disappointing. It's overpriced, and the sheets smell of cigarette smoke – presumably from the laundry room where they were hung to dry. But there's a fine Italian restaurant in the old town, and the magnificent stone bridge, built between 1135 and 1146 by Duke Henry the Proud, is the oldest on the whole of the Danube. It is built of rectangular blocks of yellow sandstone, each column resting on a hull-shaped island, with twelve arches which slope gently to a peak in the middle. It is both simple and austere, like a crusader's helmet, with none of the baroque flourishes that later infected Germany and Austria.

I escape my hotel room in the early morning to watch the sun rise over the river. The cathedral is closed, but I find *Laugenbrötchen* – alkaline rolls, so named because of their peculiar orange-white glaze – and take them down to the bridge for my breakfast. Pigeons coo loudly under the arches and in the tall towers, and the cobblestones are already peppered with people cycling to work or walking to school. The bridge, reads the plaque, was blown up on 25 April 1945, but subsequently restored. The astronomer Johannes Kepler came from Regensburg. I imagine him crossing and recrossing this bridge, gazing up at the stars. The clock tower at the south end of the bridge has a particularly beautiful weather vane, of a quarter moon attached to a silver sun emerging from leaves, as though the sun is a head of thistledown. The Danube is dark green here, like jade, and the bridge makes intricate, filigree patterns in its waters.

Close by, on the Marcus Aurelius bank, the diesel tug *Freudenau* is moored. Built during the Second World War, she was withdrawn from service in 1993 after fifty-one years' work on the Danube, the last spent manoeuvring barges in the harbour in Linz. Next to her is another museum ship, the *Ruthof / Érsekcsanád*, built in Regensburg in 1922. Launched as the *Ruthof*, she was sunk in the Danube in southern Hungary near Érsekcsanád by the Royal Air Force in 1944. Raised from the riverbed by the Hungarian Mahart shipping company in 1956, the year of the Hungarian revolution, she was restored and put back into active service. In 1979 the Hungarians sold her to the city of her birth, and the ship has housed a shipping museum since 1983.

Kelheim is the highest navigable point on the Danube. From here the Altmuhl river forms the final section of the Danube–Rhine–Main canal, which connects the Danube waterway to the North Sea. Completed in 1993, this makes it possible to cross Europe from north to south by boat, without ever going ashore. This was much heralded by the transport lobby, and feared by the ecologists, as the precondition for a massive surge of river transport – a breakthrough in efforts to turn the Danube into a watery motorway. That has not happened, partly due to the blow all shipping received from NATO in 1999, partly due to the falling water level in the Danube as a result of climate change.

The high ground between the Danube and the Altmuhl at Kelheim was the site of an important *oppidum* or urban settlement of the Celts. The archaeological museum has a rich collection of Celtic and Roman finds.[14] It is still shut for its winter break, but the staff are already preparing for the first exhibition of the new season and let me in to look around. While the kilns found at Vinča and elsewhere in the Lower and Middle Danube were for smelting copper and possibly gold, of the Celts excelled at extracting iron. 'Kelheim ramparts' are known by archaeologists the Celtic world as ramparts of earthworks around hill fortresses, with protruding wooden poles for the defensive walls that were also made of thick wood. The *oppidum* at Kelheim is enormous, with ramparts all along the Altmühl river and to the west, eight kilometres long, linking the Altmühl to the Danube. No ramparts were necessary on the Danube side of the triangle – the tall, limestone cliffs along the left, northerly bank form excellent defences. Inside the ramparts iron ore was mined. These now appear like dimples in the thickly forested plateau. Twenty-one ovens and slag heaps have been found where iron was smelted. Kelheim (Alcmoenna to the Celts) was a centre of weapons production. In the grave of one warrior his full military equipment is buried with him: lance, spear, shield, bow and arrows. The jewellery found in the women's graves is particularly beautiful – necklaces of polished glass beads of red, blue, green and yellow, Bernstein pearls, fritte and millefiori.

The Danube gorge runs six kilometres between Kelheim and Weltenburg, with cragged limestone cliffs eighty metres high, like a baby version of the Iron Gates between Serbia and Romania. The lime was valuable to the Celts in their smelting work. The cliffs have been given nicknames through the ages because of the faces which appear to travellers by boat, especially if they've had a bottle or two of the dark beer of the Weltenburg Abbey which claims to be the oldest brewery in the world, dating back to 1050. The 'three brothers', the 'stone virgin', and the 'two kissers' gaze down on me. I park my car as close to the abbey as I can and cycle beside the Danube. On the river bank is a monument to three US servicemen, 'who lost their lives at this spot in the Danube on September 16th 1975. They met their deaths on active service for our freedom', reads the inscription on the white stone plinth. According to American War Memorials Overseas Inc., Lucky J. Cordle, Robert S. Adams and Dennis M. Reihan drowned in a training accident. 'They were in a rubber dingy with twelve other soldiers attempting to cross the Danube in a manoeuvre using a rope by pulling the boat across hand over hand. The current plunged the boat into the rope, flipping it over.' The conflict they died in is listed as the 'Cold War'.

The city of Ingolstadt is dedicated to the motorcar. Driving along the highway, I pass parking lots of new Opels – huge meadows of them, all different colours like fields of mechanical corn. All major towns in Germany have their own vehicle registration plate, so you can work out where they come from. In October 2006, the socialist government in Hungary invited heads of state from around the world to take part in celebrations to mark the fiftieth anniversary of the Hungarian revolution. Unable to find enough smart cars in Hungary to take them around, or for some other reason, they ordered fifty identical Opels from Ingolstadt, some of them armoured. The convoy into town from the airport all had ING number plates. On the day – 23 October – the show was stolen by a single Hungarian protester who hijacked a museum exhibit – a Soviet T-54 tank – and drove it crazily at police who were firing rubber bullets into a peaceful crowd.[15]

Siegfried Geissler waits for me at the entrance to the hunting lodge at Grünau, between Neuburg and Ingolstadt. The castle is in thick woods between the main road and the Danube on our right. It was built as a wedding gift of Duke Ottheinreich for his wife Susanna in 1530, and is rented by environmentalists as an exhibition space. Hunting lodges (*Jagdschlösser*) and pleasure palaces (*Lustschlösser*) are rather interchangeable words in German. As the danger of war passed the aristocracy emerged from their fortified castles and started to enjoy themselves. The lodge at Grunau has white, rounded walls and a steeply sloping red-tiled roof. Our footsteps echo on the cobblestones as we enter the inner courtyard. Inside one of the rooms there is a model of the whole Danube river laid out on a long table. I trace my journey so far with my hand.[16] The palace stands alone in the woods, next to the long-distance cycle path. We drive down a sandy track into the wetlands towards the Danube. This is the only national park in Germany that is part of the network of wetland forest restoration projects along the Danube. Hannes Seehofer in Grimsing gave me Siegfried's number. He's in close contact with Georg Frank in Orth in Austria, Jaromír Šibl in Bratislava, and the ecologists in Hungary, Croatia and all the way to the mouth of the river – guardians of the last flood plains, restorers of kinks and twists in the river, which earlier generations had devoted themselves to straightening out. The woods are mostly oak and ash and maple with some young elm, survivors of Dutch elm disease. But the elms rarely survive beyond their twentieth year, and the ash are also threatened by disease. The whole landscape is pregnant with the expectation of spring. There are boxes on the ground and high among the trees, collecting beetles and bugs, evidence of the impact of the work being done to restore the forest to something closer to its natural state.

Siegfried has a bushy beard and hair turning grey from his drawn-out negotiations with landowners to persuade them to let the Danube return to their lands. If the environmental organisations can drum up enough money, they buy the woods from them. If they can't, they try to rent them, on behalf of the river. The negotiations are tough, and he is often dispirited. 'Many people see the forests purely as a source of income from timber, to be milked dry.' We stand on a sandy bank in the pale March woods, studying a foaming, blue marble stream gushing between deep banks. Closer examination reveals that this river is actually flowing over a creek, on a specially built bridge. It is the first water flyover I have ever seen. 'Two years ago there was no river here at all, there was no water flowing through the floodplains. Only the canalised Danube, with no connection to its surroundings. So we have created a new river! The first four kilometres we cut from the Danube bank, so that section is new. Then we reconnected it to the old meanders.' For the first time in a hundred years, water flooded the area. It was the highpoint in a project which took Siegfried and his colleagues ten years to prepare, five years to carry out, and which will affect the landscape for hundreds. When the sluices are opened, six hundred cubic metres a second flow through the new side-arm, to flood 250 hectares of forest. The old oaks have been saved from cutting. Just upstream of the Bergheim hydropower station we come to the Danube, less a river here than the storage lake of the power plant. The bed of the lake is thick with mud, while most species of fish need running water, and gravel to spawn in – which the new system facilitates.

Because the level of the lake is constant, unlike that of a normal river, the managers of the project have to imitate Nature, periodically allowing the water through the sluice gates to flood the forest. Studies carried out by researchers from the University of Munich already show excellent results: forty-two kinds of fish breeding in the flooded forest out of the forty-seven which used to be found here before the dam was built in the 1970s, and using the new system of waterways to migrate upstream. Siegfried sees the region, in its healthy state, as a game of give and take between the river and local inhabitants. The last big, natural flood was in 1999, and he's hoping the next will come soon. 'Within a couple of years, people forget about floods and the problems they cause, and look for ways of using the land for industry, or for building houses. The Danube was until recently an Alpine river here, full of gravel, with three or four branches flowing through it, five or six kilometres wide, changing dynamically all the time. This must have been a wonderful place a hundred years ago!'

All the electricity created by the four power stations on the Danube, Bertholdsheim, Neuburg, Bergheim and Ingolstadt, is used by the German railway system, the Bundesbahn. 'Is it not better that that power comes from hydroelectric, than from nuclear or coal?' I ask. He's very glad, he says, that Germany has just decided to phase out nuclear power – the result of thirty years campaigning by the Greens. But the downside is that it has increased pressure for more hydropower. He is convinced, however, that the great workhorse of German industry can be fed with renewable energy alone – more efficient, less environmentally harmful hydropower, biomass from the woods, wind-power and solar energy. 'We should use the woods more efficiently – and not sell them to Canada for toilet paper! If we can fuel Germany, as a heavily industrialised country, with renewable energy forms, then anybody can – we could be a model for the whole world! We are talking about the return of the Danube – but there's still a lot of work to do.'

We stand for a while in silence, breathing the river. That contrast of the dead mud of the storage lake and the living gravel of the shallow, unharnessed, or restored shores of the river, resonates through my journey. In the distance I see pine trees, near the shore, and remember them from the previous summer, between Ram and Golubac in Serbia.

Siegfried smiles. 'The river brings the pinecones downstream, from the Black Forest.' Nature recovers. Beavers were reintroduced into the wild here some years ago. Now there are so many of them they are exported all over Europe, to forests wherever they are needed. 'There were some left in the wild in Poland, and in the eastern part of Germany on the Elbe, but all the rest of the beavers in Europe come from here.'

I drive on main roads, then, weary of the heavy, relentless traffic, return to the river. Near Lauringen on the south bank I see strange wooden

sculptures beside the road. There is a strong scent of wild garlic through
the open window. It grows everywhere along the roadside, among the
sculptures. I stop and ring the bell of a house with a garden full of carved
wood. A woman comes to the door with intense, sparkling eyes. Jutta is
delighted to have a visitor – 'Come in, come in!' I hesitate, suddenly scared
by the staring eyes of the sculpted wood. Fairy stories from my childhood
encroach along the edges of my minds, of witches in the woods. But there
is something reassuring in her tone and generous in her welcome, so I
follow her through her house. The walls of each room are woven with
some soft, organic matter – wasps' nests she tells me proudly. They are like
a cross between a honeycomb and a snowflake. On another wall are the
curving crusts of snake skins. 'They watch me from the forest,' she says,
'then they lead me to where they have left their old skins, in spring.' There
is one particularly huge one, almost cobra-like. She laughs like a little
girl – 'Well, that one I got from the zoo!' In her living room she unwraps
for me her latest, and greatest, treasure: a crystal human skull. This she
uses for prophecy. She tells fragments of her story as we walk among her
art. She was a successful trainer of racehorses, but gave it all up to come
and live and work here. She inherited land from her father, and some of
the wood she works with is bog oak, or moor oak, dug up on her own land.
Before I leave I ask if I can write about her in my book. She consults her
spindle, which she produces from a pocket and dangles in mid-air from a
thread. The thin wooden object like a spinning top starts to revolve, clock-
wise. 'Yes!' she says happily. She gives me her card, handmade, with a four-
leafed clover carefully mounted on the top.

Not far from Jutta's house, huge meadows of black solar collectors tilt
towards the sun like sunflowers. I can almost imagine them turning to
follow the sun all day, but not even the Germans have thought of that yet.
Or perhaps they have, but these look rather static. And beyond the
meadows, the arch-enemy of the solar panels: a nuclear power station. I see
it first in double, its cooling towers reflected in what might be a lake, or
flooded fields between pollarded willows. The vast, concave concrete
towers look almost beautiful, four of them rather than two, in the still
waters fringed by trees. But I am still under Jutta's spell.

CHAPTER 14

The Tailor of Ulm

Und er predigte ihnen lange durch Gleichnisse . . . – And he taught them
many things by parables . . .[1]

ULM IS the last city before the source of the Danube. I arrive in the evening
with nowhere to stay, and wander enchanted through this old town
of fishermen and boat-builders. Down by the water's edge is a labyrinth of
houses leaning into the River Blau. I ask for a room in the most ancient,
most beamed, most leaning house I can find, which looks like the stern
of a battleship from the Spanish Armada. No space. I would probably
need to book it years in advance. But Ulm is so beautiful, I wouldn't mind
if I have to sleep on the riverbank. These three-letter German towns, Ilz
and Ulm, have a certain power, like words in an incantation. I find a room
in a clean, more modern place, eat pikeperch in a leaning pub washed
down with local beer, and fall asleep to the music of water. Wherever you
go in Ulm, you can hear the rivers flowing. And the bells of the Minster
chiming.

The next day I make my way to the ancient church. The massive Bible
on the pulpit is open at Saint Mark's Gospel: '*Und er fing abermals an, zu
lehren am Meer. Und es versammelte sich viel Volks zu ihm, also daß er mußte
in ein Schiff treten und auf dem Wasser sitzen; und alles Volk stand auf dem
Lande am Meer. Und er predigte ihnen lange durch Gleichnisse . . .*' 'And he
began again to teach by the sea side: and there was gathered unto him a
great multitude, so that he entered into a ship, and sat in the sea and the

whole multitude was by the sea on the land. And he taught them many things by parables . . .'

Along the choir stalls, in oak reddened by age, are the heads of women on one side, men facing them on the other. Carved by Jörg Syrlin between 1469 and 1474, they represent the wise women and men, philosophers and oracles of Greek and Roman times. All are magnificent, but the Cumaean Sibyl has the best bonnet, a sort of horned construction sprouting from her head, with a diadem in the middle. In a side chapel are stained glass windows from the 1430s, their colours as bright as the day they were made. My favourite is of Noah, climbing up through what looks like the big white chimney of his ark to greet the returning dove, white on a deep blue sky. Noah himself, bearded and patriarchal, wears a purple jacket that Mick Jagger would be pleased to be seen in, and what looks like a heaven-blue kippa on the back of his head. His chimney protrudes from a house with rather medieval-looking roof tiles, while the faces of his sons gaze out of the windows below. The house is the centrepiece of his ark, golden-coloured with a fine prow which looks like a pulpit, on a stormy, light blue sea.

The young woman selling postcards at the entrance to the cathedral is big with child, and her face angelic enough to inspire another Jörg Syrlin. She seems aglow like a stained glass figure in astonishment at her precious cargo. The cathedral boasts the tallest cathedral spire in the world, at 161.53 metres, 534 feet. Begun by several generations of master builders from the Parler family, who also built the St Vitus cathedral in Prague, the spire was only completed in 1890, 513 years after the then mayor, Lutz Krafft, laid the foundation stone.[2] It towers over the marketplace, which swarms with stalls selling all the fruits of Bavaria, Baden-Württemberg and beyond. Ulm is a town that, like Passau, grew rich as a river trading post on the Danube. It has kept that sense of prosperity, though today it is a quiet backwater compared to cities it must once have considered its inferiors. In the excellent market I count fourteen different kinds of potato on one man's stall, and buy cheeses and salads for a picnic by the river.

One of the side streets off the cathedral square leads down towards the Bread Museum. I spot a small tailor's shop and go inside to negotiate emergency repairs to the increasingly precarious button which holds my trousers up. The Turkish tailor gallantly offers to sew it back on immediately, then gets into deep conversation with one customer after another. Meanwhile I sit, trouserless and rather self-conscious, behind a curtain. The bells chime noon and I put my head round the corner. 'Are you still there? A thousand apologies!' Turgut comes from Erzurum, in the far east of Turkey, where his father ran a coffee shop. He moved first to Ankara, then to Germany in 1964 at the age of twenty-six. He came for better work and better money than he could earn at home. First he got a job as an interpreter, in Hanau near Frankfurt, because his German was rather good. Then a friend told him there was a shop to rent in Ulm. He's been here ever since, for forty-four years. The Danube dilutes his home-sickness. 'I'm glad that I live so close to a river which flows all the way to the Black Sea.' Turkey, he reminds me, is sandwiched between the Black Sea and the White Sea – the Mediterranean. Then he teaches me some Turkish Black Sea dialect. In everyday Turkish *ben gidiorum* means 'I go', but on the Black Sea coast they say *ben jideirum*. He has two sons and two daughters. The two sons stayed in Germany when they married, and each has a three-year-old child, but both his daughters went back to Turkey. One teaches German in Ankara – to inspire another generation of Turguts, perhaps, to come west up the Danube to seek their fortune. His workshop is spick and span, but crowded with the tools and finished items of his trade. There are Pfaff sewing machines mounted on the tables, clothes on hangers all around the room, and yellow and orange tape-measures like strands of spaghetti. Turgut wears a grey suit, black cardigan and a light orange shirt. On one window ledge is a vase full of fresh roses and carnations. In the window is a big sign – 'We alter and repair all items!'

At the bottom of his road, the Bread Museum reminds me of the Paprika Museum in Kalocsa, but without that intense burning sensation in the eyes.[3] 'Documentation of the great famines of history, and of the current food shortage in the world is a special task of the museum,' reads the sign at the entrance. 'What is not put on display, however, is bread, because bread is not the stuff of museums, but of everyday nourishment.' A little didactic, I think, but true enough. There is a reconstruction of an Ulm bakery in 1910, with great vats for the dough and mannequins shaping loaves with their bare hands. There are oil paintings of people returning from the fields after a long day harvesting wheat. There is a model of a rotating stone mill from 4000 BC, and a sign that once hung outside a local baker's shop, of two wolves rampant supporting a magnificent golden pretzel. Ulm Minster is mounted on the top with the date 1657.

Back on the shore of the Danube there is a monument to the Danube Swabians, who boarded their boats here in the seventeenth and eighteenth centuries, and rowed and sailed downriver in search of a better life in the East.[4] The Habsburg Queen Maria Teresa offered them hard work and rich rewards to replace a Hungarian population devastated by war and disease. A hundred thousand Germans emigrated to the Hungarian kingdom between 1740 and 1790, and most set out from the landing-stage in Ulm. They settled in five main areas, in the south and west of Greater Hungary, and in Transylvania. Their diligence in draining the marshes beside the Danube and its tributaries transformed the landscape, and laid the foundations for the agricultural prosperity of many districts. But the chance for younger generations to enjoy that heritage was undone in eight brief years during the mid-twentieth century. Accused of collabo-ration with the Nazis, they were expelled from their lands, abused, and, in Yugoslavia at least, starved to death in the years following the Second World War. Two girls and a boy perch on the steps of the monument, watching the river go by. Theresa and Geraldine are both aged eighteen, born in Ulm, and thinking of moving on. Geraldine has a job for the summer in the café of a swimming pool, Theresa isn't working at the moment, but prefers not to say why. She dreams of going 'somewhere up-river . . . maybe to Stuttgart', to start a new life. Erdem has a dark, Turkish complexion, compared to the pale German girls. He wears a black and white woolly hat from Guatemala, and talks about leaving too. But he would go further north, to Hamburg, if he gets the chance. We talk near the Schwal, a small island with a backwater just off the main Danube. From the landing stage here, from 1570 onwards, the flat-bottomed barges known as *Zille*, or 'Ulm-boxes', carried people, animals and goods all the way down the Danube as far as the Black Sea. It was on the *Zille*, too, that the famous clay Ulm pipes were carried to market, while the tobacco to fill them came upstream, from the warmer lands to the south. The last freight barge left here in 1897, bound for Vienna. Erdem, Geraldine and Theresa pose for a photograph. Erdem puts his arms around the girls. The Danube flows behind them, with a weeping willow glowing almost fluorescent on the bank and seagulls diving in the dark waters. The horse chestnuts are just coming into bud. Three kids, just starting out. An image of a harmonious, modern Germany.

By now the Danube is barely more than a stream. There are outcrops of limestone cliffs, capped by the castles of Württemberg dukes. Rocky crags sprout whiskery pine trees, forerunners of the Black Forest. The last museum dedicated to the Romans on the Danube is at Mengen-Ennetach.

On a map showing the disposition of Roman troops, I understand for the first time the relationship of the Danube to the Rhine. The Rhine forms an L-shape around the Black Forest, out of which the two-prongs of the Brig and Bregach rivers flow, to become the Danube at Donaueschingen. A little to the north, also in the Black Forest, the River Neckar rises, to flow northwards to join the Rhine. Another map shows the wine route, for barrels of the precious liquid from southern France, Italy and Spain, from the sea coast near Marseilles, northwards to southern Germany. Little wonder that so many vines were planted in the fertile soils of southern Germany to avoid the need for such expense. The final exhibit in the museum is a relief from a gravestone from around AD 200 of two oxen pulling a cart loaded with barrels of wine, on which a hungry-looking dog perches, his ribs showing through his coat. The driver wears a hooded jacket from the region of Gaul.

Gerhard Obstle remembers when the meadows beside the Danube were blue with wild flowers – *bauernbübchen* as they are called in the Swabian dialect. He shares a little of that pride; he won a prize two years ago for the flowers on his own land. He farms ninety-five hectares beside the Danube at Scheer, slightly bigger than the average size farm in Württemberg, slightly smaller than the German average. Half he ploughs, half is meadow. He switched to organic farming after the Chernobyl nuclear disaster in 1986, and has never regretted it. Conventional farmers, he says, constantly face the dilemma of '*wachsen oder weichen*' – to expand, or disappear. They use more and more chemicals on their fields to increase the yield. He didn't want to take part in that race any longer. As the German government turned away from nuclear energy after the Fukushima disaster, many farmers in Germany began growing maize as a biofuel. But Gerhard hasn't been tempted. 'There's nothing "organic" about the process – just the fermentation of the mass of the crop, until it turns to gas. I don't like maize because it cannot tolerate weeds – its growth suffers. It's not so competitive, and it's hard to grow without chemicals. But there are organic farmers in the Rhineland, where the soil is more fertile, who are doing it well.' There would be no point in ploughing more land as it would be under water when the Danube floods. Climate change he notices very exactly. In his childhood, a temperature of 32 degrees Celsius in July was unusually hot. Nowadays it is often 35 degrees in July. I drink cool, home-made organic apple juice with Gerhard and his wife, watched by their peaceful oxen. The walls of the barn have been painted by their daughter, with a huge mural of the same brown and white cows on one, of a little girl blowing dandelion-seeds in a meadow in the other. Gerhard breaks into song – the 'Blankenstein Hussar':

> *Dort drunt im schönen Ungarland,*
> *Wohl an dem schönen Donaustrand . . .*

> Down there in the lovely Hungarian lands
> Along the lovely Danube strand
> There lies the land of the Magyar.
> As a young lad I set out there
> Leaving neither wife nor child at home
> to be a Blankenstein hussar . . .[5]

The Hussars were the light cavalry of the Hungarian army, famed for their courage and gallantry. Young men from across central and western Europe were drawn to serve in their ranks, to fight the French in the early 1800s.

In Sigmaringen the castle rises steeply from the Danube and is reflected in its still waters, sailed over by swans, a majestic white against the vigorous, dark red shoots of the new bushes along the banks. I sleep in the attic room of an old inn and drink wine from the Kaiserstuhl, the Emperor's Seat, a long, low hill between Freiburg in Germany and Coburg in Alsace. When I was a student in Freiburg we would pass that hill when we hitch-hiked to France, in search of disorder and laughter when German orderliness got too much. The *spätlese*, late-harvested grapes from the Kaiserstuhl, make the most delicious, orange coloured wine.

I reach Donaueschingen at dusk, dump my bags at the hotel, and rush down the hill in search of the source of the river before it gets dark – just as I went in search of its mouth at Sulina exactly a year earlier. I find the Fürstenberg park first of all, through which the Brigach flows. Expecting at any moment to reach the point where the Breg flows into it from the south, I strike out on foot, but the walk gets longer and longer. At one point, the 'Danube Temple' appears on the far shore, at the spot where the spring, regarded by many as the true source of the Danube rather than its two-parent tributaries, flows down to the Brigach. The temple was built in 1910 by order of Kaiser Wilhelm II, who was a frequent visitor to the Fürstenberg palace. I pass a riding stable, a dog-kennel, a playground and a sports club. Just before a concrete bridge leads traffic on to the ring-road, I come across the Breg flowing, small but vigorous, into the Bregach. It is my journey's end.

There's a large marble statue of a stern matriarchal figure: Mother Baar – the name of this region of the southern Black Forest – holding a child in her lap, the young Danube. The child, in contrast to his mother, smiles with delight, and pours the first waters of the river from a small bucket, with all the rapt attention of childhood. Beneath the statue are the words: 'For our beloved hometown, Donaueschingen, Irgon and Max Egon, to commemorate our golden wedding anniversary, 19 June 1939.' There's a simple bench for young lovers to sit on, and a couple of spindly silver birch trees. The leading edge of a cloud blocks out the sun, and a high foreheaded, youthful male face appears – Danubius himself.

I take off my socks and shoes and wade out into the start-waters of my river. I was afraid that Donaueschingen might be an anticlimax, a patch of sleepy suburbia after the spectacular sights of the journey, but it is far from that. The water is deliciously cold. The row of beech trees along the Breg shore give a certain dignity to the scene. The freshly mown grass, the statue, the people dotted about, each with their own relationship to this enormous river, add to the nobility of the Danube. Even the plain concrete bridge, the traffic passing over it, and the electricity pylons cannot rob the source of the Danube of its grandeur. A sign offers a choice of 2,840 kilometres, 2,845 kilometres or even 2,779 kilometres to the mouth. It's a long way to Sulina.

I walk back slowly to the gardens of the Fürstenberg palace, my head in the clouds, overwhelmed with happiness. The river turns black and yellow and blue in the dying light. Steps lead down beside St John's church to a circular pool. It's almost dark now. The twin towers of the church are reflected in the deep, blue-black water. The statue of another mother, holding her daughter close, oversees the pool. Her left hand is suspiciously close to the girl's young breast, suggesting a particular interest of the sculptor. The mother's right hand points the girl's way, eastwards. The daughter-Danube gazes innocently downwards at a shell she holds in her right hand. At the foot is a small, cherubic boy, blowing on a conch. Both the girl and her mother have garlands in their hair.

I throw a Hungarian twenty forint coin into the pool, watch it spiral downwards, to join thousands of others at the bottom. Bubbles rise from the source of the Danube. Then all is still.

A Kind of Solution

Why this sudden restlessness, this confusion?
(How serious people's faces have become.)
Why are the streets and the squares emptying so rapidly,
Everyone going home so lost in thought?

Because night has fallen and the barbarians have not come.
And some who have just returned from the border say
There are no barbarians any longer.

And now, what's going to happen to us without barbarians?
They were, those people, a kind of solution.
CONSTANTIN CAVAFY[1]

The next morning I wake early in the Hotel zur Linde, walk out into the sunshine, and buy a local newspaper to devour with my toast, in the black and white breakfast room. A headline in the *Stuttgarter Zeitung* announces the centenary of Karl May's death, at the age of seventy, on 30 March 1912.[2] May was the German poet of the American Wild West, without ever going there in person. He taught himself to write during spells in prison for petty theft, and created two of the most endearing characters in German fiction: Old Shatterhand, the German emigrant to America, and Winnetou, the Apache Indian chief he befriends.[3] When US troops occupied western Germany at the end of the Second World War, they were astonished at the romantic vision of the United States entertained by their hosts, faithfully learnt from May's novels. In central and eastern Europe, children in playgrounds to this day choose to be Indians, largely thanks to Karl May, while their peers in western Europe mostly want to be cowboys. His detractors like to remind readers that Adolf Hitler loved his novels, while his defenders point out that Albert Einstein did too. The books have never really taken off in English translation. May confused readers, and quite possibly himself in later life, by identifying so closely with Old Shatterhand, that the two characters rolled into one. 'And so I found myself in a new and strange life,' writes Old Shatterhand, 'and beginning it with a new name, which became as familiar and dear to me as my own.'

'The paths we really took are overlaid by the paths we did not take,' wrote the East German novelist Christa Wolf, 'I can already hear words that we never spoke.'[4] Eastern Europe is a kind of mirror image of the Wild West in the west European imagination: the Wild East, where priests crucify nuns to exorcise them, where factories smoke like chimneys, and from whence swarthy Gypsies emerge to slaughter swans in the parks of London or Vienna. That is the tabloid version, but there is also a more intellectual variety, of various peoples caught up in a kind of eternal hostility to one another. But the Danube washes all of them, reminding them of other lands, from which visitors arrive – to trade, or rest or settle. The Danube offers solace, and preaches tolerance. And in countries far from the sea coast, the river reminds people of the power of nature.

Just as I found no barbarians in the east, I didn't find any in the west either. The east Europeans come to the west to work, not to steal, at what are often the most menial jobs. The care with which the river environment, in its tamer or wilder fragments, is protected in Austria and Germany, offers a model of civilised behaviour from which many in the East could learn.

The traveller puts her, or his best foot forward, and comes not to speak, but to listen. By accident I left my tape recorder by the source of the Danube, recording the waters of the Breg and the Brigach flowing together. When I came back, hours later, I found it still there, in the darkness, recording every cry and whisper.

Notes

Introduction. The Lips of the Danube

1. T. S. Eliot, 'The Dry Salvages', from *Four Quartets*, Harcourt, New York, 1943.
2. Friedrich Hölderlin (1770–1843), *Sämtliche Werke*, trans. Maxine Chernoff and Paul Hoover, Berlin, 1846. See <http://jacketmagazine.com/27/hold-trans-2.html>.
3. Andrei Ciurunga, *Canalul*, trans. Mihai Radu and Nick Thorpe, from the booklet available at the memorial at Poarta Albă to those who died building the canal.
4. See <http://en.wikipedia.org/wiki/Dobruja#Etymology>. For a background to the archaeology of the Dobrogea region, see Valentina Voinea and Glicherie Caraivan, *Human-Environment Coevolution in Western Black Sea Coastal Region (5th Millenium BC)*, Proceedings of an International Conference, Alexandria, 3–5 November 2010, Editura Renaissance, Bucharest, 2011, pp. 49–60.
5. *The Lost World of Old Europe: The Danube Valley, 5000–3500 BC*, ed. D. W. Anthony, Princeton University Press, Princeton, NJ, 2011, pp. 179–89.
6. John Chapman and Bisserka Gaydarska, 'Colour in Balkan Prehistory', in *Early Symbolic Systems for Communication in Southeast Europe*, ed. L. Nikolova. *BAR Intern. Series 1139*, Archaeopress, Oxford, 2008, pp. 31–56; John Chapman and Bisserka Gaydarska, *Spondylus gaederopus / Glycymeris exchange networks in the European Neolithic and Chalcolithic*, Durham University, Department of Archaeology, 2011.
7. Philip L. Kohl, *The Making of Bronze Age Eurasia*, Cambridge University Press, Cambridge, 2009, pp. 23–56.
8. L. Séfériadès, '*Spondylus* and Long-distance Trade in Prehistoric Europe', in David Anthony, ed., *The Lost World of Old Europe: The Danube Valley, 5000–3500 BC*, Institute for the Study of the Ancient World, New York University and Princeton University Press, Princeton, NJ, 2010, pp. 179–90.
9. *Kingdom of Salt, 7000 Years of Hallstatt*, ed. Anton Kern, Kerstin Kowarik, Andreas W. Rausch and Hans Reschreiter, Natural History Museum, Vienna, 2009.
10. Marija Gimbutas, *The Goddesses and Gods of Old Europe*, Thames and Hudson, London, 1982.
11. See *The Lost World of Old Europe*, ed. Anthony.
12. *The Danube Script, Neo-Eneolithic Writing in Southeastern Europe*, Exhibition Catalogue, Brukenthal Museum. See especially Harald Haarmann and Joan Marler, pp. 3–9.

13. See <www.viminacium.org.rs>.
14. Herodotus, *The Histories*, Book II, Ch. 5, trans. Aubrey de Selincourt, Penguin Classics, Harmondsworth, 1954.
15. Nick Thorpe, *'89 – The Unfinished Revolution – Power and Powerlessness in Eastern Europe*, Reportage Press, London, 2009.
16. Yehuda Bauer, *A History of the Holocaust*, Franklin Watts, New York, 1982.
17. *Danube Bike Trail*, Vols 1–4, Bikeline, Verlag Esterbauer, Rodingersdorf, 2008.
18. 'Fukushima radiation spread as far as Romania', 25 August 2011: <http://iopscience.iop.org/1748-9326/6/3/034011/fulltext/>.

1. The Beginning of the World

1. Herodotus, *The Histories*, trans. Aubrey de Selincourt, Penguin Classics, Book 5, ch 10, Harmondsworth, 1954 p. 317.
2. <http://molluscs.at.gastropoda/index.html?/gastropoda/freshwater/neritidae.html>
3. Mór Jókai, 'Arany Ember, 1872, The Man with the Golden Touch', in Mór Jókai, *Timar's Two Worlds*, trans. Hegan Kennard, M. J. Ivers, New York, 2010.
4. See <http://norwaygrants.org/en/Activities/Project-events/Biology-sociology-and-tourism-to-preserve-the-Danube-beluga-sturgeon/>; <www.ddbra.ro>.
5. Neal Ascherson, *Black Sea – The Birthplace of Civilisation and Barbarism*, Jonathan Cape, London, 1995.
6. For much of the data on sturgeon in this book, I am indebted to Radu Suciu, and to his teacher, Nicolae Bacalbaşa-Dobrovici (1916–2010).
7. Razvan Voiculescu, *Dobrogea inceptul lumii* (Dobrogea – The Beginning of the World), bilingual Romanian and English edition, Editura Q-T-RAZ, Bucharest, 2008.
8. On silkworms in the Ottoman empire, see <http://www.academia.edu/168776/Patterns_of_Proto-industrialization_in_the_Ottoman_Empire_The_case_of_eastern_Thessaly_ca.1750–1860>.
9. Gavrila Derzhavin, old Russian national anthem, trans. Alexander F. Beck. See <http://en.wikipedia.org/wiki/Grom_pobedy,_razdavajsya!>
10. Patrick Kinross, *The Ottoman Empire*, Jonathan Cape, London, 1977; The Folio Society, London, 2003.
11. Constantin Ardelean, *The European Commission of the Danube and the Results of Its Technical and Administrative Activity on the Safety of Navigation, 1856–1914*. See <http://www.academia.edu/1016592>.
12. For Ceauşescu's attempts to drain the Danube, see inter alia: Daily News, 22/2/90: http://news.google.com/newspapers?nid=1241&dat=19900222&id=dGhTAAAAIBAJ&sjid=DYYDAAAAIBAJ&pg=2806,2185405.
13. Well illustrated by the statement of the Romanian Communist Party dissident Silviu Brucan to this author, November 1987 in Silviu Brucan, *The Wasted Generation – Memoirs of the Romanian Journey from Capitalism to Socialism and Back*, Westview Press, Boulder, CO, 1993.
14. Jacques Cousteau studied the Danube with his team from 1990 to 1992. See <http://www.cousteau.org/expeditions/danube>.
15. ICPDR Joint Danube Survey 2, Vienna, 2008.
16. See <http://www.bestcombat.cc-intro.info/beluga-sturgeon-community-based-tourism>.
17. Kindly translated by Onur Yumurtaci of the Anadolu University Faculty of Communication Sciences, Department of Film and Television, Eskişehir.

2. The Kneeling Oak

1. In Gerard Casey, *Between the Symplegades – Revisions from a Mythological Story*, Enitharmon Press, London, 1980.

2. See <http://en.wikipedia.org/wiki/C._A._Rosetti>.
3. For a good summary of the case against more barge traffic on the Danube, see <http://www.wwf.hu/media/file/1180873628_danubereport_4.pdf>.
4. The letter begins: 'Hear now, my son, those things of which I think you should not be ignorant, and be wise that you may attain to government. For I maintain that while learning is a good thing for all the rest as well, who are subjects, yet it is especially so for you, who are bound to take thought for the safety of all, and to steer and guide the laden ship of the world.' Byzantine emperor Constantine VII Porphyrogenitus, *De Administrando Imperio*, *c.950 AD*, ed. Gy. Moravcsik, trans. R. J. H. Jenkins, new, rev. edn, Washington, D.C., Dumbarton Oaks Center for Byzantine Studies, 1967, pp. 49–51; 167–71, 57–63.
5. Elizabeth Taylor died on 23 March 2011.
6. Data cited by Aurel Bajenaru.
7. No English translation exists. A French translation has been made, but is out of print. There is also a film called *Europolis*, based on the life of Eugeniu Botez / Jean Bart: Cornel Georghita, *Europolis* (2010); see <http://www.europolis-film.com/?lang=en>.
8. For the water tower of Sulina, see <http://www.romguide.net/Visit/The-Water-Tower_vt5c5>; for The Danube Delta Biosphere Reserve, see <http://whc.unesco.org/en/list/588/>.
9. Interviews by the author with Maria Sterp *et al.*, Poiana Sibiului, summer 2005.
10. Sfântu Gheorghe film festival: <http://www.festival-anonimul.ro/home_en>.
11. Mak Dizdar, *Kameni Spavac – Stone Sleeper*, trans. Francis Jones, DID, Sarajevo, 1999.
12. *Jason and the Argonauts*, Stephanides Brothers' Greek Mythology, Trans. Bruce Walter, Sigma, Athens, 1998.
13. *Romanian Folk Tales*, trans. Ana Cartianu, Editura Minerva, Bucharest, 1979.
14. Nicolae Densusiana, *Prehistoric Dacia*, <www.pelasgians.org/website1/06_02.htm>.

3. Mountains of the Fathers

1. Ibn Battuta, *Travels in Asia and Africa 1325–1354*, trans. H. A. R. Gibb, George Routledge, London, 1929.
2. Andrzej Stasiuk, *On the Road to Babadag – Travels in the Other Europe*, Harvill Secker, London, 2011.
3. F. W. Hasluck, *Christianity and Islam under the Sultans*, 2 vols, Oxford University Press, Oxford, 1929; H. T. Norris, *Islam in the Balkans – Religion and Society between Europe and the Arab World*, Hurst, London, 1993.
4. Andrea Weichinger and Nick Thorpe, *The Vineleaf and the Rose, A Journey into Bosnia*, documentary, TintoFilms/ MTV, Budapest, 2001.
5. See <http://news.bbc.co.uk/2/hi/programmes/from_our_own_correspondent/8682669.stm>.
6. Hasluck, *Christianity and Islam*, Vol. 1, p. 95.
7. For a fictional, but very readable, novel based on the Leprosarium in Tichileşti, see Ognjen Spahić, *Hansen's Children*, Istros Books, London, 2012.
8. For the Lipovan Russians, see <http://www.crlr.ro/index_en.php>.
9. An Orthodox prayer from the third Sunday of Lent, which is known as the Sunday of the Veneration of the Cross: 'The Church fathers equate the life-giving cross with the tree of life and plant it in the middle of the Lenten pilgrimage. It was the tree that was planted in Paradise; it is to remind the faithful of both Adam's bliss and how he was of deprived of it.' See <http://orthodoxwiki.org/Sunday_of_the_Holy_Cross>; and: <http://byztex.blogspot.hu/2011/03/before-thy-cross-we-bow-down-in-worship.html>.

4. The Colour of the River

1. Gimbutas, *Goddesses and Gods*, p.238.
2. Bertolt Brecht, *Selected Poems*, trans. H. R. Hays, Grove Press, New York, 1959. The poem is a remarkable recognition of the failure of communism, by a believer. A section of the poem reads:

You, who shall emerge from the flood
In which we are sinking,
Think –
When you speak of our weaknesses,
Also of the dark time
that brought them forth.
For we went, changing our country more often than our shoes,
In the class war, despairing
When there was only injustice and no resistance.

For we knew only too well:
Even the hatred of squalor
Makes the brow grow stern.
Even anger against injustice
Makes the voice grow harsh. Alas, we
Who wished to lay foundations of kindness
Could not ourselves be kind.

3. Manuela Wullschleger, *Neolithic Art in Romania*, Arte-m, Bucharest, 2008.
4. Gimbutas, *Goddesses and Gods*, p. 17.
5. Chapman and Gaydarska, *Colour in Balkan Prehistory*.
6. For more on the controversy, see especially <Wikipedia talk:WikiProject Archaeology# Marija Gimbutas>.
7. Romanian Radio International, article on Anghel Saligny, 18 October 2010.
8. For the hardship experienced during the building of the canal, see, inter alia: <http://www. magtudin.org/black%20sea.htm>.
9. For the cave churches of Basarabi, see especially Constantin Chera, *Basarabi – The Cave Churches Complex – Description of the archaeological site and of the carved images*, <http:// constanta.inoe.ro/pagini/p13.html>.
10. See <http://kroraina.com/pb_lang/pbl_2_4.html>.
11. The Romanians discount the Bulgarian claims <http://constanta.inoe.ro/pagini/p13. html>.
12. Herodotus, *The Histories*, Book IV, Chapter 93, p. 272 (referring to the Getae). For the controversy over who exactly the Getae, Dacians, Scythians and Thracians were, and where they came from, see <http://www.sino-platonic.org/abstracts/spp127_getes.html>; see also *The Romanian Space in Medieval Cartographic Representations*, Radio Romania International, 27 January 2011.
13. See <http://en.wikipedia.org/wiki/Dacian_language>.
14. Marguerite Yourcenar, *Memoirs of Hadrian*, Librarie Plon, Paris, 1951, trans. Grace Frick, Penguin Books, Harmondsworth, 1959, p. 56.
15. Heraclitus, fragment LXXIX. See commentary in Charles H. Kahn, *The Art and Thought of Heraclitus*, Cambridge University Press, Cambridge, 1979, p. 201.
16. Mihai Vlasie, *How to Get to the Monasteries of Romania*, trans. Luminita Irina Niculescu and Diana Presada, Editura Sophia, Bucharest, 2003, p. 48.

5. The Dogs of Giurgiu

1. Elias Canetti, *The Memoirs of Elias Canetti – The Tongue Set Free*, Farrar, Strauss & Giroux, New York, 1999, p. 7.
2. See <http://www.romguide.net/Visit/Lower-Danube-Museum_vt44b>.
3. Pencho Slaveikoff, *The Shade of the Balkans – A Collection of Bulgarian Folksongs and Proverbs*, David Nutt, London, 1904; <http://www.archive.org/stream/cu31924029895467/ cu31924029895467_djvu.txt>.

4. For more on Eliezer Papo, see <http://www.jewishencyclopedia.com/articles/11891-papo-eliezer-ben-isaac>.
5. See WWF Factsheet: 'Navigation Project: Romania-Bulgaria', 18 January 2010.
6. Nick Thorpe *et al.*, *Tearing Down the Curtain: People's Revolution in Eastern Europe*, Headway Books, Hodder Arnold H & S, London, 1990.
7. For Ruse, see Nikolai Nenov, *Guidebook*; <www.parnas.bg>; *Thracian Treasure of Borovo*, <www.museumruse.com>.
8. Canetti, *Memoirs*, p. 7.
9. The information here is taken from notes from the museum catalogue.
10. Ali Haydar Midhat, *The Life of Midhat Pasha: a record of his services, political reforms, banishment, and judicial murder*, J. Murray, London, 1903.
11. For Ilija Trojanow's documentary (in German), 17 December 2007, see <http://www.zdf.de/Mainzer-Stadtschreiber/Gespr%C3%A4che-mit-Opfern-und-Zeitzeugen-5363280.html>.

6. Gypsy River

1. Interview with the author, May 2011.
2. Kinross, *The Ottoman Empire*, p. 56.
3. See <http://www.velikoturnovo.info/arte.php?Codf=3&Codr=29>.
4. For Aleko Konstantinov, see *The Everyman Companion to East European Literature*, ed. R. B. Pynsent and S. I. Kanikova, J. M. Dent, London, 1993, pp. 199–200.
5. Maria Todorova, *Imagining the Balkans*, Oxford University Press, Oxford, 2009, pp. 39–42.
6. Sonia Kanikova on Aleko Konstantinov, in *The Everyman Companion to East European Literature*, ed. Pynsent and Kanikova.
7. For details about the Persina Nature Park, see <www.persina.org>.
8. Kinross, *The Ottoman Empire*, p. 56.
9. Ibid., p. 58.
10. Mehmed Genç, 'L'Economie Ottomane et la guerre au xvii siècle', *Tunica* 27, 1995, pp. 177–96, cited in *The Ottomans and the Balkans – A Discussion of Historiography*, ed. Fikret Adanir and Suraiya Faroqhi, Brill, Leiden, 2002, p. 15.
11. Gábor Ágoston, 'Habsburgs and Ottomans, Defense, Military Change and Shifts in Power', *Turkish Studies Association Bulletin*, 22, 1, 1998, pp. 126–41.
12. Metternich had changed his views markedly since 1828 when he wrote: 'We look on the Ottoman Empire as the best of our neighbours: since she is scrupulously true to her word, we regard contact with her as equivalent to contact with a natural frontier which never claims our attention or dissipates our energies. We look on Turkey as the last bastion standing in the way of the expansion of another Power . . .' Metternich's Letter to Prince Paul Esterhazy, the Austrian Ambassador in London, 2 December 1828. Cited in G. de Bertier de Sauvigny, *Metternich and His Times*, Darton, Longman & Todd, London, 1962, p. 247.
13. For shipping on the Danube, see statistics published by the Danube Commission since 1963.
14. L. S. Stavrianos, *The Balkans since 1453*, Holt, Rinehart & Winston, New York, 1958; C. Hurst, London, 2000, p. 321.
15. See <http://www.firstissues.org/forum/index.php?topic=290.0>.
16. Stavrianos, *The Balkans since 1453*, p. 323.
17. The subject has also been addressed in fiction; see Boris Akunin, *The Turkish Gambit*, 1998, trans. Andrew Bromfield, Random House, New York, 2005.
18. Ian Hancock, *The Pariah Syndrome: An account of Gypsy slavery and persecution*, Karoma Publishers, Ann Arbor, Michigan, 1987.
19. Isabel Fonseca, *Bury Me Standing – The Gypsies and their Journey*, Vintage, New York, 1996.

20. For a general treatment, not on the Roma in particular, see Gerry Johnstone, *Restorative Justice – Ideas, Values, Debates*, Willan Publishing, Uffculme, 2002.
21. Thorpe, *Unfinished Revolution*, pp. 301–2.
22. See <http://www.jarokalivia.hu/en>.
23. See <http://brain.oxfordjournals.org/content/121/3/399.full.pdf>.
24. Emil Andreev, 'The Return of Teddy Braun', in *Lettre Internationale, 2011*, trans. Andrea Iván, who kindly brought my attention to it.
25. Hasluck, *Christianity and Islam*, Vol. II, pp. 391–402.
26. The Austrian 100 corona is still being minted, with a 1915 mint mark to enable Austrians to take advantage of a grandfather clause in the law regarding private ownership of gold bullion. See <http://en.wikipedia.org/wiki/Coins_of_the_Austro-Hungarian_krone>, and <http://www.taxfreegold.co.uk/1915austrian1ducat.php>.

7. River of Dreams

1. Constantin Brâncuşi, *Thus Spoke Brancusi*, Fundatia-Editura, Craiova, 2011, p. 234.
2. Interview with the author, July 2011.
3. Marian Tutie, *Ada-Kaleh, sau Orientul scufundat*, Noi Media Print, Bucharest, 2010.
4. See a short film, *Ultima Primavera in Ada Kaleh – Last Spring on Ada Kaleh* <http://www.youtube.com/watch?v=A6Td7IqThZ8>.
5. See Chapter 3, p. 41.
6. Conversation with the author, July 2012.
7. Tutie, *Ada-Kaleh*, p.187.
8. I have searched in vain for any other reference to him. He has vanished, like his clothes.
9. Brâncuşi, *Thus Spoke Brancusi*, p. 105.
10. Ibid., p. 106.
11. For information about Tania Rachevskaia, see <http://www.bbc.co.uk/news/magazine-15216513>.
12. Cited in *The Vineleaf and the Rose*, TintoFilms, Budapest, 2003.
13. Brâncuşi, *Thus Spoke Brancusi*, p. 95.
14. Ibid., p. 94.
15. Gerard Casey, *Between the Symplegades – Revisions from a Mythological Story* (a translation of George Seferis's poems), Enitharmon Press, London, 1980.
16. See Mihai Vlasie, *How to Get to the Monasteries of Romania*, trans. Luminita Irina Niculescu and Diana Presada, Editura Sophia, Bucharest, 2003, pp. 356–57.
17. *Danube Bike Trail, Vol. 4* Bikeline, Verlag Esterbauer, Rodingersdorf, 2008.
18. For a dramatic nineteenth-century lithograph of the Iron Gates, see 'Wallachei – das Eiserne Thor', by Ludwig Erminy / Franz Wolf 1840, in *Sketches on the Danube – Vedutas by 19th century artists*, Közép-európai Kulurális Intézet, Budapest, 2001.
19. Conversation with the author, Constanţa 2003.
20. Friedrich Hölderlin refers to Hercules in 'The Ister':

> Now they call Him the Ister.
> He lives prettily. His pillars' leaves
> Are burning and stirring. Wildly
> The pillars stand upright, together; above them
> A second measure, slinging forth
> From the rock, a roof. No surprise,
> Then, that He
> Invited Hercules to come as a guest,
> Shining from afar, down there at the Olymp,
> Since he who sought Shadow,
> Came all the way from hot Isthmus . . .

See <http://poetrybeingzen.blogspot.it/2007/11/hölderlin-der-ister-translation.html>.

21. Brâncuşi, *Thus Spoke Brancusi*, p. 112.
22. Mladić was arrested on 26 May 2011; Hadžić was arrested on 20 July 2011.
23. See <http://en.wikipedia.org/wiki/Trajan%27s_Bridge>.
24. Helmuth von Moltke, cited in *Die Donau – in Sagen, Mythen und Marchen*, ed. Bertram Kirchner, Anaconda Verlag, Cologne, 2007, p. 343.
25. David Ulansey, *The Origins of the Mithraic Mysteries*, Oxford University Press, Oxford, 1991.
26. Dragoslav Srejović, *Europe's First Monumental Sculpture – New Discoveries at Lepenski Vir*, Lepenski Vir, Belgrade, 1972.
27. Gimbutas, *Goddesses and Gods*, pp. 108–11.
28. Ljubinka Babović, *Sanctuaries of Lepenski Vir – Location, Position and Function*, National Museum, Belgrade, 2006.
29. See   <http://www.memorialmuseums.org/eng/staettens/view/1210/Memorial-to-the-Victims-of-the-Kladovo-Transport>.
30. See <http://forum.axishistory.com/viewtopic.php?f=61&t=73554>.
31. See <http://news.bbc.co.uk/2/hi/europe/3166863.stm>.
32. For Djordje Balašević, see, inter alia: <http://www.youtube.com/watch?v—nWdq_2otFE>.
33. For more tales of Marko Kraljević, see *The Ballads of Marko Kraljević*, trans. D. H. Low, Cambridge University Press, Cambridge, 1922. Also see <http://www.archive.org/stream/balladsofmarkokr00lowduoft#page/n7/mode/1up>.
34. H. G. Williams, and K. Hunyadi, *Dictionary of Weeds of Eastern Europe*, Akademia, Budapest, 1987.
35. See the essay by Marco Merlini in *The Danube Script – Neo-Eneolithic Writing in Southeastern Europe*, ed. Joan Marler, Institute of Archaeomythology, Sebastopol, California, 2008.
36. See Gimbutas, *Goddesses and Gods*, pp. 196–97.

8. River of Fire

1. Bernard Lewis, *The Muslim Discovery of Europe*, W. W. Norton, London and New York, 1982.
2. See <http://en.wikipedia.org/wiki/Golubac_fortress>.
3. See <http://en.wikipedia.org/wiki/Zawisza_Czarny>.
4. In Kusturica's *Underground*. see <http://www.youtube.com/watch?v=IltS4FWrwxM>.
5. On the first Ottoman soldiers in Europe, see H. T. Norris, *Islam in the Balkans – Religion and Society between Europe and the Arab World*, Hurst, London, 1993.
6. During a visit to Edirne in summer 2006, I found at least three major drum-makers in the city.
7. This story of the Smederevan origin of Tokaj wine is popular in Serbia, but seems little known in Tokaj itself.
8. See <http://www.royalathena.com/pages/prehistoriccatalog/VLF04.html>.
9. My estimates, based on Andrej Starović's figures.
10. András Rónai, *Atlas of Central Europe*, Teleki Research Institute, Budapest, 1945; digital facsimile edition, Puski, Budapest, 1993.
11. For obsidian, see John Chapman and Bisserka Gaydarska, 'The Aesthetics of Colour and Brilliance', *Geoarchaeology and Archaeomineralogy*, ed., R. I. Kostov, B. Gaydarska and M. Gurova, Proceedings of the International Conference 29–30 October 2008, St Ivan Rilski, Sofia, 2008, pp. 63–66.
12. Harald Haarmann, 'Changing the Canon: Research on Ancient Writing Systems beyond the Mesopotamian Bias' in *The Danube Script – Neo-Eneolithic Writing in Southeastern Europe*, ed. Joan Marler, Institute of Archaeomythology, Sebastopol, California, 2008, pp. 11–12.
13. See   <http://ww3.economist.com/blogs/easternapproaches/2013/03/remembering-dessa-trevisan>.

14. Tim Judah, *The Serbs – History, Myth and the Destruction of Yugoslavia*, Yale University Press, New Haven and London, 1997; Marcus Tanner, *Croatia – A Nation Forged in War*, Yale University Press, New Haven and London, 1997; Misha Glenny, *The Fall of Yugoslavia*, Penguin, Harmondsworth, 1996.

15. John Reed, *War in Eastern Europe – Travels through the Balkans in 1915*, Scribner, New York, 1915; repr. Orion Books, London, 1995, p. 32.

16. Information extracted from the museum catalogue in the military museum in Kalemegdan.

17. Kinross, *The Ottoman Empire*, p. 353.

18. For the 2000 Baia Mare disaster, see <http://news.bbc.co.uk/2/hi/europe/1146979.stm>.

9. The Black Army

1. Kemal Pasha Zade, 'Poet in the Court of Suleiman the Magnificent', cited in *Mohács Emlékezete*, trans. Nick Thorpe, p. 184.

2. Kinross, *The Ottoman Empire* p. 170.

3. Vladimir Nedeljković, *Zavod za Culturu Vojvodine* (The Boys and Girls from the Danube), 1964–1972 and 1964–80, 2 vols, Novi Sad, 2007/2010. See <http://www.vladimirnedeljk-ovic.com/news/news%20engl.htm>.

4. Quotation reproduced at the entrance to the museum in Petrovaradin.

5. See <http://news.bbc.co.uk/2/hi/world/monitoring/368817.stm>.

6. Tibor Cseres, *Cold Days, 1964*, first English language edition, Corvina, Budapest, 1993; idem, *Titoist Atrocities in Vojrodina, 1944: Serbian Vendetta in Bácska*, Hunyadi, Budapest, 1993.

7. See especially Tanner, *Croatia – A Nation Forged in War*.

8. On the trial of Goran Hadžić at the International War Crimes Tribunal, see <http://www.balkaninsight.com/en/balkan-transitional-justice/goran-hadzic-at-the-hague-news>.

9. For Ovčara farm, see <http://www.b92.net/eng/news/region-article.php?yyyy=2011&mm=11&dd=18&nav_id=77386>; also <http://iwpr.net/report-news/ovcara-survivor-recalls-day-massacre>.

10. The conversations that follow are reproduced from my written notes and audio recordings from January 1999.

11. See <http://www.amazon-of-europe.com/en/menu31/>.

12. The Croatian Society for the Protection of Birds and Nature can be found at <http://www.wiser.org/organization/view/be2c1167157a91f285466a5df5181bd5>.

13. Marcus Tanner, *The Raven King – Matthias and the Fate of his Lost Library*, Yale University Press, New Haven and London, 2009.

10. Smoke, Ash and a Tale or Two

1. Marcus Aurelius, *Meditations*, Book XII.

2. There are few good English language sources on the battle. In Hungarian there is *Mohács Emlékezete – A Mohácsi csatára vonatkozó legfontosabb magyar, nyugati és török források*, ed. Tamás Katona and László Girias, Magyar Helikon, Budapest, 1976.

3. See <http://upload.wikimedia.org/wikipedia/commons/3/3e/Orlai_perenyine.jpg>.

4. For the European Bicycle Route 6, see <http://en.eurovelo6.org>.

5. 'Only the conquest of Vienna might have rescued the Hungarian territories from their unenviable position at the center of the battlefield.' *The Ottomans and the Balkans – A Discussion of Historiography*, Vol. 25 of *The Ottoman Empire and its Heritage*, ed. Fikret Adanir and Suraiya Faroqhi, Brill, Leiden and Boston, 2002. p. 54

6. Adanir and Faroqhi, *The Ottomans and the Balkans*, p. 317.

7. Ibid., pp. 305–49.

8. Marcus Aurelius, *Meditations*, Book IV; see <http://classics.mit.edu/Antonius/meditations.html>.

9. The recipe and other information cited here all come from the museum.
10. Luigi Ferdinando Marsigli, *Danubius Pannonico-Mysicus – Observationibus geographicis, astronomicis, hydrographicis, historicis, physicis perlustratus*, Amsterdam, 1726. Reprinted as *The Discovery of the Danube*, Museum of Water Management, Budapest, 2004.
11. From the *Collected Poems of Kenneth Patchen*, New Directions, New York, 1968.
12. *Magyar Hajózási Statisztikai Kézikönyv – 1945–1968* (Hungarian Shipping Handbook), Mahart, Budapest, 1971.
13. Charles (Karl) IV was crowned in St Mátyás church in Buda on 30 December 1916, the last king of Hungary. He abdicated less than two years later, as Austria-Hungary fell apart at the end of the First World War. When he attempted to return to Hungary, to restore the monarchy in October 1921, his small force was overwhelmed by troops loyal to the Regent, Admiral Horthy, and he and his wife were escorted out of the country down the Danube on the British gunboat HMS *Glowworm*, all the way to Galaţi. He died the following year, in exile on Madeira, of Spanish flu, aged thirty-six.
14. See <http://profiles.nlm.nih.gov/ps/retrieve/Narrative/WG/p-nid/149>.
15. For László Magyar, see <http://www.wdl.org/en/item/2925/>.
16. 'Folksong', by János Arany, 28 August 1877.
17. For the fate of Csepel during the siege of Budapest at the end of the Second World War, see Krisztián Ungváry, *Battle for Budapest: 100 Days in World War II*, trans Ladislaus Lob, I.B. Tauris, London, 2003, pp. 14–17.

11. The Wind in the Willows

1. Algernon Blackwood, 'The Willows', from *Three Supernatural Classics*, Dover Mineola, New York, 2008.
2. See especially István Deák, *The Lawful Revolution – Louis Kossuth and the Hungarians, 1848–1849*, Columbia University Press, New York, 1979; Phoenix Press, London, 2001.
3. For the fate of Batthyány's silkworms, see <http://www.diszmadarmagazin.hu/hun/cikk.php?id=627>.
4. The Venus of Willendorf, a tiny item of exquisite beauty, is on display at the Natural History Museum in Vienna. See Walpurga Antl-Weiser, *Die Frau von W., Die Venus von Willendorf*, Natural History Museum, Vienna, 2008.
5. Mária Vida, *Spas of Hungary in Ancient Times and Today*, Semmelweis Kiadó, Budapest, 1992, pp. 23–25.
6. Ibid., p. 25.
7. János Arany, *The Legend of the Wonderous Stag*: <http://mek.oszk.hu/00200/00215/00215.pdf>.
8. Author's interview with István Sárvári, 1995.
9. From the album, Mihály Dresch, *Túl a Vizen*, 1996.
10. Gábor Ágoston and Balázs Sudár, *Gül Baba*, Terebess, Budapest, 2002.
11. John Kingsley Birge, *The Bektashi Order of Dervishes*, Luzac, London, 1937; reprinted by Luzac Oriental, London, 1996.
12. Ágoston and Sudár, *Gül Baba*.
13. Béla Tóth, *Gül Baba*, Lampel, Budapest, 1907, pp. 9–20.
14. See the Mahart website <http://www.mahartpassnave.hu/webset32.cgi?MAHART@@EN@@158@@GOOGLEBOT7>.
15. See <http://www.ferrexpo.com/ukraine.aspx>.
16. Photographs of Sylveszter Matuska's trial, and of the man himself, can be seen on the stairs of the Hungarian Lawyers' Association in Budapest.
17. On Nagymaros, see 'Devil Bids Adieu to a Dammed River', *Observer*, October 1992.
18. For the sad fate of the *Tatabánya*, see <http://iho.hu/hir/a-tatabanya-vontato-vegnapjai>, 26 July 2011.
19. Marko Pogačnik, *Nature Spirits and Elemental Beings – Working with the Intelligence in Nature*, Findhorn Press, Findhorn, 2009.

20. The text of the treaty is at: <http://www.gabcikovo.gov.sk/doc/it1977en/treaty.html>.
21. Ibid.
22. Author's conversation with János Betlen.
23. From the documentary film *The Fairy Island*, TintoFilms/ Duna TV 1993 – Thorpe/ Weichinger.
24. Ibid.
25. See Danubiana <http://www.danubiana.sk/eng/index.html>.
26. William Blake, 'The Tyger' *Songs of Experience*, 1794.
27. See <http://www.broz.sk/organizacia/en>.
28. See <http://www.icjcij.org/docket/index.php?p1=3&p2=3&code=hs&case=92&k>.
29. For Donauauen National Park, see <www.donauauen.at>.

12. Danube Fairytales

1. Friedrich Hölderlin, Book III, Ch. 10.
2. Bernard Grun, *Gold and Silver: The Life and Times of Franz Lehár*, David McKay, New York, 1970.
3. See <http://www.hgm.or.at/index.html?&L=1>.
4. Kinross, *The Ottoman Empire*, p. 324.
5. See <http://www.muzeum.krakow.pl/Arms-and-Uniforms-in-Poland.350.0.html?&L=1>.
6. Noel Malcolm, *Bosnia: A Short History*, New York University Press, New York, 1996, pp. 153–55.
7. See <http://www.sagen.at/texte/sagen/oesterreich/niederoesterreich/wienerwald/schleier-fuerklosterneuburg.html>.
8. See <http://www.tibetforum.at/>.
9. The Roman *Limes* along the Danube are receiving increasing attention in each riverside country as a focus for tourists. See in particular <http://www.danube-limes.eu/homepage>.
10. See <http://www.tulln.at/?lang=1&dok_id=6429&kat=345&mkat=374&op=307>.
11. For 'the miracle of the rain', see <http://www.livius.org/le-lh/legio/rain.html>.
12. For Florianus, see <http://www.catholic.org/saints/saint.php?saint_id=149>.
13. Marcel Brion, *Attila – The Scourge of God*, trans. Harold Ward, Cassell, London, 1929.
14. Mihály Hoppál, *Hungarian Review*, 3, 1, January 2012, pp. 79–91.
15. Notes taken from the Tulln Museum.
16. See <http://www.bbc.co.uk/news/world-europe-16359991>.
17. See <http://www.hpkuhn-art.de/hpk.html>.
18. For Alemu Aga, see <http://www.youtube.com/watch?v=Qnes19ERSBM>.
19. On Richard the Lionheart's heart, see <http://www.nature.com/news/king-s-lionheart-gets-a-forensic-exam-1.12521>.
20. See <http://www.jstor.org/stable/20538124>.
21. For a summary in German, see <http://www.arbeitskreis-wachau.at/downloads/Landschaften11_2.pdf>; <www.naturatrails.net>; <www.danubeparks.org>.
22. http://www.coronelli.org/index_e.html.

13. Oh Germany, Pale Mother

1. Miklós Radnóti, *Under Gemini – A Prose Memoir and Selected Poetry*, trans. Kenneth McRobbie, Zita McRobbie and Jascha Kessler, Corvina Press with Ohio University Press, Budapest and Ohio, 1985, p. 362.
2. *Mauthausen Guide*, Osterreichische Lagergemeinschaft Mauthausen.
3. Radnóti, *Under Gemini*, p. 105.

4. Bertolt Brecht: 'O Deutschland, Bleiche Mutter!', in English: <http://permanentred.blog-spot.com/2009/11/o-germany-pale-mother-by-bertolt-brecht.html>.

5. *Passau – Mythos & Geschichte*, Oberhaus Museum Passau, Verlag Friedrich Pustet, Regensburg, 2007.

6. On wolves in Germany, see, inter alia: http://www.spiegel.de/international/spiegel/the-return-of-wolves-to-germany-fears-are-being-stoked-a-467205.html

7. Boria Sax, *Animals in the Third Reich: Pets, Scapegoats, and the Holocaust*, Continuum International, London, 2000.

8. Ibid.

9. Interview with the author, Switzerland, October 2011.

10. *Kingdom of Salt – 7000 Years of Hallstatt*, ed. Anton Kern, Kerstin Kowarik, Andreas W. Rausch and Hans Reschreiter, Natural History Museum, Vienna, 2009.

11. For the capture of the crown near Mattsee in Austria by the US 86th Infantry Division in 1945, see Richard C. Briggs, *Black Hawks over the Danube: The History of the 86th Infantry Division in World War II*, Western Recorder, Louisville, 1954, pp. 94–5.

12. *Danube Bike Trail*, Vol. 1, p. 116.

13. Ibid., p. 110.

14. See <http://www.museen-in-bayern.de/inhalt/content.php?type=&objID=464&lang=en>.

15. See <http://news.bbc.co.uk/2/hi/europe/6078052.stm>.

16. See <http://international.naturpark-altmuehltal.de/en/>.

14. The Tailor of Ulm

1. Luther Bible, 1534, Wittenberg. See <http://*lutherbibel*.net/>.

2. For Ulm Minster, see *Ulm Minster*, revised English guide (Munich, 2010), <www.dkv.kunstfuehrer.de>.

3. For the Museum der Brotkultur, Ulm, see <http://www.museum-brotkultur.de/index.php?option=com_content&view=article&id=77&Itemid=59>.

4. For the Danube Swabians, see <http://www.danube-swabians.org/>.

5. 'Blankenstein Hussar' (my translation).

Afterword. A Kind of Solution

1. Constantin Cavafy, 'Waiting for the Barbarians', from *Collected Poems*, trans. Edmund Keeley and Philip Sherrard, Princeton University Press, Princeton, NJ, 1992; see <http://www.cavafy.com/>.

2. 'Blutsbruder auf ewig: unser Karl May', *Stuttgarter Zeitung*, 30 March 2012.

3. Rivka Galchen, *The New Yorker*, 9 April 2012.

4. Christa Wolf, *The Quest for Christa T.*, Farrar, Straus & Giroux, New York, 1979.

Select Bibliography

Gábor Ágoston and Balázs Sudár, *Gül Baba*, Terebess, Budapest, 2002

Boris Akunin, *The Turkish Gambit*, 1998, trans. Andrew Bromfield, Random House, New York, 2005

Emil Andreev, 'The Return of Teddy Braun', trans. Andrea Iván, *Lettre Internationale*, no. 81, 2011

David W. Anthony, ed., *The Lost World of Old Europe – The Danube Valley 5000–3500 BC*, Institute for the Study of the Ancient World, New York University and Princeton University Press, Princeton, 2010

Walpurga Antl-Weiser, *Die Frau von W., Die Venus von Willendorf*, Natural History Museum, Vienna, 2008

Neal Ascherson, *Black Sea – The Birthplace of Civilisation and Barbarism*, Jonathan Cape, London, 1995

Marcus Aurelius, *Meditations*, Books IV and XII. See <http://classics.mit.edu/Antoninus/meditations.html>

Ljubinka Babović, *Sanctuaries of Lepenski Vir – Location, Position and Function*, National Museum, Belgrade, 2006

Ibn Battuta, *Travels in Asia and Africa 1325–1354*, trans. H. A. R. Gibb, George Routledge, London, 1929

Andrew Beattie, *The Danube – A Cultural History*, Signal Books, Oxford, 2010

Algernon Blackwood, 'The Willows' in *Three Supernatural Classics*, Dover Publications, Mineola, New York, 2008

The Boian Civilisation on Romania's Territory, Lower Danube Museum, Calarasi, 1999

Constantin Brâncuşi, *Thus Spoke Brâncuşi*, Fundatia-Editura, Craiova, 2011

Marcel Brion, *Attila – The Scourge of God*, trans. Harold Ward, Cassell, London, 1929

Silviu Brucan, *The Wasted Generation – Memoirs of the Romanian Journey from Capitalism to Socialism and Back*, Westview Press, Boulder, Colorado, 1993

Muhammed Fatih Calisir, 'A Long March: The Ottoman Campaign in Hungary, 1663'. Unpublished Masters thesis, Central European University, Budapest, 2009

Elias Canetti, *Memoirs – The Tongue Set Free*, Farrar, Straus & Giroux, New York, 1999

Gerard Casey, *Between the Symplegades – Revisions from a Mythological Story*, Enitharmon Press, London, 1980

John Chapman and Bisserka Gaydarska, 'Colour in Balkan Prehistory', in *Early Symbolic Systems for Communication in Southeast Europe*, ed. L. Nikolova. BAR International Series 1139, Archaeopress, Oxford, 2003, pp. 31–56

John Chapman and Bisserka Gaydarska, *Spondylus gaederopus / Glycymeris exchange networks in the European Neolithic and Chalcolithic*, BAR International Series, 2216, 2011

V. Gordon Childe, *The Danube in Prehistory*, Oxford University Press, Oxford, 1929

V. Gordon Childe, *What Happened in History*, Penguin, Harmondsworth, 1942; rev. edn, Penguin, Harmondsworth, 1976

David M. Crowe, *A History of the Gypsies of Eastern Europe and Russia*, St. Martin's Press, New York, 1994

Evlia Cselebi, *Török Vilagutazó Magyarországi Utazásái 1660–1664*, Gondolat, trans. into Hungarian by Imre Karacson, Budapest, 1985

Tibor Cseres, *Cold Days*, 1964, first English language edn, Corvina, Budapest, 1993

Karoly Csonkaréti, *Hadihajók a Dunán* (Warships on the Danube), Zrinyi Katonai Kiadó, Budapest, 1980

Culturá şi Civilizaţie La Dunărea de Jos, vols XXII and XXIV, Editura DAIM, Bucharest-Calarasi, 2005 and 2008

Krzysztof Czyzewski, *The Path of the Borderland*, Boderland Publishing House, Sejny, 2001

Robert Dankoff, *An Ottoman Mentality – The World of Evliya Celebi*, Brill, Leiden and Boston, 2006

Danube Bike Trail, Vols 1–4, Bikeline, Verlag Esterbauer, Rodingersdorf, 2008

The Danube Script – Neo-Eneolithic Writing in Southeastern Europe, ed. Joan Marler, Institute of Archaeomythology, Sebastopol, California, 2008

István Déak *The Lawful Revolution – Louis Kossuth and the Hungarians, 1848–1849*, Columbia University Press, New York, 1979; Phoenix Press, London, 2001

Mak Dizdar, *Kameni Spavac – Stone Sleeper*, trans. Francis Jones, DID, Sarajevo, 1999

Andrew Eames, *Blue River, Black Sea: A Journey Along the Danube into the Heart of the New Europe*, London, 2009

The Everyman Companion to East European Literature, ed. R. B. Pynsent and S. I. Kanikova, J. M. Dent, London, 1993

Patrick Leigh Fermor, *A Timer of Gifts*, John Murray, London, 1977

Patrick Leigh Fermor, *Between the Woods and the Water – The Middle Danube to the Iron Gates*, John Murray, London, 1986

Marija Gimbutas, *The Goddesses and Gods of Old Europe*, Thames and Hudson, rev. edn, London, 1982

F. W. Hasluck, *Christianity and Islam under the Sultans*, 2 Vols, Oxford University Press, Oxford, 1929

Herodotus, *The Histories*, trans. Aubrey de Selincourt, Penguin Classics, Harmondsworth, 1954

The History of the Hungarian Pipemaker's Craft, Hungarian National Museum, Budapest, 2000

Nicolae Iorga, *Byzantium after Byzantium*, Bucharest, 1935; trans. Laura Treptow, Center for Romanian Studies/ Romanian Institute of International Studies, Bucharest, 2000

Jason and the Argonauts, Stephanides Brothers' Greek Mythology, trans. Bruce Walter, Sigma, Athens, 1998

Barbara Jelavich, *History of the Balkans, Vol. 1, Eighteenth and Nineteenth Centuries; Vol. 2 – Twentieth Century*, Cambridge University Press, Cambridge, 1983

Gerry Johnstone, *Restorative Justice – Ideas, Values, Debates*, Willan Publishing, Uffculme, 2002

Tim Judah, *The Serbs – History, Myth and the Destruction of Yugoslavia*, Yale University Press, New Haven and London, 1997

Charles H. Kahn, *The Art and Thought of Heraclitus*, Cambridge University Press, Cambridge, 1979

Kemal H. Karpat, 'The Memoirs of N. Batzaria: The Young Turks and Nationalism', in *Studies on Ottoman Social and Political History*, Brill, Leiden, Boston and Cologne, 2002

Tomás Katona and László Ginács, eds, *Mohács Emlékezete – A Mohácsi csatára vonatkozo legfontosabb magyar, nyugati es török forrasok* (The battle of Mohács from the most important Hungarian, Western and Turkish sources), trans. Nick Thorpe, Magyar Helikon, Budapest, 1976

Kingdom of Salt – 7000 years of Hallstatt, ed. Anton Kern, Kerstin Kowarik, Andreas W. Rausch and Hans Reschreiter, Natural History Museum, Vienna, 2009

Patrick Kinross, *The Ottoman Empire*, Jonathan Cape, London, 1977; The Folio Society, London, 2003

Bertram Kirchner, ed., *Die Donau – in Sagen, Mythen und Marchen*, Anaconda Verlag, Cologne, 2007

Philip L. Kohl, *The Making of Bronze Age Eurasia*, Cambridge University Press Cambridge, 2009

Bela Köpeczi *et al.*, eds, *History of Transylvania*, Akademiai Publishing House, Budapest, 1994

Marko Kraljević, *The Ballads of Marko Kraljević*, trans. D. H. Low, Cambridge University Press, Cambridge, 1922

Bernard Lewis, *The Muslim Discovery of Europe*, W. W. Norton, London and New York, 1982

Allan Little and Laura Silber, *The Death of Yugoslavia*, Penguin, Harmondsworth, 1996

Claudio Magris, *Danube*, trans. Patrick Creagh, Collins Harvill, London, 1989

Magyar Hajózási Statisztikai Kézikönyv – 1945–1968 (Hungarian Shipping Handbook), Mahart, Budapest, 1971

Sándor Márai, *Memoir of Hungary 1944–48*, trans. Albert Tezla, Corvina, in association with CEU Press, Budapest, 2005

Luigi Ferdinando Marsigli, *Danubius Pannonico-Mysicus – Observationibus geographicis, astronomicis, hydrographicis, historicis, physicis perlustratus*, Amsterdam, 1726. Reprinted as *The Discovery of the Danube*, Museum of Water Management, Budapest, 2004

Melk Abbey, official guide, Stift Melk, 2008

Thomas Merton, *Memoirs of a Guilty Bystander*, Doubleday, New York, 1965

Military Museum collections, ed. Sadik Tekeli, Istanbul, 2006

Simon Millar, *Vienna 1683 – Christian Europe repels the Ottomans*, Osprey Publishing, Oxford, 2008

Museum Guide, Baranya County, Collections of Janus Pannonius and Dorottya Kanizsai Museums, Pecs, 2009

Nikolai Nenov, ed., *Sexaginta Prista-Intrus*, Ruse History Museum, Ruse, 2007

H. T. Norris, *Islam in the Balkans – Religion and Society between Europe and the Arab World*, Hurst, London, 1993

Dimitri Obolensky, *The Byzantine Commonwealth: Eastern Europe 500–1453*, Weidenfeld & Nicolson, London, 1971

George Ostrogorsky, *History of the Byzantine State*, trans. Joan Hussey, Basil Blackwell, Oxford, 1956

Mirko Peković, *Archaeological Collection of the Military Museum*, Belgrade, 2006

Marko Pogačnik, *Nature Spirits and Elemental Beings – Working with the Intelligence in Nature*, Findhorn Press, Findhorn, 2009

Constantine Porphyrogenitus, *De Administrando Imperio*, ed. Gy. Moravcsik, trans. R. J. H. Jenkins, new, rev. edn Dumbarton Oaks Center for Byzantine Studies, Washington, D. C., 1967, pp. 49–51, 57–63 167–71

Prehistory of the Lower Danube, Editura CARO, Bucharest-Calarasi, 1997

Miklós Radnóti, *Under Gemini – A Prose Memoir and Selected Poetry*, trans. Kenneth McRobbie, Zita McRobbie and Jascha Kessler, Corvina with Ohio University Press, Budapest and Ohio, 1985

John Reed, *War in Eastern Europe – Travels through the Balkans in 1915*, Scribners, New York, 1915; repr. Orion Books, London, 1995

Romanian Folk Tales, trans. Ana Cartianu, Editura Minerva, Bucharest, 1979

András Rónai, *Atlas of Central Europe*, Teleki Research Institute, Budapest, 1945; Digital Facsimile Edition, Puski, Budapest, 1993

Rough Guide to Bulgaria, Jonathan Bousfield and Dan Richardson, 5th edn, London, 2005

Ruse Tell, Guidebook, Ruse, 2009

L. Séfériadès, 'Spondylus and Long-distance Trade in Prehistoric Europe', in David Anthony, ed., *The Lost World of Old Europe: The Danube Valley, 5000–3500 BC*, New York University and Princeton University Press, Princeton, NJ, 2010

George Seferis, *Collected Poems*, Ikarus, Athens, 1965; trans. Edmund Keeley and Philip Sherrard, Princeton University Press, Princeton, NJ, 1967

Serbo-Croatian Heroic Songs, collected Milman Parry, Harvard University Press, Cambridge, MA, 1979

Gary Snyder, *The Practice of the Wild*, Counterpoint, Berkeley, 1990

Andrzej Stasiuk, *On the Road to Babadag – Travels in the Other Europe*, Harvill Secker, London, 2011

L. S. Stavrianos, *The Balkans since 1453*, Holt, Rinehart & Winston, 1958; C. Hurst, London, 2000

Marcus Tanner, *Croatia – A Nation Forged in War*, Yale University Press, New Haven and London, 1997

Marcus Tanner, *The Raven King – Matthias and the Fate of his Lost Library*, Yale University Press, New Haven and London, 2009

Nick Thorpe *et al.*, *Tearing Down the Curtain, People's Revolution in Eastern Europe*, Headway Books, Hodder Arnold H & S, London, 1990

Maria Todorova, *Imagining the Balkans*, Oxford University Press, Oxford, 2009

The Tragedy of Slovak Jews, Proceedings of the International Symposium, Banska Bystrica, Ministry of Culture and Museum of the Slovak National Uprising, Banska Bystrica, 1992

Martin Trancik, *Between the Old and the New – The History of the Bookseller Family Steiner in Pressburg*, trans. Julia Sherwood, Albert Marencin Vydavatel'stvo, Bratislava, 2006

Turkish Flowers – Studies on Ottoman Art in Hungary, ed. Ibolya Gerelyes, Hungarian National Museum, Budapest, 2005

Marian Tutie, *Ada-Kaleh, sau Orientul scufundat*, Noi Media Print, Bucharest, 2010

Krisztian Ungvary, *Battle for Budapest: 100 Days in World War II*, trans. Ladislaus Lob, I. B. Tauris, London, 2003

Mihai Vlasie, *How to Get to the Monasteries of Romania*, trans. Luminita Irina Niculescu and Diana Presada, Editura Sophia, Bucharest, 2003

Razvan Voiculescu, *Dobrogea inceptul lumii* (Dobrogea – The Beginning of the World), bilingual Romanian and English edition, Editura Q-T-RAZ, Bucharest, 2008

H. G. Williams and K. Hunyadi, *Dictionary of Weeds of Eastern Europe*, Akademia, Budapest, 1987

Marguerite Yourcenar, *Memoirs of Hadrian*, Librarie Plon, Paris, 1951; trans. Grace Frick, Penguin Books, Harmondsworth, 1959

Filmography

David Barison, Daniel Ross, *The Ister*, 2004; see <http://www.theister.com>

Cornel Gheorghiță, *Europolis*, 2010; see <http://www.europolis-film.com/?lang=en Ultima Primavera in Ada-Kaleh>

Andrea Weichinger, Nick Thorpe, *The Vineleaf and the Rose*, TintoFilms, Budapest, 2001

Andrea Weichinger, Nick Thorpe, *The Fairy Island*, Duna TV, Budapest, 1993

Index